# GOVERNANCE OF A PARTY-STATE

Ling Li unveils the often-hidden inner workings of China's Party-state. The Chinese Communist Party has crafted and relied on an integrated regulatory system, where politics and law are fused, to govern both its internal operations and its relations with the state. Drawing on two decades of in-depth research, Li delves into the "black box" of decision-making in the Party-state, analyzing the motivations and strategies that drive individual and institutional choices in corruption, anti-corruption investigations, and power struggles at the Politburo. This insightful book reveals the critical role of rules and institution-building within the Party, illuminates the complex relationship between corruption and regime stability, and captures the evolving dynamics of Party-state relations. A must-read for students, academics, business leaders, and policymakers alike, this book is an indispensable guide for anyone seeking a deeper understanding of law, politics, and governance in China and its global implications.

LING LI teaches China Studies at the University of Vienna, specializing in Chinese law and politics. She holds a doctorate in law from Leiden University and has published extensively on corruption, anti-corruption, and the political-legal system of the People's Republic of China (PRC).

This comprehensive and impressive work represents the culmination of two decades of research on China's courts, corruption, and the Chinese Communist Party's disciplinary apparatus. The author's unparalleled command of the sources yields a portrait of corruption in the courts that is Boschian in its detail, and her account of the disciplinary system is the most thorough to date.

Donald C. Clarke, Professor Emeritus,
George Washington University Law School

This book will be welcomed by all those interested in comparative law and government. With the perspective of an "insider," Ling Li analyzes the history, achievements, flaws and challenges, as well as implications of the Chinese Communist Party's seventy-five-year effort to govern China as a Party-state. Based on two decades of deep research and sharp observation, it offers a stimulating view of both the evolving theory and expansive practice of the country's transformative but secretive political-legal process.

Jerome A Cohen, Professor Emeritus,
New York University; adjunct Senior
Fellow for Council on Foreign Relations, United States

Dr. Ling Li's exceptional comprehension of China's political and legal institutions offers readers an insightful exploration of the intricate workings of law and political power, both in the public eye and behind closed doors. With her penetrating analysis of the governing rules that dictate political disciplines and corruption, she presents a persuasive and thought-provoking perspective on the power dynamics within the political and legal sphere. Dr. Li's argument considers the significance of both the symbolic and legitimizing values of legal rules and the practical functions of political prerogatives and imperatives, providing a nuanced understanding of the subject matter.

Hualing Fu, Dean and Professor of Law,
Hong Kong University Faculty of Law

Ling Li's book is an impressive and penetrative study of the evolution of China's Party-state through the lens of corruption and anti-corruption. Theoretically informed, the book offers a rare and important contribution to our understanding of the rules and institutions that stabilize single-party rule and shape decision-making. It is essential reading for those who wish to deepen or reassess their understanding of the formal and informal structures and mechanisms through which the Chinese Communist Party governs itself and China.

Ben Hillman, Director of Australian Centre on China
in the World Professor, Crawford School of Public Policy,
Australian National University

This is an extremely important contribution to the study of the Chinese Party-state, the relationship of the Party-state to the legal system, and how these relationships have evolved and changed over time. Likewise, anyone seeking to understand the dynamics between corruption, anti-corruption and power struggles in China under Xi Jinping will find this to be an extremely valuable book.

Benjamin L. Liebman, Professor of Law, Director of Hong Yen Chang Center for Chinese Legal Studies, Columbia Law School

A valuable work by one of the leading scholars of corruption in China. Dr. Li expertly details the day-to-day experience of corruption within the Chinese state, as well as the grand historical evolution of the Party's disciplinary apparatus aimed at checking such practices, and tying both to core institutional choices made by China's leaders from Mao to Xi.

Carl Minzer, Professor of Law, Fordham Law School; Senior Fellow for China Studies, Council on Foreign Relations, United States

This meticulously researched study of the opaque nature of China's Party-state relationship provides us with a vivid X-ray of not only its veiled structure but also how subject it is to manipulation, corruption, power struggles, and influence-seeking. As we seek to divine the enigma of Xi's new China, Ling Li's roadmap is like being given a set of night vision goggles that help us see what otherwise remains obscure.

Orville Schell, Director of the Center on U.S.-China Relations, Asia Society, New York; former Dean of the Graduate School of Journalism, University of California, Berkeley

By focusing on the legal system and the problem of judicial corruption, Ling Li incisively penetrates the "black box" of China's "Party-state," disaggregates the formal rules and concrete practices that structure how it functions, and thus deepens our understanding of how the party governs China.

Andrew Wedeman, Professor of Political Science, Georgia State University

# GOVERNANCE OF A PARTY-STATE

## Corruption, Law, and the Modus Operandi of the Chinese Communist Party

**LING LI**
*University of Vienna*

CAMBRIDGE
UNIVERSITY PRESS

CAMBRIDGE
UNIVERSITY PRESS

Shaftesbury Road, Cambridge CB2 8EA, United Kingdom

One Liberty Plaza, 20th Floor, New York, NY 10006, USA

477 Williamstown Road, Port Melbourne, VIC 3207, Australia

314–321, 3rd Floor, Plot 3, Splendor Forum, Jasola District Centre, New Delhi – 110025, India

103 Penang Road, #05–06/07, Visioncrest Commercial, Singapore 238467

Cambridge University Press is part of Cambridge University Press & Assessment, a department of the University of Cambridge.

We share the University's mission to contribute to society through the pursuit of education, learning and research at the highest international levels of excellence.

www.cambridge.org
Information on this title: www.cambridge.org/9781009275002

DOI: 10.1017/9781009275033



When citing this work, please include a reference to the DOI 10.1017/9781009275033

First published 2025

Cover image: Qweek / E+ / Getty Images.

*A catalogue record for this publication is available from the British Library*

*Library of Congress Cataloging-in-Publication Data*
Names: Li, Ling (Writer of Governance of a party-state), author.
Title: Governance of a party-state : corruption, law, and the modus operandi of the Chinese Communist party / Ling Li.
Description: Cambridge, United Kingdom ; New York, NY : Cambridge University Press, 2025. | Includes bibliographical references and index.
Identifiers: LCCN 2025002715 (print) | LCCN 2025002716 (ebook) | ISBN 9781009275002 (hardback) | ISBN 9781009275040 (paperback) | ISBN 9781009275033 (epub)
Subjects: LCSH: Political corruption–Law and legislation–China–History. | Corruption investigation–China. | Corruption–Prevention–China. | Political ethics–Law and legislation–China–History. | Zhongguo gong chan dang–Rules and practice. | Rule of law–China–History. | China–Politics and government–History.
Classification: LCC KNN4516 .L5 2025 (print) | LCC KNN4516 (ebook) | DDC 324.251/075–dc23/eng/20250118
LC record available at https://lccn.loc.gov/2025002715
LC ebook record available at https://lccn.loc.gov/2025002716

ISBN 978-1-009-27500-2 Hardback

To *mom* and *dad,* for their infinitely selfless support, and to *Friedl* – for being the *Basis und Überbau* of my intellectual, emotional, and social life.

# CONTENTS

# ILLUSTRATIONS

## Figures



## Tables

# ACKNOWLEDGMENTS

Research for this project began in 2005, the year I embarked on my doctoral study at the Van Vollenhoven Institute (VVI) of Leiden University Law School, laying the groundwork for Chapters 1–3. I remain deeply grateful to my promoter Benjamin van Rooij for his boundless energy, passionate guidance, and generous friendship over the years, as well as Jan Michiel Otto, my other promoter and the director of the VVI, for his steady support.

The endogenous approach adopted in this book germinated during my five-year stint at the US–Asia Law Institute (USALI) at New York University Law School, led by the legendary Jerome A. Cohen. On a personal level, I remain, like many, in awe of Jerry's intellectual rigor and unparalleled academic achievements – not to mention his charm, humility, integrity, and generosity. Professionally, USALI was nothing short of an intellectual magnet, drawing together sharp minds from different disciplines and jurisdictions. There, I enjoyed engaging with many scholars, including Ira Belkin, Ben Liebman, Carl Minzner, and Frank Upham, whose deep knowledge of both the US and PRC legal systems continues to leave me astounded and full of admiration. It was during this time that I gained my first real glimpse into the workings of the US criminal justice system – its flaws and struggles – prompting me to investigate China's political-legal system based on its own internal logic.

My journey into the governance of China's Party-state took a decisive turn in Vienna. I am grateful to Christian Göbel for inviting me to teach at the Sinology Institute at the University of Vienna, and to Susanne Weigelin-Schwiedrzik for leading me into the deeper currents of Party history. Teaching PRC history and engaging in spirited exchanges with historians enhanced my appreciation of the wealth of information embedded in historical materials. These materials proved to be treasure maps full of insights into Chinese elite politics – territories often impenetrable due to their opacity. The hybrid approach that ultimately shaped this project required absorbing a towering stack of reading – a feat made manageable thanks to the exceptional library service provided by the University of Vienna, especially from the sinology desk of the East Asian Studies Library, whose dependable support I appreciate greatly.

Over the past two decades, I have had the great fortune of crossing paths with many outstanding China scholars who have supported my research in diverse and meaningful ways. I thank Björn Ahl, Sue Trevaskes, Ben Hillman, Xin He, Wei Cui, Mary Gallagher, Björn Dressel, Elif Akcetin and Maura Dykstra for involving me in workshops, talks, and conferences that helped shape various chapters of the book at different stages of its development. My deepest appreciation goes to Sida Liu, Will Low, Grace Mou, Christoph Steinhardt, Stein Tsui, and Juan Wang whose critical insight, collegiality, friendship, and generosity of spirit have been a constant source of inspiration and encouragement – and a lasting reminder of the value of community in academic life.

I am also grateful to Hualing Fu, whose exemplary scholarship has guided my work since he served on my doctoral examination committee fifteen years ago. I also wish to thank Donald Clarke, from whom I have learned a great deal over the years – particularly about professionalism, fair-mindedness, and a meticulous attention to detail. Don was generous enough to read the draft manuscript of this book and, in doing so, rescued me from a number of otherwise embarrassing errors, for which I am truly grateful.

Earlier versions of some chapters have appeared in various publications, including Corruption in China's courts in Judicial Independence in China (2010); Production of Corruption in China's Courts in *Law & Social Inquiry* 37(4), Performing Bribery in China and Politics of Anticorruption in China in *Journal of Contemporary China* 20(68) and 28(115), respectively, and The Rise of the Discipline and Inspection Commission 1927–2012 in *Modern China* 42(5).

Lastly, I am indebted to all those – Orville Schell, Andrew Wedeman, and others acknowledged earlier – whose eloquent and humbling praise has graced this book. Their endorsements have provided not only invaluable affirmation of the work itself but also deep personal reward for what has been a long and challenging journey.

# NOTE ON PARTY-STATE NOMENCLATURE

**Party Center** (*dangzhongyang*) is an official name used by the Party in its normative documents without a definition. In practice, it refers to any or any combination of the Central Committee, the Politburo, and the Politburo Standing Committee of the CCP.

**State** (*guojia*) is used throughout the book to denote the power structure and associated institutions established under the PRC Constitution. In this book, the term "state" is used to contrast the Party structure and its associated Party institutions established under the Party Charter. A *state organ* refers to a branch of the state, as stipulated in the PRC Constitution. *Government* is used to denote the executive branch of the state structure at any administrative level.

**Subnational units** refer to all administrative units below the national level, including provinces, prefecture, county/urban district, and townships and street blocks, consistent with the usage of "local (*difang*)" in state laws and Party regulations. When a specific tier is referenced, it will be explicitly indicated – for example, "provinces" or "units with provincial ranks."

**Leaders** refer to civil servants, including political leaders, who perform "leadership" functions (*lingdao zhiwu*), such as "organizational (*zuzhi*), managerial (*guanli*), decision-making (*jüece*), and command (*zhihui*) functions" (NPC, 2005). In China, political leaders and the civil service are integrated. Public posts are generally divided into two categories: leader positions and non-leader positions, based on whether the individual is appointed to perform a "leadership" function.

**Leader judges** are judges who hold leadership positions and perform a supervisory role in the administration of court affairs. They include the court president, vice-presidents, members of the adjudicative committee, divisional leaders, and when applicable, sub-divisional leaders.

A **territorial Party Committee** is a Party organization established within an administrative unit. It holds plenipotentiary authority over all affairs within its territorial boundaries and serves as the highest decision-making body in that unit.

# NOTE ON SOURCES

1. The sources that are used for the factual summary of each cited case are provided where the case was first mentioned in this book unless indicated otherwise. Due to space constraints, not all sources of all cases are listed in the book. However, readers can find details of a list of representative corruption cases in the Appendix.
2. The source of cited regulation is either indicated in the texts or in the footnotes. Sources of regulations that have been consulted but not necessarily directly cited in the book are included in a selective reference list in the Appendix.
3. Pinyin and corresponding Chinese characters are provided in two separate glossaries in the Appendix – one for key Chinese words and phrases and one for names of corrupt officials in important cases and main political figures.
4. All Chinese names in the texts follow the order of family name first and first name second, unless the individual has indicated a different preference.

# PRINCIPAL ABBREVIATIONS

| | |
|---|---|
| CAC | Central Advisory Committee |
| CCDI | Central [Party] Committee of Discipline and Inspection |
| CCP | Chinese Communist Party |
| CDI | [Party] Committee of Discipline and Inspection at subnational levels |
| COD | Central [Party] Organizational Department |
| CPLC | Central Political-Legal Committee of the Party |
| CPS | Central Party School |
| CPSU | Communist Party of Soviet Union |
| CSC | Central Supervision Committee |
| GITIC | Guangdong International Trust and Investment Corp. |
| GPS | General Party-Secretary |
| KPGK | Party-State Control Committee of the Soviet Union |
| KNK | People's Control Committee of the Soviet Union |
| KQL | Kai Qi Lai Company |
| Xmei | Xi'an Mineral Exploration Institute |
| MPS | Ministry of Public Security |
| MOS | Ministry of Supervision |
| MSS | Ministry of State Security |
| NPC (State) | National People's Congress |
| NPC (Party) | National Party Congress |
| NSC | National Supervision Commission |
| PEP | Political Education Programs |
| PLC | Political-Legal Committee of the Party at subnational levels |
| PRC | People's Republic of China |
| SOE | State-owned enterprise |
| SPC | Supreme People's Court |
| SPP | Supreme People's Procuratorate |
| UCOPC | Unified (Absolute) Command of the Party Center |
| YARC | Yan'an Rectification Campaign |

# Introduction

## What Is a Party-state and Why Study It?

"Party-state" is a descriptive term for the political system of the People's Republic of China (PRC). In comparative political studies, the PRC political system is often referred to as a "one-party system" or a "single-party state." Such labels are avoided in this book, because when numerals are used to define a political system, they obscure significant qualitative differences in the infrastructural capacities achievable by a political party in a Party-state compared with what is possible in a multi-party system. Such labels create a misleading impression that the political system of, for instance, the United States (a two-party system), is closer to China's (a one-party system) than to the Dutch multiparty system. Interestingly, "Party-state" is not a term of reference employed by the Party either.[1] In the PRC Constitution (2018), China's political system is described as "a socialist system" with the leadership by the Chinese Communist Party (the Party or the CCP) as its "defining feature."

To facilitate analysis, Party-state is used in this book not only as a descriptive but also an analytical term. It is analytical because the term addresses not only the state of connectivity between its two components, the Party and the state, but also their distinction. It means that both components have their own identities and self-contained organizational structures, which are not erased by their connectivity. This feature of distinction is critical because it allows the Party to operate both inside and outside of the state organs. It is functionally valuable for the Party and the state to retain separate identities, which is highlighted by the

[1] The reason is perhaps partly due to the term's historical association with the Republic of China (1911–49) and partly due to the PRC constitutional arrangement, which allows a pocket of space for consultative "multi-party collaboration" with eight nominal "democratic" political parties through the Chinese People's Political Consultative Conference.

recent expansion of practices of "conjoined-offices" and "wearing two hats." Both practices allow the Party to retain double identities, one of a Party and one of a state organ, and exploit the prerogatives of both by switching identities when circumstances so require.

This book explores two themes in parallel. The first is the operation of the Party both inside and outside of the state and the second is corruption, with an institutional focus. The objective of my analysis is to understand the meanings of consequential actions taken by relevant actors, both at the institutional and personal levels. To that end, I combine macro-level normative analyses of the rules enacted to enable or constrain conduct with micro-level case studies that address the actions of individual actors, who may or may not observe the rules depending on the circumstances. My investigative focus is decision-making, namely, asking how decision-making is shaped by the formal-normative structure and how individual actors interact with it. In order to gain a deeper understanding of the operation of the Party-state, I also adopt a historical perspective, placing the subject matter in a broader historical context to reveal structural patterns that stabilize the Party-state as well as contingent forces that drive institutional changes. Next, I will situate the two themes in a set of broader topics to provide a more contextualized background of this study.

## Opacity of the Party-State

For evident reasons, researchers generally face greater challenges on any topic when studying a closed political system compared with a more open system. But, of the compounded structure that we call a "Party-state," the component that is most challenging to study is the Party. This is manifested by the predominance, in contemporary China studies, of literature on the structure and operation of various state institutions, contrasted by the paucity of academic outputs on the inner workings of the Party.

The reason for this disproportionate distribution of academic attention is in large part attributable to the fact that the operation of the state is relatively more open and transparent, whereas the operation of the Party is notoriously opaque. The opacity of the Party stems from the fact that the Party adheres to a practice of self-governance. This means that the Party is regulated like a quasi-private club, despite being the largest and most important single public institution of the country. The Party decides what information to share with the public, when to share it, and whom to share it with. For instance, the recommendation, nomination, and selection of the top leaders of the Party-state organs are not disclosed to the public until the completion of the election. Similarly, the Party's internal disciplinary process, which can either absolve a person of criminal liability or trigger prosecution, is carried out in complete secrecy.

In the past two decades, the Party has made efforts to make its operation more public, which is accompanied by a drive to enhance institutionalization. To that end, the Party has standardized many practices and turned them into an "intra-Party regulatory system." More central directives, regulations, and operational guidelines have been promulgated and published in the past two decades than in the previous eight decades combined. Such an abundant pool of information provides a precious window of opportunity to look inside the operation of the Party. However, these Party rules are often written with an esoteric nomenclature and terminology (Barnett, 1969) that would appear alien even to a Chinese lawyer, let alone to those who do not speak the language and/or are untrained in this regard.

Of the Party-state construct, the other component that remains opaque and difficult to study is the "-" between the Party and the state. The "-" embodies the critical link that binds the two systems together. One of the most important but the least studied conceptual features of China's Party-state is the set of structural elements that chain the state, a self-contained institutional structure, to the Party, itself a distinct institutional structure, and subjugate the former to the latter. In multiparty systems, political parties exert control over state offices primarily, if not exclusively, through winning elections and making political appointments. In China's Party-state, mechanisms that are installed for the Party to control the state are multidimensional and permanent. They are multidimensional because such mechanisms apply not only to persons but also to institutions. They are permanent in the sense that they are not dependent on electoral outcomes but are deployed without interruption, either before, during, or after political elections and appointments.

These mechanisms are often hidden and difficult to study because decision-making in state organs is bifurcated, which obscures the Party's participation. Bifurcation means that decision-making in state organs is divided into two phases, one taking place backstage, as it were, in Party organs and the other taking place "onstage" in state organs (Li, 2015a). The bridge between them is the Party-group, the members of which constitute the absolute majority if not the entirety of the decision-making body of a state organ. The Party-group answers first and foremost to the superior Party committee and its function is to translate the instructions and priorities of the latter into formal decisions of the state organ concerned. Information about the Party's involvement in the decision-making process is subject only to voluntary disclosure by the Party itself.[2] The depth of the opacity is best illustrated by the most recent disappearances of the now ex-foreign minister Qin Gang and ex-defense minister Li Shangfu. Both had disappeared from public view for months at the time of writing without any information about their current whereabouts or explanation of their disappearance and their later removals despite heightened public interest.

## Party's Normative System

Within the Party-state construct, the primary and dominant actor is the Party. As a political organization, it has more than 90 million members and enjoys the plenipotentiary power to oversee "all areas of endeavor" in "every part of the country" (Xi, 2019). The Party's self-governing regime consists of a complex multilayered and multidimensional system in which both formal and informal institutions operate. Among the earlier generations of China scholars, a lot of investigative energy had been dedicated to the study of the informal practices, especially in the field of elite politics. Many factors contributed to this selection bias: prohibition to conduct field research in China, fragmented sources of information with limited perspectives, mixture of scholarship and intelligence gathering, and the fact that, at the time, the Party was poorly institutionalized (Barnett, 1969; Oksenberg, 1969).

Before 1949, the Party was an underground political organization, scattered in pockets of remote areas across the country, constantly under siege or the threat of it by its adversary. The rules developed by the Party in this period were scant and rudimentary and focused mostly on military and underground operations. After seizing power in 1949, the Party started to build a Party-state, combining practices learned from the Communist Party of the Soviet Union (CPSU) and China's imperial past. However, top leaders of the Party differed on the exact approach through

[2] Such information constitutes "process information" and is exempted from mandatory disclosure. See Article 16, State Council Open Information Act (2019).

which the country should be governed and to what extent the Party should be institutionalized.

Discord between top Party leaders, compounded with ideological differences and individual vindictiveness, had led to persisting political turmoil. Efforts made toward institutionalization were frequently undermined and certainly overshadowed by incessant ideological drives favored by Mao, the Party's paramount leader, who saw institutionalization as an encroachment on and threat to his personal power. Mao's endeavor to stymie institutionalization reached its peak during the Cultural Revolution. It resulted in the dissolution of the Party's institutional seats of power, the breakdown of its organizational cohesion, and the imposition of military rule on the country. The destructive force of the masses unleashed by the Cultural Revolution had destroyed the nascent normative system of the Party-state, leaving the Party debilitated for years.

In the late 1970s, following Mao's death, the crackdown on the Gang of Four, and the return to power of Deng Xiaoping, Chen Yun, and other veteran revolutionary leaders, the Party embarked on a remarkable path of institution-building.[3] Copious literature has documented this process. Studies of the normative system of the Party-state have mushroomed, especially on the emergent PRC legal system. Publications on various branches of Chinese law filled international and comparative law journals and bookshelves. In parallel, the Party's own normative system was also rebuilt. This process began with the promulgation of a new Party Charter (functions as the Party Constitution) in 1982. Compared with its previous versions, the 1982 Party Charter is much more elaborate, being three times longer than the one passed in 1977 and five times longer than the most infamous one passed at the height of the Cultural Revolution in 1969. The Party Charter (1982) contains basic constitutional elements and principles of the Party that still guide its operation to the present day.

Under the Party Charter, a sprawling formal (written) normative system has been developed in the past four decades. After revamping and recompiling, this normative system (referring to the written, formal

[3] The result was nothing short of a spectacle. For instance, between 1979 and 2005, the number of primary laws promulgated by the National People's Congress and its standing committee was 6.3 times higher than that of the 1949–78 period. Similarly, the number of administrative statutes issued by the State Council was thirteen times greater, while ministerial administrative acts increased by an astonishing ninety-nine times compared to the previous thirty years combined. Source: Zhu (2007; Tables 1-01, p. 2).

norms unless indicated otherwise) comprises 3,615 intra-party regulations as of July 1, 2021.[4] Among them, 211 regulations were issued by the Central Committee, 163 by the Central Committee of Discipline and Inspection (CCDI) and the Central Committee work organs, and 3,241 by regional and local Party Committees. In 2018, the Party initiated an amendment to the PRC Constitution, where the Party crossed the normative divide between the Party and the state and put itself in the main text of the PRC Constitution with a provision stipulating that "the Party's leadership" is a defining feature of the PRC socialist political system.[5] In the meantime, a large-scale governmental overhaul was authorized, which conferred upon the Party more direct administrative control over state agencies through devices of conjoined offices (Committee, 2018).

The Party's normative system comprises critical information of how the Party operates. As the Party-state grows in maturity, it relies more and more on this normative system not only for self-governance but also for its means of control over the state and, by extension of state activities, over society. It is due to these normative rules that the Party organizes its members, regulates the power relations between them, and standardizes their practices. From this normative system, we can study not only routine political operations of the Party but also contentious elite politics. Winners of any political struggle consider it an important prize to consolidate their gains by shaping or reshaping the normative system that would systematically affect future routine political operation of the Party to their advantage. During the past two decades, we have witnessed consistent efforts by the Party to expand its normative system, which has been accelerated during Xi Jinping's rule. Regrettably, such development has largely eluded the attention and grasp of China watchers in the English-speaking world.

[4] According to the survey of the Legal Department of the General Office of the Party Center, as of July 1, 2021, there were 211 valid regulations promulgated by the Party Center, 163 regulations promulgated by the CCDI and other central Party organs, and 3,241 regulations made by provincial-level Party institutions. Available at https://rb.gy/8msl0, last visited on August 6, 2023. Also see Feng (2019).

[5] The normative divide means that, since the Party is not a sovereign power, its regulatory reach is limited to Party members and Party organizations. It oversees the operation of state organs only through its members and organizations embedded in them. In other words, without formal membership or institutional connection, the Party does not interact with the state directly. As a result, for a long time until 2018, the Party was absent in the PRC constitution, except in the historical narrative of the developmental path of the PRC outlined in the document's preamble.

## Academic Backwater

Whereas the Party's formal-normative system provides ample information about its mode of operation, its sustained development has, however, barely been reflected in academic studies published outside China. Several factors have contributed to this neglect. First, a long disciplinary tradition that focuses on the informal instead of formal politics in China[6] because of the (mis)belief that formal rules are either nonexistent or unimportant. Scholars of informal politics rely on a set of established methods and a toolbox based on accumulated knowledge of their pioneers (Carlson, 2010). By contrast, formal politics in China is still an uncharted field in which most scholarly work has not ventured beyond analysis of ideological discourses embodied in the Party's policy documents.

Second, in contrast to the state legal system, which has derived much of its content from established democracies and is therefore more familiar to West-based China scholars, the Party's normative system is rather an alien entity. One can find terms, principles, and doctrines in the PRC laws that trace back to, for instance, the Anglo-American, Germanic, or Japanese legal systems. But for the Party's normative system the only foreign source that one can refer to is the Soviet system. However, Sovietology and Sinology cross-fertilize less frequently than is expected. After the collapse of the Soviet system, scholars who are versed in both languages have become an even rarer breed.

In addition, despite its shared historical roots, China's Party-state is not identical to that of the Soviet Union. Under the general framework of the Party-state structure that both systems share, the operation of the CCP is distinguishable from that of the CPSU in almost all policy fields. For instance, in military affairs, strategically, the CCP's revolution deviated from the Soviet model and was anchored in rural rather than urban areas and favored guerrilla rather than conventional warfare (Fairbank, 1983; Fairbank & Feuerwerker, 1986). Structurally, the Party-army relation in China follows an "infused" pattern, whereas it was more "separated" in the Soviet Union (Zhou, 2019). In economic affairs, the CCP administered the planned economy quite differently from the CPSU:

[6] It is impossible to present an exhaustive list of scholarship on informal Chinese politics within the affordable space here. However, some representative studies include Dittmer (1990, 1995; Fewsmith, 1996, 2021b; Goldstein, 1991; Huang, 2000; Li, 2012a; Nathan, 1973; Shih, 2022; Tsou, 1995; Unger, 2002).

Even before the Great Leap Forward, economic decision-making in China had been much more decentralized than in the Soviet Union (Hu, 1994; Pei, 1996; Wang, 2021a).

In political affairs, the CCP has an additional tier of a formal decision-making body above the Politburo, namely, the Politburo Standing Committee, while the CPSU did not; in China, Party leaders taking executive positions in state organs are organized in a collective body called Party-group, an institutional design that was seemingly nonexistent or insignificant in the CPSU (Sperber, 2023). In legal affairs, the CCP relies on the Party *zhengfa* committee to coordinate affairs between courts, procuracy, the police and the justice department, which was either nonexisting or operated in obscurity under the Soviet system. The above-mentioned list of differences between the CCP and the CPSU is by no means exhaustive but merely exemplary of the most obvious. These divergences have only expanded since the Sino-Soviet split in the late 1950s. After the collapse of the Soviet Union and the East European Bloc, the CCP has been completely on its own track.

The third factor contributing to the neglect of the Party's normative system in the field of China studies is a significant cognitive barrier to comprehend it. First, the Party's normative system is heuristically developed, which means that it is not systemized despite recent efforts of codification (Snape, 2019b). Second, originally, the system was exclusively written for and addressed to insiders. One should recall that, for a long time, Party regulations were not open to the public (Hamrin, 1995; Oksenberg, 1974; Wu, 1995) but only for internal use. Since these rules were written only for insiders, they did not follow the requirements of legislative drafting. For instance, clarity and precision are not necessarily the primary drafting criteria for Party regulations. To the contrary, "strategic ambiguity" is employed more frequently than desirable to allow regulatory fluidity. Consequently, many key concepts in Party regulations remain undefined, the legislative intents of the drafters undisclosed, and the reasoning behind the normative provisions unexplained.

Adding to the cognitive barrier is the fact that, unlike standard legal documents, Party regulations are filled with political exhortations and historical references. Sometimes, metaphorical language is employed to communicate punitive sanctions. To decipher these rules and to fully understand their functions and significance, one would need to have a solid knowledge of the bureaucratic practices of the Party, both at present and in the past, involving a skillset that not every China scholar is willing or able to invest time and effort to acquire.

Lastly, the public disclosure of the Party's normative system is incomplete. At least two important categories of information remain undisclosed. The first concerns normative documents issued by the Politburo and its standing committee, the executive bodies of the Central Committee that possess legislative power on their own and the power to approve drafts submitted by their work organs. However, few regulations enacted by these two bodies are published and the rules, if any, that guide their conduct of business are also not disclosed. The second type of information that is undisclosed is the process information, including information explaining the drafting process, such as disagreements that were debated and compromises that were reached. Such information is treated as state secrets and regularly omitted in published documents or reports.

All these factors make the Party's normative system hopelessly pedantic and difficult to penetrate. Hence, we witness a situation that would be rare in any academic field where the object under observation is rapidly growing but has somehow passed by us and escaped our attention. With such a static and limited understanding of a rapidly growing system, it is no surprise that questionable judgments frequently appear in op-eds and other unscrutinized political analyses.

## Party's Disciplinary System

Among all Party apparatuses, none other can reflect the evolution of the Party's normative system more fully than its disciplinary institutions. This is because the disciplinary system has been an integral part of the constitutional makeup of the Party since its establishment. Hence, the normative development of the Party's disciplinary system is, in a way, a reliable barometer of the Party's institutionalization.

In 1982, as an important step to reconstruct its normative system, the Party rebuilt the CCDI, which was mandated by the Party Charter to enforce Party policies and disciplines. The CCDI expanded steadily in the 1980s and began to shift its focus to corruption, which had spiked during the country's market economic transition. In 1992, three years after the anti-corruption protests in 1989, the CCDI was authorized to use coercive investigative methods and its investigative capacity started to grow rapidly. Throughout the 1990s–2000s, the increased enforcement of anti-corruption laws of the Party-state has gradually stamped out the more visible types of corruption, whereas the less visible type – namely, the parochial or *guanxi*-facilitated corruption – continued to spread and intensify (Guo, 2008; Wedeman, 2005b, 2012).

During that period, corruption and anti-corruption seemed locked in an equilibrium. Corruption is occasionally exposed through scandals but manages to survive both routine oversights and periodical anti-corruption campaigns until the next scandal. This equilibrium was, however, broken in 2012 after Xi Jinping took office. He launched an unprecedented anti-corruption campaign, bringing down more corrupt officials than his predecessors had done in previous decades. At the height of the campaign, an intersectional institutional reform was launched that has further expanded the reach and investigative capacity of the Party's disciplinary system.

Among all Party organs, the CCDI is the one that has attracted the most attention from China scholars because of its dominant role in anti-corruption investigation. So far, dozens of monographs and hundreds of journal articles have been published regarding anti-corruption in China.[7] Any study on this topic would be considered seriously flawed if the CCDI's role is not properly addressed. However, due to the narrow anti-corruption focus, the functions and operation of the Party's disciplinary system in the broader political context remain unexplored. For instance, why are the CCDI and its lower counterparts elected instead of appointed like all other Party organs? Does this electoral status give the CCDI any prerogative that is not afforded to other Party organs? Which one holds the highest disciplinary power, the CCDI, the Central Committee, the Politburo, or the General Party Secretary (GPS)? What are their respective roles in the disciplinary process? Why are the Party disciplinary institutions subject to "dual-leadership" instead of vertical control by the CCDI exclusively? What is the original purpose of the Party's disciplinary system? How did the disciplinary system operate before anti-corruption became a prioritized mandate of the Party? And lastly, how does the Party's disciplinary system regulate power struggles at the top and how has it evolved over time?

## Elite Politics under the Party's Disciplinary System

One salient feature of the Party's disciplinary system is its attachment to elite politics at the Politburo. The most evident example is Xi Jinping's rise in power, which was paced in lockstep with his anti-corruption campaign, a campaign that was carried out by the Party's disciplinary

[7] For a more comprehensive overview of this body of literature, see Li and Kautz (2021).

institutions. This process was closely observed and widely reported in international media, propagating the view that the emergence of Xi's personal rule has upended the previous institutionalization process of the Party. The most recycled "proof" that was employed to support this view concerns succession politics of the Party. It was believed that before Xi's coming to power, the Party regulated its leadership succession through a provision of the PRC Constitution (1982) that imposes a two-term limit on the PRC chairman. This "term limit" was considered the main factor contributing to the "normalization" of elite politics at the top of the Party. According to this view, the "normalization" began in 2002 when Jiang Zemin passed power to Hu Jintao and it was reaffirmed when Hu Jintao passed power to Xi Jinping (Xi) in 2012.

This peaceful transition was seen as strong evidence of the formation of a "succession norm" that has abolished life-tenure of top Party leaders, forestalled personalistic politics, and prevented nationwide political turmoil driven by power struggles, as witnessed during the Cultural Revolution. As a result, elite politics appeared to have become more predictable and the regime more stabilized. If elite politics in China had indeed been dictated by this perceived succession norm, then Xi should have left office in 2022 and allowed himself to be succeeded by one of the two heirs apparent anointed by Xi's predecessor Hu Jintao. However, as history has unfolded, Xi did not leave office but started a third term and both heirs apparent were banished. To explain what had happened, Xi was portrayed as a treacherous dictator who squandered the Party's political legacy and wantonly broke the most precious norm that his predecessors had painstakingly built and protected, thus reversing the normalization process of Chinese politics. This view has been turned into a popular narrative that has dominated the international news media.

Since Xi's rise to power is inextricably linked to his anti-corruption campaign, it is necessary to note that the Party's disciplinary system regulates not only the conduct of the rank and file, or the "flies," but also of the "tigers," including those sitting in the Politburo. In fact, a survey of major historical power struggles at the Politburo reveals that the Party's disciplinary procedure was a decisive element in all these conflicts, as each ended with the losing side receiving disciplinary sanctions. Why is this the case? In what way has the disciplinary system shaped the approach and outcome of various power struggles? What kinds of constraints does it impose upon individual actors? How do actors with high agency shape the outcomes of the power struggles differently from actors with low agency? How has the regime changed over time and to whose advantage?

To answer these questions, a thorough investigation of disciplinary decision-making and of its historical vicissitude is required. Such an endeavor will improve our understanding of Xi's meteoric ascent to power, which is nothing less than extraordinary in a political environment where power is closely guarded, frequently contested, and fiercely competed for. Such an institution-oriented historical investigation will also aid our efforts to incorporate formal politics into analyses of elite politics in China, which has long been an exclusive subject of informal politics.

## Deviation and Corruption

As explained earlier, the Party's normative system provides abundant information that can be mined for the study of the operation of the Party-state. However, the same as in all normative systems, there exists a significant gap between what is dictated by the norms and what is implemented in practice. Any study of the system necessarily has to contend with multiple variances, inconsistencies, and deviations (Zhou, 2017b). To gain a better understanding of how the Party-state operates, one must examine not only what the rules are but also how they are applied in practice. Therefore, to complement my study of normative system of the Party-state, I use corruption as the empirical base to observe and analyze deviations from these Party-enacted rules.

Corruption is the most transparent evidence of behavioral deviation because the Party has never condoned corruption. To the contrary, all Party rules have introduced measures to punish corruption. Normally, deviation from rules is nothing unusual if occurring in isolated and exceptional instances. This, however, is not the case for China. In this book, I use judicial corruption to showcase that corruption is not a simple aggregation of idiosyncratic behavior of a few officials who have gone rogue, as it were. Rather, it is regular though hidden conduct that is produced and reproduced at every level of the government despite continued purges.

At the time of writing, Shen Deyong, former first vice-president of the Supreme People's Court (SPC) and the second most senior judicial official of the country, has just been convicted and has received a fifteen-year sentence for corruption. Shen was not the first SPC justice convicted for corruption. In Qincheng Prison, home for privileged high-profile prisoners, Shen may meet two of his former colleagues. One is Xi Xiaoming, also a vice-president and an associate justice of the SPC who was convicted of bribe-taking of 115 million *yuan* and sentenced to life imprisonment in 2017; and the other is Huang Songyou, who received the same sentence for bribe-taking of a smaller sum in 2010.

Some may argue that the investigations against these SPC justices might have been politically motivated. Indeed, as one will find in Chapter 6, corruption investigations have become increasingly politicized since the end of Xi Jinping's first term of office. However, whether the investigations of Shen Deyong and other SPC justices were initiated due to their political conduct is irrelevant to the discussion of the entrenchment of judicial corruption in China, unless the cases against them were fabricated. All three SPC justices in question have deep expertise in law and are highly knowledgeable about the inner-workings of the legal processes both inside and outside the courtroom. Framing them for egregious corruption involving extraordinarily large sums of money seems less likely, as it would require blatant evidential fabrication and tampering – overt violations of the law on multiple levels.[8]

Judicial corruption remains a serious problem in China because of its pervasiveness and persistence in the entire judicial system. Its pervasiveness is manifested by the fact that the crime is not limited to those who are ignorant of law or those who suffer from endemic or contingent economic hardship. Instead, it has infected the entire judiciary of all ranks, at every level of the judiciary, from all corners of the country. And, it can occur at any stage of the litigation in any type of cases, civil, commercial, and criminal, even in administrative litigation. Circumstantial factors, such as personal disposition, educational background (Zhang, 2006; Zou, 2000), or income of a judge (He, 2008; Wang, 2013), fail to explain its ubiquity.

In addition, judicial corruption occurs with such a high frequency and regularity, featuring such a long latency period, that it came to look like a business model. For instance, Zhang Jiahui, vice-president of the High

[8] Framing a person of power for corruption is not as straightforward as it may seem, even in a system where the investigating authority enjoys overwhelming power. Under current practices, proving corruption in court typically requires not only matching confessions from the bribe-giver and the bribe-taker but also a verifiable account of the transfer of the bribe(s). Dai Chunning, a former State-owned enterprise (SOE) executive, was confronted with this challenge when he falsely confessed to having accepted a bribe. Once he did so, he struggled to provide an explanation for where the bribe had gone. See the transcript of the interview of Dai Chunning by his lawyer Chen Jiangang, conducted on August 8, 2017.

Court of Hainan province, had taken money from thirty-seven bribers in sixty court cases over thirteen years without being detected. Shen Deyong, above-mentioned former SPC vice-president, had a history of bribe-taking that lasted for twenty-seven years until his arrest. In a recent scandal of the Intermediate Court of Ji'nan City, Shandong province, home of Confucius, three judges were caught for corruption and their history of bribery spanned for more than one decade and together they had taken bribes in 122 instances.

The long latency of these cases indicates that corrupt judges much more frequently succeed with their corrupt activities than are being caught. In other words, corruption being undetected is the norm rather than the exception. What, then, is sustaining corruption and insulating it from detection? Some scholars attribute judicial corruption to the Party-state structure because the Party's political control over courts renders the latter weak, dependent, and, rather paradoxically, also unaccountable (Gong, 2004; Henderson, 2007; Ip, 2008). However, others question this explanation based on two observations, first, the Party has never condoned judicial corruption and, second, the Party rarely directly interferes in individual cases because most court cases are neither political nor politically sensitive (Fu, 2010). Some scholars even argue that the Party is the most important progressive political force that empowers courts, promotes justice, and fights corruption (Huang, 2020; Jiang, 2019a; Wei, 2018; Zhang & Ginsburg, 2019; Zhu, 2010), which suggests that judicial corruption would have been worse without the Party's intervention.

My analysis of judicial corruption in this book stems from the hypothesis that when judicial corruption as a delinquency has become the norm, immune from countermeasures, the mechanism that creates the delinquency must be something that is entrenched in the normative prescription of routine judicial practices. Following this hypothesis, the first step of my investigation is to uncover the normative factors that would affect judicial impartiality in routine judicial decision-making in these courts. This is made possible due to the fact that the operation of courts, compared with other state organs, is more open and public. It means that their decision-making process is relatively more procedurally regulated. Relevant rules and some of their decisions are published. In addition, courtrooms and judges are relatively more accessible to researchers for field studies.

Consequently, empirically grounded research on China's courts has burgeoned during the past two decades, covering a broad range of topics, including judicial dependence or "embeddedness" (Li, 2012b; Ng & He, 2017), the configuration of the *zhengfa* system under the Party's rule (Li, 2015a, 2016a; Yu & Yang, 2019; Zheng, 2020), the operation of the Party's *zhengfa* committee (Ge, 2020; Hou, 2013; Liu, 2012a; Xu, 2016b), judicial appointments and personnel management (Liu, 2012c, 2013; Zuo, 2016a), decision-making at the adjudicative committees (He, 2011; Wang & Liu, 2017; Zuo, 2016b), and the more theoretical exploration of the relation between power and law in judicial decision-making (Li, 2017c, 2023). All these studies will enrich the empirical base of my analysis.

The second step of my analysis is to identify mechanisms of judicial corruption that make such an illegal conduct safe. This low chance of detection is particularly noteworthy because judicial corruption takes place in a highly adversarial environment, which means whatever advantages gained by the bribing litigant will result in the direct loss of the opposing party, who therefore has every incentive to prevent it or, if failing that, to expose it. What has enabled judges such as Shen Deyong and Zhang Jiahui to continue to commit corruption for several decades without being discovered? This question will be answered in Part I of the book.

## *Guanxi* and Corruption

To address the prevalence of judicial corruption in China, one cannot evade the topic of *guanxi*. *Guanxi* is commonly understood as social connections. In essence, its function is not so much different from how social connections are utilized in Western democratic societies to gain business advantages or to facilitate political appointments. What is distinctive about *guanxi* is its salience, namely, its omnipresence and omnipotence in Chinese society. It is therefore no surprise that *guanxi* has been a staple topic in China studies (Gold, 2002b), covered by a wide array of disciplines, including anthropology (Kipnis, 1997; Smart, 1993; Yan, 1996; Yang, 2002), sociology (Barbalet, 2017; Zhai, 2004), political science (Guo, 2001; Pye, 1995), as well as governance (Harding, 2014) and business management (Luo, 1997; Su, 2001). In this well-trodden field, sociologists and anthropologists generally emphasize *guanxi*'s social and moral functions and see it as a voluntary social and cultural practice, driven by emotions and sentiments, whereas corruption, in their view, is coerced (Barbalet, 2017) and driven by pure instrumentality and wanton and cold material calculation (Jones, 1994; Yang, 1994; Yang, 2002). Some scholars go further and consider *guanxi*-practices as a remedy for

China's weak and underdeveloped legal system (Jones, 1994; Potter, 2000).

This perception of corruption being "cold" and driven by pure economic calculation may be fitting for "market corruption." According to James Scott, corruption takes place in one of two forms, parochial and market corruption (Scott, 1972). In parochial corruption, opportunities to exchange are highly discriminatory and offered only to participants with distinctive identities, while in market corruption, opportunities to exchange are open, nondiscriminatory, and offered to anyone who pays or pays the most. Market corruption is predicated on the openness of its transactional environment, which contributes not only to its efficiency but also to increased exposure and risk of detection. Consequently, this form of corruption is particularly susceptible to anti-corruption efforts if such efforts are credible and sufficiently punitive. Corruption facilitated by *guanxi* epitomizes parochial corruption because the access to opportunities of corruption is conditioned by the identity of the participants, restricting such access only to those who share social ties, either endowed at birth or cultivated afterwards, with those who provide corrupt services.

Our foggy understanding of the relation between *guanxi* and corruption is to a considerable extent attributable to the semantic fluidity of how the term "*guanxi*" is used in Chinese conversations. At the same time, the fogginess is also attributable to the lack of exposure to the practice of corruption, which leads to the failure to appreciate the complexity of the contracting process of corruption as an illegal activity. Informed by institutional economic studies of corruption (Lambsdorff, 2002, 2004b; Schramm, 2002), I will illustrate, with real-life examples, the contracting process of corruption, including initiation, negotiation, and enforcement. Only when we can put ourselves in the shoes of corruption participants can we understand the constraints that they are facing when engaging in a legally and morally challenged transaction. And only then can we understand the measures that have been taken to reduce the legal, moral, and cognitive barriers that would otherwise prevent the transaction from taking place.

Another paradoxical phenomenon of *guanxi*-facilitated corruption in China's courts is its prevalence. Given its discriminatory and restrictive nature, this type of corruption ought to be a rare privilege reserved only for a limited number of court users, since few litigants have pre-established social ties with the judges hearing their case. In addition, the litigation process in China's courts has multiple phases and involves interactions with multiple judges at each phase. To cultivate ties, socially, with so many decision-makers within a limited span of time seems like a mission impossible. Even if one can prepare in advance, the transaction costs that the practice would entail would be prohibitively expensive. Given these constraints, how to explain the prevalence of *guanxi*-facilitated corruption in China's courts?

## Research Design and Book Structure

As explained earlier, the book investigates the operation of the Party-state both inside and outside of the state. In Part I of the book, I use court and judicial corruption as a window to examine how the Party controls decision-making in a state organ. In this part, I first seek to identify the structural mechanism that allows the Party to control judicial outcomes in China's courts. Then I will illustrate how certain features of this mechanism make it susceptible to abuse. Next, my investigation turns to the causal relation between *guanxi* and corruption in China, two inseparable phenomena. The purpose of my investigation is not to reaffirm their correlation but to identify and demonstrate the exact causal mechanism that links them. The goal of my investigation of these two mechanisms is to reveal the political and social institutional roots of corruption in China and explain two intriguing phenomena: transactional efficiency of corruption despite its illegality, and its resilience despite the severe punishment and intensified anti-corruption efforts. Part I ends with a survey of past anti-corruption judicial reforms and an assessment of the effects of these reforms against the findings of the previous chapters.

Part II of the book focuses on the self-governing regime of the Party itself. Specifically, I examine the structure, principles, and functions of the Party's formal-normative system and illustrate it with an analysis of the institutional design of the Party's disciplinary system. Part II starts with a historical survey of the normative development of the Party's disciplinary system, based on a normative analysis of a sizable body of Party regulations. This survey focuses on the power relations between various political actors involved in disciplinary matters, especially mechanisms that are installed to regulate delegation and control. Then, I will zoom in on Xi Jinping's anti-corruption campaign and disciplinary institutional reform in 2012–2022 and use it as a case study to show the centrality of the disciplinary system in Chinese politics, how it is both the starting and finishing points of Xi's campaign. Next, taking inspiration from the scholarship of historical institutionalism (Capoccia, 2016;

Capoccia & Kelemen, 2007; Hall, 1996; Thelen, 1999; Thelen & Steinmo, 1992), I will zoom out to survey major power struggles at the Politburo and examine different paradigms that have been developed to initiate a disciplinary action against a Politburo member. By historicizing the disciplinary mechanisms that have been used to facilitate power struggles, I hope to highlight how different political actors respond to institutional constraints differently and when and how institutional changes occurred.

As mentioned at the beginning of this chapter, corruption is a parallel theme that underpins the main investigation in this book. Unlike existing literature on corruption in China, which usually sets out to measure the trend of corruption and its correlations with various factors in which corruption is situated, my investigation focuses on the intrinsic causal mechanisms (Beach, 2016; Bennett & Checkel, 2015; Falleti & Lynch, 2009; Hedström & Ylikoski, 2010; Tilly, 2001) that explain the link between corruption and the deeper structural causes. To identify and explicate such causal mechanisms will help bring the analysis of interactions between corruption participants and their environment to the causal level, thus reducing the space of ambiguity where the causal attribution may be diverted or even reversed. My investigation of corruption also includes an examination of the political logic of the anti-corruption institution. This analysis will reveal a positive – from the viewpoint of the Party Center – externality of pervasive corruption, that contributes to the transition from the previous ideologized model to the anti-corruption model regulating elite politics of the Party.

## Sources

This book engages with a copious and eclectic collection of primary sources generated by the Party-state. These sources concern hundreds of normative enactments that were decreed by Party-state authorities, which are supplemented by (1) countless explainers, interpretations, and commentaries disseminated by these authorities in training materials and research publications and (2) more than a thousand cases regarding normative violations and malpractices that had been investigated and denounced by Party-state authorities. Different combinations of these sources are used in different chapters.

Specifically, the sources used in Part I of the book can be divided into three groups. The first comprises empirical materials concerning regular judicial practices, which consist of both primary and secondary sources.

Primary sources include, inter alia, courts' internal regulations, witnesses' accounts of court practices, leaked internal communications documenting the judicial decision-making process, investigative journalistic reports of corruption scandals, and occasionally released court decisions or criminal complaints regarding corruption cases. Secondary sources include empirically grounded legal studies on court administration and the operation of court decision-making bodies, most of which are written in Chinese and published in China as monographs or in academic journals, conference proceedings, or book volumes.

The second group brings together a collection of more than a thousand corruption cases for both statistical and qualitative analyses. For statistical analysis of judicial corruption, I use a self-compiled Dataset consisting of 349 cases. The cases are gathered through regular screening of major online news portals, newspapers, and news magazines focusing on corruption issues between 2005 and 2010.

I had attempted to update the Dataset but such attempts produced little benefit. When I compiled the Dataset in 2005–2010, courts and anti-corruption agencies were much more open in sharing information on judicial corruption with the public. After 2010, such practice became significantly restricted, making it impossible to rely on media outlets for national-level statistical analysis. Additionally, the National Database on Court Judgments, which was made publicly accessible in 2013, cannot be used for such statistical analysis either, as judicial corruption cases are heavily censored within the database.

Post-2010 cases are, however, collected and used for qualitative analysis, which is less sensitive to distortion due to selective reporting. Sources that are used to build this collection of case files include media reports published by investigative journalists or court documents occasionally leaked by litigants or their lawyers until 2023. Cases in this category are not limited to judicial corruption but include corruption committed by public officials in other legal institutions, including procuratorates,[9] police, Committee of Discipline and Inspection at subnational levels

[9] Procuratorates (*jiancha yuan*), a legacy of the Soviet legal system, wield a broader range of powers in China than their counterparts – prosecutors – in Western legal systems. In addition to prosecuting crimes, they are also authorized to conduct criminal investigations of certain offenses (most notably corruption, before the supervision reform in 2018), initiate public-interest civil actions in courts, and, albeit largely symbolically, oversee court activities to ensure the proper application of laws in both adjudication and enforcement.

(CDI) agents, as well as high-ranking Party leaders overseeing political-legal affairs. Except for court documents directly leaked through social media, all sources used for analysis in this book came from official sources, such as courts and anti-corruption agencies, or reputable media. Single-source uncorroborated and unsubstantiated complaints of corruption are excluded from the analysis.

The third group of sources consists of over 100 hours of semi-structured interviews with legal professionals, including lawyers, judges, procuratorates, and other law officials, conducted between 2005 and 2019. Some interviews were one-time only, while others included follow-ups through face-to-face meetings, phone calls, or emails at various stages of the research. Due to the sensitive nature of the interview content, most of the information obtained is not directly cited in this book but serves as a guide for understanding the motivations behind certain corrupt practices, particularly *guanxi*. Gaining this understanding is crucial for the qualitative analysis of real corruption cases discussed later. In this context, two autobiographies are particularly valuable for exploring *guanxi* and corruption in Chapter 3. Both books offer intimate first-person accounts of how corruption unfolds through *guanxi*-practices, aligning with the patterns and narrative revealed in my interviews.

Sources for Part II of the book can be divided in two categories. For the normative analysis of the Party's disciplinary system, the sources comprise (1) a copious body of primary sources, including Party directives (*tiaoli*), measures (*guiding*), methods (*banfa*), decisions (*jueding*), notices (*tongzhi*), and other normative documents, a selection of which are listed in the Appendix III, and (2) a pool of secondary sources, including interpretations and explainers of Party regulations compiled and disseminated by the Party for training purposes as well as scholarly studies published in Chinese academic journals. The data supporting the statistical analyses are primarily derived from the annual work reports of the CCDI.

For the historical analysis of major power struggles at the Politburo, I have consulted two types of primary sources, which consist of (1) official records of disciplinary decisions or announcements in the form of Party decisions and associated supplementary materials circulated by the Party; Party regulatory measures, internal communication records, Party conference proceedings, speeches of Party leaders, including self-criticism letters written by Party leaders; (2) witness accounts of historical events in the forms of memoirs, diaries, biographies, interviews, and oral history records. A selection of the first type of primary sources is included in the Appendix III. Secondary sources are also consulted in this study and are of equal value to the primary sources. These sources include Party histories, biographies, chronicles of major Party leaders, written by both Party-sponsored and independent Party historians.[10]

[10] For a more detailed account of Party historiographers, see Weigelin-Schwiedrzik (1987).

# PART I

# Corruption, Law, and Politics

# 1

# Corruption in China's Courts

Judicial corruption has long been a specter haunting Chinese legal scholarship. Despite widespread recognition of its persistent prevalence, few studies have ventured to delineate its exact scope, nature and manifestation. As a covert activity, the actual rate of corruption can never, it must be acknowledged, be accurately measured in quantitative terms, as such analysis can account only for what has been exposed.

When corruption is measured as such, two imperfect methods are commonly employed.[1] The first method gauges the perception of corruption by asking respondents how frequently they have encountered or engaged in corrupt behavior. The second method relies on statistics detailing the number of corruption cases detected, investigated, and punished.

Each method, however, has limitations. The first, measuring perceptions, can be unreliable, as respondents' answers may be influenced by subjective personal experience or distorted by actual or perceived external pressure to provide the "appropriate" answers. Survey results can also be skewed by researchers' biases, either in the sampling process or in the formulation of survey questions, leading to an over- or understatement of the actual situation. The second method, tracking anti-corruption activities, also risks misrepresenting the reality. For instance, an apparent increase in recorded corruption cases might indicate an improvement in anti-corruption efforts rather than a genuine rise in corruption, making it difficult to discern the true trend without considering other variables.

In this chapter, I will first offer a broad overview of the scope of judicial corruption in China, employing the second method – using court statistics on detected corruption among court personnel – to expose its limitations. Subsequently, I will analyze the distribution of judicial

[1] UNODC (2024).

corruption based on a self-compiled dataset. Throughout this chapter, "court personnel" primarily refers to judges, who comprised approximately 55 to 60 percent of the total court personnel at the time when the data were collected.[2] It also includes support staff such as clerks, administrators, stenographers, forensic examiners, and bailiffs. The term "judicial corruption" follows the definition provided by the Supreme People's Court (SPC), referring to conduct that seriously violates ethical discipline or even the criminal law, involving the use of adjudicative or enforcement power to engage in fraud, favoritism, or bribery (SPC, 1998, 2004, 2008).

## Official Statistics

The SPC regularly publishes annual statistics of court personnel subjected to disciplinary sanctions, either criminal or administrative, in the Annual Work Report (AWR), with a few exceptions. Since the predominant cause of these sanctions is corruption-related conduct, these figures provide a historical snapshot of judicial corruption in China. Figure 1.1 illustrates the fluctuation in the number of disciplined court personnel over time from 1985 to 2023, with three spikes, respectively, in 1998, 2017 and 2021–22.

Two key findings emerge from Figure 1.1. First, the statistics published by the SPC in its AWR likely underreport judicial corruption. This conclusion is drawn from a comparison of the SPC statistics with aggregated local court statistics on punished judicial personnel from 2003 to 2007. The comparison reveals a significant disparity (see Table 1.1), as the SPC's figures – which should ideally reflect the total number of reported judicial misconduct cases nationwide – are consistently lower than the sum of local reports of the same period. For instance, the SPC reported 218 punished court personnel nationwide in 2007, whereas the combined figure from just four provincial regions and one prefectural level district court (Note: China has in total 31 provincial level administrative units on the mainland) amounted to 252. This discrepancy sug-

2 The percentage dropped significantly after the introduction of the "quota-judge" in the 2016–17 judicial reform, which raised the qualification standards for judgeship and significantly reduced the number of judges. At the end of the reform, the reported total number of judges was 120,000, which dropped nearly 40 percent from the total number in 2013. See Xu (2017). Earlier judicial statistics are available in Zhu (2007, p. 154).

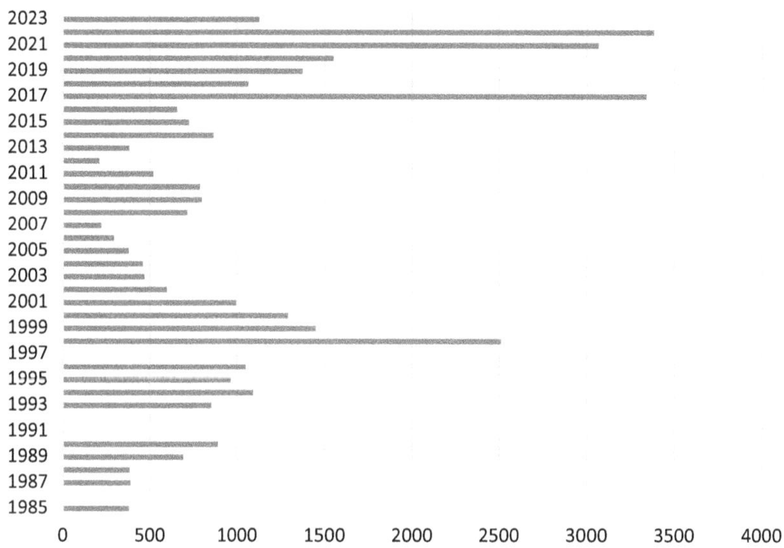


**Figure 1.1** Court personnel punished for corruption (1985–2023).

gests that the official statistics published by the SPC in the AWR do not capture the full extent of detected corruption, let alone of actual corruption within the judicial system.

Second, the fluctuations in judicial corruption shown in Figure 1.1 coincide with the launch of anti-corruption campaigns. These campaigns are designed to generate deterrence of corruption in a short period through mobilizing investigative resources and increasing both the chance of detection and the severity of punishment. Although the durability of such deterrence is debatable, it is evident that these campaigns lead to an increase in investigations (Manion, 2004b). This relationship is clearly reflected in the trends shown in Figure 1.1.

For example, the first spike of judicial corruption in 1998 coincided with an anti-corruption campaign launched by the Central (Party) Political-Legal Committee (CPLC) in 1997 (Wang & Chen, 1998). At that time, rampant corruption in law enforcement institutions had sparked massive grievances and discontent. The level of public dissatisfaction was so extreme that nearly half of the National People's Congress (NPC) delegates voted against approving the work report submitted to them by the SPC in 1997 – a highly uncharacteristic move (Caixin, 2016).

Table 1.1 Disparity of numbers of corruption offenders between the SPC and local court reports

| Year | Partial aggregation based on lower court reports | AWR National figures |
|---|---|---|
| 2007 | **252 – aggregation of cases reported from the following courts:**<br>4 provincial regions: Shaanxi, Hebei, Jiangxi, Hubei;<br>3 cities: Nanjing (Jiangsu), Linfen (Shanxi), Shizuishan (Ningxia)<br>1 basic court: Beilin District of Suihua city (Jilin) | **218** |
| 2006 | **697**<br>8 provincial regions: Shanxi, Henan, Ningxia, Hunan, Liaoning, Hubei, Hainan, Shanghai<br>2 cities: Harbin (Heilongjiang), Xuzhou (Shandong) | **292** |
| 2005 | **677**<br>8 provincial regions: Liaoning, Hainan, Zhejiang, Shanxi, Henan, Guangdong, Jilin, Shanghai | **378** |
| 2004 | **329**<br>5 provincial regions: Hunan, Hainan, Fujian, Jilin, Liaoning<br>1 city: Guilin (Guangxi) | **461** |
| 2003 | **884**<br>9 provinces: Shanxi, Liaoning, Shaanxi, Henan, Anhui, Hainan, Jiangsu, Hubei, Xinjiang<br>1 city: Cangzhou (Hebei) | **794** |

Note: Due to unstandardized statistical practice, the figures in the middle column do not always accurately correspond to the time period indicated in the first column. While some figures cover only a particular month of a calendar year, some cut through two consecutive calendar years. All data and sources are on file with the author.

The second spike in judicial corruption, observed in 2017, similarly aligned with an anti-corruption campaign launched by the Party, targeting law-related institutions, including courts. This campaign emerged at the tail end of the larger anti-corruption initiative led by General Party Secretary (GPS) Xi Jinping that began in 2012. Initially, the campaign focused on other governmental agencies and did not extend to courts until a special task force was dispatched to conduct an onsite inspection of the SPC in late 2016. The inspection focused on the performance of the leadership of the SPC in terms of discharging their supervisory duties, including their duties to monitor and control corruption in the judiciary. Subsequently, the SPC ramped up the efforts to clean its own house. The number of court personnel punished for corruption had quadrupled in the SPC alone and quintupled in all courts nationwide in 2017 compared with the previous year.

The third spike came in 2021, when the Party launched a disciplinary rectification campaign specifically targeting courts, procuratorates, and the police nationwide, underscored by the stark slogan "driving the blade in" to signal its resolve (Buckley, 2020). As shown in Figure 1.1, the campaign had doubled the total number of punished court personnel nationwide in 2021 compared with that in 2020. The trend continued in 2022 as the campaign was extended beyond 2021, reflecting the impact of these intensified efforts.

## A Judicial Corruption Dataset

Given the doubtful reliability of the official statistics, I have compiled a dataset (hereby the Dataset) that allows me to examine distributional patterns of different types of corruption, thereby painting a more contextualized picture of corruption in China's courts. This Dataset consists of 349 cases of judicial corruption publicized in press releases of courts and anti-corruption investigative authorities and in media reports, which I gleaned from the Internet during 2005–2010.[3] The 349 cases involve 340 judges, 4 court clerks, 4 court accountants, and 1 court bailiff (hereinafter judges for the sake of brevity). In some cases, multiple crimes were committed by one judge, for instance, bribe-taking, embezzlement, and abuse of power. Altogether, these 349 judges had committed 468 corruption-related criminal offenses.[4]

[3] These sources include the legal sections of www.sina.com and www.xinhuanet.com, fazhi ribao (Legal Daily), jiancha ribao (Procuracy Daily), jiancha fengyun (Procuracy Affairs), nanfang zhoumo (Southern Weekly), Caijing Magazine, minzhu yu fazhi (Democracy and Rule by Law), and Anti-corruption Weekly, published on *zhengyiwang* (Justice Network), an online magazine run by the Supreme Procuratorate. A considerable proportion of the cases were initially posted at Archives of Corruption Officials (*tanguan dangánguan*)," a blog hosted by Zhang Hongjian, a procurator in Heilongjiang province.

[4] Different counts of the same crime are recorded as a single offense in this Dataset. For instance, if a judge is accused of thirty-eight counts of bribe-taking, it is registered as one offense.

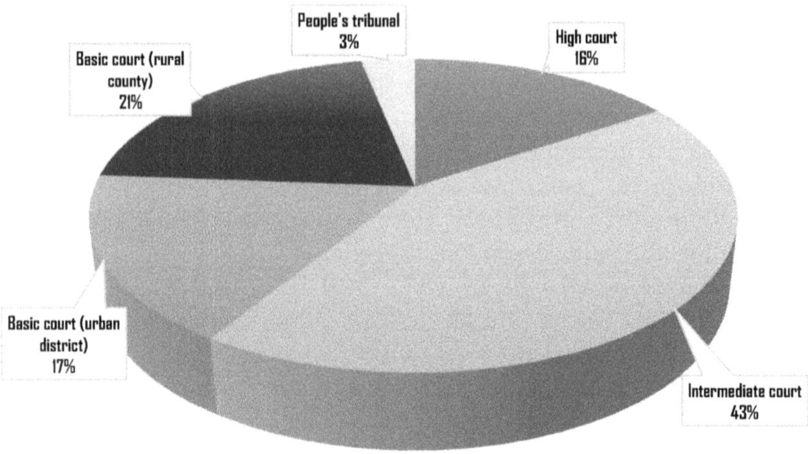


**Figure 1.2** Composition of the Dataset – divided by court levels.

Despite its temporal distance, this Dataset is nevertheless valuable for our understanding of judicial corruption in China. Over the past decade, information on corruption has become more restricted, notwithstanding improvements of judicial transparency in other areas. Case documents involving judicial corruption are generally excluded from the National Database on Court Judgments, and courts have long ceased issuing press releases on corruption within their own ranks. Nongovernmental anti-corruption watchers have also diminished their activities due to a crackdown on civil society. Therefore, while the Dataset was compiled a decade ago, it remains useful for illustrating enduring structural patterns of corruption. For clarity, my analysis in this chapter is limited to this Dataset alone; cases collected after 2010 will be incorporated and analyzed in subsequent chapters.

As shown in Figure 1.2, among the 349 cases, 43 percent occurred at intermediate courts, 16 percent at high courts, and the remaining 41 percent occurred at basic courts. It shows that high courts and intermediate courts (hereafter, higher courts) are overrepresented in this Dataset relative to their sizes. Currently, high courts comprise only 1 percent of the total number of courts in the country, while intermediate courts comprise 12 percent and basic courts 87 percent. The overrepresentation of higher court judges relative to their total number does not necessarily imply that judicial corruption is more prevalent at the higher than the lower levels of the judicial hierarchy. Rather, it is likely due to media bias, which placed more focus on high-profile cases. When the Dataset was compiled, no corruption at the SPC had been reported.

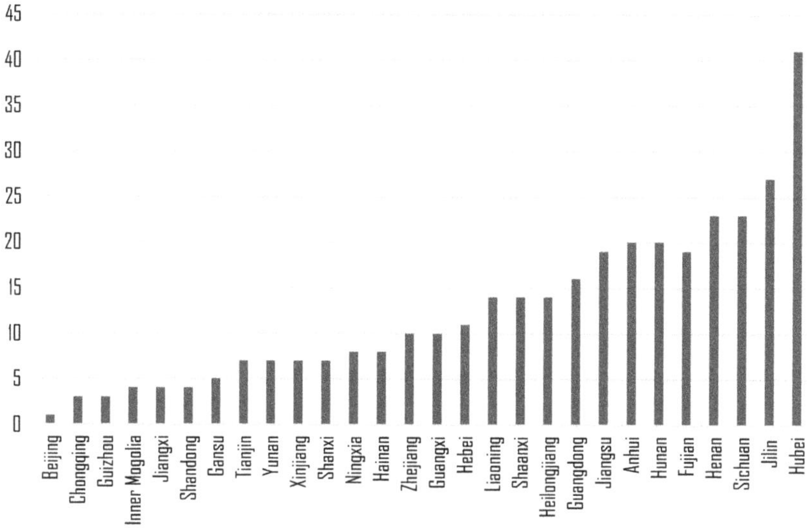


**Figure 1.3** Composition of the Dataset – divided by region.

Figure 1.3 shows regional representation of the Dataset. Specifically, the Dataset covers all provincial-level administrative regions except Shanghai, Qinghai, and Tibet. It needs to be stressed that the regional representation in the Dataset should not be mistaken as a reflection of the actual occurrence of corruption for reasons explained earlier. Rather, the representation should be read as a mixed result of the actual rate of corruption, the intensity of anti-corruption efforts, and varying media coverage policies across regions.

In terms of the temporal dimension, the Dataset is organized according to the year when corruption was investigated rather than the year when the offense was committed. This is due to the fact that in some cases, information about the exact timing of the corruption is unavailable, while in others, the allegations involve multiple offenses spanning several years, making standardized indexing challenging, if based on the investigation's launch date. Nonetheless, one should note that 73 percent of the cases were investigated in or after 2004, 27 percent before 2004, and fewer than 3 percent before 2000. Several factors may have contributed to this imbalance: greater online visibility of more recent cases, increased incidence of violations over time, enhanced anti-corruption efforts, or a combination thereof.

## Unpacking Judicial Corruption

Corruption is a considerably broad concept. The most popular definition, though sometimes contested, is that proposed by Transparency International and the World Bank: abuse of public power in exchange for private gain (Tanzi, 1998). Since this definition emphasizes the feature of "exchange," corruption is often equated with bribery, which includes the offering, giving, receiving, or soliciting of something of value to influence an official's action to discharge their public or legal duties. "Judicial corruption" in media reports encompasses a much broader range of misconduct by judges or other court personnel at any stage of litigation or in the administration of court affairs. It includes, for instance, physical abuse of litigants or other court users, extortion, embezzlement, fraud, and bribery. In order to gain a better understanding of judicial corruption in China, I unpack and classify different types of judicial corruption based on the nature of the power misused, where and how it is misused, and by whom.

To this end, I developed a subtractive classification scheme (see Figure 1.4) to classify the offenses represented in the Dataset through four filters.

**Step 1**: Distinguish cases with physical violence (Type A1) from those without (Type A2).

**Step 2**: Split the resulting A2 cases into B1 (*not involving self-enrichment*) and B2 (*involving self-enrichment*).

**Step 3**: Subdivide the dominant B2 cases into C1 (*non-transactional*) and C2 (*transactional*), namely, involving exchange, monetary or non-monetary.

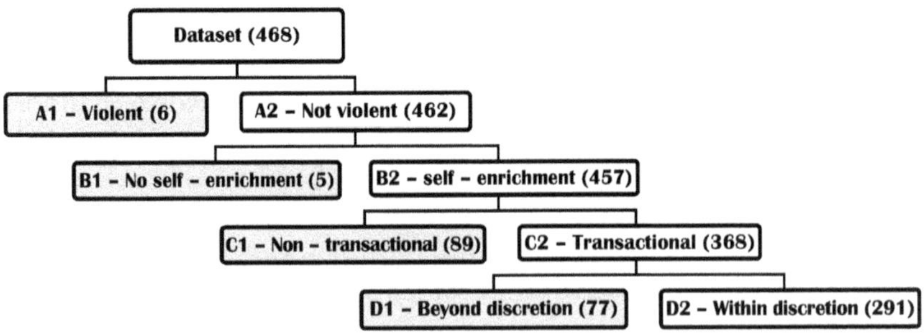


**Figure 1.4** Data composition based on a schematic classification of judicial corruption.

**Step 4**: Further subdivide the dominant C2 cases into D1 (*involving miscarriage of justice, namely, exceeding one's judicial discretion*) and D2 (*not exceeding one's judicial discretion*).

## Atypical Judicial Corruption

My study finds that the absolutely dominant type of judicial misconduct in China's courts involves transactional corruption where the corrupt service is delivered within the judge's discretion (D2). Misconduct involving physical harm (A1) and misconduct resulting from culpable incompetence or negligence instead of self-enrichment (B1) is extremely rare. Among the 468 offenses, only 6 fall in Type A1 and 5 in Type B1, all taking place at basic courts, the lowest level in the judicial hierarchy. Physical abuse (A1) is unsurprisingly rare (1.28 percent): courts have minimal police force and their authority to exercise physical coercion is limited to maintaining order in courtrooms and curtailing resistance when enforcing court decisions outside of courtrooms. Judicial misconduct due to incompetence or negligence (B1) is also rare (1.06 percent) because such conduct is generally not disciplined unless it has resulted in serious damage.

Corruption driven by self-enrichment is largely transactional (C2) instead of non-transactional (C1). Only 89 offenses in the Dataset are non-transactional and 368 are transactional. Typical transactional corruption includes bribery and favoritism, which require an exchange of benefits between two parties. Non-transactional corruption – embezzlement, misappropriation of assets, and fraud – does not necessarily involve another party.

Figure 1.5 shows the distribution of the 89 non-transactional cases (C1) based on the type of power misused. It is not surprising that more than one-fifth of these offenses were committed by court officials with access to court funds. For instance, Cheng Wei, an accountant in Tianjin Maritime Court, embezzled 1.69 million *yuan* and misappropriated 140 million *yuan* from the court's bank accounts in 1992–2004 and managed to conceal it by colluding with his colleagues in the Tianjin Maritime Court and with investigators in the local procuratorate. Cheng's activity had nearly paralyzed the court, which was compelled to temporarily rely on emergency funds from the superior court to remain operational.

Such non-transactional offenses (C1) also commonly occur during enforcement of civil and commercial court judgments. Here, judges

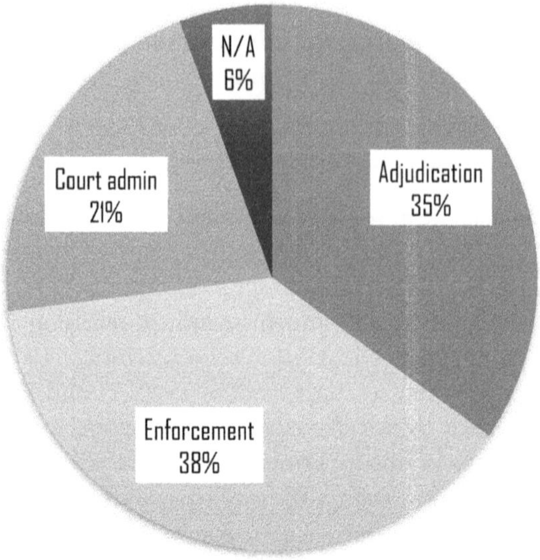


**Figure 1.5** Unpacking Type C1 by court functions.

exploit their authority to hold or manage seized assets for embezzlement, misappropriation, and bribery. For instance, Tan Yongxing, an enforcement judge in Longgang District (Basic) Court, Shenzhen City, misappropriated 13 million *yuan* earmarked for the victorious litigants and used it for gambling. In another case, Li Zhengda, an enforcement judge in Jilin High Court embezzled 40 million *yuan* during 1994–2001. He was arrested only after an investigation was ordered by the superior procuratorate following complaints submitted by a procuratorate from a different region.

In terms of corruption committed in the enforcement process, the cases included in the Dataset involve only civil and commercial but not criminal cases. It is not because criminal judgment enforcement is corruption-proof. Rather, it is because criminal judgments are not executed by courts but by prisons overseen by the Ministry of Justice, except for death execution. Corruption in sentence reduction in prisons is well-documented. A two-month campaign in 2021 reportedly screened 13,750,000 leads of problematic cases, rectifying 15,291 cases and disciplining 854 justice officials, with 121 prosecuted (Liu, 2021c).

Apart from embezzlement and misappropriation of assets, non-transactional corruption also involves fraud. Nine judges were accused of defrauding litigants. One judge from a county court in Liaoning province faked court auctions of seized assets worth a million *yuan* to swindle prospective buyers. Another judge, Yu Junyi, vice-president of a county court from Hebei province, used a forged court order to seize assets worth 7 million *yuan* from a state-owned enterprise. Afterwards, he made up a fake case against the enterprise brought to his court by fake plaintiffs and then ruled against the defendant based on fabricated evidence. This scandal came to light only after protests erupted, leading to violent clashes with the local police.

These examples highlight long-standing lapses in public accounting and auditing in China's courts, particularly prevalent in the 1990s. Those courts that were implicated in these cases typically suffered from chronic problems of low accounting standards, absence of internal or external audits, as well as non-transparent operation vis-à-vis court users, all of which cultivated a fertile ground for abuses. Such abuses were committed primarily by the administrative personnel who have direct access to the public coffer. In the past two decades, significant improvements have been made to narrow or close these regulatory loopholes with more stringent accounting and auditing protocols, reducing opportunities for non-transactional corruption.

## Transactional Judicial Corruption

Among the 468 offenses in the Dataset, 368 (78.63 percent) are transactional. Seventy-seven (20.92 percent) of these involve violation of Article 399 of the PRC Criminal Code, which targets miscarriage of justice driven by personal interests, typically through forging or manipulating evidence or knowingly applying the wrong law, in order to produce a favorable judicial outcome for a particular party. The remaining 291 (79.08 percent) offenses involve bribery without miscarriage of justice.

Unlike bribe-taking, which punishes violation of the integrity and honesty of judicial offices, the *actus reus* of Article 399 punishes intentional miscarriage of justice. According to a prosecutorial guideline issued by the Supreme People's Procuratorate (SPP) in 2006, a judge can be prosecuted for miscarriage of justice for fabricating, tampering, concealing, or destroying evidence, suborning witnesses, intentionally admitting inadmissible evidence, refusing to admit evidence that should have been admitted, or intentionally violating procedural rules or applying the wrong law. Also, unlike bribe-taking, a judge can breach Article 399 without committing monetary transactions. For example, Su Jiafu, a

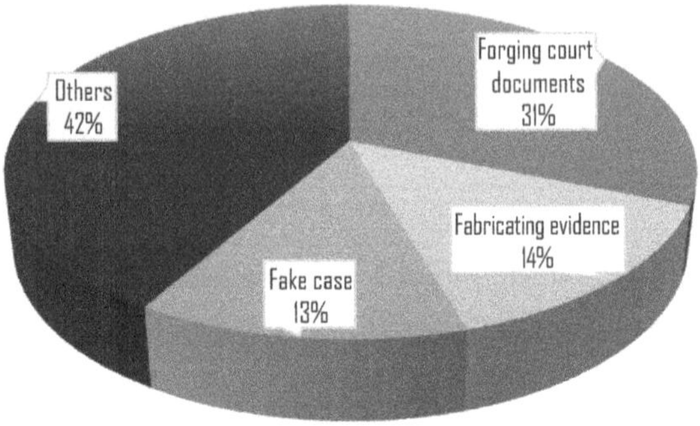


**Figure 1.6** Unpacking Type D1 by methods of corruption.

judge from a county court in Fujian province, once acquitted three defendants on a rape charge because one of the defendants was the son of the local police chief, who had previously done a favor to the judge in a battery case involving the judge's brother.[5] Of course, a judge can commit both bribery and a miscarriage of justice within a single criminal act, in which case the offender is usually prosecuted for the crime that carries the heavier sentence.

The Dataset contains 77 Article 399 violations. As Figure 1.6 shows, offenders in nearly 60 percent of these instances had taken brazen measures, including forging court documents, fabricating evidence, and creating fake cases with made-up disputes (usually for the purpose of seizing assets from the victims).

The Dataset contains a total of 291 offenses of bribery without miscarriage of justice.[6] These offenses are further divided into five crimes: soliciting bribes, bribe-taking, brokering bribery, bribe-giving, and possession of a large sum of unaccounted assets (hereinafter "unaccounted assets"). While the first four offenses are self-explanatory, the last one perhaps needs some explanation. The crime of "unaccounted assets" is similar to "illicit enrichment" defined in Article 20 of the United Nations Convention against Corruption,[7] to which China is a signatory. Such a crime is deemed to have been committed if a public official has been

[5] Tan (2000, p. 123).

[6] It should be noted that a judge may commit both D1 and D2 offenses on different occasions. There are twenty-two such cases in the Dataset.

[7] Article 20 of the United Nations Convention against Corruption defines illicit enrichment as an offence that is committed intentionally resulting in a significant increase in the assets of a public official that they cannot reasonably explain in relation to their lawful income.

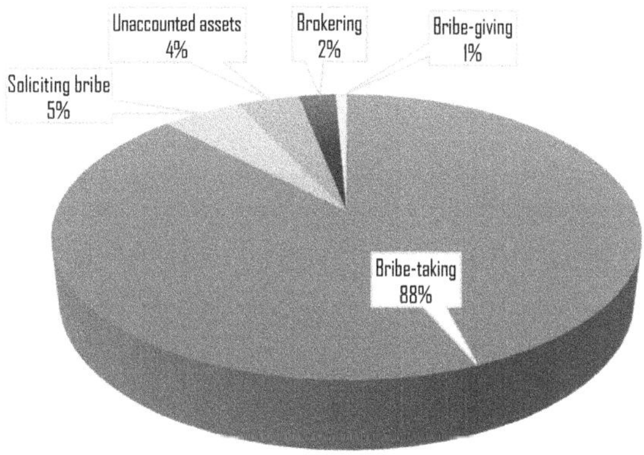


**Figure 1.7** Unpacking Type D2 by methods of corruption.

found in possession of a significant amount of tangible assets that cannot be reasonably explained in relation to lawful income. The criminalization of unaccounted assets has been criticized for shifting the burden of proof from the procuratorate to the defendant, thus violating the principle of assumption of innocence until proven guilty (Lewis, 2012). This is an important subject for academic and policy discussions but irrelevant to our analysis here.

Figure 1.7 unpacks transactional judicial corruption cases (D2) of the Dataset. Nearly 90 percent of D2 offenses are bribe-taking, initiated by bribers. Only fifteen bribe-taking offenses involve judges who actively solicited bribes, all of which were committed before 2004, with five found at intermediate courts and the rest at basic courts. Twelve judges were accused of unaccounted assets and seven of brokering bribery. Interestingly, whilst two judges were charged for giving bribes to their superiors for promotion, thirteen were charged for taking bribes from their subordinates for promotion. This gap is noteworthy because the number of offenses of bribe-taking should normally equal the number of offenses of bribe-giving. The cause for this gap is an asymmetrical procuracy policy, where the procurator offers to drop the charge or defer prosecution for bribe-givers in exchange for their cooperation to provide evidence against their bribe-takers (more will be discussed on this point in Chapters 2 and 3).

Figure 1.8 unpacks D2 offenses, namely, transactional corruption where a court official, in their capacity as either a judge or a court administrator, uses their discretion in the course of exercising judicial

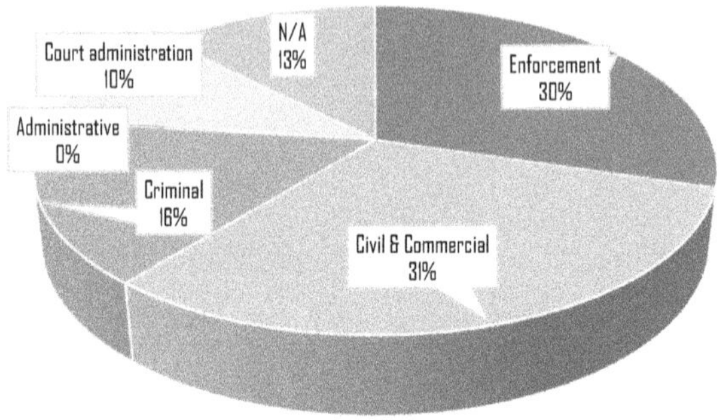


**Figure 1.8** Unpacking Type D2 by types of court activities.

or administrative power in exchange for bribes or other benefits. These cases are then disaggregated by the types of court activities where corruption occurred. Figure 1.8 shows that among the 291 D2 offenses, 30 took place in court administrative activities, including allocation of court public procurement contracts and personnel matters; 7 occurred at the case-acceptance phase, 153 in the adjudicative phase, and 86 in the enforcement phase. Particulars for the rest of the cases cannot be ascertained.

## Distributional Patterns

Based on the classification of judicial corruption shown in Figure 1.4, we can examine how each type of judicial corruption (A1, B1, C1, D1, and D2) is distributed across various court levels, divisions, and judge groups. As shown in Figures 1.9 to Figure 1.11, three patterns emerge.

First, the most prevalent type of judicial corruption is D2, namely, transactional corruption for self-enrichment without miscarriage of justice or overt misapplication of law beyond one's discretion.[8] D2 takes

[8] The PRC criminal law punishes misuse of power for self-enrichment when it involves receiving money or monetary assets, classifying it as the crime of bribe-taking. However, misuse of power in exchange for personal interest that are not easily quantifiable in monetary terms, for instance, sexual favors, personal affection, or securing a lucrative job for a family member, is typically not prosecuted. Exceptions arise when the misuse of power leads to a miscarriage of justice, such as wrongfully convicting an innocent person or acquitting the guilty party, or issuing judicial decisions without a legal basis or based on forged evidence.

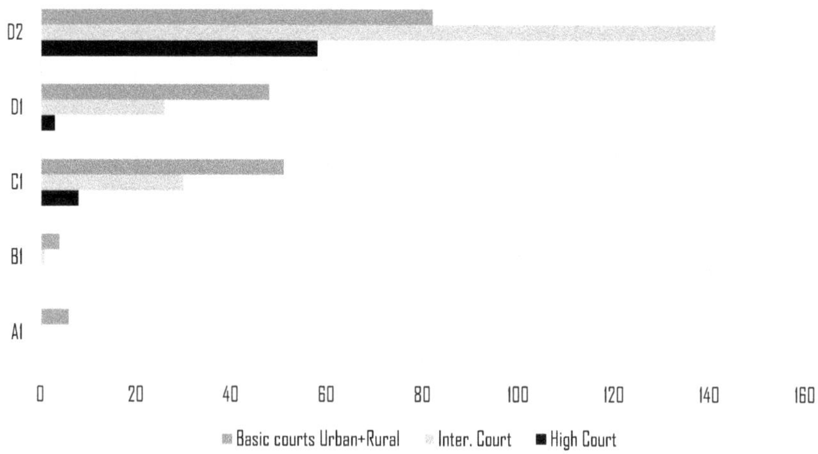


**Figure 1.9** Unpacking Type A–D by level of courts.

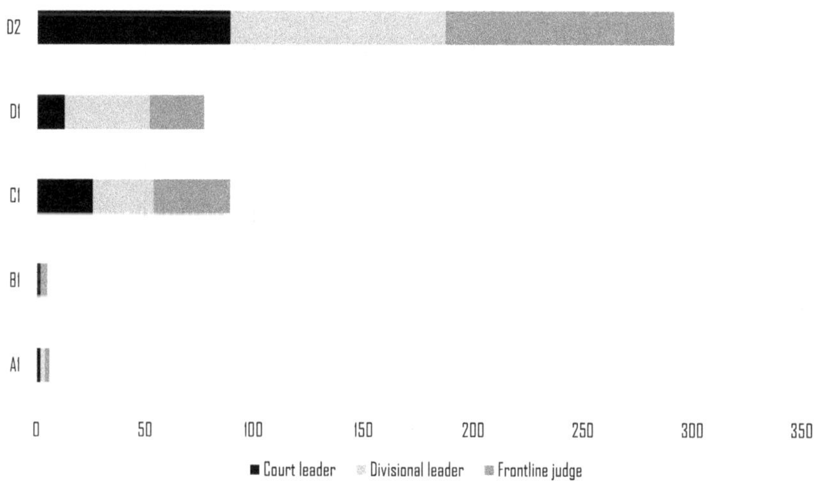


**Figure 1.10** Unpacking Type A–D by judge groups.

place across all court levels (Figure 1.9) and judge groups (Figure 1.10). Its distribution is disproportionately higher at higher-level courts (intermediate courts and above) relative to their case intake. Almost half of D2 offenses (48 percent) were committed by judges from intermediate courts, which constitute only 12 percent of the judiciary, in terms of

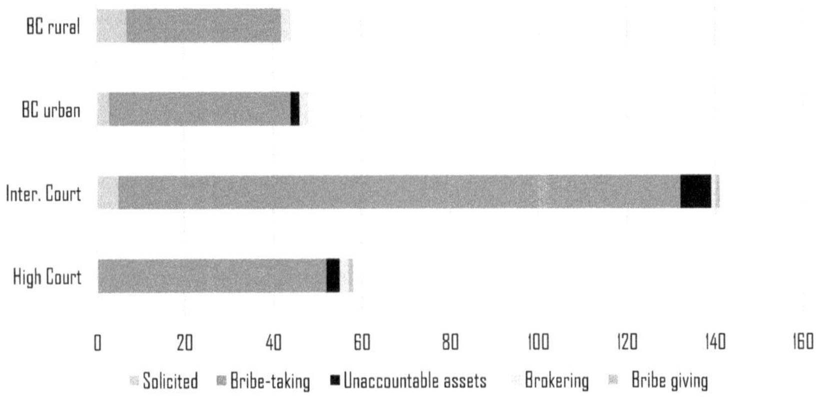


**Figure 1.11** Unpacking Type D2 by level of courts.

the total number of courts.[9] High courts, which constitutes less than 1 percent of the judiciary, nevertheless account for 20 percent of D2 in the Dataset. This finding contradicts the propagated discourse that judicial corruption is chiefly a local problem concentrated at lower courts.

Secondly, among D2 offenses, *passive* bribe-taking predominates in the Dataset across different court levels (Figure 1.11). The Dataset also indicates that D2 offenses are equally salient in rural and urban areas at the grassroots level since it shows a nearly equal amount of D2 offenses in both rural and urban basic courts. In contrast, *proactive* bribe-taking, namely, soliciting bribes, occurs much more frequently in rural basic courts, whereas no judge from high courts in the Dataset committed such an offense. Meanwhile, no judge from rural basic courts in the Dataset was found in possession of a large sum of unaccounted assets, likely because the criminal threshold of this offense is much higher than that of

9 The SPC publishes only nationally aggregated case intake numbers categorized by trial instance, without providing breakdowns by court level. As a result, numbers of cases heard at different court levels are unavailable. However, since the majority of first-instance cases are handled by basic courts, the ratio of first-instance versus second-instance cases can be used as a reference for estimating caseload differences between basic courts and higher courts. According to Zhu (2007, p. 206), approximately 90 percent of court case intakes nationwide were first-instance cases, heard primarily by basic courts. This ratio remained consistent throughout the observed period of 1988–2004 by Zhu (2007). Given the absence of significant policy changes affecting the division of trial instances, it is reasonable to expect that the ratio has remained relatively stable in subsequent years.

bribe-taking in terms of the value of corruption gains.[10] Compared with judges from urban and higher courts, rural court judges typically receive smaller bribes from engaging in judicial corruption because of (1) fewer corrupt opportunities arising from lower case intake and (2) lower exchange value of their judicial power, given that cases handled by them generally involve smaller stakes. These findings indicate that there is no definitive rural versus urban divide in the overall *prevalence* of judicial corruption but rather differences in the *forms* of corrupt offenses and their impact.

Thirdly, leader judges, namely, court leaders and divisional leaders combined, constitute the majority of corruption offenders in the Dataset across all types of corruption offenses, despite their smaller overall number compared to frontline judges. According to Sun and Fu (2022, p. 6), in 2002, the average ratio of leader versus frontline judges in a court was 1:2.5. Given this disparity, the overrepresentation of leader judges in the Dataset is particularly evident for non-transactional corruption offenses (C1) and transactional corruption without exceeding judicial discretion (D2), as illustrated in Figure 1.8. This finding challenges the conventional belief that judicial corruption primarily affects the lower ranks of the judiciary and that the problem can be resolved by centralizing judicial power in the hands of higher-ranking judges and in higher courts.

## Conclusion

No country that maintains some form of governance through public institutions and offices is free from corruption. Among such institutions, courts are typically the most insulated from corrupt practices. One key reason is that, by profession, judges are usually expected to hold higher moral and ethical standards than other public officials (SPC, 2010). In addition, disputes handled by courts typically involve zero-sum game scenarios, where any advantage gained by one party, with or without corruption, comes at the direct expense of the opposing party. Therefore, both sides have strong incentives and unambiguous responsibility (except in class actions where free rider problems may arise) to prevent and, if detected, expose corruption by the other side. Moreover, compared with decision-making in other public institutions, the judicial

[10] As of 2023, the prosecution threshold for bribe-taking under the PRC law is 30,000 *yuan*, while the threshold for unaccounted assets is 300,000 *yuan*.

process provides the parties with more procedural instruments to safeguard fairness. Under such conditions, one would expect corruption in courts, monitored by highly motivated litigating parties, to be particularly risky, thus relatively rare. How, then, is it so prevalent in China's courts?

Previous studies have pointed to various factors, such as low salaries, judicial incompetence, local protectionism, and insufficient court funds, to explain the phenomenon (He, 2009; Li, 2002; Wang, 2013; Zou, 2000). If these were the decisive factors, corruption would presumably be more common at lower courts, in less economically developed areas, and among the lower ranks of the judges (with lower pay and judicial training). However, the findings of this chapter contradict these predictions. As demonstrated, corruption, in particular bribery, appears in courts of all levels and across regions and all judge groups. It is not confined to remote, underfunded, and resource-deprived judicial institutions. Nor is it limited to judges who are underpaid, undereducated, or occupy the lowest rung of the judicial hierarchy. Judges at higher courts and in senior positions can be equally susceptible, if not more so, compared with other groups. At the time of writing, former SPC standing vice-president Shen Deyong was convicted for taking bribes amounting to 65 million yuan, spanning twenty-seven years. Clearly, the notion that he accepted all these bribes due to economic hardship or ignorance of the law does not withstand scrutiny.

To explain the prevalence of corruption in China's courts, we need to look beyond idiosyncratic traits of individual offenders and focus on structural factors or mechanisms that affect all courts, regardless of case type, court level, litigation stage, location, or judges' personal backgrounds. Although it is tempting to directly ascribe judicial corruption to the Party-state system – where the judiciary is dependent on rather than independent from the Party – this causal link is not straightforward. For instance, some scholars argue that the Party's interest and political intervention extend only to "politically sensitive" cases whilst corruption occurs predominantly in non-sensitive cases. In the next chapter, I will examine the courts' embeddedness within the Party-state and explain how this embeddedness shapes judicial decision-making and generates negative spillover effects extending far beyond the relatively small group of cases that the Party micromanages.

# 2

# Normalization of Political Prerogative in Courts

In the People's Republic of China (PRC), politics and law are merged into a single concept known as: *zhengfa*. Courts (*fayuan*) are a type of *zhengfa* organs. Higher educational institutions where law is taught and studied are called *zhengfa* universities, and the Party's specialized apparatus that oversees court affairs is called the *zhengfa* committee. In these references, *zhengfa* is not merely a linguistic convention that suggests a closer than usual proximity between politics and law. Rather, *zhengfa* is an alloy in which politics and law are amalgamated into an institutional structure that is designed to normalize political interference in judicial decision-making whenever and wherever the competent Party authority sees fit.

Put differently, as a measure to safeguard the Party's continued rule, political considerations are mandated priorities that courts must take into account throughout the entire judicial decision-making process. These political considerations are present from the very beginning of the process, concerning decisions on, inter alia, whether to accept a case, which decision-making procedure is to be followed, which judge(s) should be assigned to a case, and how the laws, both substantive and procedural, should be applied to achieve the maximum political and social impact. To establish and sustain such a *zhengfa* order in any court anywhere in the country, the Party has built courts into a regimented power structure that allows continuous oversight and intervention in judicial decision-making without legal scrutiny.

In this chapter, I will first explain the construct of this *zhengfa* order in China's Party-state. I will then identify the mechanisms through which political interference in judicial decision-making is normalized in all courts, before explaining why and how the very same mechanism that is used to normalize political interference has also contributed to the normalization and proliferation of corruption in these courts.

## *Zhengfa* System of the Party-State

The foundation of the *zhengfa* institutional design is a command structure that binds courts to the Party. This structure ensures not only the political monopoly of the Party but also the enforceability of the Party's commands.[1] Each court is supervised by the Party Committee at the same administrative level, which wields plenipotentiary power to oversee all public affairs on its turf.[2] A local Party Committee answers to the Party Committee at the next upper administrative level and is linked all the way up to the Politburo, which operates most often under the name of the Party Center (*dangzhongyang*) or, in short, the Center (*zhongyang*). According to the Party's Political-Legal Work Directive (2019; hereinafter, the 2019 Political-Legal Directive), the Party Center exercises absolute leadership over *zhengfa* work, setting down fundamental principles and making decisions on matters with overarching and long-term effect on *zhengfa* work (Article 7).

Regional and local Party Committees lead the *zhengfa* work within their territorial jurisdiction and are responsible to implement the Party Center's *zhengfa* policies, operationalize its directives, carry out its instructions, and execute its decisions (Article 9). In earlier decades of PRC history, Party Committees had micromanaged court activities, in particular, on criminal matters (Tian, 2016). For instance, when the Supreme People's Court (SPC) held, upon the Party Center's instruction, the first trial against Pan Han'nian (a vice-mayor of Shanghai) in 1963 for treason, the court president handpicked three politically trustworthy judges to handle the case. These judges were required to regularly report to the SPC Party-group, who in turn consulted Central Party leaders at every step of the judicial process. Both legal matters, such as the sentencing range, and logistic matters, such as when the trial should be held and who would be allowed to attend, were determined before the trial started (Peng & Li, 2011).

In 1979, the Party ceased the practice of reviewing all criminal sanctions indiscriminately and started to selectively intervene only in "important cases." What makes a case "important" depends on the

[1] See more detailed discussions on this topic from various authors (Li, 2015a; Liu, 2012b; Zheng, 2020).

[2] There are many types of Party organizations that share the name "committee." To avoid confusion, only territorial Party committees that have plenipotential power over their jurisdictions are fully capitalized (appearing as "Party Committee").

nature of the case and the Party's priorities at the time. As an illustration, Zhou Daoluan, a former member of the SPC adjudicative committee, once gave a talk to judges at lower courts. He said in a sympathetic tone: "courts have no freedom in deciding when to finalize a decision and close a case if the case is processed as a part of a 'strike-hard' campaign. Sometimes a judgment had already been signed off by the court president, but then the territorial Party Committee or the Party Center held a meeting [and changed the judicial policy], then the previously concluded judgment could not be announced [before it is modified to reflect the new policy]" (Tian, 2016; Zhong, 2012).

In the 1990s, the task of reviewing court cases was largely relegated by the Party Committee to one of its specialized units: the Party's *zhengfa* committee (Political-Legal Committee (PLC)). It is important to note in this context that the PLC is not autonomous but performs routine supervision on behalf of the Party Committee over the work of *zhengfa* organs, including courts, procuratorates, the police, and the judicial administrative bureaus. The PLC answers to the Party Committee at the same level. The committee comprises a head called *zhengfa*-secretary, sometimes also a deputy secretary, and a high-ranking representative from each of the *zhengfa* organs. The PLC ensures coordinated implementation of the Party Center's initiatives among *zhengfa* organs, resolves conflict or entanglement among these organs in the handling of individual cases, and fosters complementary rules and policies in these organs to carry out the Party's political line and policies. Unlike the Committee of Discipline and Inspection (CDI), another specialized Party organization set up at both the central and subnational levels, which I will elaborate on in Chapter 5, the PLCs do not have their own agents to enforce their policies or decisions.

The PLCs conduct oversight by earmarking cases or categories of cases and demanding to be notified and consulted in decision-making by relevant *zhengfa* organs that handle these cases. These categories are broadly and subjectively defined, such as "cases concerning national security, regime security and social stability." There are no rules or procedures through which one can challenge a PLC's decision to earmark a case for close supervision. Sometimes, when the leader of a *zhengfa* organ is uncertain about how the Party wants a case handled or needs assistance in securing cooperation or compliance from another state organ in a legal procedure, they can request PLC intervention.

A PLC and its leader may also receive requests for intervention from other concerned parties, including court users.[3] Such requests often come with case memorials and other supplementary materials. A PLC leader can then forward the request, with written instructive remarks called *pishi* attached to the request and case materials, to relevant *zhengfa* organs, including courts, and bring the case to the latter's attention. Depending on the extent to which the PLC leader wants to get involved, the instruction can be formal and specific, detailing how a case is expected to be handled, or informal and vague, leaving it to the addressee to work out the details (Hu, 2010; Tian, 2016).

In high-priority criminal cases, PLC leaders used to hold committee meetings with representatives from the court, the police, and the procuratorate – in the absence of the defendant or their representative – to hash out their differences and coordinate a unified decision. The outcome of such meetings might be summarized briefly, sometimes consisting of only a few bullet points, indicating whether a suspect should be formally arrested, prosecuted, or given a particular sentence. All concerned *zhengfa* organs would receive a copy of this "meeting memo (*huiyi jiyao*)," which can be used internally to justify decisions on arrest, prosecution, conviction (or, though rarely, acquittal). Normally, all internal communications should be kept in a sealed, classified case dossier (*fu juan,* the classified copy) for internal use only. But occasionally they ended up in the public case dossier, the official/public copy), which the defense could access. The media reported several wrongful convictions in the 2000s, where innocent people were convicted for crimes that they did not commit based on their coerced confessions.[4] After having spent decades in prison, these convicts were absolved only because critical new evidence accidentally surfaced (in one case, the presumed victim of a murder showed up home alive). Some cases were directly supervised by local PLCs, leading to public outcry.

Against this backdrop, the central PLC – supported by the then newly elected General Party Secretary (GPS) Xi Jinping – introduced reforms to

[3] Governmental court users, for instance, defendants in administrative litigations, and politically connected private court users can send the requests through various channels, while court users without political connections often wait outside the office building or residential compounds of Party leaders and hope to have a chance to capture their attention and hand in their requests. A documentary film about a Chinese mayor captures several such scenes; see Zhou (2015, Time stamp: 31:47 and 1:02:32).

[4] A list of some of the reported wrongful conviction cases can be found at News (2018). For a more detailed analysis of some of the cases in English, see He (2016).

prevent and reduce wrongful convictions in 2013. Under these reforms, the PLCs were barred from issuing concrete instructions on how to characterize a case and from dictating substantive decisions (Article 15). "Individual case coordination" was officially removed from the PLC's mandate, replaced by vague language about "coordinating important issues between *zhengfa* organs and between these organs and other agencies to ensure unified thinking and actions" in the 2019 Political-Legal Directive (Article 12). At the same time, protection of "state secrets" was strengthened to prevent leaks. Records of internal communications within courts and between courts and Party authorities are now labeled as "adjudicative secrets." Those who leak protected secrets could face disciplinary sanctions and even criminal prosecutions.[5] Since then, incidents of leaks have drastically decreased.

In addition to supervision by the Party Committee and its specialized *zhengfa* committee, a court is also under supervision from the superior court, which is linked level by level all the way to the SPC. This judicial hierarchy constitutes a vertical line of control in the domain of justice administration transmitted from Beijing down to the nearly 3,000 basic courts at the grassroots level. Superior courts hold appellate review, issue judicial policies and evaluate lower court performance. They also wield a broad spectrum of judicial administrative power over lower courts.

The most evident is the power of judicial appointment. Starting in the 2000s, superior courts began sharing local Party Committees' authority to appoint leader judges at lower courts (Liu, 2012b). The 2014–2017 judicial reform expanded this power further, granting high courts greater authority over selecting, certifying and appointing judges in courts under them. Somewhat less evident is the power to reallocate jurisdiction. Since the 1990s, high courts have been allowed to remove a specific case from a court's jurisdiction and assign it to another court of its choosing for judgment enforcement. Although this authority may sound technical and innocuous, it proves immensely valuable, which will be shown in later sections.

## Mechanisms of Political Supervision in Courts

Under this *zhengfa* system, courts are designated as one of several "special forces engaged in *zhengfa* work under the Party's leadership." (Article 3, 2019 Political-Legal Work Directive). According to the same directive, the

[5] See more detailed discussions in Eva (2021), Liu and Halliday (2016), Lu (2018), and Pils (2015).

first principle governing the work of courts is to uphold the absolute leadership of the Party and to implement the Party's leadership in all aspects and the entire process of its work . . . (Article 6). To achieve this level of political control, the Party staffs or "equips" courts with politically vetted cadres to be appointed to all senior posts with supervisory functions. Other than political vetting, the Party has also instituted two additional mechanisms to monitor the judicial decision-making process.

The first mechanism is to circumscribe judicial autonomy through a hierarchical cluster of supervisory powers. This is achieved by incorporating courts and judges into an administrative ranking system, linking courts to the Party and judges to a string of supervising leader judges with higher ranks. Judges at the lower end of the power structure can enjoy judicial autonomy only to the extent permitted by their superiors.

The second mechanism is collective decision-making, a signature feature of the self-governance of the Party. It is designed to address agency problems and prevent high-ranking leaders, who enjoy significant unchecked discretionary power, from exploiting it for personal gain. To that end, collective decision-making bodies, composed of judges of similar ranks, are called upon to make decisions in a collective fashion on important cases (General Office, 1985).

### *Court Party-Group*

Like other state institutions, each court has a Party-group installed in its decision-making body. This Party-group is composed of the first-tier ranked court leaders (often referred to as "court leaders"). Its regular members include the court president, vice-presidents, the heads of key functional departments, and a CDI representative. The Party-group answers to the territorial Party Committee, and its members – being Party members – are bound by Party rules. The Party-group observes the *zhengfa* principles set down by the Party Center, implements the latter's directives and decisions, executes its instructions and carries out its assignments (Article 20, 2019 Political-Legal Directive). Furthermore, it must seek instructions or obtain approval from the PLC and/or the Party Committee on matters of importance, such as:

a. system-wide policy issues concerning *zhengfa* work;
b. contested cross-region or cross-institution *zhengfa* affairs where an agreement on a legal issue or on a case cannot be reached among the state organs involved;

c. major *zhengfa* reform plans and measures;
d. release of major judicial interpretations and other normative documents, or submission of legislative recommendations;
e. important tasks assigned by the Party and important issues that require the Party's assistance to coordinate; and
f. measures or issues involving national security, especially regime security.

Below court leaders are divisional heads, each leading a division. Currently, a typical basic court might have from five to ten functional and administrative divisions and an intermediate court from fifteen to twenty divisions, depending on the size of the population and the volume of case intake. As in other judicial systems, different divisions are set up for different subject matters, such as civil, criminal, and administrative divisions, and so on, each of which can be subdivided into smaller units depending on the case intake. Specialized court divisions, such as bankruptcy division, intellectual property division, and juvenile division, can also be set up when necessary.

Unlike many judicial systems elsewhere, each court in China also has a case-acceptance division, which examines and determines whether a plaintiff's filing of a case is acceptable. Each court also has an enforcement bureau/division that handles the enforcement of civil and administrative judgments. In addition, each court has several units providing administrative and logistical support. Such units include a political department, which handles personnel dossiers, carries out ideological work and ethical training, and in some courts also conducts performance evaluations of judges, and a case-management office, which assigns cases and monitors the case flow and deadlines.

Each court division has one head, and if justified by the workload, one or two deputy heads. Divisional heads and deputy heads of different divisions together constitute the mid-level management of the court. They oversee the operation of their divisions and answer to court leaders. Heads of key court divisions are usually admitted as members of the adjudicative committee. The head of the political department is regularly admitted as a member of the court Party-group.

Under the divisional leaders are frontline judges who directly handle cases. Frontline judges meet litigants and/or their lawyers before and during the trial, preside over the fact-finding process, conduct occasional investigations, admit evidence, and draft opinions. A frontline judge exercises adjudicative power by one of two approaches. The first is to rule as a sole adjudicator in fast-track cases, which involve mostly small-claim, simple, and uncontested cases.

The second is to rule as a member of a collegial panel on cases that follow the standard adjudicative procedure. The collegial panel usually consists of three members. When warranted by circumstances, the panel can be enlarged up to seven members. A mixed panel with both judges and laypersons is common in lower courts due to the mismatch between the supply of judges and the demand. Laypersons are selected from a roster of vetted candidates who are appointed by the local people's congress and trained, evaluated, and managed by the court. In general, laypersons have very limited influence in the decision-making process and on its outcome. The autonomy of the collegial panels or individual judges is circumscribed by leader judges – including court leaders, divisional leaders, and sub-divisional leaders when applicable – either through the adjudicative committee or the internal case-review procedure.

### *Adjudicative Committee*

Every court has an adjudicative committee that is set up to control the adjudicative quality of cases that are considered controversial, challenging, or bearing significant political and social implications. In practice, cases reviewed by the adjudicative committees are predominantly criminal cases (Zuo, 2016b). The committee, as prescribed by law and judicial policies, must review and rule on cases involving, for instance, criminal offenses punishable with life imprisonment or a death sentence, acquittals, the opening of a new trial, prosecutorial appeals, and so on.

Members of the committee typically include the court president, vice-presidents, heads of key divisions, and several "senior and experienced" judges. According to a survey carried out in a province in Southwestern China, court leaders constitute half of the committee members. The other half comprises divisional leaders (33 percent), designated full-time members (10 percent), and senior and experienced frontline judges (7 percent) (Zuo, 2016b). The court president can add any additional case to the committee's docket.[6] A collegial panel can also request the adjudicative committee to review a case.

When the adjudicative committee convenes, it makes decisions more as a partial bureaucracy instead of a collegial body of professional judges.

[6] See more detailed discussions in Ng and He (2017) and Zuo (2016b).

The discussion is often outcome-oriented (Ng & He, 2017). Typically, a committee meeting lasts 3–3.5 hours, during which time multiple cases will be discussed. Given that the discussion must allocate considerable time for the frontline judge to introduce the facts of a case, little time is left for legal discussions (Wang & Liu, 2017, p. 89).

In some courts, the adjudicative committee observes a routine of conveying Party instructions before discussion begins (Wang & Liu, 2017, p. 89). Some instructions are concrete, indicating specific preferences for the outcome of the cases; some are vague, only indicating which litigant should be "taken care of," without specifying the preferred outcome in concrete terms (Ng & He, 2017, p. 116). The committee makes decisions under majority rule. While nominally all committee members vote equally, in practice, however, the court president and involved vice-presidents, who are usually the chairs of the committee meetings, have a much greater say in setting the direction of the deliberation and in shaping the outcome.[7] As members of the court's Party-group, the court president and vice-presidents have an obligation to safeguard the Party's interest and take political or "extralegal" factors into account in the deliberation process.[8]

### *Internal Case-Review Procedure*

Despite the lack of national statistics, it is well understood that the proportion of cases reviewed by the adjudicative committee is only a fraction of the total case intake of any given court.[9] The vast majority of court cases are decided by the collegial panel or a single judge. To safeguard political control in these cases without necessarily invoking the adjudicative committee, judges are required to observe an internal case-review procedure (known as "case review/approval" or "document sign-off" procedure) regardless of whether or not the case is to be reviewed by the adjudicative committee.[10]

Before the 2014–2017 reform, a wide range of court-issued legal documents had to be signed off by the responsible division leader, and depending

[7] Ng & He (2017); Wang & Liu (2017).

[8] Ng & He (2017); Wang & Liu (2017).

[9] According to Zuo's study based on a survey of twenty-three courts in one province, cases heard by the adjudicative committees of these courts in 2014 range from 1 percent to 5 percent. See Zuo Weimin (2016a, p. 164).

[10] Zhang (2000, p. 4) and Ng and He (2017, pp. 114–15). For more discussions on this topic, see Gao and Zhao (2018), Hu (2002), Li (2017b), Luo (2002), Wu and Dong (2016), and Yin (2013).

on the issue, also by a responsible court leader.[11] For instance, at Beihai Intermediate Court, Guangxi, frontline judges must obtain approval from the court president in five categories of court orders or decisions, approval from the corresponding vice-president in eight categories of court orders or decisions in criminal law cases, fourteen categories in civil law cases, eight categories in administrative law cases, and sixteen categories in civil judgment enforcement cases (Court, 2015). Similarly, a basic urban district court in Xi'ning City, Qinghai, listed twenty-nine types of judicial documents for which approvals from court leaders were required (Court, 2014).

At the same time, it is also worth noting that the rigidity of top-down control varies from court to court, and such variances are generally correlated to case intake. In a court with a high volume of case intake, to subject a wide scope of judicial decisions to the approval of leader judges would simply overwhelm the latter and significantly slow down the decision-making process. Hence, courts in more developed areas, where the case intake tends to be high in both volume and stakes (value of claim), the scope of judicial decisions that are subject to internal review is generally narrower than that of courts with lower case intake in less developed regions. For instance, a basic urban district court of Wenzhou, a rich coastal city of Zhejiang, only listed five types of judicial documents that were subject to approvals from court leaders (Court, 2012).

Nevertheless, regardless of its regional variances, this internal case-review procedure operates under the same political logic as the adjudicative committee but with even less transparency. The practice has long been criticized for misplacing the judicial power in the hands of those who do not directly hear the cases, thus compromising judicial accountability. In 2015, the SPC took a progressive step to limit the case approval procedure to four circumstances (SPC, 2015a):

a. a case that concerns multiple persons and may disrupt social stability;
b. a case that is complex, with facts that are difficult to ascertain and a significant social impact;
c. the proposed decision of the case may clash with a previous decision of a similar case rendered by the court or a superior court;
d. judicial misconduct is reported in the course of litigation.

According to the same SPC opinion, if a leader judge disagrees with the decision of a collegial panel or a solo-judge (i.e., a judge acting as sole

[11] See Huang (2008) and Yin (2013).

decision-maker) in a case that falls in any of the above categories, the former cannot directly change the latter's decision but can submit the case to the adjudicative committee for final decision. In 2017, the SPC issued a supplementary opinion to further stress that leader judges shall not deceptively reinstate the internal case-review procedure by overusing their supervisory power (SPC, 2017).

However, merely three years after the introduction of these measures, the SPC started to reverse them. In 2021, the SPC issued a new opinion to require judges to earmark or label a case for top-down supervision if the case falls in "four categories of cases (*silei anjian*,)" which is an expanded version of the four "circumstances" mentioned in the 2015 Opinion as listed earlier. Unlike the 2015 Opinion, which focuses on empowering frontline judges and only mentions top-down supervision as a marginal reservation, the 2021 Opinion, however, focuses on strengthening mandatory top-down supervision by leader judges, thus renewing leader oversight. In the revised four categories of cases that are subject to mandatory top-down supervision, the first concerns important (*zhongda*), uncertain and difficult (*yinan*), complicated (*fuza*), or sensitive (*mingan*) cases, which can be any case that meets one of the following conditions:

a. cases involving national interests or social public interests;
b. cases involving considerable controversy in terms of ascertaining the facts and/or application of law;
c. new types of cases with precedent-setting potentials;
d. cases in which the application of law can be generalized to have an exemplary effect for other cases;
e. cases involving national security, foreign relations, ethnic groups, religion, and other sensitive issues.[12]

The 2021 SPC Opinion permits lower courts to expand the list when necessary.[13]A judge is required to mark the case if it meets the indicated criteria and must submit it for mandatory top-down supervision. The same opinion also provides leader judges with a set of tools to execute their supervision, which include the following:

a. to take a case out of the random case-assigning system, if a case is earmarked at the case-acceptance phase, and assign the case to a panel or a judge who is deemed appropriate to take the case;

[12] See SPC (2021b, Article 3).
[13] See SPC (2021b, Article 7).

b. to reassign a case from a solo-judge to a collegial panel; to change the responsible judge; to change members of the collegial panel; to appoint him or herself to head the collegial panel, if a case is earmarked at the adjudication stage;
c. to command the collegial panel to report its work progress and the result of case deliberation to the supervising judge;
d. to command the collegial panel to provide court judgments of similar cases or to provide relevant research reports;
e. to review the outline of the trial and trial report;
f. to review the case dossier and to audit the trial;
g. to request the collegial panel to reconsider and re-deliberate its decision, but no more than twice;
h. to submit the case to the specialized judicial conference for deliberation;
i. to submit the case to the court adjudicative committee for deliberation;
j. to submit the case to the superior court to handle; or
k. to take other permissible measures.[14]

At a high-level judicial conference in the summer of 2023, the newly appointed SPC president Zhang Jun made a speech, which indicates a further backslide of the 2014–2017 judicial reform.[15] In the speech, Zhang Jun blamed the reform that abolished the internal case-review procedure for having caused a decline of adjudicative quality because more cases were appealed and fewer decisions were affirmed by the appellate courts.[16] Furthermore, Zhang Jun stressed the necessity not only to strengthen top-down supervision in the four categories of cases but also to introduce a new case review and approval procedure (*yue-hezhi*) applicable to possibly all cases (SPC, 2023a). In an effort to give the new case-review procedure a more progressive appearance, Zhang made a distinction and said that unlike the previous case-review procedure, the new procedure does not permit a leader judge to directly change

[14] See SPC (2021b, Article 9–10).

[15] See SPC (2023a). After the conference, a lot of courts have started to operationalize the case-review procedure. For an incomplete compilation on these activities, see Yanyu (2023).

[16] See SPC (2023a). This narrative has an uncanny resemblance to the discourse employed to resist a similar decentralizing reform attempt launched by the SPC in the 2000s. For a more comprehensive analysis of the historical vicissitude of past reforms on the restriction and expansion of top-down adjudicative supervision within courts, see Huang (2008).

the decision of a solo-judge or a collegial panel (SPC, 2023a). This restriction on the power of leader judges is, however, not new because the SPC had issued a regulation concerning the operation of collegial panels in 2002, barring court leaders and divisional leaders from changing the decision of a solo-judge or a collegial panel, which has been either ignored or circumvented in practice.

Thus, any attempt to reverse the power structure in which courts and judges are embedded, or to weaken hierarchical oversight in judicial activities, has been short-lived. This is because this power structure, which directs and facilitates top-down supervision, is the bedrock of the *zhengfa* construct of the Party-state. It links frontline judges to court leaders and court leaders to Party leaders through a chain of command, enabling anyone higher in the chain to decide, approve, or influence judicial outcomes based on rank or superiority of their power rather than on law and legal reasoning. Since the exercise of this power is outcome-oriented, the law inevitably becomes pliant, malleable enough to accommodate the personal interests of individual power-holders as much as the institutional interest of the Party.

## Interference of Party Leaders

Due to the authoritarian nature of the Party's rule, a Party leader who directs a court leader to make a partial decision in favor of a particular litigant to safeguard the Party-state's interests is not required to provide legal reasoning to justify the instruction. When receiving such an instruction, a subordinate is required to implement it without questioning unless the instruction overtly violates the law, for instance, if the implementation requires one to commit a crime.[17] When a court leader, who is also a Party member, receives such an instruction, they are obliged to

[17] See Article 60 of the PRC Public Servants Law (2018): When a public servant, in the course of performing official duties, deems that a decision or order from a superior is erroneous, they may present their views to the superior and request its correction or withdrawal. If the superior upholds the decision or order or demands immediate execution, the public servant must comply, with any resulting consequences borne by the superior. However, if a decision or order is clearly illegal, the public servant shall bear corresponding legal responsibilities for carrying it out. Also see Center (2023a, Article 78): If a subordinate Party organization refuses to implement or unilaterally alters the decision of a superior Party organization, those who are directly responsible, including leaders, shall be served with a warning or severe warning. If the refusal results in serious consequences, the responsible person may be removed from office or have their Party membership suspended.

deliver the desired outcome as conveyed in the instruction. In such instances, the role of the court is more like that of an advocate for the party supported by the supervising authority rather than that of an objective and impartial adjudicator.

Party leaders are authorized to exercise this arbitrary power primarily for the purpose of safeguarding the Party's interests. However, since the Party's interests are so broadly defined and freely interpreted, a Party leader can characterize any instruction as the effort to advance the Party's interests in one direction or another. These conditions create an environment that allows a Party leader to advance personal interests under the guise of protecting the Party's interests because it is impossible for a subordinate to discern a leader's transgression beyond doubt.

For example, since the PLC is mandated to oversee the administration of justice by accepting and examining petitions from aggrieved citizens, Gan Rongkun, a former PLC leader of Heilongjiang, instructed his bribers to present their requests in the form of petition letters. Gan would then make instructive remarks (*pishi*) on the petition letters and forward them to relevant *zhengfa* organs to implement. For cases that were earmarked by Gan, relevant *zhengfa* organs handling the cases, be it courts, procuratorates, or the police, would be duty-bound to brief Gan about the progress of the cases and consult him in the process of decision-making. On the surface of Gan's instructions, it would be difficult to tell whether the instructions were driven by diligence or corruption. Gan was charged in 2022 for taking bribes worth 166 million *yuan* (CCDI, 2023b).

When a Party leader shows personal interest and makes inquiries about a particular case, the act is usually referred to as "to *guowen* a case." *Guowen* could be done with a phone call or a short conversation at a brief encounter. For example, Mu Suixin, former mayor of Shenyang, capital of Liaoning, once helped a local business tycoon in a commercial case pending in Liaoning High Court by simply indicating his personal attention in this case to the court president at a brief encounter during the break of a Party meeting which both attended. The business tycoon's request was granted and Mayor Mu received cash and gifts worth 850,000 *yuan* from the litigant.

To implement a Party leader's instruction, a court leader would inform the judges handling the case as to which litigating party is to be given favorable treatment. Practices vary from court to court on whether the identity of the Party leader who has demanded favoritism would be revealed to judges handling the case. As mentioned earlier, in some courts, it is customary for court leaders to share such information. But in some, the identity of the Party leader is not disclosed. For instance, Zheng Wei, the CDI head of Yuzhong District, Chongqing, once asked the district court president to place a company, from whom Zheng had taken bribes, on the court's white list of auction houses (who will be eligible to bid for court auction commissions).[18] The court leader passed the company's name to the divisional leader and simply mentioned that "a district Party leader showed interest in this applicant" without revealing the Party leader's identity. The divisional leader dutifully complied with the instruction without further questions. Even though those who are assigned to carry out an instruction do not necessarily know who has given the instruction and why, they share an understanding that they are not in a position to question the legal merit of the instruction. In fact, what troubles some court leaders most is not the impropriety but the vagueness of the instruction.

It is important to note that courts are usually the last stop for most disputes. If a disputing party can enlist support from a Party leader, it is more effective and easier to seek that support at the beginning of a legal process, when it involves fewer decision-makers and leaves a lesser or no paper trail, than doing so toward the end of the dispute. For instance, a popular type of corrupt service involves the release of a suspect, called *laoren*, which literally means to pull someone out of water. Such intervention is most cost-efficient *before* the case is brought to court. Gan Rongkun, the former provincial PLC leader mentioned earlier, had helped favor-seekers "pull people out" of police detention by simply issuing commands to local policy chiefs by telephone. (CCDI, 2023b). As much as Gan Rongkun could pull people out of police detention, Zhang Yue, former PLC leader of Hebei province, known as the regional "*zhengfa* lord," had done the reverse: he had "ordered" multiple arrests, upon requests of his business partners, of the latter's competitors or personal foes (Gao & Cui, 2017).

Some PLC leaders' wanton abuse of their broad and arbitrary judicial supervisory power had caused many personal tragedies. In one case that took place in Yunnan, a lawyer named Liu Shaobin was prosecuted because his defense in a tort case harmed the economic interest of a local PLC leader. The tort happened to the lawyer's five-year-old nephew, who tripped over a high-voltage power cable while walking in a rural field

[18] See Appendix II, No. 35.

in 2007. The boy survived the electrocution but lost his hands. His lawyer uncle brought a tort case against a local factory, its shareholders, and the power company that was responsible for the safety of the power cables. The court ruled in favor of the boy and ordered the defendants to pay the boy's family a sum of 274,000 *yuan* as compensation. The defendants appealed, but the appellate court upheld the decision.

Displeased by the court decision, the defendants sought help from the head of the county PLC, Peng Zegao, who appeared to be a secret shareholder of the sued power company. Peng ordered the county police and the county procuratorate to put together a task force to investigate the case in the name of exercising its duty of supervision. Within days, the joint task force detained four witnesses who had previously provided testimonies supporting the boy's claims and also arrested lawyer Liu for "suborning witnesses." The witnesses withdrew their testimonies. Lawyer Liu was prosecuted and convicted. The boy's tort case was reopened and the previous decision awarding compensation to the boy was reversed. After lawyer Liu had served his sentence, he started to petition the case publicly through various news outlets. During the same period, the central PLC issued the wrongful conviction prevention opinion mentioned under the first section of this chapter. Three years later, lawyer Liu's case was reviewed. He was acquitted in 2015, eight years after his nephew's accident (Zou, 2015). It is not clear whether his nephew's tort case has been reexamined thereafter.

What happened to lawyer Liu closely resembles the case of Li Zhuang, a defense lawyer accused and convicted for suborning witnesses during the notorious anti-crime (*dahei*) campaign (2009–2010) launched by Bo Xilai in Chongqing. During the campaign, torture and other forms of coercion were applied to extract confessions from suspects. Li Zhuang, a criminal lawyer based in Beijing, was representing Gong Gangmo, a key member of a criminal gang. Gong told Li that he was tortured. Li then asked the court to exclude the evidence obtained through torture. In response, the police – seeking to deter and frustrate the defense – induced Gong Gangmo, the defendant, to turn against his lawyer in exchange for a lighter sentence. Gong cooperated with the police. Li was arrested and soon convicted for suborning witnesses based on Gong's false testimony. Li was sentenced to 1.5 years in prison, while Gong was spared death execution and received a life sentence (Luo & He, 2012). The scale of police abuse and miscarriage of justice during the campaign was exposed only after Bo Xilai's downfall in 2012.

The mechanisms that facilitated the prosecutions of Li Zhuang and Lawyer Liu are the same: the unfettered and normalized power of Party leaders to intervene in the judicial decision-making process. Although the mechanism was originally designed to safeguard the political interest of the Party, its inherent arbitrariness allows it to be easily abused by those in power for their personal interest. Take the case of Zeng Jinchun as an example. When Zeng Jinchun served as the deputy Party-secretary of Zhuzhou City, Hunan, he once asked a local court to rule in favor of the plaintiff in a case after having taken the plaintiff's bribe. The defendant appealed the case. Then, Zeng asked the appellate court to rule in favor of the defendant in the appeal after having taken the defendant's bribe. Both courts complied.

As explained earlier, a key feature of the *zhengfa* construct is the normalization of political interference in judicial decision-making. This normalization is accomplished by incorporating courts into the power structure of the Party-state and by subjugating judicial decision-making to the political order defined by this power structure. Thus, courts are turned into a "partial bureaucracy,"[19] no matter whether the case is handled by one single judge, a collegial panel, or the adjudicative committee. This partial bureaucracy allows, or even requires, partial application of the law based on the power dynamics between the parties before the court and between the political and social forces behind them.

Even though the mechanism is installed in the court system primarily to protect the collective political interest of the Party, its impact goes far beyond because it has eroded the integrity of law and courts, rendering judicial decision-making vulnerable to corruption – an issue that will be explored next.

## Proliferation of Judicial Corruption

The purpose of installing a chain of command between the Party and the courts is not to turn the Party into a full-time judicial body but to provide the Party with unfettered access to intervention in judicial decision-making. To ensure loyal implementation of the Party's command at courts whenever and wherever deemed opportune or needed, a mechanism is established to normalize the Party's political prerogative to intervene. As explained earlier, when a Party leader gives an instruction to a

[19] Ng and He (2017, p. 107).

court leader, the instruction need not be legally reasoned, relieving the former from the burden of justification based on the premises and principles of the law. Subsequently, when a court complies with the instruction and renders a partial decision by bending the law, the court can use the instruction as a source of formal authority according to which the law is interpreted and applied. This leaves the integrity of the law unguarded and vulnerable to abuse by anyone who occupies a position in a long chain of command – from Party leaders, court leaders, divisional leaders, to frontline judges. This is why and how judicial corruption proliferates in China's courts.

Compared with Party leaders, who enjoy a broad range of competences and more lucrative corruption opportunities elsewhere (for instance, allocation of public funds and commissions of public procurement contracts),[20] the power that a judge can wield is limited only to court cases. For judges, their opportunities for corruption vary depending on their scope of discretion, the case intake and the stakes involved in these cases. Below, I will survey the main sites of judicial corruption, which include the three stages of litigation – case-acceptance, adjudication, and enforcement – and court administration. The power of an ordinary frontline judge is confined to one of the sites at any given time whereas a court leader enjoys a wider scope of power, across multiple sites.

### *Case-Acceptance Phase*

In China, case-acceptance is a stand-alone standard court procedure, without which the judicial process cannot begin. It means that all actions brought by plaintiffs must first be reviewed and officially accepted by the court before the judicial process can begin. The same case-acceptance procedure is also installed in criminal investigations (Liu & Liu, 2002), which turns the launch of a criminal investigation from an obligation of the state to a state power that can be exercised in a discretionary manner.

Among the 368 transactional corruption offenses in the Dataset that I analyzed in Chapter 1, only 7 were committed by judges serving

[20] For example, according to the procurator's statement, Mu Suixin, the former mayor of Shenyang City (Liaoning province), had taken bribes on sixty occasions, among which only one was related to a court case. The rest mainly took place in the course of allocation of public funds, public procurement contracts, personnel management, and the permission for land confiscation.

in case-acceptance divisions. Two took place at intermediate courts and five at high courts. The seemingly low corruption rate in this court division, especially in the lower courts, is not, however, attributable to greater honesty of judges handling case-acceptance. Rather, the most likely cause is the lower exchange value of the discretionary power inherent in case-acceptance than in other phases of a litigation.

For a long time, court users used to complain that their cases were thrown out by case-acceptance divisions for frivolous reasons. For instance, a court once rejected a medical negligence case because the lawyer did not provide the proof of cremation of the deceased even though the lawyer had provided the death certificate. Another common complaint is the court's failure to render their rejection in written form, which made it impossible for a litigant or a lawyer to appeal the rejection. When confronted with such predicaments, court users frequently and patiently rely on their charisma and persuasive skills but rarely offer serious bribes, because an ill-tempered case-acceptance judge could make life more difficult for a court user but would eventually have to take the case after exhaustion of subterfuges.

During the past two decades, great efforts have been made to improve access to courts. Central authorities have appropriated special funds for local courts to provide more spacious waiting areas and more staff to handle case-acceptance. The reform has also limited the discretion of case-acceptance judges to reject cases. Since then, reports on difficulties to register a case have become sparse, except for administrative actions. For instance, in 2022, a group of plaintiffs went to Beijing Dongcheng Court to file a complaint against a township government for a house demolition dispute. The court rejected the case and refused to render a written decision. The plaintiffs protested against the rejection, making reference to the newly amended Administrative Litigation Law, which requires courts to accept all complaints without substantive screening. The judge repeated an unapologetic refusal, saying "no ground is to be given."[21]

Cases that are more prone to corruption at the case-acceptance stage are retrial applications. The same as in other judicial systems, the acceptance of a case for retrial is subject to a high threshold of probative criteria because courts need to uphold the finality of their judgments. This creates a large gap between the demand of discontented litigants and

[21] The encounter was recorded by a plaintiff on video, which can be seen at https://twitter.com/709wangqiaoling/status/1513777084807585794.

the supply of this service by courts. At the same time, when the criteria for acceptance of a retrial are broad and highly discretionary, space for corruption is widened. It is therefore not surprising that among the seven corruption cases committed by case-acceptance judges in the Dataset, five are retrial cases.

More corruption in case-acceptance for retrial was reported in recent years. One of them concerns Wang Hongguang, a judge, who worked at the SPC's second case-acceptance division in 2007–2012. Wang took bribes in several retrial applications and had either granted (when the briber was the applicant) or denied applications (when the briber was the opposing party of the applicant), depending on who was bribing.[22] Another example is Zheng Xuelin, who served, *inter alia*, as head of various case-acceptance divisions of the SPC between 2001 and 2014. Zheng was accused of, inter alia, interfering in cases, trading power for money, taking large sums of bribes to help others gain undue advantages in case representation and litigation, during his tenure in various judicial offices. He was expelled from the Party on February 26, 2024, and his case is pending for prosecution at the time of writing this chapter.[23]

### *Adjudication Phase*

Unsurprisingly, the adjudication phase provides most opportunities for judicial corruption. Among the 289 bribe-taking offenses in the Dataset that I analyzed in Chapter 1, 52.9 percent (153/289) were committed by judges in adjudication divisions. The adjudicative process starts with serving a defendant with a court summons or with the filing of a criminal complaint by the procuratorate, and ends with the rendering of a court judgment. During the process, a frontline judge or a collegial panel hearing the case can act partially in multiple ways. Depending on whose bribe the judge has taken, the fact-finding process offers multiple opportunities to establish a certain set of facts in favor of a particular party. Certain procedures can be expedited or stalled, evidence admitted or dismissed, forensic examination requests granted or denied, to name just a few.

Figure 2.1 shows that the majority (55 percent) of the 153 bribe-taking offenses committed by judges from the adjudication divisions occurred in commercial disputes, 30 percent in criminal cases, and less than 1 percent in administrative cases. Gan Rongkun, aforementioned PLC leader of

[22] See Appendix II, No. 23.
[23] See the official announcement of the disciplinary decision at CCDI (2024).

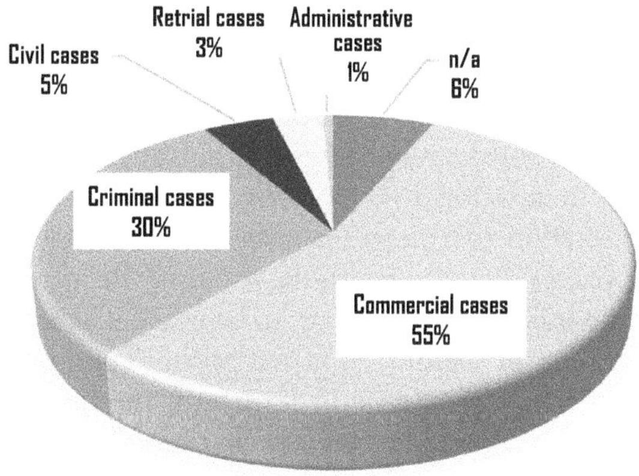


**Figure 2.1** Distribution of bribe-taking by case types.

Heilongjiang and Henan provinces for 2016–2021, confessed that he felt more comfortable taking bribes in civil rather than criminal cases because the former are less "sensitive" and "safer" (Zhong, 2016).

All three SPC vice-presidents who fell for corruption took bribes in commercial cases, including Shen Deyong, who has a criminal law background. Reportedly, the case that had triggered a corruption investigation against Shen was a commercial dispute, involving shareholding ownership in a financial arrangement that was worth 70 million *yuan*. Allegedly, the litigating party who lost the case at the first instance court appealed to the SPC. According to the account of the appellee, an intermediary invited both parties to bribe the SPC judges in a bid. The appellee declined the opportunity. But the appellant offered the judges 31 million *yuan*, half of the claim, to reverse the first-instance ruling. The SPC did (Yu, 2022).

As a rule of thumb, the more complex and technical a case is, the more room there will be for legal manipulation. And the better the judges are versed in the law, the better they can cover their tracks. Only those without sufficient legal acumen would resort to low-skill high-risk measures, such as forging or tampering with evidence.[24] By contrast, in complex cases involving, for instance, contractual disputes in complicated financial transactions,

[24] For instance, two judges from Wuhan Maritime Court once knowingly admitted a fake contract into evidence after accepting bribes from one litigant. In another case in Shangqiu Intermediate Court, Henan, a judge, seeking a favor for a plaintiff in a land

the intricacy of the transactions and relevant regulations provides sufficient room for manipulation so that a judge does not need to resort to risky measures such as forgery or evidence tempering.

Unlike civil cases, where the parties involved are or act as private persons or entities, both criminal and administrative cases, by definition, involve another state actor, which has significantly limited the scope of the judicial discretion that judges can enjoy. In criminal cases, once a procuratorate brings a case to court, the room for the court to acquit the defendant at the trial is nearly zero or, to be exact, 0.052 percent in 2021 (Zhou, 2022). Thus, as mentioned in the previous section, any effort to seek a suspect's release would be best spent at the investigation or the prosecutorial review stage. After the case has been brought to court, the chance for a defendant to obtain an acquittal with or without bribery is fairly low. However, there is considerable room for manipulation in terms of fact-finding and/or application of law that can result in a lighter sentence. For instance, in practice, if one seeks a sentence below the sentencing range, one of two circumstances has to be met, according to the PRC Criminal Law: (1) the defendant surrendered to the investigative authority before the crime was detected or before the defendant was identified as the culprit of the crime by the investigative authority, (2) the defendant performed meritoriously in providing information to the investigative authority about undetected crimes and/or assisting the investigative authority to identify the culprit(s) in open cases.

Hence, there has emerged an underground market of the selling and buying of "meritorious conduct."[25] The following example concerns Lü Zonghui, a frontline criminal judge, and Zhao Zhengbing, the former's superior, at Jingmen Intermediate Court in Hubei province. According to a court document, the two judges were once approached by the family of a defendant in a murder case, who were seeking a lenient sentence.[26] After having taken the bribes, the judges advised the family that the only way to secure a reprieve of the death sentence for the defendant was by showing proof of meritorious conduct. The judges also told the family that the only type of evidence that a court accepts as proof of meritorious conduct or self-surrender is pertinent statements from the investigative authority. Following the judges' advice, the family bought a piece of "intelligence"

dispute, forged a land certificate and entered it into evidence without informing the defendant.

25 Newsweek (2014) and Daily (2010).

26 Press (2004).

from a captain of the local police and shared the "intelligence" with the defendant. The defendant then reported the "intelligence" to the police in a staged interview. Afterwards, the police captain issued a statement certifying that the defendant's report constitutes "meritorious conduct," which was submitted to the court. During the court hearing, the judge announced the discovery of mitigating evidence and admitted it immediately. When the victim's family requested the court to disclose this evidence, the judge denied the request on the ground that the evidence constituted an "adjudicative secret." As promised to the defendant's family, the court rendered a reprieve, sparing the defendant from death.

In a more recent case, Yao Hui, head of the Second Criminal Division of Shenzhen Intermediate Court, took bribes from twenty-eight bribers involving more than forty criminal cases tried at his court from 2003 until his arrest in 2021.[27] Most corruption services provided by Yao involved the grant of suspended sentences. According to the PRC law, a defendant can**not** receive a suspended sentence if charged and convicted for multiple crimes. In several cases, Yao Hui struck down some charges to make the rendering of a suspended sentence possible. Another method used by Yao Hui was to replace the procuratorate's charge with a different crime that carries a lower sentence range. For instance, in one case, he dismissed the charge of bribe-taking [by an individual] and convicted the defendant for bribe-taking on behalf of a company or work unit, which carries a lesser sentence.

More surprisingly, Yao Hui also took bribes from at least fourteen defendants who were prosecuted for corruption. This is surprising because there was a shared presumption that corrupt judges would not dare to take bribes from corruption defendants because these cases would be considered politically sensitive and closely monitored by the Party. It appears that the Party has, at least, in some regions, relaxed its monitoring scope and delegated more decision-making power to judges in certain types of corruption cases. These types of cases encompass, for instance, (1) corruption in the private sector, such as corruption committed by corporate managers; (2) public corruption committed by low-ranking officials; and (3) corruption committed by bribers, who are in most cases business people instead of public officials. Indeed, Yao once took a bribe from a defendant who was a senior official. Sometime later Yao regretted it and returned the bribe to the latter.

[27] See Appendix II, No. 30.

Other than in sentencing, judges also have a say in post-conviction sentence reduction, another potentially corruption-prone adjudicative activity. Perhaps, the most notorious scandal in this respect was triggered by the case of Sun Xiaoguo. Sun, a bully and thug in Kunming, was sentenced to death with reprieve[28] in 1997 for several violent crimes. According to media reports, Sun was found having been released from prison after serving only 12.5 years in prison thanks to his "meritorious conduct" that his parents had bought him through collusion with the prison warden, the police, and judges. The scandal had caught the attention of the media only because Sun was caught for new offenses at the height of a nationwide anti-crime campaign. A special high-level task force was assembled to reinvestigate Sun's crimes, old and new. The investigation unveiled corruption committed by at least three judges and thirteen law and enforcement agents who helped Sun obtain his early release. Sun was executed one year later. However, sentence reduction for sale did not end with this scandal.[29] During the 2021 *zhengfa* rectification campaign alone, inspectors found 15,000 cases where sentence reduction, parole, and probation were wrongfully rendered based on bogus "meritorious conduct," fake age certificates, or forged medical certificates (Wei, 2021).

Compared with the salience of corrupt activities in civil and criminal litigation, many would expect greater restraint from judges in administrative courts. Indeed, the Dataset contains zero cases of corruption committed in administrative litigation. However, this low representation of corruption in administrative courts is first attributable to the statistical insignificance of administrative litigation in the overall case intake of courts. According to the SPC Work Report of 2023, administrative litigation constitutes less than 0.96 percent of the total case intake at first instance courts, even after a significant rise in administrative case filings following the amendment of the Administrative Litigation Law in 2015. In addition, one would also expect less instances of corruption in administrative litigation because the defendants, being governmental agencies, would have little incentive to bribe judges. In addition, they are in a better position to resist and even challenge an unfavorable court decision,

[28] Death with reprieve is a form of criminal punishment under the PRC Criminal Law. It can be and usually is commuted to life or limited term of imprisonment after two years of the conviction on the condition of good behavior.

[29] Daily (2018b).

especially when such a decision is unfairly made and driven by corruption between the judges and the plaintiff.

It is against this backdrop that the instances of corruption committed by Zhang Jiahui, a vice-president of Hainan High Court, are truly extraordinary. According to the court judgment, Zhang took bribes from thirty-seven bribers in at least fifty-nine cases over a five-year period. Among the fifty-nine cases, nine were administrative litigation cases heard at her court or courts at lower levels. All nine cases concerned land use rights of great economic value. In one of the administrative litigation cases, Zhang compelled a lower court to rule in favor of a company owned by her family concerning the floor ratio of a piece of land valued at 46 million *yuan*.

In administrative disputes, corruption could also occur during the administrative reconsideration process, which is an optional procedure that precedes a court action. For instance, in 1998, a Hainan farm owner bribed Lou Xiaoping, then deputy head of the Hainan Justice Bureau, over a land rights dispute for which the owner sought administrative reconsideration. After accepting 400,000 yuan, Lou ruled in the owner's favor. The case remained undetected until several years later, after Lou had been promoted to the vice-president of Hainan High Court, the same position that Zhang Jiahui held two decades later (Lin, 2004).

### *Enforcement Phase*

Judgment enforcement has long been a challenge for court users. A report (Meng, 2015) published by *Legal Daily*, a newspaper run by the CPLC, found that 70 percent of uncovered judicial corruption cases took place in the enforcement process of civil court judgments with 70 percent of those involving asset disposal. Enforcement procedures are particularly susceptible to corruption for several reasons. To start with, victorious litigants become more willing to pay bribes as they near the end of the litigation. Second, enforcement is subject to a range of factors to which no rule applies. For example, judges can justify inaction, thus stalling the enforcement, by citing reasons such as local protectionism, shortage of manpower, resistance from recalcitrant defendants, and even the lack of judicial autonomy. However, when offered sufficient incentives, enforcement judges can take extraordinary measures to execute a judgment, framing their actions as a commitment to rights protection and the rule of law (Shu et al., 2014).

A report by *Zhengzhou Evening Newspaper* in 2014 revealed that there were at least eleven different methods to collect bribes in the enforcement process, as disclosed by a disgraced judge (Meng, 2015). Enforcement judges, if incentivized by the winning party, could facilitate asset recovery and transfer through a number of measures, including advance enforcement, seizing assets outside of one's jurisdiction, or jurisdiction transfer. Conversely, if bribed by the losing party, they could also delay or obstruct enforcement simply by work slowdowns (Shu et al., 2014). In general, requests for inaction or delayed action are much easier to accommodate than those for proactive enforcement, which requires additional effort and resources.

Enforcement judges not only control the pace of enforcement but also the order of execution in cases involving multiple creditors. As one lawyer noted in an interview, court awards are rarely executed automatically – especially when the award involves a large sum of assets and multiple creditors – without financial incentives for enforcement judges.[30] A notable example is the bankruptcy case of Guangdong International Trust and Investment Corp. (GITIC) at the turn of the twenty-first century. GITIC, the overseas investment arm of the Guangdong provincial government, was the second largest trust company in China at the time but had accumulated massive debts, including US$1.9 billion owed to foreign creditors.

Following the company's bankruptcy declaration, a liquidation and financial restructuring process began under the leadership of Wang Qishan, then a deputy governor of Guangdong and later a prominent member of the Politburo Standing Committee and a key figure in Xi Jinping's pivotal anti-corruption campaign in 2012–2017. In managing the GITIC crisis, Wang took a ripping-the-band-aid-off approach to avert further and greater crises, which was widely praised as decisive and visionary at the time. However, beneath the surface, corruption permeated the restructuring process, with creditors or third parties securing sweetheart deals to purchase auctioned assets at heavily discounted prices. Liquidation administrators also accepted bribes from professional service providers – including auctioneers, asset assessors, accounting firms, and lawyers – in exchange for lucrative court commissions.[31] Yang Qingshan, head of the GITIC liquidation team, was found taking bribes from three auction houses. Dong Hong, a former assistant of Wang Qishan during the

[30] Interview L014.1. Also see Shu et al. (2014).

[31] See SPC (2005, Note. 13).

GITIC crisis, was found, more than two decades later, to have lined his pockets as a member of the GITIC liquidation team.[32]

Meanwhile, just a hundred kilometers away, judges at the Shenzhen Bankruptcy Tribunal were also deeply embroiled in corrupt dealings. The tribunal, soon after its inauguration, quickly became infested with corruption. In 2006, an anti-corruption crackdown led to the investigation of thirty judges in a single operation. At least seven, including the head of the tribunal, were sent to prison.[33]

Court auction is another hotbed of corruption during enforcement due to high commission fees and murky rules. In theory, public auction sales should serve as an efficient mechanism to maximize asset value by eliminating the intermediaries, fostering competition, and shortening the negotiation period, benefiting both sellers and buyers. However, they quickly became new platforms for corruption. During judicial auctions, courts could sell seized assets at half of their estimated price if they remained unsold after two attempts. Corrupt enforcement judges exploited this rule by deliberately making the auction fail. According to Huang (2015; Xinhua, 2014), 90 percent of court auctions at Chongqing High Court failed at their first attempt, leading to assets being sold sometimes at a depreciation rate of 70–80 percent. In 2009, the vice-president of Chongqing High Court in charge of enforcement matters received a death sentence with a reprieve for corruption, while the head of its enforcement bureau committed suicide while under investigation.

At the SPC, former SPC vice-president Huang Songyou, once facilitated the sale of a fifty-one-story office building located in the central business district of Guangzhou for 924 million *yuan* to a private company at a court auction. The company later resold it for over 1.3 billion *yuan*, turning an enormous profit.[34]

The enforcement process becomes even more precarious when both parties in a case seek to influence the judges. In one contractual dispute between real estate developers in Nanning, capital city of Guangxi province, the apartment building under dispute was seized and re-seized multiple times at the request of different major creditors,

[32] For more detailed reports on the GITIC case, see Chang'an (2009), Guyot et al. (1999), and Xinhua (2012b). For details on the case of Dong Hong, see Sina (2022).

[33] See Caixin (2008).

[34] See Qianjiang (2010).

leaving homebuyers – the primary victims – totally unprotected.[35] In other cases, judges from different divisions and different courts have fought over auction rights for the same asset, leading to heated jurisdictional battles.

The auction of the Oriental Gate Grand World shopping mall in Shenzhen provides a striking example.[36] The mall, valued at 400 million *yuan* at the time, was subject to competing claims from five creditors. Hunan High Court first seized the mall but internal conflicts arose between the court's economic law and enforcement divisions, each vying for auction rights. Eventually, the court split the auction into two packages, with each division in charge of one package. Each division commissioned a different auction house. Notably, the son of the then court president Wu Zhenhan had a financial stake in the auction house selected by the economic law division, while the son of a provincial Party leader had interests in the one chosen by the enforcement division.

Complications escalated when Shenzhen Intermediate Court, which had the territorial jurisdiction, also claimed auction rights. With no agreement among the three competing interest groups, the dispute reached the SPC, which ordered Hunan High Court to transfer part of the auction proceeds to Shenzhen Intermediate Court. However, Hunan High Court refused to comply, having already distributed the proceeds. The Central Committee of Discipline and Inspection (CCDI) then launched an investigation, leading to the conviction of Wu Zhenhan, Hunan High Court president, who was sentenced to death with reprieve for multiple corruption offenses. The investigation also uncovered a vast corruption network within the Hunan judiciary, implicating numerous judges.

In the 2010s, the SPC introduced online auctions to enhance transparency in court auctions. However, skepticism remained (Liu, 2014a) – and for good reasons. In 2021, after the new judicial auction regulation entered into force, an anti-corruption campaign led to the investigation of twenty enforcement judges. Among them were yet another head of the enforcement bureau of Chongqing High Court and Meng Xiang, head of the SPC enforcement bureau.[37]

[35] See Quality Watch (2006).

[36] See Appendix II, No.26. Also see (Li, (2005) and Liu, (2005).

[37] See Liu (2021b) and Sohu (2021).

### *Judicial Appointments*

Among all forms of corruption, the sale of judicial offices is the most detrimental to the administration of justice. The reason is twofold. First, when someone purchases a judicial office, they are likely to view it as an investment. To maximize their return, they may treat public services as commodities, selling favorable rulings for financial gain. The more services they sell, the higher return on investment. Second, buying a judicial office fosters a sense of private ownership of the office, motivating judges not only to render more favorable than fair decisions to bribing litigants but also to extort bribes by regularly rendering less favorable than fair decisions to litigants who do not bribe.

The sale of public offices was not uncommon in the 2000s, a period when corruption was particularly rampant. For instance, the downfall of Wang Huaizhong, a deputy governor of Anhui province, exposed an extensive network of office sales, implicating 800–900 office-buyers, including judges. Most of these officials not only remained unpunished but were also allowed to keep their offices.[38] Similar practices were also found in the military based on in-depth interviews of military personnel (Wang & Wang, 2018).

This study found three judges who had been caught for selling judicial offices. The first is Yang Duoming, former vice-president of Guangxi High Court, who accepted a bribe from a subordinate judge in exchange for the promotion to a vice divisional head post at the same court (Jin, 2005). The second is Wu Zhenhan, former president of Hunan High Court, who accepted a bribe from Tang Jikai, a vice-president of Changsha Intermediate Court, in exchange for recommending the latter for promotion to court president. However, Wu's recommendation was not adopted by the Organization Department of Hunan Party Committee, which had greater authority on this matter at the time (Jiang, 2006).

The third case involves Xiong Xiaoping, former president of Neijiang Intermediate Courts of Sichuan, who accepted, between 2005 and 2014, bribes from at least twelve subordinate judges, securing them leadership positions at various county or district courts of Neijiang through the judicial personnel transfer program (Taishan, 2023).[39]

In 2016, the 9th Amendment of the PRC Criminal Code made selling public offices an aggravated factor in sentencing for corruption.

[38] See Li (2008a).

[39] Also see Appendix II, No.27.

## Power-Based Distribution of Judicial Corruption

As explained in previous sections, the judicial interference mechanism installed between a court and the supervising Party committee is primarily designed to allow Party leaders to exercise their political objectives to implement the Party's policies and decisions through judicial activities. However, due to its inherent arbitrariness, the same mechanism also creates opportunities for Party leaders to abuse their prerogative for personal gain. When the same interference mechanism is universally installed and normalized within all courts, opportunities for corruption are extended to the entire judiciary as well. The distribution of such opportunities and associated gains is, however, uneven among judges.

### *Frontline Judges*

Frontline judges, as previously mentioned, are those judges who handle cases directly. They interact with litigants and witnesses, write case reports and draft court rulings. Their decision-making power is circumscribed by leader judges, especially for cases that are earmarked and closely supervised by the latter. However, even in these supervised cases, a frontline judge can still manipulate the adjudicative process to influence case outcomes. This is possible because, in most supervised cases, leader judges do not hear the cases firsthand; rather, they conduct supervision based on the information presented by the frontline judges – unless approached directly by litigants.

The Dataset analyzed in Chapter 1 includes 126 offenses committed by frontline judges, most of which involved misconduct in the fact-finding process. These included unethical and procedural violations such as admitting or excluding evidence without allowing the opposing party to contest it; tampering with or concealing evidence; and manipulating forensic examinations. Because such misconduct constitutes blatant violations of procedural rules, it carries a higher risk of exposure and detection.

As the lowest ranking officials in the judicial hierarchy, frontline judges not only have fewer opportunities for corruption but also receive lower returns from corrupt transactions compared to their superiors. This is partly due to the internal case-review mechanism, which selects cases for additional review based on their stakes – usually reflected in the economic value of a claim or the severity of a sentence. As a result, bribes paid to frontline judges tend to be lower, as their decision-making power is curtailed by leader judges and the cases that they are allowed to handle independently often involve lower stakes.

### *Leader Judges*

Leader judges hold supervisory roles and primarily review case summary reports submitted by frontline judges, either in written or oral forms. The extent of their supervisory authority depends on their rank within the court's power structure. Before the 2014–17 judicial reforms, leader judges made up 20–30 percent of all judges in an average court.[40]

When a court leader issues instructions regarding a case, they are not required to provide a properly reasoned legal argument to justify their instruction. Instead, the authority of their instruction stems from their superior position in the power structure of the Party-state. This was best articulated by Shen Sibao, a distinguished Chinese law professor, in his witness testimony presented in a case heard in a US court:

> Many official requirements are also transmitted through communications that may consist of department documents or oral directions, even including telephone calls. It is not the form of communication that creates its binding character, but the source and authority of the party giving the direction. Regardless of form, to the extent that these directions come from people in superior authority they are no less binding and obligatory on subordinates and the companies than any other type of "law."[41]

This decision-making mechanism, driven by political prerogative rather than legal merit, allows court leaders to influence far more cases than they could personally handle. Lü Hongmin, former vice-president of Jilin High Court, admitted that for cases he handled directly, he simply dictated his preferred outcomes to frontline judges, who then translated them into official rulings; for cases he did not handle directly, he used his supervisory authority to request updates from responsible judges and

[40] According to a study of the research team of Guangdong High Court in 2013, there were 65,136 leader judges nationwide at the time. See Sun and Fu (2022, p. 6). Also see Xu (2002).

[41] Report of Professor Shen Sibao, February 19, 2009, In re Vitamin C Antitrust Litig., 2009 WL 5133512 (E.D. N.Y.) (No. 06MD01738) (emphasis added). That case ultimately went to the Supreme Court as Animal Science Products, Inc. *v.* Hebei Welcome Pharmaceutical Co., 138 S. Ct. 1865 (2018), as cited in Clarke (2022, pp. 593–4).

then offered opinions that were subsequently incorporated into court decisions (Ji & Pan, 2020).

Different court leaders exercise their political prerogatives in different ways. Some personally introduce favor-seeking litigants to frontline judges and instruct the latter to take care of the case.[42] Others pass case materials prepared by favor-seeking litigants to frontline judges along with instructive notes such as "please expedite the case" or "please pay special attention to this case." Some adopt a more cautious approach, issuing vague instructions like "please adjudicate the case according to the law," or "this case needs careful examination," leaving frontline judges to interpret their true intent.[43] Records of such decision-making processes are not to be disclosed to court users but are kept in the classified case dossier (*fujuan*) for internal reference only (Li, 2017a; Wu, 2020).

As previously mentioned, cases subject to additional supervision by leader judges are typically high-stakes cases. The greater the stakes, the higher exchange value of the decision-making power and the greater the required level of supervision and approval. Empirical evidence overwhelmingly shows that judges of higher ranking receive larger bribes. Court records reveal the following examples:

- Zhang Jiahui, former vice-president of Hainan High Court, accepted bribes totaling 44 million *yuan*
- Zhang Jian, former president of Anhui High Court, accepted bribes totaling 72 million *yuan*
- Shen Deyong, former SPC vice-president, accepted bribes totaling 65 million *yuan*
- Xi Xiaoming, former SPC vice-president, accepted bribes exceeding 114 million *yuan*

[42] Interview W020.3.

[43] Such practices are often referred to as "*qianguize* (hidden rules)." According to Jiang Zongfu, a deputy mayor of Linxiang City, Hunan province, certain codes have developed in some institutions, requiring the instruction recipient to decipher the true intent of their superiors by analyzing subtle cues, such as the choice of punctuation marks in written instructions. See Jiang (2010). Readers interested in a more in-depth exploration of the psychology and strategic thinking behind such practices may find insight in a genre of literature known as "officialdom fictions." A notable example is *guohua* (*Chinese Painting*) by Wang Yuewen (Wang, 1999), a fiction so strikingly true to life that it underwent five reprints in two months after publication and before being banned. Additional real-life examples can be found in case reports on figures such as Zhou Wenxuan, Mai Chongkai, and Wu Zhenhan.

## Conclusion

Governed by an authoritarian approach to judicial decision-making, judges in China's courts are required to answer first and foremost to the political demands of their superiors, both within and outside the judiciary. To fulfill these demands, courts function as a partial judicial authority where the law can be interpreted flexibly to produce the desired judicial outcome. The normalization of the Party's political prerogative allows Party leaders to dictate court decisions in cases of interest without needing to oversee routine matters.

What distinguishes the Chinese judiciary is not its bureaucratic and hierarchical structure – a feature common in many civil law systems that do not necessarily lead to systemic judicial corruption. Rather, the Chinese system is distinctive in two significant ways. First, judges are expected to apply the law selectively and partially to satisfy their political superiors' preferences whenever required. The absence of judicial scrutiny allows corruption-driven instructions to be processed and implemented through the adjudicative process, provided that they are marked by broad and vague claims of serving the Party-state's collective interest. This practice erodes the authority of the law and undermines judicial impartiality. Such a decision-making mechanism serves to safeguard the Party's political interests, while simultaneously facilitating the corrupt interests of individual powerholders. Judges accustomed to applying the law selectively and partially for political purposes may just as readily accept private incentives to favor particular litigants, mirroring the way they uphold Party interests.

The second defining characteristic of the Chinese judiciary is the institutionalization of this decision-making mechanism across all courts to ensure the nationwide enforcement of political directives whenever necessary. This arrangement has expanded opportunities for corruption, allowing opportunistic leaders to engage in corruption more efficiently. It has also fostered a mutual dependence between superior and subordinate judicial officials, enabling them to advance their respective interests. Superior judges rely on subordinates to carry out their instructions at the operational level, while subordinate judges depend on their superiors for favorable task assignments, career advancement, and political protection. This interdependence leads to a tacit tolerance of corruption shared by them, provided that their interests do not collide. As a result, corruption becomes structurally embedded at all levels of the judiciary, making it widespread and persisting. It is this combination of factors that has made judicial corruption an endemic problem in China rather than an isolated and anomalous occurrence that may occur in any legal system.

# 3

# "Marriage" of *Guanxi* and Corruption

In the autumn of 2003, five judges from three different courts in China received an identical letter from Zhai Xuejun, a lawyer who had just started legal practice in Beijing. The letter, to which the lawyer's business card was attached, read, "I would like to cooperate with you . . . to share litigation resources and the profits. You are welcome to introduce me to litigants in cases you hear . . . under the following conditions: 1) the dispute's claim exceeds 300,000 *yuan*; 2) the litigant has not yet retained a lawyer or is represented by someone who could be easily replaced; 3) the litigant is likely to win the case or to have the opposing party's claimed damages reduced . . . I will share 40 percent of my retainer as your commission fee [author's translation]" (Niu, 2005).

To Zhang's surprise, a few judges handed the letter in to the local justice bureau. The bureau initiated an investigation. A couple of months later, Zhai was disbarred on the grounds of ethical violation of the People's Republic of China (PRC) Lawyers' Law. After the event, one judge told a reporter (Niu, 2005): "When I received the letter, I found it amusing at first but then thought it had crossed a line. I knew many people tried to engage in *guanxi*-practice with judges. But the way this lawyer did it is truly exceptional." It seems that what had caught the judge's attention was not merely the lawyer's audacity in soliciting corruption but the specific manner in which it was conducted. It raises important questions: What makes Zhai's "way" "exceptional"? What is the appropriate "way" in which bribery is expected to be conducted? And, why are *guanxi* and *guanxi*-practices such integral components of corruption in China?

According to sociological studies, *guanxi* represents a particularistic relationship used to facilitate favor-exchange. It is considered a close equivalent to *blat* in Russia, *vruzki* in Bulgaria, *pistolão* in Brazil, *wasta* in the Middle East, *protektzia* in Israel, or *compadrazgo* in Latin America. In China, *guanxi* wields considerable influence over political, economic, and social affairs and remains a persistent topic of ethical debate regarding its role in corruption.

Some scholars argue that *guanxi* and corruption are so closely linked that *guanxi* constitutes the cultural foundation of corruption (Gold, 2002a; Yu, 2008). Others contend that the two are different: while corruption involves "an impersonal" exchange for "short-term immediate gain," *guanxi*-practice is geared towards cultivating long-term mutual trust and strengthening relationships (Jones, 1994, p. 205), thereby adding "an element of humanity to otherwise cold transactions" (Gold, 2002a, p. 3). Following this line of analysis, some scholars believe that *guanxi* embodies "a culture of civility" (Lo, 2003, p. 143), serves as a "stabilizing alternative" (Jones, 1994, p. 125), and compensates for the absence of the rule of law (Potter, 2000, p. 194).

This chapter addresses two central questions. First, it investigates precisely how corruption, particularly bribery, operates between the briber and the bribed. Second, it examines where and how corruption and *guanxi*-practice intersect and why *guanxi*-practice has become an indispensable conduit of corruption in China. For the purpose of this discussion, "*guanxi*" is defined as a social tie or connection, while "*guanxi*-practice" refers to the act of soliciting, receiving, offering, or delivering a service among two or several parties who share one or more social connections under the following conditions: (1) the service involves the exercise of public power by one party, resulting in favorable treatment for another; (2) the service is provided by one party either in reciprocation for a favor previously received or as a means to generate future reciprocation from the other party. Equivalent Chinese expressions for this concept include "*gao/la guanxi*" (to cultivate guanxi) "*zou/tuo guanxi*," (to solicit favorable treatment from guanxi)" or "*guanxi yunzuo* (guanxi operation)."

## *Guanxi*-Practice – An Exemplar

Although lawyer Zhai's overt approach to bribery was quickly deemed unacceptable by the judges, as shown at the beginning of this chapter, one may wonder what an acceptable approach would look like. How should bribery ideally be executed? Direct observation of a bribery would offer the best insight. However, such access is nearly impossible for external researchers due to the inherently clandestine nature of bribery. Consequently, the most comprehensive accounts come from corruption participants themselves. Although these individuals are typically disincentivized from revealing incriminating details about these practices, some have overcome this barrier.

*Celadon*, a quasi-autobiography (Fushi, 2006) authored by an auction house owner, offers "textbook" material for studying "the art of guanxi", as proclaimed on its book cover. Centered on the life of Zhang Zhongping, a successful auctioneer, the book paints a vivid portrait of how the protagonist managed his business by engaging in *guanxi*-practices with court officials. The book's author, Hu Gang (aka Fushi), was involved in the 2004 Hunan judiciary scandal – a case discussed in Chapter 2 – that shook the Hunan judiciary, resulting in the arrests of at least a dozen judges, including then Hunan High Court president, Wu Zhenhan.[1] In *Celadon*, the protagonist, Zhang Zhongping (hereinafter Boss Zhang), runs an auction house in a provincial capital city. Boss Zhang's business primarily comes from court commissions, which he procured by leveraging the smooth *guanxi*-practice skills he had mastered. To demonstrate the thought process behind *guanxi*-practice, I have summarized and translated into English one episode of Boss Zhang's story as shown here.

> Boss Zhang learned from his contacts that Judge Hou was the person directly in charge of a court auction involving a large sum of assets. To obtain the court commission, Boss Zhang needed first to obtain Judge Hou's recommendation. But at this moment, the judge hardly knew Boss Zhang. During one of his regular visits to the court enforcement division's office, Boss Zhang discovered that Judge Hou had a drinking habit. One day, Boss Zhang delivered a full case of "health-preserving" baijiu (a type of distilled spirit) to the judge's home. This baijiu featured a mysterious aphrodisiac formula and was bottled in fine porcelain. The liquor case was heavy and Judge Hou lived on the 7th floor of a walk-up apartment building. Although Boss Zhang could have the baijiu delivered by his assistant, he chose to do it himself to make the encounter personal.
>
> When Boss Zhang finally showed up at Judge Hou's doorstep, panting and puffing, the judge was slightly surprised and immediately invited Boss Zhang in. Setting the case down, Boss Zhang explained, "It is a gift to me from a distiller friend. I don't drink. But I want someone who would enjoy it to have it." Judge Hou asked, "How much does it cost?" Boss Zhang replied, "The product has not been released to the market yet. I don't know the price. But I do know that it cost my friend millions just for the trademark and the formula." Judge Hou said nothing. During the visit, Boss Zhang learned that Judge Hou had a son, Xiaoping, who was studying calligraphy. He did not mention the court commission. Soon

[1] Gong (2007). Also see Appendix II, No. 26.

> after the visit, Boss Zhang arranged for a famous calligrapher to tutor Judge Hou's son and paid the tuition fee. The judge did not object.
>
> Since then, Boss Zhang was treated almost like a family member by Judge Hou's wife. He now had the privilege to make casual visits to the judge's home without an appointment. During one such visit, Boss Zhang took an interest in the calligraphy of the judge's son and asked for two exercise pieces for his personal collection. He later consigned them to an artwork auction, purchasing them at an inflated price under a friend's name. A few days later, Boss Zhang visited Judge Hou at home again, this time bringing an envelope containing 3,600 *yuan* in cash. "This," Zhang explained, "is the proceeds from Xiaoping's calligraphy". Judge Hou hesitated, "Tell me the truth. Are you behind this arrangement?" Boss Zhang replied, "How could that be? The auction was not even hosted by my company." Boss Zhang showed Judge Hou the auction certificate and added: "I even deducted a 10 percent commission fee from the sales proceeds. It can withstand any investigation." Boss Zhang put the envelope on the table. Judge Hou asked no further questions.
>
> Just as Boss Zhang was about to leave, Judge Hou broached the topic of the court auction. "The court will soon decide which bidding auction house will handle the auction," the judge said, "but the selection procedure is not yet clear . . ." He then casually mentioned the name of the auction applicant. Zhang immediately proposed, "How about we go fishing together another day, you, me, and Manager Yan (the auction applicant) . . . No agenda, no business talk. We will simply spend some time in nature and enjoy some fresh air. What do you say?" Judge Hou said, "Boss Zhang, I am not consulting you on anything . . . I have mentioned nothing about the auction . . . you arrange as you see fit." Zhang said, "Of course, of course."[2]

When placed side by side, Boss Zhang's career bore many similarities to that of the disbarred lawyer Zhai Xuejun. Both started their business from scratch, relocated to a new city in search of opportunities, and built their work around the same institution – the courts. However, their approaches and outcomes differ markedly. To start with, lawyer Zhai offered a business prospect to the targeted judges, while Boss Zhang provided unconditional gratuities before any business arrangements were made. In addition, lawyer Zhai sent a proposal for an illicit business deal by post to a group of judges who did not know him, while Boss Zhang deliberately refrained from uttering, let alone putting down in writing, anything that might incriminate Judge Hou. In essence, Lawyer Zhai treated corruption as a straightforward market transaction, whereas Boss Zhang embarked on a painstaking process of trust building, deploying

[2] Fushi (2006, Chapter 8).

gifts and gratuities before presenting his request. In an interview, Hu Gang, *Celadon's author*, revealed that he had spent half a year building trust with a high-court judge before securing his first court commission (Xiao, 2006). This strategic trust-building process is precisely what *guanxi* and its associated practices are about.

## Gifts and Initiation of Corruption

According to a survey among 100 individuals prosecuted for bribe-giving, 94.2 percent stated that they would first "warm up the relationship" before offering money.[3] The "warm-up" phase almost always starts with the offering of gifts or other gratuitous services that benefit the bribed at the briber's expense. Asking someone for a favor without first offering a gift would be considered mannerless and rude (Shin & Lui, 2022, p. 8). The reasoning behind this is simple: a favor is not an obligation. A favor-seeker must first cultivate a sense of indebtedness in the favor-provider to initiate the exchange (Mauss, 1967). Experienced *guanxi*-practitioners often remark: The "thing" is half done once the gift is accepted. This is because, after accepting a gift, the recipient is less likely to reject further interactions with the gift-giver. Gift-giving is, therefore, the most fundamental skill in the repertoire of any successful *guanxi*-practitioner.

### *Choosing a "Gift"*

A well-chosen gift draws the recipient into a relationship, while a poorly chosen one repels them and invites rejection. Boss Zhang's first gift to Judge Hou, a case of premium liquor, is a thoughtful choice. First, the gift is valuable, as he emphasized: "It costs millions just for the trademark and formula." At the same time, because the liquor has not yet been released on the market, as Boss Zhang took time to explain, its exact value remains ambiguous, allowing it to serve as a defense should any investigation arise in the future. Boss Zhang's meticulous planning impressed the judge, who responded, "You really thought this through.

[3] The research team surveyed eighty-five respondents. The survey was conducted by the Haizhu District Procuratorate in Guangdong Province in collaboration with the Clean Governance Research Center of Tsinghua University. See Huang (2006). A news report about the survey can be found in You (2006).

If people from the procuratorate ever ask about it, we can simply say I am helping you conduct a pre-marketing consumer evaluation."[4]

Boss Zhang's second gift, a private calligraphy tutor for Judge Hou's son, is even more subtle and appreciated. What made the service particularly appreciated by Judge Hou was not just its financial value but its demonstration of Boss Zhang's *sincere* care for the judge's family. Only after winning Judge Hou's trust did Boss Zhang offer cash bribes, which were then perceived acceptable.

Evidently, what constitutes a good gift varies for different recipients and at different times. Choosing the right gift is not always easy. From a briber's viewpoint, the first consideration is how much to spend. The gift should not be too expensive so that the briber would avoid suffering a great loss if the recipient fails to deliver the expected service. At the same time, it should not be so cheap that it is dismissed outright. For instance, offering two packs of cigarettes would constitute an insult when trying to secure a multimillion-yuan public procurement contract.

From an economic standpoint, the value of a gift should be commensurate with the benefit that the gift-giver expects to receive in return. *Red Roulette*, an autobiography by Desmond Shum, a shrewd and charismatic businessman, details how he and his then wife Whitney Duan cultivated guanxi with high-ranking officials in Beijing, particularly, then PRC premier Wen Jiabao's family. Shum explains, with striking clarity, how, at that level of power, fine-dining is no longer about appreciation of food but about "value proposition":

> We turned the Grand Hyatt's Yue Ting Restaurant into our private canteen. Our backup was the Lei Garden, a Michelin-starred restaurant situated on glitzy Jinbao Street near the Beijing branch of the Hong Kong Jockey Club. Sea bass at $500 a pop was a favorite dish of ours, as was a $1,000 soup made out of fish maw, the air bladder of big fish . . . Neither Whitney nor I felt much discomfort spending more than a thousand dollars on lunch. To me, it was just the cost of doing business in China in the 2000s. That is how things were done. A big element was the Chinese concept of "face." Everybody knew we were paying ridiculous prices for the soup, the fish, and even the veggies. And it was precisely that fact that gave our guest face. If I had been buying lunch for my personal consumption, I would have looked at it as a value proposition. But I was not there for fun, I was there for business, and if I wanted to do business in Beijing, that is what lunch cost. (Shum, 2021, p. 88)

[4] Fushi (2006, Chapter 2, p. 18).

As China's economy has developed, traditional gifts have lost their appeal. Thirty years ago, treating an official to a good dinner at a restaurant was an inducement in itself. Today, it is a challenge to persuade an official to accept a dinner invitation.[5] Ordinary gifts are unlikely to impress, let alone please, sophisticated officials who regularly receive bribes from countless favor-seekers. To overcome this barrier, bribers often conduct extensive research into their targets' hobbies or pastimes. As one interviewee remarked: "One *has to* have *some* kind of hobby."

Many officials do. For instance, Mai Chongkai, the former president of Guangdong High Court, perfected his golf skills after numerous all-expenses-paid rounds on courses across the country, courtesy of favor-seekers (Liu, 2004). At the turn of the twenty-first century, officials nationwide seemed to have been gripped by "golf fervor." During a 2000 anti-corruption campaign in Guangdong province, 135 golf club gift-vouchers were confiscated from officials and five officials were forced to resign from honorary positions in various golf associations (Ji, 2004). Even global financial institutions such as Deutsche Bank, J. P. Morgan, and Goldman Sachs took note of this trend. Their China representatives busied themselves with organizing golf outings, sponsoring trips, and gifting premium golf equipment and vintage wines such as Château Lafite Rothschild, all in an effort to court top Party leaders or their relatives for contracts and licenses, according to a 2019 New York Times report (Forsythe et al., 2019).

*Mahjong*, a popular gambling game in China, has long provided a convenient cover for bribery. For a long time, playing *mahjong* had been a standard program of *guanxi*-practice after banquets. The service was provided in almost all teahouses, nightclubs, or other entertainment establishments. It was common for bribers to deliberately lose to targeted officials during the game, a practice known as *yewupai* (game-for-business).[6] However, this method has a flaw, from the briber's perspective. The flaw is that the official could attribute their winnings to luck or skill rather than to the briber's generosity. To avoid such "misunderstanding," experienced bribers arranged for officials to play on their behalf against others while covering their losses. If the officials won, the briber would insist they keep the winnings as compensation for their "labor" or

[5] Interview T.028.

[6] *Celadon* has an elaborate description of the scene in chapter 3.

"*xinkufei*," as the briber would put it. If they lost, the briber would simply cover the loss (Zhou, 2005).

For some officials, gambling extended beyond *mahjong* tables to casinos. Ma Xiangdong, former deputy mayor of Shenyang City of Liaoning province, visited Macau seventeen times over two and a half years, accumulating massive gambling debts. When he ran out of money, his bribers stepped in. Once, a briber complained about financial strain after covering Ma's US$500,000 debt. As a response, Ma, who oversaw zoning and public construction of Shenyang city, granted a tax credit of 12 million *yuan* to the briber's construction company in exchange.[7] Bribing through gambling was so popular that it was explicitly listed as a form of criminal offense in the laws against bribery in 2007.[8]

Of course, not all officials are drawn to gambling. Some prefer cultural pursuits. For example, some corporations once sponsored the Chinese State Orchestra to perform a symphony composed by Wang Yi, then vice-chairman of the China Securities Regulatory Commission, who "accidentally" discovered his "talent" for musical composition in his late forties during a trip to Tibet.[9] Some officials who were less "talented" but otherwise also "artistically inclined" showed a strong interest in art collections, a trend that coincided with a surge in China's antique and art markets (Barboza et al., 2013). In China's loosely regulated auction industry, artwork became an ideal vehicle for bribery due to its advantage in money-laundering. A common practice involves the briber first arranging the sale of an antique to the bribed official at a flea market for a minimal price. The official would then put the item up for auction, where the briber would discreetly repurchase it at a significantly inflated price – much like what Boss Zhang did with the calligraphy of Judge Hou's son in *Celadon*.[10]

In general, gifts are favored over cash at the initial stage of *guanxi*-practice when trust has not yet been fully established. However, gift vouchers are an exception to this rule. Gift vouchers or shopping-cards (*gouwuka*) remain popular despite repeated efforts to restrict their use by the central government.[11] Their appeal lies in their quality as the perfect

[7] See Appendix II, No. 14.
[8] SPC and SPP (2007, Art. 5).
[9] A special website is dedicated to Wang Yi's case on the finance section of sohu.com. See Sohu (2010).
[10] China (2005) and Newspaper (2005).
[11] For instance, see Jiufeng Office (2001).

bridge between money and gift: they are transferable and function as cash without carrying the overt stigma of venality that cash does. A local procuratorate reported that in 2007, 92 percent of the officials prosecuted for bribe-taking in their jurisdiction had accepted shopping-cards. Not a single official had declined a shopping-card when offered (CCDI, 2023c; Lu, 2007). Some officials felt completely at ease receiving stacks of shopping-cards but were uncomfortable to accept cash. For instance, a county official in Shandong province twice refused a 5,000-*yuan* cash bribe but readily accepted a shopping-card of the same value when offered by the same briber.[12]

To curry favor with those in *zhongnanhai* – the Party's headquarters – one would need something better than shopping-cards. For Desmond Shum, author of *Red Roulette*, a US$15,000 timepiece was merely "pocket change" to his VIP patrons. Such gifts would not even be considered as bribes but merely "a sign of affection" (Shum, 2021, p.106). In the line of businesses that Desmond Shum operated, *guanxi*-practices involved, for instance, a spontaneous wine-tasting trip to France with three private jets carrying four couples (two jets flew empty, kept on standby just in case any guest required an earlier return ride), card games where the host deliberately lost US$100,000–US$200,000 per sitting, extravagant wine-tasting dinners at Pavillon Ledoyen and Rothschild's castle, followed by luxury shopping sprees in Milan (Shum, 2021).

Shum's story is not unique. Josef Ackermann, chief executive of Deutsche Bank (2002–2012), put it succinctly, "this was part of doing business in this country" (Forsythe et al., 2019). A US Securities and Exchange Commission investigation found that Deutsche Bank had once spent US$200,000 on gifts for Chinese bank officials to cultivate relationships. Notable recipients of the gifts included Premier Wen Jiabao, who was gifted a US$15,000 crystal horse – his zodiac animal – and a top-ranking Chinese banking official, described as "a son of one of China's founding fathers", who received a US$4,254 bottle of Château Lafite Rothschild, vintage 1945 – the year of his birth (Forsythe et al., 2019).

## *Addressing a "Gift"*

After a bribe has been chosen, the next step is its delivery. It is only at that point one would realize that referencing a bribe becomes "an issue." As

[12] Daily (2007).

Noonan detected, "there is no specific, unambiguous word for bribe" and "no common terms designating and denigrating the briber and the bribee" (Noonan, 1984). Bribers with even basic common sense understand that a bribe should never be labelled as a "bribe" or described as an "inducement" for a service. Instead, effective bribers would go to great lengths to obscure both the transactional and illegal nature of the exchange.

As demonstrated in the story between Boss Zhang and Judge Hou in *Celadon*, word choice is of utter importance. Certain words should be avoided at all costs. In all the cases examined in this research, corruption participants never employed explicit terms such as bribe (*huijin*), bribery (*huilu*), and bribe-giving/taking (*xinghui/shouhui*) when discussing their own corrupt activities. Instead, when referencing a bribe, they rely on euphemisms such as "a token of expression [of gratitude])." In sectors where corruption is entrenched and bribery is routine, euphemisms become more direct, using terms such as benefit-fee (*haochufei*), fee for the labor (*xinkufei*), or kickback (*huikou*). When greater discretion is required, coded language is employed. For example, a briber used the expression *mi*, which means money in Cantonese slang, when he gave a shopping bag containing cash to Tang Jikai, former vice-president of Changsha Intermediate Court, as payment for a favor.[13] Bribes involving larger sums often require a structured payment scheme, posing challenges that extend beyond mere euphemism.

References to the act of bribery are often drawn from *guanxi*-related expressions, for instance, *zou guanxi* (pulling guanxi), *tuo guanxi* (leveraging guanxi), *huodong guanxi* (mobilizing guanxi), *dadian guanxi* (greasing guanxi), and *goudui guanxi* ("mixing" connections). A recent study based on interviews of business elites in Guangdong found that none of the interviewees saw themselves corrupt, despite acknowledging that bribery was an essential practice for doing business in their region. Instead, they framed their actions as mere *guanxi*-practices and explained that they engaged in "*guanxi*" simply to obtain officials' "help and support," – thus, positioning their behavior "within moral parameters" (Shin & Lui, 2022, p. 8).[14] This finding is hardly surprising. In everyday life, we frequently resort to euphemisms to soften unsettling topics. Similarly, at the scene of corruption, nothing is more "unsettling" than the direct invocation of moral impropriety, or worse, the potential legal liability for oneself or one's partner in crime.

[13] Also see Appendix II, No. 21–22.

[14] Shin and Lui (2022, p. 8).

### *Acceptance of a "Gift"*

When dealing with an official who is "troubled" with the implications of venality, employing euphemisms alone may not be enough to ensure the acceptance of a bribe. According to a survey among 100 convicted bribe-taking officials, the most persuasive framing they had heard include: "This is what you deserve. Don't be too courteous." and "You are not giving me 'face' (*mianzi*) if you don't accept it."[15] Another common tactic is to attribute the bribe to an unknown third party, according to an interviewee, who once managed to persuade a hesitating official by saying, "Please take it. What I am requesting is not an easy task. This (money in the envelope) is not for you but for you to cover expenses when dealing with other officials." The envelope was accepted.[16]

In the episode from *Celadon* presented earlier in this chapter, Boss Zhang gave a mastery performance of the art of persuasion in bribery. To prevent rejection of his gifts or gratuities, he carefully framed his offerings in narratives that neutralized their venal implications. For example, during his first visit, he personally carried a heavy case of liquor to the top floor of Judge Hou's walk-up apartment building. When the judge opened the door and saw Boss Zhang struggling under the weight of the liquor case, he felt morally compelled to accept the gift – refusing it would have meant making Boss Zhang carry it all the way back downstairs, which would have been a breach of social etiquette and interpersonal obligations (*bujin renqing*).

A striking resemblance can be found in a gift-acceptance speech delivered by Empress Dowager Cixi over a century ago at her lavish sixtieth birthday celebration, an event that took mandarins two years to prepare. Though she had previously declared that she did not wish to impose any burden on her court and the country, the Empress ultimately accepted the extravagant gifts on the grounds that the officials who presented them were "sincerely persistent" and merely complying with tradition. The Dowager said, "If I do not accept them … it will be *me* being unreasonable (Ren, 2003, p. 125)."

To further obscure the venality of bribe-taking, many bribers choose to deliver gifts during traditional holidays or other ritual occasions, such as

[15] Shin and Lui (2022, p. 8).

[16] Interview H.022.

weddings and funerals, when gift-giving is customary. According to another survey conducted by the same research team of Haizhu procuratorate, the most popular occasions for bribe-related gift-giving are the Spring Festival and Mid-Autumn Festival (You, 2006). Such occasions even normalize the use of cash bribes wrapped in red envelopes (*hongbao*). Over time, this practice has expanded beyond major holidays to include any situation requiring an official to incur special expenditures, such as travel, illness, moving to a new home, and opening of school terms if the targeted officials have young children.

For risk-averse officials, whether to accept a bribe depends not only on what is offered, how it is offered but also on who is offering it. Most officials preferred to accept bribes from individuals who "looked loyal and trust-worthy" or "appeared wealthy" (Mo & Li, 2006). The officials become more selective when the value of their services increases.[17] To secure a lasting business relationship with such officials, one needs to be not only generous with "gifts" but also "likable." Of course, what one official considers "likable" might be despicable to another. However, in the context of bribery, certain characteristics are universally appreciated – generosity, loyalty and discretion – all of which signal that the briber is less likely to act opportunistically.

When cultivating *guanxi* with top-echelon officials, outstanding personal attributes become crucial. In *Red Roulette*, Desmond Shum presents a richly detailed account of how his then wife, Whitney Duan, meticulously cultivated *guanxi* with Auntie Zhang, wife of then premier Wen Jiabao. According to Shum, Whitney had a photographic memory, was well-versed in both Chinese and Western classic literature, and had an acute understanding of "the psychology of China's elite" – qualities that allowed her to impress the right people and make them feel good about themselves (Shum, 2021, p. 68). Whitney was always prepared. To cultivate *guanxi* with Auntie Zhang, she discreetly gathered information about Auntie Zhang's preferences and habits so that she could anticipate and fulfill Auntie Zhang's needs before the latter even recognized them herself. For high-power players like Desmond and Whitney, cultivating *guanxi* with the inner circle of power required self-erasure. As Desmond explained in a TV interview, "To abandon your own identity, to suppress your own needs and desires, and to always place

[17] For example, Xu Guoyuan, former mayor of Chifeng City of Inner Mongolia, confessed that so many people had offered him bribes that he could more easily recall those who had not bribed him rather than those who had. See Network (2009a).

yourself entirely in the other party's shoes – that is what it takes." He even likened this role to that of a eunuch serving royalty in a Chinese imperial court.[18]

Similarly, when Gu Kailai, the wife of Bo Xilai, then a Politburo member and Party-secretary of Chongqing City, was interrogated about her family's relationship with Xu Ming, a businessman who had bribed them with a luxury house in Nice, France, she gave the following statement:

"We have known Xu Ming for about 20 years. We have always had a good impression of him. Over time, through careful observation, we found him to be honest and trustworthy (*houdao*), someone who understood his place and how to behave (*dongshi*). He did not exhibit the [despicable] bad habits (*xiqi*) of a businessman ... His company has a secretarial office that can organize trips and book flight tickets for us, which is very convenient. We felt we could dispense with formalities and treat him like family (*bujianwai*) [and accept his help]."[19]

The strongest connection that a briber can hope to forge with a targeted official is a sense of bonding that is established in times of crisis. In *Red Roulette*, Desmond Shum recounts how an unexpected crisis transformed his relationship with a local Party leader in Shunyi County, where Shum's airport warehouse project was located. This crisis provided Shum an opportunity to forge a bond with the Party leader in ways that he did not know was possible.

At the time, Shum's previous government contact – with whom Shum had cultivated *guanxi* with over the years – was transferred to a different post, leaving Shum's project in bureaucratic limbo. He desperately needed new allies in Shunyi government to help him clear bureaucratic hurdles and mobilize resources to demolish several buildings where Shum's airport warehouses were to be built. As an icebreaker, Shum organized a junket to the United States for a group of officials from Shunyi, including Li Yousheng, who ran the district's planning and land department. Soon landing in Los Angeles, their first stop, Li Yousheng, who had a preexisting heart condition, collapsed at the hotel from heart failure. Shum immediately called an ambulance and accompanied Li to

[18] This study has consulted approximately a dozen interviews given by Desmond Shum in 2021–2023. The most informative ones were those he gave to Chinese-language media outlets during his book tour in Taiwan, for instance, (Shum, 2023a) (Shum, 2023b,c,d). All these interviews are available on YouTube.

[19] Bogu (2013, Timestamp 1:20).

hospital, where Li underwent a 7-hour triple bypass surgery. Throughout the ordeal, Shum remained by Li's side, offering both financial and emotional support.

Li made a swift recovery. From that moment on, he saw Shum as his personal savior. Upon returning to China, Li began introducing Shum to various Shunyi officials. Whenever they dined together, Li seated Shum at a place of honor and would recount the story of how Shum had not only saved his life but "given him a new heart." Other county officials working for Li also viewed Shum as a benefactor of the county, a man who had rescued their "big brother" "from near death in a foreign land." The dynamics of negotiation between Shum's company and the Shunyi Government shifted. Instead of officials asking, "what are you (Shum) going to do for me (the county and the bureau)?" to "how do we solve this problem of yours together?" For Shum's good luck, Li was later promoted to executive district chief, further smoothing the path for Shum.

Shum estimated that he had spent about US$300,000 covering Li's medical expenses in Los Angeles, half of which was reimbursed a few years later by the Shunyi District government. Reflecting on this experience years later, Shum remarked, the money did not matter because "the goodwill that experience bought was priceless" (Shum, 2021, p. 119).

## Transactional Risks of Corruption

Research indicates that, over time, corruption in China has become more "intensified" and "institutionalized."[20] At the same time, these corrupt activities have grown more hidden and involve increasingly complex arrangements (Gong, 2002; Ma, 2004). Unlike the practice of a traffic officer dropping a ticket in exchange for a small bribe, an interaction that is completed on the spot, most corrupt activities in China involve multiple interactions, taking months, if not years, to complete. At the same time, corruption has become riskier as anti-corruption has been moved to the top of the political agenda. While the absolute apprehension rate of corruption remains relatively low, the chance of detection has significantly risen thanks to an intensified anti-corruption enforcement campaign launched in 2012 (see more details in Chapter 6).

This illicit feature of corruption as well as its criminal implications exposes its participants to two primary types of risk (Graeff, 2005;

[20] Wedeman (2005b, p. 920) and Guo (2008, p. 364). Also see Ren (2008).

Lambsdorff, 2004b). The first is the risk of external exchange safety, which concerns the detection and punishment of corrupt activities. The second is the risk of internal exchange safety, which arises when one of the exchange parties behaves opportunistically (Lambsdorff, 2004a). Opportunism typically occurs when the execution of the corruption transaction is asynchronous – that is, when one party must act first, exposing themselves to the risk that the other may not fulfill their end of the bargain. Compared with legal transactions, the risk of opportunism in corrupt transactions is far greater because any loss incurred cannot be remedied through legal recourse due to the illicit nature of the exchange.

Deterrence stemmed from moral repugnance and condemnation of corruption is presumably weaker in China, where the boundaries between state and society, and between public and private domains, are more blurred than that in Western societies. Nevertheless, corruption still carries moral costs for individuals, particularly as ethics have become increasingly emphasized in political education among public officials in recent years. Cognitive dissonance, arising from moral contradictions, also serves as a psychological barrier impeding the contracting process of corrupt exchange. Cognitive dissonance occurs when an individual experiences discomfort due to conflicting cognitions[21] – such as when one's professed values contradict one's actual behavior. For instance, an official who publicly advocates for integrity and honesty in governance may experience cognitive dissonance if shortly afterwards, he personally accepts a bribe.

The risk of detection and punishment, the potential opportunism of the other party, moral costs and cognitive dissonance collectively constitute the main barriers that impede the contracting process of corrupt exchange. A direct manifestation of such obstacles is the labored initiating process, in which the intent to engage in corrupt exchange must be established and communicated. While intent is a prerequisite for any transaction, it rarely attracts our attention because the exchange that we frequently engage in in our lives take place in legitimate marketplaces, where such an intent is evident or can be explicitly communicated.

[21] Cognitive dissonance is a key theory in social psychology. It suggests that when two cognitions are related, they are either consonant (aligned) or dissonant (contradictory). People naturally seek cognitive consistency, as dissonance creates discomfort. The theory posits that individuals are motivated to reduce dissonance by changing their attitudes, beliefs, or behavior, or by rationalizing inconsistencies. See more in Festinger (1957) and Harmon-Jones (1999).

In corruption, however, openly revealing such an intent can be incriminating, which raises the risk of exposure and sanction. Moral awareness and cognitive dissonance will also hold potential corruption participants back from manifesting their intent. Thus, *guanxi*-practitioners resort to practices of social exchange to obscure their intent. In ordinary social exchange, transactional intent is often concealed through a deliberately placed time lag between when a gift or a favor is provided and when reciprocity is called upon. Shrewd *guanxi*-practitioners invest a considerable amount of time in cultivating trust with targeted officials – lavishing them with gifts and gratuitous services long before making any specific requests. In Jiangsu, for example, a businessman once confessed that when he offered bribes to the deputy mayor of Suzhou City, he never attached his bribe to any specific request, explaining that it would be "too distasteful" if gifts were only given at the moment of a transactional need (Li, 2008b).

Beyond being a matter of style, this deliberate time lag plays a critical role in corruption defense. By distancing the act of bribe-giving/taking and from the delivery of corrupt service, corruption participants can obscure the quid pro quo, a key element required to establish bribery in a court of law. This temporal separation allows corruption to be reframed as favor-exchange, a product of moral fulfillment in an affective relationship instead of a premeditated abuse of public power. It is, therefore, unsurprising that in some companies *guanxi*-maintaining activities become routinized and are formulated as a part of the business plan. For instance, a leaked company spreadsheet revealed that in 2009, Xin Ao, a gas boiler company in Shandong, had 212 local officials on its *guanxi*-maintenance plan. The first person on the list was the local Party-secretary, for whom the company's general manager was responsible for the following tasks:

a. quarterly treats to banquets or gifts, budget at 2,000 *yuan*/per time or occasion;
b. gifts for special occasions, e.g., the Mid-Autumn Festival and Spring Festival, budgeted at 5000 *yuan*/per occasion;
c. arranging an inspection tour for the officials to visit the company, budgeted at 50,000 *yuan*;
d. spontaneous arrangements, budgeted at 10,000 *yuan*.[22]

[22] The spreadsheet is on file with the author.

Concealing the intent to exchange not only minimizes the legal risk but also reduces the moral discomfort that corruption participants may experience when engaging in unlawful conduct. As shown in the previous section, *guanxi*-practice dulls the sense of immorality of corruption by transplanting it to a social framework, where exchange of gifts and services is not only permitted but even expected. Within this framework, the intent to exchange is subtly signaled and communicated through mutual acknowledgments of friendship and endorsements of goodwill while the venality associated with corruption is neutralized and rationalized. In this redefined social reality of corruption, the moral censure that would otherwise have been called upon is replaced with moral commitment and obligation that social interactions require. Recontextualized, the meaning of gift is no longer what is embodied in the traditional custom of gift-exchange.

However, the thin veil of *guanxi*-practice is often insufficient to completely disguise bribery. Three key indicators distinguish guanxi-based inducements from genuine social exchanges. First, *guanxi*-practices always take place within a principal-agent-client relationship while ordinary social exchanges are not bound by such a structure. In guanxi-practices, the recipient of the gift or gratuities always holds an entrusted office, most commonly in a public institution, from which the gift-giver has either already received or expects to receive special treatment. Second, unlike reciprocal gift exchanges in social relationships, the flow of gifts in guanxi-practices is overwhelmingly one-way, moving from the individual with little or no power to the one with greater power. Third, in traditional social exchange, gifts typically hold symbolic value, whereas in guanxi-practices the gift is no longer merely a "token" of friendship or affection but instead carries significant economic value, far exceeding what customary social interactions would entail. In short, *guanxi*-practice operates on the basis of a mutual understanding between both parties regarding what it signifies and what it will ultimately lead to, even if the exact terms remain unstated and obscured.

## Asymmetry of Risks

Catching and punishing the bribe-taker has always been the primary focus of China's anti-corruption efforts. The success or failure of anti-corruption campaigns has always been measured by the number of bribe-taking officials apprehended and punished – not by that of the bribers.

The risks of legal punishment, moral scrutiny and cognitive dissonance are distributed unevenly between bribers and bribe-taking officials.

Firstly, bribe-taking carries more severe legal consequences than bribe-giving. Historically, the threshold of prosecution had long been lower for the bribed than the bribers. According to the Chinese Criminal Law (1997), the offense of bribe-giving was prosecutable when the bribe exceeded 10,000 *yuan*, whereas bribe-taking was indictable at just 5,000 *yuan*. Additionally, bribe-taking carried a much heavier sentence than bribe-giving. Only in the last decade have new laws been introduced to close or narrow these disparities.[23]

Nevertheless, significant disparities remain. When all other factors being equal, taking a bribe is still punished more harshly than giving a bribe. For instance, according to the current sentencing standard, taking a 3.5 million *yuan* bribe, without any mitigating or aggravating factor, will result in a minimal sentence of ten years; while giving a bribe under the same conditions will result in a maximal sentence of ten years. In addition, bribe-giving is never punishable by death but bribe-taking can warrant the death penalty, both before and after recent legislative changes. Furthermore, bribe-giving does not incur criminal liability if the bribe is rejected; however, soliciting a bribe, regardless of whether a bribe is ultimately accepted, constitutes an aggravating factor for sentencing.[24]

In prosecutorial practices, far fewer bribers than the bribed are prosecuted and punished – sometimes as an inducement for their cooperation in testifying against the bribed, and sometimes without any particular reasons revealed publicly.[25] For instance, in the recent corruption scandal at Ji'nan Intermediate Court, sixty-four lawyers were found to have bribed judges of that court (Huang, 2021). More than one-third of these lawyers held leadership positions in city and/or provincial bars. While the judges were convicted, the lawyers remained free, with no official explanation given for the lack of prosecution. Similarly, in the aftermath of the scandal of Zhang Jiahui, only four out of the thirty-eight lawyers who had given Zhang bribes were referred to the procuratorates for prosecution and the rest received only administrative sanctions (Cai, 2021). Even more astonishing was the case of former president of Neijiang Intermediate Court Xiong Xiaoping, who accepted bribes from twelve judges for promotions. Despite clear evidence of bribe-giving,

23 SPC and SPP (2016).

24 Chinese Criminal Law (1997). Art. 386, 383, 390.

25 Chinese Criminal Law (1997). Art. 68, 390.

these twelve judges were neither prosecuted nor dismissed – they were even allowed to keep their positions after Xiong's conviction.[26]

Secondly, bribe-taking officials are subjected to stronger moral scrutiny than the bribers. The public is generally more likely to sympathize with bribers and relate to their experiences, whereas bribe-taking officials are often perceived as privileged, venal, and greedy. This perception is reinforced by governmental propaganda, which frequently attributes corruption to individual moral degradation rather than systemic institutional dysfunction.

Thirdly, bribe-taking officials experience or are expected to experience stronger cognitive dissonance compared with the bribers. Between the two, it is the bribed who need to maintain a moral image and publicly declare their commitment to honesty and integrity in public office. These expectations and requirements normally create a moral cognition that clashes with the self-serving desire for illicit gain, leading to heightened cognitive dissonance. In contrast, the briber is not subject to the same moral conditioning, or at least not to the same extent, as the bribed official.

## Asymmetry of Bargaining Power

Similar to the asymmetric distribution of legal, moral, and cognitive constraints between the bribers and the bribed, bargaining power is also unevenly distributed between them – except in this case the bribed official holds the advantage. This imbalance primarily stems from the scarcity of valuable public resources, which are controlled by a select few, compared to the high demand for these resources from many (Ren, 2008). In other words, there are usually more potential bribers than the bribed officials. As Desmond Shum exclaimed, if one can tolerate the exaggeration, all 1.4 billion Chinese people would appreciate the opportunity to cultivate *guanxi* with high-powered officials like Wen Jiabao or their family members. Thus, it is entirely at the discretion of these powerful officials to decide whom they choose to engage in *guanxi*-practice with.

[26] The case came to light when a defense lawyer revealed a judge's prior misconduct – bribing a superior for promotion – as grounds to request the judge's recusal from a corruption trial at the Neijiang Intermediate Court. For more, see Weibo posts of the said lawyer Zhou Lixin at https://rb.gy/cddrc9.

Bribers also suffer from a disadvantage in the negotiation of exchange terms due to information asymmetry. This asymmetry arises when public institutions operate in opacity, with unclear or inconsistent rules, creating process information that is known only to insiders. Thus, officials can easily manipulate this information to their advantage (Song, 2005).

Pressurized by their weaker bargaining position and encouraged by the lower risk of legal sanction, bribers often take a proactive role in initiating corrupt exchange. They are sensitive to cues and keenly observe opportunities. As depicted in *Red Roulette*, navigating this intricate process requires exceptional interpersonal skills, emotional intelligence, entrepreneurial acumen, and meticulous planning. Desmond Shum revealed that he and Whitney Duan would methodically discuss issues such as how to approach their targets and what responses to anticipate, and how to strategize each subsequent move.

In contrast, bribed officials often adopt a passive and responsive stance as their optimal strategy. However, passivity does not equate to weakness. On the contrary, as this chapter has demonstrated, it is ultimately the bribed official who dictates the terms of engagement. They typically retain full control over whether, when, and to what extent they will commit to an exchange, ensuring its safety before they deliver the requested service or promise to do so.

Once again, Desmond Shum's words perhaps best illustrate such asymmetry. When asked about the nature of their investment partnership with Auntie Zhang, Desmond Shum explained, "We had an unwritten understanding that [for each investment] Auntie Zhang would contribute one-third of the capital . . . However, whether her promised capital would arrive, and when, was left for later discussion. We could not possibly chase after her, insisting that she cover any shortfall . . . and frankly, if our joint investment had failed, it would be impossible [for us] to ask them to share the loss. This was as clear as day."[27]

## Self-Enforcement Mechanism

In corruption, participants are compelled to conceal their intent to exchange due to its illegality, creating significant obstacles in negotiation and enforcement. In ordinary social exchanges, negotiation is often unnecessary. People readily sign for a neighbor's package when they

[27] Shum (2023a, Timestamp 28:09).

are not at home, without considering whether the favor will be reciprocated or under what terms, because such exchanges involve low stakes and minimal costs. However, in corrupt transactions, where the stakes are significantly higher, negotiation and enforcement become essential.

This raises two key challenges: How can participants negotiate exchange terms when the intent to exchange must remain hidden? Similarly, how can corruption participants monitor and control opportunism when they cannot openly acknowledge their intent and seek legal recourse?

This study finds that corrupt transactions are negotiated and enforced through a self-enforceable operating mechanism. This mechanism differs from the informal social reputational system, commonly found in ordinary social exchanges, which relies on network gossip to circulate evaluative information to third parties (Barbalet, 2014). Such a word-of-mouth-based enforcement mechanism may effectively regulate low-stakes social exchange within small, close-knit communities. It cannot, however, explain the type of exchange that involves high stakes, where the benefit of defaulting far outweighs the repercussions of any social sanction imposed by intra-network gossip.

The limits of the word-of-mouth mechanism are not unique to corruption. Economic historians have detailed how medieval European traders (Milgrom, 1990; North, 1990) faced similar risks of default, as cross-region trade preceded the emergence of nation-states, with no centralized authority to enforce contracts or punish cheaters and defaulters. At the beginning, traders relied on word of mouth to create a "virtual" bulletin board of performance records for prospective trading partners. However, this informal reputation system eventually collapsed when trade volume, scope, and scale outgrew the capacity of this reputational system to manage information (Milgrom, 1990; North, 1990). In response, traders developed the Law Merchant system, where private judges appointed by trade fair organizers would hear complaints, adjudicate disputes, and impose punitive measures on defaulting parties.

However, the solution adopted by medieval European traders would not work for corrupt transactions, as traders did not need to conceal their intent to exchange and could explicitly negotiate terms (Quinn, 1996; Read, 1926). Corruption, by contrast, requires secrecy. This study finds that corruption operates on a self-enforceable mechanism comprising two key components: partial performance and voluntary restitution for default.

Partial performance is very common in cases examined in this study. Bribers rarely offer the full bribe upfront but instead pay in increments, with each installment corresponding to the value of the service that has been received or is expected to be received. Similarly, the bribed officials also negotiate the terms by delaying or withholding services until an adequate bribe is provided. Thus, partial performance not only minimizes risks for both parties – ensuring that if either side defaults, the financial loss remains limited – but also serves as a negotiation tool – allowing both parties to adjust exchange terms without explicitly discussing them.

Therefore, the pricing of corrupt services remains fluid and dynamic except in cases where the economic value of a corrupt service is clear and straightforward and when the same service is rendered routinely by the bribed official. In such corrupt transactions, bribes are fixed at predetermined rates, similar to a tax system. For example, according to a 2006 internal report on judicial corruption, a common bribery practice emerged in court auction commissions in the studied region. This unwritten rule dictated that the auction commission be divided in a 4:3:3 ratio, with 40 percent allocated to the judges involved, 30 percent to the auction house, and 30 percent to cover operational costs, including payoffs to other officials (Fan, 2006). Similarly, at Beijing West District Court, former president Guo Shenggui frequently referred litigants whose cases were pending before his court to lawyers with whom he had personal connections with pre-determined kickbacks. A lawyer named Zhang Ruping represented forty-five cases in Guo's court during 1999–2002, most of which were referred to him by Guo. In each, Guo took a 20–30 percent cut of Zhang's retainer fees. Between 2002 and 2005, Guo referred twenty-six cases to Wu Min, a former judge of the same court, and took half of the retainers after tax (Jing, 2009; Wang, 2007).

The second component of the self-enforcement mechanism is restitution, which means that if an official accepts a bribe but fails to deliver the promised corrupt service, they would voluntarily return the bribe in part or in full to the briber. The motivation for returning a bribe is twofold. First, fairness. As the Chinese saying goes: one should not retain an undeserved reward. Since the bribe is offered in exchange for a service, it would be unethical to keep it if the service is not delivered. Second, risk management. If a briber is unable to recover their money, they may be incentivized to report the corruption to authorities. Officials with a long-term perspective tend to avoid opportunism, as cheating a briber increases the risk of exposure.

On the other hand, a briber with long-term interests may choose not to reclaim their bribe even if the corruption service is not delivered. Some choose to leave the balance sheet uneven in favor of the official as a gesture of goodwill, locking in opportunities for future exchanges. For instance, Yao Hui, head of the Second Criminal Division of Shenzhen Intermediate Court, was convicted for twenty-eight counts of bribery, primarily involving lawyers paying him for favorable rulings. Despite failing to deliver on some cases, Yao was able to keep the bribes in full, except in one instance, where he voluntarily returned the bribe. That case involved the corruption trial of a ranked official heard by Yao. He refunded the bribe when the investigation into the official escalated, significantly increasing the risk of exposure (Cui, 2022b).

## Detection of Corruption

Previously, I have explained that the dominant form of transactional corruption is facilitated by *guanxi*-exchange, wherein corrupt dealings occur only after a trusting relation has been established between the parties involved. This trust serves to conceal and insulate the transaction from external scrutiny. Given this built-in safeguard, how is it, then, that many corruption perpetrators are caught? This study finds that insider whistleblowing is the primary cause for corruption detection. Whistleblowing typically occurs when a bribe-taking official engages in opportunistic or provocative behavior, prompting the briber or other witnesses to expose the corruption. It can also arise from internal strife over the distribution of corruption spoils or other domestic disputes. In some instances, corruption was exposed inadvertently due to an official's association with other exposed crimes and offenders. The following three cases illustrate these dynamics.

The first case involves a broker named Zhang Xiangying, who entered into a corrupt agreement with a judge from Liaoning High Court concerning an appeal heard by that court (Jia, 2021). The judge agreed to rule in favor of Zhang's client in exchange for a bribe of 200,000 *yuan*. However, the final court ruling took Zhang by surprise as the court ruled against his client. When confronted, the judge explained that he had mistakenly assumed Zhang was acting on behalf of the opposing party. Zhang's client was, however, unconvinced and suspected that the judge had been bribed by their opposing party. The judge offered to refund the bribe, but it was insufficient to offset the client's losses. Seeking an alternative solution, the judge also offered to find a way to reopen the case through a contact at the SPP, but these efforts proved fruitless. Ultimately, Zhang's client leaked the story – along with a secretly recorded conversation between Zhang and the judge – on social media.[28]

The second case involves the downfall of Zhang Jiahui, the former vice-president of Hainan High Court. According to court files and media reports,[29] Zhang rose rapidly in the Hainan judiciary, being promoted from an assistant judge to the high court vice-president in just ten years. Her husband, Liu Yuansheng – a former judge and then lawyer – operated a business conglomerate valued over 20 billion *yuan*. Unbeknownst to them, their eventual downfall would be set in motion by what seemed to be an insignificant business dispute that occurred 1,000 miles away in Chongqing.

The dispute stemmed from a real estate development project Liu undertook in Chongqing, where he hired a local contractor but refused to pay for the completed work. Desperate to recover his dues, the contractor obtained a recording of a *mahjong* party hosted for Zhang Jiahui by her favor-seekers, along with evidence of Liu's illegal business dealings. He then blackmailed Liu, threatening to leak the materials unless he received his payment.

Under pressure, Liu made a partial payment to the contractor to de-escalate the situation but soon retaliated by reporting the contractor to the police for blackmail. The contractor was arrested, but his lawyers released the recordings, exposing Zhang and her family's corrupt dealings. The revelations prompted the Hainan Party authorities to launch a disciplinary investigation, which uncovered Zhang's extensive network of judicial corruption. She was ultimately convicted for thirty-eight counts of bribe-taking, one count of rendering a wrongful administrative court decision in violation of the law, and one count of fraud. In 2020, she was sentenced to eighteen years in prison and her husband was sentenced to 14.5 years. Yi Zhenwu, the contractor, was acquitted two years after Zhang and her husband's convictions.

Whistleblowing can also arise from disputes over the distribution of corruption spoils. A notable example is the court auction commission for the sale of Oriental Gate Grand World Shopping Mall, where three court

[28] One can find the recording of the conversation between the judge and the broker as well as the transcript at Jia (2021).

[29] See Appendix II, No.33. Also see Paper (2020, 2022).

authorities laid jurisdictional claims over the case (see details in Chapter 2). The dispute remained unresolved until the Central Committee of Discipline and Inspection (CCDI) was brought in to investigate. The investigation ultimately led to the dismantling of a vast corruption network within Hunan High Court, involving its president Wu Zhenhan.

A similar story unfolded in Chongqing High Court, where disputes over auction commission allocations led to irreconcilable conflicts among competing interest groups. As tensions escalated, anti-corruption authorities intervened, exposing an extensive corruption network led by a court vice-president (Yin, 2011; Zhu, 2009). As in the Hunan scandal, the investigators found that corruption had been entrenched in Chongqing High Court for years (Yin, 2011). The absence of earlier investigations into these practices underscores a critical reality: when corruption is deeply rooted, only a more powerful force can expose it. High-stakes court cases often draw multiple interest groups backed by different powerholders of higher offices. As the financial interests rise, conflicts intensify – sometimes to the point where eliminating a rival becomes the only solution. In today's political climate, few things can end an official's career as decisively as a CCDI-led corruption investigation.

However, not all whistleblowers catch the attention of anti-corruption authorities. To do so, they need either special access or compelling evidence – such as tapes capturing officials red-handed – amplified by a media campaign. Most corruption victims lack both. Since 2003, a judge couple – Zhan Zhiliang, a civil divisional leader at Changsha Intermediate Court, and Zeng Xintian, a divisional leader at Hunan High Court – had engaged in judicial corruption either independently or in collusion. At least eight litigants had reported them to the authorities (Zhai & Chen, 2022). Yet, none of these reports resulted in a criminal investigation until 2019.

As will be explored in Part II of this book, anti-corruption investigations are highly selective and require multiple layers of approvals before being launched. The more powerful and influential a corrupt official is, the more approvals are necessary to authorize the investigation. In extreme cases, individuals with strong connections with law enforcement agencies, including the police, the procuratorates, and the Committee of Discipline and Inspection at subnational levels (CDIs), can even leverage these relationships to eliminate competition. For instance, Guo Wengui (aka Miles Kwok) was notorious for his ability to weaponize the legal system for his personal interests thanks to his deep connections or affiliations with the intelligence agency, CCDI officials and high-ranking Party officials.[30]

## "Marketization" of *Guanxi-Practice*

As discussed earlier, *guanxi*-practice provides its participants privileged access to public services and resources. This privilege is generally limited to two groups: individuals in possession of preexisting social ties – often through kinship – with officials in power, and those with sufficient resources to cultivate *guanxi* with those in power. However, cultivating *guanxi* is neither cost-free nor instantaneous; it requires advance planning and a significant investment of time, resources, and efforts over a prolonged period, with no guaranteed return. Given these barriers, one might expect *guanxi*-facilitated corruption to be relatively rare in judicial settings due to two primary constraints.

First, the time constraint. As discussed previously, *guanxi* cultivation is inherently personal and requires a deliberate time lag between the investment phase (building *guanxi*) and the return phase (seeking for favor). This time lag presents a major challenge for litigants. For instance, a plaintiff usually does not know in advance which judge(s) will be assigned to their case before taking it to court. This uncertainty prevents early strategic guanxi cultivation. A defendant, on the other hand, has even less time for preparation, as they lack control over when the dispute is brought to court. If a litigant only begins to cultivate *guanxi* with a judge after the case is filed, the instrumentality of *guanxi* cultivation becomes obvious. Moreover, judges in China's courts are overburdened by their workload and strict deadlines, which leaves limited availability for *guanxi* cultivation.

Second, the transaction cost constraint. As explained in Chapter 2, the litigation process in China is fragmented in three respects. First, multiple phases of litigation. Each case progresses through three distinct stages at three distinct court divisions: case filing, adjudication, and enforcement. To secure a favorable outcome, a litigant needs to engage in corrupt dealings with multiple judges across several court divisions at different phases of the case. Second, hierarchical court bureaucracy. The court is bureaucratically structured, meaning that court rulings are determined by a number of decision-makers. A litigant seeking to influence a case

[30] Newspaper (2017) and Wang and Lu (2015). Also see Appendix – court judgment on Meng Huiqing.

needs to cultivate *guanxi* not only with the judges who directly handle the case but also with their superiors, who hold oversight and review authority. Finally, judicial hierarchy and appeals. Court cases do not end with a single ruling. If the opposing party appeals a court decision, the case moves up the judicial hierarchy. A case does not end with the appeal either. An appellate ruling can be remanded for retrial, restarting the litigation process, further multiplying the costs.

Under these circumstances, an average litigant is unlikely to possess the necessary number of preexisting social ties to readily connect with multiple judges when a dispute arises. Establishing these social ties through *guanxi* cultivation within a short time frame is equally difficult. If that is the case, how can we then explain the widely acknowledged pervasiveness of *guanxi*-facilitated corruption in China's courts, as demonstrated in the previous two chapters? What – or who – has lifted these constraints?

The answer lies in the emergence of professional *guanxi*-brokers.[31] These brokers specialize in establishing, cultivating and maintaining *guanxi* with judges and court officials, monetizing these connections for financial gain. Their brokering activities have effectively transformed *guanxi* into a marketable service that extends *guanxi*-based corruption to any litigant with the financial means to participate.[32]

Currently, professional *guanxi*-brokers in judicial corruption fall into three main categories. The largest group consists of lawyers, who possess several advantages to act in this role. First, preexisting social ties with judges. Many lawyers developed *guanxi* with judges through a shared educational background. Trained in the same law schools, some even shared dormitories before diverging onto separate career paths. These connections create a natural foundation for *guanxi* cultivation.

Second, open access to bribers. As intermediaries between litigants and courts, lawyers enjoy lawful and unrestricted access to litigants and can freely market their services. Some lawyers and law firms openly advocate their *guanxi* connections. Some, especially, elite law firms, are more discreet. However, most lawyers disclose little or no details of the bribery

[31] The presence of *guanxi*-brokers in courts is by no means a new phenomenon. Legal historians have documented cases from the Qing dynasty, where "litigation masters" – court clerks and family members of corrupt officials – acted as intermediaries, offering brokerage services to litigants in need (Lin, 2009; You, 2015).

[32] *Guanxi*-brokers are by no means limited to the judiciary. Research has shown that such brokers were prevalent even in highly disciplined institutions such as the People's Liberation Army (Wang, 2017a).

to their clients. This opacity enhances the security of bribery for all parties involved: the litigant remains distanced from direct involvement of the bribery, while the judges appear to operate within ethical bounds. As a result, in criminal proceedings, lawyers are often prosecuted not as mere bribery facilitators but as independent bribers.

Third, integrated service. As the intermediaries between litigants and courts, lawyers can bundle their legitimate legal services (e.g. legal consultation and representation) with illicit corruption brokerage, offering both to clients. In doing so, lawyers can simultaneously enhance the chance of winning a case while reducing the risk of corruption detection. When a judge rules in favor of a bribing litigant with a poorly argued claim, the decision is more likely to attract scrutiny and be challenged by the opposing party. Therefore, strong legal advocacy that emphasizes the legal merits of a case helps mitigate the violation of the law, thus concealing corruption.

Four, money laundering. By bundling legal representation with corruption brokerage, lawyers can effectively launder bribes by invoicing them as part of their legal fees. This arrangement provides litigants with a distinct financial benefit, allowing them to claim bribes as tax deductible expenses – a benefit that would be impossible if the litigant were to bribe a judge directly.

Last, repeated players and the reduction of transaction costs. As discussed in previous sections, *guanxi* cultivation requires a significant entry cost, involving investments of time, money, and effort. In terms of institutional economics, such expenditures constitute sunk costs – investments that have already been incurred and cannot be recovered (Schramm, 2002). However, these costs can be distributed and minimized when the briber (investor) has repeated interactions with the bribed over time. No one is better positioned for this than lawyers, who – unlike litigants – engage in frequent, ongoing interactions with judges. Most lawyers practice locally, and most judges remain stationed in the same court for the majority of their careers.[33] Put differently, lawyers are far more likely than individual litigants to repeatedly appear before the same judges, thereby lowering the transaction costs of guanxi-facilitated corruption.

[33] In fact, when high-valued officials are transferred to different jurisdictions, their close business associates would move their businesses with the officials. For instance, see reports in Xinhua (2015), Xue a Jia (2015), and Yue (2017).

Given all the above advantages, it is unsurprising that lawyers consistently emerge as the largest group of bribers in high-profile judicial corruption scandals. Examples include:

2002 Wuhan Intermediate Court scandal – forty-four lawyers implicated.

2019 Hainan High Court Zhang Jiahui scandal – thirty-seven lawyers implicated.

2021 Ji'nan Intermediate Court scandal – fifty-eight lawyers implicated.

2022 Changsha Intermediate Court Zhan Zhiliang scandal – fifteen lawyers implicated.

The second group of professional brokers in judicial corruption consists of judges and court officials, who do not necessarily handle court cases but have close working contacts with those who do. Their insider position grants them unique access to the judicial system, allowing them to operate as "key bridges" that facilitate the delivery of corrupt services (Wang & Liu, 2022).

For example, Huang Jianzhong, a former deputy divisional head of the SPC Research Office, accepted 2.16-million-*yuan* in bribes from favor-seekers in exchange for "getting a word" to judges in lower courts – judges whom Huang had met at training conferences or other professional gatherings.[34] Similarly, in the 2005 Hunan High Court corruption scandal, Li Xiaohua, the head of the political department of the court, played a dual intermediary role. He introduced bribers to the corrupt court president, Wu Zhenhan, while also acting on Wu's behalf, relaying his instructions to judges handling the cases that the two had promised to "take care of." These services earned Li Xiaohua 370,000 *yuan* in bribes.[35] In the 2021 scandal in Changsha Intermediate Court, Zhan Zhiliang, a civil division leader, was found to have accepted bribes not only in cases heard in her own court but also in cases adjudicated in the superior court, where her husband held a divisional leadership position.

Some judges, after leaving the judiciary, transitioned to private legal practices and capitalized on their ties with former colleagues. For instance, in the 2021 corruption scandal at Ji'nan Intermediate Court, five of the fifty-eight bribing lawyers were former judges from the same court (Huang, 2021). Similarly, in the recent SPC corruption scandal, Shen Deyong, the third SPC vice-president to fall for corruption, was

[34] See Appendix II, No.6.
[35] See Appendix II, No.26.

found to have accepted bribes from law firms owned by his former assistants. One such assistant had represented clients in fifty-nine cases heard at the SPC in 2012–2019, when Shen served as the executive vice-president (Yu, 2022).

The last and most privileged group of brokers consists of family members or close relatives of court leaders. These brokers benefit from unfettered access to key judicial decision-makers by virtue of family ties, making them highly effective conduits for corruption. For instance, in 2011, a former vice-president of Qingdao Intermediate Court was convicted for accepting bribes brokered by his wife and two mistresses, all of whom were lawyers representing cases in his court. Wu Zhenhan of Hunan High Court accepted bribes regularly brokered by his wife, son, and nephew. Xi Xiaoming, another fallen SPC vice-president, accepted 114-million-*yuan* in bribes, many of which were brokered by his son. Zhou Yongkang, former Politburo Standing Committee member in charge of courts, procuratorates, and the police, was also convicted for bribe-taking through his son.

## Conclusion

This chapter began with the case of Lawyer Zhai, who proposed a corrupt transactional arrangement to a group of judges, only to be reported by them and subsequently disbarred. Zhai's critical mistake was treating a corrupt exchange as though it were a straightforward market transaction. In so doing, he skipped the trust-building process and failed to recognize, let alone remove, the legal, moral, and cognitive barriers that prevent the exchange from taking place. His plan was poorly conceived and demonstrated his fundamental misunderstanding of how corrupt exchange operates.

As demonstrated in this chapter, the illegality of corruption compels its practitioners to conceal their intent to exchange while conducting it. To achieve this, they rely on an alternative contracting mechanism embodied in *guanxi*-practice, which allows the intent to exchange to be safely communicated. In addition, *guanxi*-practice also minimizes the otherwise prohibitive transaction costs of corruption while also helping to overcome the moral and cognitive barriers that could deter targeted officials from participating. Gifts, its main instrument, serve as an informal down payment, signaling the briber's commitment to the exchange. More importantly, it sets up an alternative social context, in which the exchange can be redefined. Performed with discreet tactics and proper etiquette, *guanxi*-practice seamlessly grafts a corrupt and immoral agreement onto a social setting, in which venality is neutralized and rationalized. Within this redefined social reality of corruption, an instrumental and transactional relationship can be presented as an affective relationship based on social commitment. The art of *guanxi* is to conceal the intent to exchange, blur the line between gifts and bribes, and moralize corruption through a set of shared social norms and codes of conduct.

At the same time, concealing the intent to exchange also introduces challenges in negotiating the exchange terms and enforcing them. When the stakes are low, this problem is negligible. However, in high-value corruption transactions, ensuring compliance becomes a critical challenge. To counteract the risks of opportunism, corruption participants rely on a self-enforcement mechanism that consists of partial performance and voluntary restitution for default. The effectiveness of this self-enforcement mechanism is closely tied to the credibility of anti-corruption efforts, a topic that will be further elaborated in Part 2. As long as this self-enforcement mechanism remains intact, *guanxi*-based corruption is almost impervious to detection, unless internal strife or external contingencies break the equilibrium.

Given that only a limited number of individuals possess preexisting social ties with the "right" judge at the right time and place, a significant gap emerges between high demand and limited supply for privileged access to *guanxi*. This imbalance has led to the rise of professional *guanxi*-brokers, who have commercialized access to *guanxi*-facilitated corruption. The most prominent of these brokers are lawyers, who cultivate social ties with judges and sell their *guanxi*-practice as a part of their legal services to court users. Together, these factors explain the paradox of parochial corruption in China's judicial system – hidden yet pervasive, privileged yet widespread.

# 4

# Survival of Corruption under Court Reforms

Judicial corruption in China is an unintended consequence, not a goal of its political-legal system. The ideal judiciary envisioned by the Party is politically compliant, professionally competent, and morally upright. Over the years, the prevalence of judicial corruption has spurred a series of court reforms initiated by the Supreme People's Court (SPC). These reforms aimed at redistributing judicial power, restructuring incentives of judges, and tightening judicial ethics in an effort to contain corruption. Despite improvements in judicial professionalism and efficiency (Liebman, 2007), the success of these reforms in curbing corruption remains questionable, as for every judge who was removed, another often takes their place or "*qianfu houji*," quipped in Chinese.

A case in point is the recurring corruption scandals in the Intermediate Court of Wuhan, the capital of Hubei province with a population of more than 10 million. In 2002, a scandal led to the arrests of a vice-president, a former vice-president, three divisional leaders, and eight frontline judges. Following this, Zhou Wenxuan was appointed court president, who, immediately upon taking the office, launched an anti-corruption campaign, replacing one-third of the court's judges. Less than four years later, Zhou himself was convicted for corruption and sentenced to ten years in prison. Subsequent years continue to see a cycle of corruption scandals at the court, with major purges in 2011 and again in 2018, culminating in the massive arrests of a new corruption network, involving leaders from the court, the procuratorate, the police and the political-legal committee (PLC) (Jiang, 2019b).

What happened in Wuhan is not exceptional. Courts across China – including Shenzhen Intermediate Court, Fuyang Intermediate Court (Anhui), Jilin High Court (Jilin), and Chongqing High Court (Chongqing) – have experienced similar cycles of judicial corruption. Even the SPC has not been immune. Three of its vice-presidents – Huang Songyou (convicted in 2010), Xi Xiaoming (convicted in 2017), and Shen

Deyong (convicted in 2023) – fell to corruption scandals, despite being regarded as eminent academic judges.

In 2014–2017, under Party General Secretary Xi Jinping's leadership, the Party authorized a nationwide judicial reform to enhance judicial fairness and authority, with the stated goal of ensuring that every court case "instills a sense of fairness among the populace." Did these reforms make a substantive difference in curbing judicial corruption? This chapter examines key anti-corruption judicial reform measures implemented by the SPC from the 1990s till the present.[1] In the final section, a commercial case heard at the SPC between 2008 and 2018 is discussed to illustrate the deeper political constraints that hinder anti-corruption efforts within these courts.

## Dividing Power

A fundamental anti-corruption strategy in China has been the redistribution of power to address power over-concentration. Redistribution can take many forms. The first is dividing power.

As discussed in Chapter 2, the litigation process in China is divided chronologically into three phases: case-acceptance, adjudication, and enforcement. This structure, introduced through judicial reforms in the 1990s, replaced an earlier system where a single court division managed cases from initiation to resolution. Previously, the same judge or panel of judges handled all stages of a case, from its acceptance, hearings, ruling and enforcement. This system was widely believed a major driver of judicial corruption (Court, 2001, p. 95), prompting the reform that segmented litigation into three phases handled by separate court divisions.

Following the reform, a typical first-instance court was restructured to include a case-acceptance division, multiple adjudication divisions specializing in different subject matters and a separate enforcement division. At the same time, the same judicial decision-making mechanism that normalized and institutionalized political prerogative in judicial decision-making (see Chapter 2) remains intact.

Unsurprisingly, the reforms failed to eliminate judicial corruption. Instead, corruption became more diffuse, involving a larger number of judicial actors. Some litigants lamented that the reform merely increased the number of "*bodhisattvas*" to whom they had to "pay tribute" (He,

[1] For a wider discussion on the functions of the SPC, see Finder (2024), Hou (2021), and Ip (2011).

2006). As cases were now handled by multiple divisions and judges, the transaction costs of judicial corruption rose, as discussed in Chapter 3, because a briber had to navigate a more complex network of decision-makers. When the increase of transaction costs outweighs the gains from corruption, it may deter some litigants from engaging in corruption, but may also prompt some judges to integrate their corrupt businesses through collusion.

Economics theories suggest that institutional integration reduces transaction costs. While it is uncertain whether those implicated judges were secret admirers of economic theories, they certainly demonstrated acute business instincts – consolidating the otherwise fragmented corruption services through collusion – thereby reducing the complexity of these transactions and associated transaction costs.[2] Since the late 1990s, "nested corruption" cases (*wo'an*) surged, involving multiple judges coordinating their corrupt activities. In some instances, informal markets of judicial corruption had been uncovered, governed by trade rules (*hanggui*) that regulated client sharing and profit distribution.[3]

When collusion is entrenched, corruption becomes even more resistant to monitoring, detection, and investigation. There are two primary reasons for this resilience. First, whistleblowers face heightened risk when more people are participating in and benefit from the misconduct that they intend to expose (Lui, 1986). Second, these networks often involve high-ranking court leaders, who shield them from oversight and scrutiny. As illustrated in Chapter 3, the exposure of collusive corruption is rarely the result of routine supervision and more often a consequence of internal strife, opportunism, miscalculations, or mistakes made by corruption participants themselves.

## Centralizing Power

Centralization of power is another prominent instrument employed by judicial authorities to address judicial corruption. Reforms have been launched to shift power from local to regional and central judicial

[2] For a more in-depth discussion and analysis on the incentives, modes, and dynamics of collusive behaviors in corruption across various sections in China, see Pei (2016). For insights into the operation of patronage networks as a spoil system in local PRC politics, see chapters 5 and 6 of Hillman (2014).

[3] See Huang and Chen (2005). The distribution of illicit profits typically aligns with a judge's position in the power hierarchy. Frontline judges, positioned at the bottom of the pecking order, usually handle all the "legwork" but receive the smallest share of the profits.

authorities. The effectiveness of this strategy hinges on the assumption that judges at higher courts and Party officials of higher ranking are more honest than those at lower levels, which is, however, not supported by empirical evidence.

Two recent disciplinary decisions issued by the Central Committee of Discipline and Inspection (CCDI) illustrate this point. The first concerns Gan Rongkun, who had served as the head of the PLC in two provinces. The CCDI decision stated:

> Gan Rongkun lost his ideals and beliefs, was disloyal and dishonest to the Party . . . He accepted gifts and money without limit, repeatedly accepted travel arrangements and banquets that may affect the fair execution of his public duties . . . He used his decision-making power in the legal process as a private instrument for money-making; he abused his power to interfere with judicial activities. Gan Rongkun pursued vulgar interests, had long-term addiction to gambling, traded power for money without fear, and took advantage of the prerogatives granted to his office to seek profits for others in . . . and case handling (in judicial institutions) in exchange for huge amounts of bribes. (Issued by the CCDI on December 2, 2021)

The second case concerns Shen Deyong, who served as the first vice-president of the SPC in 1998–2018. According to the CCDI:

> Shen Deyong lost his ideals and beliefs, abandoned his duties and missions, disregarded repeated instructions of the Party Center, and wantonly intervened in judicial activities. He turned himself from a guardian into a transgressor of justice, destroying the credibility of the judiciary. He accepted gifts, bribes, invitations to banquets and sponsored travel arrangements that compromised the fair discharge of his duties. He manipulated judicial cadre selection and appointments for personal gain, turned his office into an instrument for private benefits, and condoned his family members and secretaries, who acted as judicial [corruption] brokers, selling services that abused his office in exchange for bribes. (Issued by the CCDI on September 7, 2022)

Therefore, it should not be surprising that corruption among high court judges increased as the centralization reforms unfolded. A prime example is the centralization of enforcement power. As discussed in Chapter 2, enforcement has long been a challenge for litigants due to the lack of voluntary compliance with a court ruling by the losing party and the lack of cooperation from local governments and regulatory agencies, such as banks and property registrars. To solve the problem, the SPC issued a policy in 2000 that has granted higher courts' extensive supervisory power to oversee enforcement matters at the courts below them, including to organize enforcement campaigns, to review and alter enforcement decisions made by lower courts, to mediate enforcement disputes between lower courts, or to transfer cases between courts (SPC, 2000).

The enforcement centralization reform was founded on the rationale that power could and could only be checked by an authority with greater power, acknowledging the semi-hidden order of power that conditions the order of law in China's legal system.[4] Since higher courts by definition enjoy a higher rank than the lower courts, the reformers assumed that granting more enforcement power to higher courts would allow them to command greater compliance and cooperation from other institutions to enforce court judgments.

Like the redistribution of power through dividing power, centralization reforms have primarily relocated authority from one institution to another without changing the mechanisms through which power is exercised. As a result, corruption opportunities are not eliminated but redistributed within the judicial hierarchy. This phenomenon is evident in the case of Yang Xiancai, head of the enforcement division of Guangdong High Court, who was convicted for corruption in 2011. Court records reveal that Yang had accepted a bribe of HK$6 million from a Hong Kong real estate developer, marking the largest single illicit payment he received. In exchange, Yang repeatedly altered the enforcement jurisdiction of a case until it was transferred to Huizhou Intermediate Court, where the developer wielded greater influence to secure a favorable outcome in a court auction. Yang employed similar jurisdictional manipulations in at least four other cases, illustrating how the centralization of judicial oversight expanded corruption opportunities upwards.[5]

Similarly, the centralization of judicial appointments through inter-court personnel transfers has also expanded corruption opportunities for higher court leaders. In the late 2000s, to enhance judicial professionalism, higher courts were granted more authority *vis-à-vis* local Party authorities to appoint leadership positions in courts below them (Liu, 2012b). As a result, some leaders exploited this expanded power for personal enrichment. Prior to the reform, Wu Zhenhan, former president

[4] Underlying this rationale, as I have argued elsewhere, is the operation of an "order of power" in China's legal system, where law is relativized by the power relations between litigating parties. For more on this topic, see Li (2023).

[5] See Magazine (2011).

of Hunan High Court, accepted a bribe from a subordinate for promotion but failed to deliver because his recommendation was overruled by the local Party authority. In contrast, following the reform, Xiong Xiaoping, president of Neijiang Intermediate Court of Sichuan, successfully facilitated the promotion of twelve judges to leadership positions at lower courts through the transfer program (Taishan, 2023).

## Checking Power

As in many other legal systems, the People's Republic of China (PRC) law allows a court to reopen a closed case under special circumstances. The process can be initiated by different actors, including litigants, courts at different levels, or the procuratorate. In 1999, the SPC launched a restructuring reform that introduced a separate adjudicative supervision division handling retrial cases in courts nationwide. The purpose of this reform was to create a layer of insulation, ensuring that retrials would be conducted by a new panel of judges to avoid conflicts of interest.

In theory, this additional layer helps address judicial mistakes. However, if the exercise of this checking power is subject to the same decision-making mechanism that normalizes political prerogative and interference, then it is equally susceptible to corruption. After all, there is no evidence indicating that judges working in this new division are more honest than those in other divisions. In practice, retrial judges are exposed to the same set of incentives and temptations to engage in corruption as those who handled the cases in earlier proceedings.

Among the cases examined, Meng Laigui, head of the Adjudicative Supervision Division of Shanxi High Court, appeared to have an unmatched appetite for bribes. Meng was notorious for his audacity in accepting bribes from both sides of the same case – a practice described as "eating off the plaintiff's hand and then the defendant's." During his three-year tenure (2003–2006) at the adjudicative supervision division, Meng accepted bribes in fourteen cases. Many of the bribes came in the form of cash, which he stored under his bed, a sight to be wondered at.

In retrial proceedings, the first and most important step for a litigant is to have a retrial application accepted, or, in the case of the opposing party, to have such an application rejected. Zhang Jiahui, during her tenure as the deputy head of the Adjudicative Supervision Division of Hainan High Court, pocketed 6.8 million *yuan* in bribes in six retrial cases. In two of them, she approved the retrial applications upon requests from the retrial applicants, while in the remaining four, she denied the applications upon requests from the responding parties.[6]

Similarly, Wang Hongguang, an SPC judge convicted for corruption in 2018, had accepted bribes in at least five retrial applications submitted to the SPC.[7] Another SPC figure was Huang Jianzhong, a deputy director of the SPC research office. With no judicial decision-making power to abuse himself, Huang had, however, accepted requests and bribes to broker corrupt deals for litigants with his colleagues. Among the fourteen counts of bribery of which Huang was convicted, four involved retrial applications submitted to the SPC.[8]

## "Delocalizing" Judicial Power

In 2014–2017, the SPC launched an ambitious "delocalization" reform, advancing its centralization campaign to a new level.[9] Previous centralization reforms, such as the one concerning enforcement power discussed earlier, were limited in scope, with power redistribution occurring solely within the judiciary. The delocalization reform affected courts' external power structure, with implications for local Party Committees, people's congresses, and the relationships between courts at different levels. This reform was designed to remove the appropriation power of court funds and the power to appoint judges in intermediate and basic courts from their corresponding Party Committees and transfer these responsibilities to the provincial high courts. The primary goal, as pronounced, was to enhance the judicial autonomy of these courts and free them from "local protectionism."

Before the reform, an intermediate court was funded by the prefecture government where it was located, and a basic court by the county or district government. Judicial appointments, except for the post of court president, were overseen by the local Party Committee (Liu, 2012b, 2022; Zuo, 2016a). These "local attachments" were believed to have rendered courts vulnerable to pressure and interference from local authorities,

6 See Appendix II, No. 33.
7 See Appendix II, No. 23.
8 See Appendix II, No. 6.
9 Based on the interviews conducted by the author of the cited article, several court officials and lawyers believed that the expansion of judicial power, especially at the appellate level, had "spun out of control." See He (2021, p. 66).

preventing them from upholding the law against narrow local interests protected by local governments.[10]

This argument must have resonated with the new Party administration, as the reform was quickly approved by the central Party authority and rolled out nationwide in 2015. By 2017, the reform had been launched in most provinces, though its implementation varied considerably across regions due to the fiscal burden and administrative costs imposed on provincial governments (Yang & Li, 2023; Yu, 2017). Contrary to what was promised, many courts and judges experienced a reduction of funds and salaries. A survey of 1,535 basic courts located in 14 provinces found that 55 percent reported budget cuts in operational costs (Fan, 2021; Yang & Li, 2023). Twelve percent of the surveyed courts noted an increase in case handling budget but this raise was disproportionate to the increase in their caseloads. Another research revealed that 42 percent of the judges in a surveyed province saw a reduction in salaries (Ning, 2020; Zhang, 2019).

Centralization of judicial appointments was also unevenly implemented, as many local Party authorities continued to oversee judicial appointments for local courts, partly because provincial high courts lacked the necessary administrative resources to fully assume their responsibility and partly because of deeper structural constraints that are not addressed in the reform.[11]

Beyond logistical constraints, the delocalization reform was poorly equipped to tackle judicial corruption for two reasons. First, shifting the budgetary and appointment power from local to provincial authorities merely redirected judicial loyalty from one political institution to another. To bind a court's loyalty not to the law but to its financial and appointment strings meant that the court is still expected to serve the needs of whichever authority administered its affairs one way or the other. Rather than eliminating judicial favoritism or partiality, the delocalization discourse has, in fact, given legitimacy to it by affirming the notion that courts are obligated to accommodate special interests, even at the expense of the integrity of the law.

Second, the reform did not fully detach courts from local Party-state authorities. It affects only the appropriation of court funds and appointments of some judicial posts, leaving many existing Party oversight mechanisms intact. Even before the reform, court presidents were

[10] For a more elaborate description of this discourse, see Ding (2023).

[11] See He (2021), Wang (2021b), Yu (2018), and Zuo (2016a).

appointed by higher Party authorities, in consultation with higher courts, not by local Party authorities, and court divisional leaders were largely selected internally rather than by local Party Committees. These practices remained largely intact. In addition, despite losing their appropriation and appointment powers, local Party authorities still have the mandate to conduct routine supervision over court affairs. Article 12 of the 2019 Political-Legal Directive explicitly mandated them to "supervise and inspect courts regarding the implementation of the Party lines, principles, and policies . . . to guide and coordinate the work between courts and other *zhengfa* organs, and to guide and promote the Party building and political work in courts." In other words, local Party authorities continue to bear the responsibility of monitoring and, when necessary, intervening in court affairs regardless of whether they hold direct control over budgets and appointments.

Finally, the delocalization discourse falsely equates favoritism with local protectionism, assuming that courts favor local litigants simply because of geographic proximity. This characterization is false because disputes arise just as frequently, if not more so, between local parties as they do between locals and nonlocals. The key factor driving corrupt collusion between a court and a local litigant is not merely spatial proximity of their places of residences but social connections and associated *guanxi*-practices that emerge from it. A rational corrupt judge would accept bribes from any trustworthy litigant, regardless of the latter's place of residence or origin. For instance, Zhang Jiahui, former vice-president of Hainan High Court, accepted bribes from several litigants outside Hainan province. In fact, the two largest single bribes she received, 5 million *yuan* each, were both offered by nonlocal litigants. Local litigants, undoubtedly, have an advantage in guanxi-cultivation with local judges due to their deeper integration into local social networks. However, outsider litigants can mitigate the disadvantage by engaging the service of a local law firm or a large firm with an office in the place where the litigation takes place (see more in Chapter 3).

## Internal Decentralization of Power

As a part of the 2014–2017 judicial reform package, a key initiative was to decentralize power within courts by restricting the scope of the internal case-review procedure. This push for internal decentralization was a renewed effort that had already been attempted nearly two decades ago. Many of the measures featured in the 2014–2017 reform had been introduced in 1998, including the requirement for court leaders to sit on collegial panels and hear cases, the expansion of the fast-track simplified procedure, the restriction of the internal case-review procedure, and the enactment of judicial accountability rule (SPC, 1999). However, the previous reform encountered strong resistance from lower courts and was more or less reversed within a few years after the introduction. Opponents of the 1998 reform blamed it for its "disastrous" consequences, including a decline in the quality of court decisions and the marginalization of leader judges' supervisory power.[12] Some contended that the reform had created "isolated information islands" within courts, leaving court leaders unaware of developments in their own courts or units and unable to respond promptly to inquiries from external supervisory authorities (Yin, 2013, p. 83). By 2005, the internal case-review procedure had been essentially reinstated nationwide (Yin, 2013, p. 83).

The 2014–2017 decentralization reform closely resembled the 1998 reform, aiming to narrow the scope of the internal case-review procedure and grant frontline judges greater autonomy. A central component of the reform was the introduction of quota-judges. Before the reform, only 70 percent of the appointed judges were actually hearing the cases,[13] while the remaining 30 percent performed administrative or other supporting functions, such as political supervision, personnel management, workflow management, and statistical analyses (Xu, 2017).

The 2014–2017 reform aimed first to separate those responsible for judicial activities from those performing administrative functions, creating two distinct tracks, and second, to select the most qualified judges through a re-qualification process, appointing them as "quota-judges,"[14] with greater decision-making power over a wider range of cases.

Anticipating resistance from leader judges, the reform has also introduced a built-in compromising safeguard to prevent the "marginalization" of the supervisory power of leader judges and avoid the formation of "isolated information islands." The safeguard requires judges to identify and label four categories of significant cases for mandatory top-down supervision (SPC, 2015b, 2021a). This safeguard would inevitably undermine the core

[12] Gao and Zhao (2018, p. 65) and Yin (2013, p. 83).

[13] Before the reform, there were approximately 210,000 judges, 150,000 of whom were frontliners, according to Sun and Fu (2022, p. 6).

[14] These quota-judges include not only judges who adjudicate the merit of a case but also those working at the case-acceptance divisions and the enforcement divisions, the latter of which can account for up to 30 percent of all judges in some regions, according to one statistical report. See Sun and Fu (2022, p. 7).

objective of the decentralization reform, which was to minimize top-down supervision and grant frontline judges greater autonomy.

As a result, the compromised reform not only failed to resolve previous issues but also added to the bureaucratic complexity of court administration for judicial personnel at all levels, leading to widespread discontent among them. Toward the end of 2023, following a change in her leadership, the SPC began introducing a review-and-approve (*yuehezhi*) practice (Yanyu, 2023), which closely resembles the previous internal case-review procedure that required judges to obtain approval from their superiors before rendering decisions. It is likely that this practice will be standardized and extended to all courts, which would then mean a full reversal of the internal decentralization reform, like what happened to the 1998 reform.

## Eliminating Improper Interference

Throughout the 2014–2017 judicial reform, the SPC made it clear that the goal of the internal decentralization was to improve judicial efficiency and professionalism, not to introduce judicial independence. To secure the Party's approval for the reform, the SPC vowed to decouple judicial professionalism and judicial independence, promising that the reform was not a "Trojan horse" aimed at seeking judicial independence (Sun & Fu, 2022, p. 3). Zhou Qiang, the SPC president, openly pledged that courts and judges nationwide must unequivocally distance themselves from wrongful Western ideas, such as the separation of powers and judicial independence (Zhou, 2017a). This reaffirms that the judicial reform would never question or challenge, let alone seek to abolish, the Party's political prerogative to interfere in judicial affairs.

At the same time, the SPC reformers convinced the Party Center to introduce two new regulations aimed at preventing Party leaders from abusing their political prerogative for self-enrichment. The first is entitled "Measures on Documenting, Reporting and Sanctioning Interference with Judicial Activities by Leader Officials of Party-State Authorities (2015)" (External Interference Regulation). This was accompanied by a matching regulation entitled "Measures on Documentation and Accountability for Case Interference by Employees of Judicial Institutions" (Internal Interference Regulation).

Both regulations were designed to distinguish between "proper" and "improper" interference, banning the latter (Jiang, 2020a). Under both regulations, an act of interference is deemed legitimate or "proper" when carried out by an individual who has a mandate, the ranking authority, and jurisdictional competence to oversee the matter at hand. For instance, according to the External Interference Regulation, a Party authority in charge of political-legal affairs has the mandate to, *inter alia*, check case progress, formulate or review judicial policies, coordinate activities between various judicial organs, urging and monitoring them to fulfill their duties, and provide a conducive environment for them to dispense justice (SPC, 2015c).

The 2019 Political-Legal Directive issued by the Party Center explicitly mandates Party authorities to interfere in court affairs. Courts, in turn, are not only required to accept the interference but also to proactively inform and invite the Party to intervene whenever they are in doubt. What then constitutes *improper* interference?

According to Article 8 of the External Interference Regulation, an act of interference is considered "improper" when a ranked official engages in any of the following:

i. Seeking favorable treatment for a litigant at any stage of a case;
ii. Demanding a judicial personnel handling a case of interest to meet privately with a party, their lawyer/legal representative, family members or other individuals related to the case;
iii. Authorizing or condoning their staff or family members to influence judicial outcomes in favor of a litigant;
iv. Overstepping their mandate to impose partial opinions or concrete instructions, in various forms, on judicial personnel for the purpose of protecting their parochial interests.

Similarly, under the Internal Interference Regulation, a court leader may provide "guidance" to a judge at any time as long as it falls within their "supervisory and monitoring duties." Improper internal interference, on the other hand, primarily comes from court personnel who have no assigned functions in handling a case. Article 9 of the Internal Interference Regulation defines improper interference as:

i. Seeking favorable treatment for a litigant at any stage of the litigation process;
ii. Asking a judicial personnel to privately meet a party, their lawyer or legal representative, family members, or other individuals related to the case that they are handling;
iii. Passing case materials for a litigant, their representative, or family members to a judicial personnel handling the case;

iv. Asking for information from a judicial personnel handling a case about progress or expected outcome of a case on behalf of a litigant, their representative, or family members.

According to the two regulations, two factors determine whether an act of interference is proper or improper: (1) whether the person exerting the interference has the competence and the authority to do so; and (2) whether the interference is driven by corruption. Here, "competence" refers to the jurisdictional scope of the office held by the person exerting interference and the "authority" refers to the ranking status of that person. Based on these criteria, "improper" interference falls into three categories: (1) interference by someone with neither the competence nor the authority; (2) interference by someone with the authority but not the competence; or (3) interference by someone with the competence and authority but for improper purposes (self-enrichment or parochial interests).

The first type of interference typically comes from one's colleagues or social contacts and is the weakest in terms of compelling power since commands flow from higher to lower ranks, not between equals or in reverse order. A judge cannot impose instructions on a colleague of equal rank. For example, if a civil division frontline judge wants information about a criminal case heard by a colleague at the criminal division, they may request it informally by currying favors, which the criminal division judge is free to ignore or reject.

Studies indicate that this type of improper interference is the easiest for judges to resist (He, 2021; Sun & Fu, 2022). In earlier years, when judicial corruption was rampant and the risk of detection low, judges might have granted such requests simply out of courtesy alone, without requiring any substantive incentive. However, as anti-corruption efforts intensified, judges became more cautious. For instance, in 2013–2015, Huang Jianzhong, a deputy director of the SPC research office, accepted bribes from litigants and promised to approach judges handling the bribers' cases to seek favorable treatment on their behalf. In nine out of twelve cases, the judges whom Huang had approached ignored his requests.[15]

The second type of improper interference occurs when a leader oversteps their jurisdictional boundaries. In any given court, supervisory power is divided between the court president and vice-presidents based on case specialization. For instance, one leader oversees the civil division,

[15] See Appendix II, No.6.

another supervises the criminal division, and another monitors the enforcement bureau, and so on. Each leader is expected to operate within their designated jurisdiction except for the court president who has broader authority and the residual responsibility. Instructions must pass through proper channels. It would be improper, for instance, if a vice-president in charge of civil cases were to summon a criminal division judge to report on a criminal case. Similarly, under the new External Interference Regulation, it would be improper, if, for example, a Party leader in charge of agricultural matters were to demand information about a murder case without a valid justification.

To curb improper interference, regulations now require judges to document and report any instruction or request for favoritism. Such reports are compiled periodically and submitted to the court's supervisory body, such as the PLC. It is then up to the Party to assess the propriety of these instructions and authorize investigation, and sanction, if warranted. However, in practice, how regularly would a frontline judge report on improper interference?

A study, based on interviews of judges in three different locations, found that not a single judge under interview had ever reported a superior or knew a colleague who had done so (Wang, 2020). Nevertheless, some judges reported that the mere possibility of being reported served as a deterrent (Wang, 2020). Another study also reported that judges became more cautious in their interactions to avoid giving the impression of improper interference (He, 2021). Indeed, Zhang Jiahui, former vice-president of Hainan High Court, appeared more cautious in her interactions with the collegial panel after the introduction of the document-and-report measure. Court records detailing her forty-seven counts of bribe-taking reveal a pattern: she would first hear the opinions of the collegial panel who handled the case of interest; then if the collegial panel's intended ruling aligned with the interest of the litigant who had bribed her, Zhang would let the judicial process unfold naturally; if the panel planned to rule against the briber, she would then decide whether, when and how to interfere, based on the level of risk and the size of the bribe.

The last type of improper interference comes from those with competence and authority but for the illicit purposes of self-enrichment or parochial interests. To be clear, the Party has never condoned interference for self-enrichment. Nevertheless, it remains widespread and persistent. Its resilience stems from the fact that when a court leader or a Party superior interferes with a case, such interference is justified as an exercise of political prerogative – a power granted by the Party. The exercise of political prerogative is exempted from legal scrutiny as there is no structured venue and mechanism through which the legal merit of such a political imposition can be challenged. This legal exemption allows a court or Party leader to conveniently disguise an improper interference as legitimate intervention.

As discussed in Chapter 2, corrupt leaders routinely framed their instructions as "proper" by citing broad political objectives. Depending on whose interests they sought to protect, they could even justify contradicting impositions, such as favoring a local litigant so as to protect local economy in one case and favoring a nonlocal litigant to encourage investments in another, or lower the prosecutorial threshold in order to crackdown on crime in one case or to raise the prosecutorial threshold to educate offenders by showing leniency in another.

A few years into practice, the document-and-report measure had received strong resistance from leader judges who, fearing the risk of being documented and reported by their subordinates, became reluctant to exercise any form of supervision. In 2021, the SPC responded by modifying the policy, excluding certain practices from document-and-report scrutiny, thereby restoring the chain of command that facilitates, legitimizes and normalizes interference in the judicial process. Below is a list of interfering activities that are now excluded from document-and-report scrutiny:[16]

[for external interference]

a. Suggestions or opinions pertaining to national, social or public interests submitted by the following bodies in accordance with relevant work protocols: Party-state organs, trade associations, chambers of commerce, public-interest social organizations, and other public institutions that undertake administrative functions as authorized by law or requested or permitted by courts;
b. Materials, complaints, claims or inquiries about the progress of a case submitted by litigants or their representatives in accordance with relevant work protocols.

[for internal interference]

a. Intervention undertaken by a court leader or division leader as an act to discharge their supervisory responsibility in cases that fall in the

[16] Based on two policy documents circulated by Guangdong High Court. See Guangdong (2021a,b).

white-list [four categories of cases] and by a superior court to discharge their supervisory and advisory duty vis-à-vis a lower court;

b. Instructions sent by a responsible leader judge to a frontline judge together with case materials that are rendered or submitted by the following bodies: Party-state organs, law-related supervisory organs, superior courts, or leaders of these bodies on the grounds of task reprioritization, stability maintenance, law supervision or coordination in important cases;

c. Instructions sent and case materials forwarded by a responsible leader judge to a frontline judge pertaining to litigants' complaints or requests.

## Accountability

Changing the incentive structure for potential corrupt offenders is a key element in standard anti-corruption strategies. The 2014–2017 judicial reform promised to provide newly selected quota-judges with stronger incentives for better performance, including pay raises, clerk support, and greater autonomy. To balance these positive incentives, the SPC also promised to introduce stricter accountability measures to deter unethical and unlawful judicial conduct. In 2015, the SPC issued the Opinions on Enhancing Judicial Accountability (Accountability Opinions). However, most forms of misconduct prohibited by the Accountability Opinions had already been banned under previous regulations. After all, the prevalence of judicial misconduct in China's courts does not stem from ambiguity about the illegality of corruption. Judges may engage in corruption for various reasons, but not because they are uncertain about whether it is ethical or lawful to accept bribes or other forms of inducements from court users in cases that they hear.

One measure introduced in the Accountability Opinions attracted particular attention: "lifetime accountability." As its name suggests, this measure holds judges responsible for their judicial activities throughout their lifetime. In the past, officials generally enjoyed a degree of immunity after retirement for actions taken while in office. Lifetime accountability revokes that immunity, potentially enhancing deterrence – but only if the chance of detection of misconduct also increases.

As already discussed in previous chapters, parochial corruption facilitated by *guanxi*-practice is particularly difficult to detect. Such corruption typically comes to light only in cases of egregious judicial misconduct, such as fabricating, altering, concealing or destroying evidence.

Corruption exercised within a judge's discretion or concealed under the cover of proper interference is difficult for victims to detect and for anti-corruption authorities to uncover through routine monitoring.

Whistleblowing witnesses face similar obstacles. To expose corruption, whistleblowers need media collaboration, but investigative journalism in China has largely vanished due to tightened censorship. Social media platforms are heavily monitored for "harmful contents" and "negative news." In addition, whistleblowers without political connection also risk serious personal consequences. The case of SPC judge Wang Linqing (discussed in the next section) highlights how exposing misconduct can backfire, serving as a powerful deterrent for potential whistleblowers.

Would the document-and-report measure discussed earlier help detect corruption? Possibly, but with significant limitations. First, a corrupt leader can earmark a case for supervision either through the internal case-review procedure or through the adjudicative committee, thus justifying "proper interference." Second, even when a judge receives a clearly improper instruction from a superior, they have more to gain by staying silent than by reporting it. Silence carries little risk and can even earn the superior's favor.[17] Reporting, on the other hand, offers no reward and no guarantee of an investigation. Worse, if the report reaches the implicated superior, the judge may face retaliation.

It is no coincidence that judicial corruption in China has a long latency period before detection, a defining feature of corruption in the country (Guo, 2008). Zhang Jiahui of Hainan High Court, for instance, began accepting bribes in 2006 and continued without consequence for thirteen years. Shen Deyong engaged in judicial corruption in 1995, during his time at Anhui High Court, and continued during his long tenure at the SPC until his departure in 2022. In the recent scandal at Ji'nan Intermediate Court, all involved had engaged in judicial corruption for decades before being punished.

More strikingly, the 2014–2017 judicial reform, designed to curb judicial corruption, failed to deter these judges. Of the forty-nine counts

[17] According to one of six "typical cases" of judicial interference published by the SPC in February 2024, six judges from a Beijing basic court were internally reprimanded for failing to document requests for favoritism from their colleagues. This study has not come across a single case where a judge received a punishment for failing to report an instruction from a superior that was later deemed as improper. So far, internal reprimand appears to be the harshest punishment for not recording interference. For further reflections on the ineffectiveness of the three regulations in corruption prevention by a practicing PRC lawyer, see Yan Yu (2024).

of bribe-taking that led to the conviction of Song Yunyi, vice-president of the Ji'nan Intermediate Court, 70 percent occurred during and after the 2014–2017 judicial reform. Similarly, Dai Wujian, a frontline judge at the same court, committed 90 percent of his bribery offenses in the same period.[18]

## The "100-billion-yuan Mining Right" Case

The "100-billion-yuan mining right" case commands a prominent place in studies of the PRC legal system as it reveals, through an unprecedented whistleblowing campaign and a counter-campaign, how normalized political intervention operated at the highest level of the judiciary through the internal case-review procedure. For a long time, the SPC has been China's most secretive judicial institution, known primarily for its roles in judicial policymaking and death penalty review. However, its role as an appellate court is rarely acknowledged outside those who work within or directly with the court. Despite this relative obscurity, the SPC's appellate function is significant. In one of its busiest years, it handled nearly 40,000 cases.[19] Cases heard by the SPC necessarily involve high-stakes claims. In civil and commercial cases, "high-stakes" refers to claims ranging from 100 million to 500 million yuan, depending on regional differences (SPC, 2019).[20]

Given its importance, the level of secrecy surrounding SPC decision-making is striking. The SPC website has been geo-blocked (as of March 8, 2025) and cannot be visited from outside China. Forty percent of the SPC decisions are not published, and those that are often appear in abridged form. Compared to their counterparts in many other legal systems, these rulings are far less rigorous in legal reasoning. The "extra-legal" factors influencing judicial outcomes of cases heard by the SPC remained unknown to external researchers until this whistleblowing campaign by an SPC judge called Wang Linqing.

Notably, the scandal exposed by this whistleblowing campaign surfaced amid the SPC's 2014–2017 judicial reform, which, as readers may recall, aimed to curtail internal case reviews, promote judicial autonomy for frontline judges and collegial panels, and reduce political interference

[18] See Appendix II, No.20, 2, 18.

[19] According to its own statistics, the SPC had accepted 149,000 cases and closed 145,000 between 2018 and 2022. In 2020 alone, it accepted 39,347 cases. See SPC (2023b).

[20] The range reflects regional variations in the jurisdictional threshold for economic claims.

from local protectionism. The revelations from this case highlights the reform's limitations, showing that political interference is not just an aberrant and localized problem but a systemic issue embedded in the PRC's *zhengfa* system, affecting judicial decision-making at all levels. The following account of the scandal is based on a careful study of diverse materials, including media reports, accounts of involved parties, whistle-blowers' statements, public records released by official authorities, and press releases from courts and other investigative bodies.[21]

### *The Dispute*

Zhao Faqi, a self-made entrepreneur, began to invest in the mining business in northern Shaanxi, a region where vast coal deposits were discovered in the 1990s. At the time, mining was a high-investment, high-risk business, and private investment was actively encouraged by the government. In August 2003, Zhao's company, Kai Qi Lai (KQL), signed a mining contract with Xi'an Mineral Exploration Institute (Xmei), a licensed mining entity established by Shaanxi Geology Mining Exploration and Development Bureau (Shaanxi Mining Bureau). Under the agreement, KQL would pay Xmei 12 million *yuan* to explore a mineral prospect in Hengshan county, northern Shaanxi. The contract stipulated that, if the exploration proved successful, the two parties would share the resulting gains, including profits from mining operations or the transfer of mining rights to a third party, at a ratio of 8:2 in favor of KQL. However, two months later, in October 2003, the Shaanxi government issued **Document 21**, revoking the freedom previously granted to Xmei to transfer or trade its mining rights.

In March 2005, acting on orders from the Shaanxi Mining Bureau, to which Xmei was affiliated, Xmei terminated its contract with KQL, citing Document 21 as justification. Shortly after, Xmei discovered a coal mine in Hengshan County containing an estimated 1.56 billion tons of reserves. Seeking recourse, Zhao brought the dispute to then deputy

[21] The sources that I have consulted on this case include, but are not limited to, the following: Bai (2019), BBC (2019), Cai (2018), Chen (2019), Cui (2022a), Huang (2018), SPC (2011), Team (2019), Wang (2018a,b,c,d,e, 2019), Xu (2018), Yan (2018), Zhao (2016), and Zhen (2019). The author has scrutinized the factual accuracy of the whistleblowing statements by verifying the times, locations, and the names and positions of key actors involved in the mentioned events against available official sources. The SPC has not disputed the factual information disclosed by the judge concerning its handling of the '100-billion-yuan Mining Rights' case.

Shaanxi governor Chen Deming, who instructed the Shaanxi Land Resources Bureau to investigate. The Bureau's findings, recorded in **Document 65**, affirmed the validity of the contract between KQL and Xmei, concluding that Xmei was obligated to honor its contractual commitments. Despite this, Xmei disregarded Document 65 and instead transferred the mining rights to another company, Hong Kong Yi Ye (HKYY). In response, Zhao took the case to court in May 2006.

### *First Trial and Appeal*

The first instance trial was heard at the Shaanxi High Court, which ruled in KQL's favor in October 2006. The court found the contract valid, reasoning that it was based on the truthful intentions of both parties and did not violate any laws or regulations. Xmei appealed to the SPC. While the appeal was pending in 2008, SPC vice-president Xi Xiaoming[22] invited the Shaanxi government – despite it not being a party to the case – to submit an opinion. In its submission, the Shaanxi government exhorted the SPC to void the contract, arguing that failure to do so would result in a significant loss of state-owned assets.

Zhao Faqi questioned the merit of the reasoning, noting that the Shaanxi government had not objected to the transfer of the mining rights to HKYY, a private company registered in Hong Kong.[23] Moreover, HKYY appeared uninterested in actual mining operations and instead sought to "flip" and resell the mining rights for profit.[24]

In 2009, the SPC remanded the case back to the Shaanxi High Court, effectively returning it to the same court that had initially ruled on it. Such rulings are common for appellate courts when they intend to avoid "taking sides" in contentious local disputes.[25]

[22] Xi Xiaoming was convicted for corruption in 2017 but details about his crimes are classified. It remains unclear whether he had committed bribery in this mining right case.

[23] Available information suggests that HKYY had exceptional political connections in both Shaanxi and Beijing, enabling it to secure multiple licenses and approvals from various ministries and other regulatory bodies within months – an achievement that typically took others years to pursue, sometimes without success.

[24] Such practices are not uncommon. For instance, Zhou Bin, the son of former Politburo Standing Committee member Zhou Yongkang, profited over 500 million yuan by flipping the mining rights of an oil field in northern Shaanxi, not far from the coal mine in the KQL vs. Xmei case. For details of the case, see Xie (2014).

[25] Hu and Chen (2012). For more discussions on the subject, see Chen (2012).

### *Retrial – First Instance*

By the time the case was remanded, Zhao Zhengyong had become Shaanxi governor.[26] In November 2010, Zhao Zhengyong convened a Party-group meeting to discuss the KQL dispute. The meeting concluded that the contract was void and the Shaanxi High Court had erred in its initial ruling. Relevant agencies were instructed to take necessary measures to implement the Party-group's decision. Even the Shaanxi CDI (Committee of Discipline and Inspection at subnational levels) was brought in to oversee the implementation process.

The greatest obstacle to annulling the contract was the aforementioned Document 65 issued by the Shaanxi Land Resources Bureau in 2005, which explicitly affirmed the contract's validity. To overcome this, Shaanxi Land Resources Bureau convened a meeting immediately after the Party-group's decision and issued **Document 67**, revoking Document 65.

In March 2011, the Shaanxi High Court ruled that the contract was void, arguing that the contractual parties had maliciously conspired to use the contract to infringe on the Shaanxi Government's rightful interests. The court ordered Xmei to refund KQL's initial investment without compensation. KQL appealed to the SPC.

Meanwhile, the Shaanxi Public Security Bureau launched an investigation into Zhao Faqi. In August 2011, police arrested Zhao on charges of false declaration of registered capital of a company – an offense enforced in a highly selective manner. The Shaanxi Industry and Commerce Administration Bureau revoked the business license of Zhao's company. Zhao spent 133 days in police custody before being released on bail, and the criminal charge was later dropped.

### *Retrial – Second Instance*

By the time the second appeal reached the SPC, the case had attracted significant media attention, making it a "hot potato" that few judges wanted to touch. Eventually, a collegial panel was formed, with Judge Wang Linqing assigned as the responsible judge. Judge Du Wanhua, a standing member of the SPC Adjudicative Committee, was assigned to oversee the case. A court record later disclosed by Wang Linqing revealed

[26] Zhao was convicted for corruption in 2019 but details about his crimes are classified. It remains unclear whether he had committed bribery in this mining right case.

a hierarchical chain of internal instructions on the case: beginning with SPC President Zhou Qiang, followed by Vice-President Xi Xiaoming, designated Adjudicative Committee member Du Wanhua (assigned to supervise the case), the head of the First Civil Division, and finally reaching the collegial panel.

While the case was pending, Shaanxi High Court sent a vice-president and a divisional leader to the SPC to lobby for the annulment of the contract. They conveyed that they were under direct order from the Shaanxi government to ensure that the Shaanxi High Court's ruling would be upheld by the SPC. In 2012, for unclear reasons, the SPC suspended the appeal, only resuming it in March 2016.

The same collegial panel, with Judge Wang still acting as the responsible judge, unanimously decided that the contract was valid based on Document 65 and that Xmei had breached the contract. Between March and November 2016, Judge Du held several meetings with the collegial panel to discuss the case. In one meeting, Judge Du relayed that the SPC president wanted the case remanded again to the Shaanxi High Court to avoid offending the Shaanxi government. Judge Du explained, "after the case is remanded, [we] can instruct the Shaanxi High Court to assign it to the Xi'an Intermediate Court (a lower court of Shaanxi High Court) for retrial. This way, even if the case is appealed again, it will stop at Shaanxi High Court [and not reach the SPC]." This approach sparked controversy within the collegial panel. Judge Cheng Xinwen, the divisional head, supported it as a way to remove the SPC from a politically difficult situation. However, Judge Wang objected, citing the Civil Procedure Law, which prohibits an appellate court from remanding a case to the same court more than once.

In a follow-up meeting, Judge Du instructed the collegial panel to assess the legal viability and social impact of three possible rulings: sustaining, remanding, or reversing the initial ruling. The panel recommended reversing the ruling of Shaanxi High Court and upholding the validity of the contract, arguing that any other outcome would misinterpret or disregard existing laws.

At the final meeting that Judge Wang attended, Judge Du presented a new plan, which he claimed had been approved by the SPC president. The plan was to affirm the contract's validity but avoid specifying Xmei's contractual obligations. This, Judge Du reasoned, would allow the SPC to appear upholding the law while "kicking the ball" back to Shaanxi and distancing itself from the dispute.

Judge Wang expressed reservations, arguing that such a decision would be unenforceable. If the court did not specify Xmei's obligations, the ruling would fail to solve the dispute and violate an SPC judicial policy requiring courts to determine and specify contractual obligations in rulings on contractual performance. Despite those concerns, the collegial panel ultimately agreed to follow Judge Du's plan, given that it had, according to Judge Du, already been approved by the SPC president.

### *Missing Case Dossier*

In November 2016, just as Judge Wang was preparing to draft the ruling on the KQL case, he discovered that the classified copy of the case dossier, which contained the internal communication records, had disappeared from his filing cabinet. Judge Wang immediately reported the incident to the head of the division, Judge Cheng. Despite a thorough search, the dossier was nowhere to be found in his office. Judge Cheng reviewed the court's surveillance tape, which showed that Judge Wang had returned to his office with the case dossier after the last meeting with Judge Du and later left empty-handed. No footage of what happened afterwards was found. Since the case dossier disappeared under Judge Wang's custody, making him accountable, he was removed from the case and replaced by another judge.

The adjudication of the case continued without Judge Wang's participation. To his bewilderment, the court showed little interest in investigating the missing case dossier. More than a year later, Judge Wang noticed that certain documents previously declared "lost" had resurfaced in the new KQL dossier. By the end of 2017, the SPC ruled that KQL's contract with Xmei was valid but denied KQL's claim on the mining right. The SPC ordered Xmei to refund KQL its initial investment and pay, in addition, a minor penalty.

### *The Whistleblowing*

In 2018, after the SPC had rendered its decision, Judge Wang launched a whistleblowing campaign, reporting the disappearance of the case dossier to various authorities. When none responded, he reached out to Cui Yongyuan, a former journalist and television personality known for his outspoken stance on social justice.

In a taped video statement, Judge Wang detailed the disappearance of the case dossier. Cui posted clips of the interview on his Weibo account – which had 20 million followers – accusing the SPC of a cover-up. The

SPC initially dismissed his claims, but Cui then released a copy of the aforementioned SPC internal communication record.

The leaked documents were a major embarrassment for the SPC on multiple levels. First, how could a case dossier vanish without a trace from the tightly guarded and surveilled SPC office building, only to reappear without any explanation? Second, what was so special about the KQL case that it drew attention from the SPC president and warranted a top-secret classification? Third, what did the incident reveal about the centralization judicial reform based on the premise that higher courts could better uphold the law and resist political interference? Fourth, what did it imply about the internal decentralization reform, which promised to curtail the internal case-review procedure and grant the collegial panel greater autonomy? These questions put the SPC under intense scrutiny.

In January 2019, one week after Cui Yongyuan posted the SPC internal communication record on Weibo, Judge Wang disappeared from public view. At the same time, the Central (Party) Political-Legal Committee (CPLC) assembled a special investigation team comprising agents from the CCDI/National Supervision Commission (NSC), the Supreme People's Procuratorate (SPP), and the Ministry of Public Security (MPS). While Judge Wang remained incommunicado, several prerecorded video statements, along with audio recordings and a written statement of Judge Wang, were released on social media, recounting the decision-making process of the KQL case at the SPC.

Two months later, the investigative team concluded that Judge Wang staged the disappearance of the case dossier to settle a personal vendetta against the court. A televised confession of the judge was broadcast on national television.[27] Later, Judge Wang was officially arrested for leaking state secrets and later also charged with corruption. In 2022, he was convicted for both crimes and sentenced to fourteen years in prison. Two days earlier, Zhao Faqi, who had also been arrested after the whistleblowing campaign, was sentenced to seven and a half years for illegally obtaining state secrets and bribe-giving. Cui Yongyuan, who had helped expose the story, withdrew from public view.

[27] It is worth noting that Judge Wang made two inconsistent statements regarding the disappearance of the case dossier. In the first statement, given voluntarily before his arrest, he claimed that he recused himself from the case after the disappearance of the dossier. In the second statement – the confession made after his arrest – he admitted that he staged the disappearance of the dossier to pressure the court into keeping him on the case, indicating that he was removed from the case before the disappearance of the dossier.

### *Implications*

The KQL case dealt a major blow to the credibility of the 2014–2017 SPC-led judicial reform, exposing its structural limitation rooted in the institutional design of the *zhengfa* system.

First, the KQL case challenges the assumption that the local Party-state authorities and local courts primarily act to protect local interests. In this case, the Shaanxi authorities went to great lengths to safeguard the interests of HKYY, an external entity or at least one that appeared to be external, while obstructing a local business run by a local entrepreneur.

Second, the case challenges the notion that transfering judicial administrative power from lower to higher courts can curb collusion between courts and local Party-state authorities. According to this logic, the SPC, as the country's highest judicial institution, should have exercised maximum autonomy in adjudicating a local dispute like the KQL case. Instead, from start to finish, the SPC abandoned its role as an impartial arbiter and guardian of the law, using every tool available to accommodate the interests of the Shaanxi authorities and those of the HKYY, neither of which was listed as a party to the case.

Third, the case shows how essential and indispensable the internal case-review procedure is to the political-legal system of the Party-state. It allows superior political prerogative to be transmitted and implemented in judicial decision-making through a reliable chain of command with minimal encumbrance. It is necessary to note that the revelation of the KQL case results from a unique convergence of extraordinary factors: the persistence of a resourceful litigant Zhao Faqi, the single-minded determination of the SPC judge Wang Linqing, the involvement of Cui Yongyuan, the unwavering efforts of Shaanxi authorities to obstruct KQL's goals, and the SPC's ill-conceived and desperate attempts to cover its tracks. Only the rare alignment of these extraordinary circumstances has given us a glimpse into the political and power dynamics that shape decision-making at the country's highest and most insulated court.

## Conclusion

In this chapter, I have sought to explain the persistence of judicial corruption despite successive waves of judicial reforms. To that end, I have examined and analyzed major reforms launched by the SPC designed to curb judicial corruption. Most of these reforms, I find, revolve around the same theme: redistributing judicial decision-making power. Such reforms failed to address the root cause of the problem: normalization of judicial interference as a political prerogative in judicial decision-making in all courts.

Rather than addressing this fundamental issue, past reforms have focused on dividing, centralizing, decentralizing, and recentralizing judicial decision-making power. Since these measures do not tackle judicial partiality or the arbitrariness of political prerogative, they redistribute corruption opportunities rather than eliminate them. However, there have been cautious efforts to limit the number of individuals entitled to exercise this political prerogative by distinguishing between "improper" and "proper" interference. Although this measure cannot eliminate corruption, it can raise its costs, thereby reducing its prevalence to some extent.

In the final section of this chapter, I presented a case study to highlight the inherent limitations of the 2014–2017 judicial reform and to illustrate how deeply entrenched the *zhengfa* logic remains in the administration of justice, even at the SPC. The case exposes an inconvenient truth: if even the SPC is vulnerable to interference, what can be expected of lower courts? As long as judicial interference remains a legitimate political prerogative and continues to be normalized in judicial decision-making, courts will continue to function as a "partial judicial bureaucracy," siding with those in power or backed by power instead of serving as impartial arbiters and guardians of law.

# PART II

# Modus Operandi of the Party

# 5

# Evolution of the Party's Disciplinary System

Based on global anti-corruption experiences, the efficacy of an anti-corruption program is positively correlated with, if not dependent upon, the independence of anti-corruption institutions, including the judiciary and the investigative agencies.[1] In China, the opposite is the case: both the judiciary and the anti-corruption investigative authorities are dependent on the Party, the very institution that is most susceptible to corruption. How does such a system function?

To understand how anti-corruption investigations operate in China, it is essential to recognize that, in a Party-state, the Party operates on two seats of power: one of the Party and one of the state. State power is derived from the principle of popular sovereignty, while Party power is realized through its actual control over the state bureaucracy, safeguarded by its exclusive control over the military, and justified both through its revolutionary legacy and performance legitimacy. The Party operates autonomously through a self-contained and multilayered bureaucracy that operates separately from the state. Meanwhile, the state, though also structured as a self-contained bureaucracy, remains chained to the Party through a series of administrative arrangements (Li, 2015a). These administrative arrangements bind the two seats of power, the Party and the state, into an integrated superstructure.

The Party regulates itself through a body of internal rules and an internal disciplinary system. For instance, Party elections, which determine the holders of the most powerful public offices, occur entirely outside the scope of state regulation. Additionally, the Party also retains preemptive investigative authority over disciplinary violations committed by its members, a power justified by these members' voluntary acceptance of its jurisdiction. This acceptance is formalized through a pledge of

[1] Doig and Moron (2000) and UNDOC (2012, 2020).

allegiance that all Party members must take upon joining. The current wording of the pledge is as follows:

> I solemnly swear to voluntarily join the Chinese Communist Party (CCP), uphold its program, abide by the Party Charter, fulfill my duties as a Party member, implement the Party's decisions, strictly observe Party discipline, safeguard Party secrets, remain loyal, work diligently, dedicate my life to the cause of communism, and be ready at any time to sacrifice everything for the Party and the people, and never betray the Party.

Constructing a self-governing disciplinary system is no simple task for an organization of the Party's size and mission. Its fundamental challenge lies in how to empower a disciplinary subsystem without creating a rival power center that can potentially challenge the authority of the plenipotentiary authority of territorial Party Committees and, in turn, weaken the absolute power of the Party Center. In this chapter, I will trace the institutional evolution of the Party's disciplinary system from 1927 to 2012, revisiting its Soviet origin, examining the shifting jurisdictional boundaries between the Party and the state, highlighting the Party Center's unified and absolute power, and delineating the disciplinary decision-making structure and procedures that have emerged since 1982.

## Soviet Origin

Fearing that the communist party might evolve into a bureaucratic machine over time and lose its revolutionary character, Lenin conceived an intra-Party disciplinary institution known as the Central Control Committee (Sullivan, 1984). According to the Rules of the All-Union Communist Party (Bolsheviks) of the Soviet Union (hereinafter the CPSU Constitution), the Central Control Committee was set up as an equal counterpart to the Central Committee, designed to serve as a check on its power. Members of the Central Control Committee were to be elected by the Party Congress – the same electorate responsible for electing the Central Committee itself.

The presidium, or executive body, of the Central Control Committee was entitled to delegate three members and three alternates to attend Politburo meetings and five members and five alternates to participate in meetings of the Central Organization Bureau and of the Secretariat of the Central Committee, all acting in a consultative capacity (Article 66). In addition, the Central Control Committee had the authority to assign tasks, within its jurisdiction, to all Party members and organizations (Article 67).

The elective status of the Central Control Committee was abolished when the CPSU Constitution was amended in 1939.[2] Under the new Constitution (1939), the Control Committee was restructured as an organization "attached to the Central Committee" (Article 35),[3] thereby losing its nominal autonomy. This arrangement remained in place until the last congress of the CPSU in 1991, when a new Party Constitution resurrected the elective status of the Control Committee. However, the CPSU soon lost power before it could implement these changes.

Alongside the Party's Control Committee, the Soviet Union also maintained a state supervision institution known as the People's Commissariat of the Workers and Peasants' Inspection or *Rabkrin*, which operated in parallel (Rees, 1987). *Rabkrin* was a ministerial governmental body tasked with scrutinizing state, local, and enterprise administrators for inefficiency and corruption (Deutscher, 1967). However, Lenin was dissatisfied with its performance and, in 1923, three years after its creation, merged *Rabkrin* with the Party's Control Committee, for the purpose of restoring the Central Committee's authority, revitalizing internal party democracy, and granting the Party's proletarian activists more influence in policymaking (Rees, 1987). After Lenin's death, Stalin repurposed the Control Committee as an instrument for his personal rule and, in 1934, established the People's Control Committee, which focused on improving industrial productivity.

Under Khrushchev, the Party disciplinary institution was merged with the state disciplinary institution to form the Party-State Control Committee, known as KPGK. The KPGK was a super agency, straddling the dual hierarchies of the party and the state. It wielded significant power to conduct surveillance, inspection, and disciplinary sanctions across all branches of the state administration.[4] Under the leadership of the ambitious Central Committee secretary Alexander Shelepin, the KPGK grew so powerful that it alarmed his political opponents, triggering efforts to rein in its influence.[5]

In 1969, a new statute established the People's Control Committee, known as KNK, to replace the KPGK. Unlike its predecessor, the KNK no

[2] According to Sullivan (1984), the elective status of the control commission was abolished already in 1934. If that is accurate, then the abolishment is not codified in the CPSU Constitution in 1934 but 1939. See Sullivan (1984, p. 599).

[3] For a full text English translation of the CPSU Constitution, see Gill (1988).

[4] See Adams (1978, p. 458).

[5] See Adams (1978).

longer held the same level of authority. Instead, it functioned as a compliant state agency, serving the interests of the Party.[6] The KNK was also designed as a grassroots organization, relying heavily on volunteers rather than a permanent staff. At its peak, it mobilized approximately 10 million volunteers to monitor government and economic activities.[7]

## Mao's Disciplinary Regime

The first disciplinary body of the Chinese Communist Party was the Central Supervision Committee (CSC), which was established at the fifth National Party Congress in 1927, following the Leninist model.[8] The tasks of the CSC were to "restrain the bureaucratic power of the new Soviet state, maintain the honesty and efficiency of the rapidly expanding Party organization," and "assist the Party and the state in selecting leading cadres" (Sullivan, 1984, p. 598). Like its Soviet counterpart, the CSC was also to be elected by the Party Congress.

According to the CCP Charter (1927), the Central Committee could not overturn a decision made by the Central Supervision Committee; nor could the Central Supervision Committee implement a decision without the Central Committee's approval. It further stipulated that any disputes between them should be resolved by a joint committee, the Party Congress, or the superior supervision committee.[9] These provisions were almost verbatim copies of the 1925 CPSU Constitution. However, they were never put into practice as the CCP, in its earlier years, was fragile and constantly purged by the Kuomintang (KMT). The first CSC members were wiped out by the KMT soon after their election (Peng, 2010; Wu, 2009).

Over the next two decades, the Party gradually recovered from the KMT's purges. During this period, several disciplinary bodies were created at different junctures and under different names, including the Inner-Party Review Committee, the Central Party Affairs Committee, and the Central Party Reviewing Committee (Wu, 2009). Their functions ranged from political vetting and financial auditing to disciplinary indoctrination, performance inspection, and investigating and punishing

[6] See Adams (1978).
[7] See Adams (1978, p. 460).
[8] Gong (2008b, pp. 140–41). Also see Wu (2009), Zuo (2010), and Party Charter (1927).
[9] Party Charter (1927, article 64).

violations (Wu, 2009). However, little documentation exists on their activities. When the CCP Charter was amended at the seventh National Party Congress (1945), establishing a disciplinary body became an optional decision left to individual Party committees. In the meantime, many responsibilities that would later be regarded as disciplinary work were carried out by the Party's organizational apparatus, which oversaw the political vetting of Party cadres.

Upon taking power in 1949, the Party established the Central Committee of Discipline and Inspection (CCDI), modeled after the Central Control Committee of the CPSU (Center, 1949). The CCDI's mandates were outlined in a draft edict announcing its creation, later published with Mao's handwritten revisions (translation by the author, with Mao's edits in bold):

> "The Party has established itself as the ruling party nationwide, **democratic coalition governments have been or will be established across the nation, and collaboration between the Party and non-Party members is increasing day by day**. Against this backdrop, the Central Party has decided to establish Discipline and Inspection Committees at all levels in order to better implement the Party's political line as well as various **concrete** policies and **to safeguard the secrets of the Party and the state**, to strengthen the organizational and disciplined characters of the Party, to maintain close ties with the masses so as to combat bureaucratism, and to ensure the correct implementation of **all** Party decisions." (Center, 1949)[10]

At the time, the CCDI was a relatively small organization, compared to what it would become decades later. The first CCDI consisted of just eleven members, led by Zhu De, and its members were appointed rather than, per requirement of the Party Charter, elected (Center, 1949). Despite its broad mandate, the CCDI had only one office with limited staff (Dong, 1957; Politburo, 1950). It left behind few public records of notable activities (Young, 1984). Below the central level, Committees of Discipline and Inspection at subnational levels (CDIs) had little or no presence, especially in the newly "liberated" regions where the Party's authority was not yet consolidated (Province A, 1953). In regions where

[10] Mao made it a political imperative for the CCDI to protect Party-state secrets likely because the Party had committed to a coalition government at the time. This commitment required the Party to share power with other social and political forces in governmental organs, whose political loyalty to the Party remained in question. However, this mandate was never incorporated in the Party Charter.

CDI offices were established, their main activities were to assist the Party committees in Party education and implementation of prioritized Party policies (Xu, 1953). The Party Center also used the CDIs to gather feedback on central policies and to monitor noncompliance (Wan County, 1951).

During the first two decades after 1949, the Party launched numerous political campaigns, often punitive and violent. These campaigns were directed from the Party's own seat of power and executed through its primary chain of command, with orders passed down from the Party Center to the territorial Party Committees of various administrative levels until they reached the grassroots. In these campaigns, the Party mobilized the masses to identify, punish, and in many cases, eliminate perceived enemies. As an integral part of the Party-state building process, these campaigns were essential in eradicating opposition, silencing dissent, and, most importantly, establishing the Party Center as a seat of power independent from that of the state. Many of these campaigns were initiated by the Party without any form of authorization from state organs. The state authority was invoked only when severe criminal punishments, especially the death penalty, were to be meted out (County A, 1960).

In 1951, the Party launched its first nationwide anti-corruption campaign, known as the "three-antis." The campaign's name was derived from its stated goals: anti-embezzlement, anti-waste, and anti-bureaucratism. It originally began as a local austerity initiative led by Gao Gang, head of the Party's North-Eastern Bureau,[11] as an effort to alleviate the fiscal strain by China's engagement in the Korean War.[12] Gao expanded the austerity program beyond industrial and productive units, introducing it to all governmental departments and agencies while incorporating an additional political dimension, anti-bureaucratism.[13] In the campaign, all public employees were required to engage in self-criticism, confessing their own corrupt and unethical behavior and reporting others who had engaged in such conduct.[14]

When Mao first learned about Gao Gang's campaign, he showed great interest.[15] A week later, he received a report from the Party's Northern

[11] Xu (2004) and Yang (2006).
[12] Xu (2004).
[13] Yang (2006).
[14] Xu (2004) and Yang (2006).
[15] Yang (2006).

Bureau revealing that two senior Party leaders in Tianjin had embezzled and misappropriated large sums of public funds.[16] The case reinforced Mao's belief in the corrosive dangers of capitalism and the susceptibility of Party members to the so-called "sugar-coated bullets" of capitalist influence. In response, he sanctioned the execution of the two Tianjin Party leaders,[17] and at the same time, demanded that Gao Gang's three-antis campaign be expanded nationwide.[18]

The campaign was given a short deadline, as Mao believed that it should be swift.[19] Its primary objective was to capture "tigers" – a metaphor Mao used to portray an image of arrogant Party officials who saw themselves untouchable – "like a tiger's bottom."[20] Mao had firm ideas about the "appropriate" size of the "tiger" population. In a telegram to the Northern-China Theatre Command, he stated, "the estimated number of big tigers [in your region] shall be at least 200 . . . Do not by any means let them get off scot-free."[21] Similarly, in a directive to the leader of Hebei Province, Mao affirmed , "Hebei province has a population of 30 million. Your plan to capture 2,300 small tigers and 200 big tigers is appropriate."

The numbers of large, medium, and baby tigers "captured" across different regions were updated every three to five days and reported to Mao. Upon reviewing the reports, Mao would annotate them and circulate his remarks, praising strong performance and embarrassing regions that lagged behind. Under peer pressure, those underperformed regions scrambled to meet expectations. For instance, on January 26, 1952, the Party's North-Eastern Bureau submitted a plan to capture 500 big tigers, which failed to impress Mao. A week later, on February 3, the Bureau raised its target from 500 to 2,000, and by February 6, it had further increased the number to 4,000.[22]

By the end of the campaign, an estimated 3 million public employees had participated in the three-antis campaign, resulting in the capture of 1.22 million corrupt "tigers" of various ranks within three months.[23]

16 Yang (2006).
17 PeopleNet (2015) and Wang and Zhang (2011).
18 Yang (2006).
19 Xu (2004).
20 Mao (1962) and PeopleNet (2011).
21 Yang (2006).
22 Yang (2006).
23 Yang (2006).

## Deng's Disciplinary Regime

Although widely recognized as a founding father of the Party and the "architect" (Faison, 1997) of China's economic reform, Deng Xiaoping's role in shaping the Party's disciplinary system has been largely overlooked, rarely studied, and seldom discussed.

When the People's Republic of China (PRC) was founded in 1949, a state supervision organ was created under the Central Government, following the Leninist model. This institution later became the Ministry of Supervision (MOS) in 1954, tasked with overseeing the performance of public employees and holding them accountable for misconduct and dereliction of duty. Unlike its Soviet counterpart, however, the PRC's state supervision organ was never designed as a grassroots organization to facilitate bottom-up oversight of the state apparatus. On the contrary, the MOS had only limited authority, and its activities remained largely obscure. In 1959, it was dissolved, with its functions and personnel absorbed by the CSC (Liu & Xiao, 2022), a Party disciplinary institution that was reinstated by the Party in 1955.

Deng Xiaoping had already been in charge of supervisory work at the State Council in 1953 (Center, 1953). In 1954, the Gao/Rao Affair erupted (the case will be discussed in greater details in Chapter 7). Gao Gang, the original creator of the Three-Anti Campaign, was accused of attempting a coup against senior Central Party leaders. Deng was one of the first to report Gao's misconduct to Mao and was later tasked to lead the investigation (Chung, 1999). A year later, Deng's investigation confirmed the allegation against Gao Gang and attributed the affair to the weakness in the Party disciplinary system. The investigation concluded that the existing disciplinary institutions lacked the capacity to detect and prevent disciplinary violations because they were under the control of the very Party organizations they were tasked to oversee (Deng, 1955).

Against this backdrop, the CSC was reinstated. The new CSC was headed by Dong Biwu, one of the Party's founding members who had attended the first Party conference in 1921 and fought in the revolution. At the Politburo, it was Deng Xiaoping who oversaw the CSC operations and made key policy decisions. Following the Gao/Rao Affair, Deng took over important portfolios previously held by Gao and Rao, expanding his influence in both the Party and the military. He was also promoted to the head of the Central Secretariat, granting him authority over the Party's day-to-day operation across all policy areas, including disciplinary matters. This allowed Deng to breathe life into the Party's disciplinary institutions. Historical records show that Deng personally issued directives to the CSC leaders on a range of issues, including policy priorities, budgetary approvals, the establishment of supervisory outposts in state organs, case-handling protocols, and critical operational matters, such as whom the supervision committee could monitor and to whom it should be accountable (Wang, 1962).

Between 1949 and 1954, the Party relied primarily on Party Committees to drive political campaigns. While these campaigns were effectively enforced, they also revealed several problems. First, unresolved disciplinary cases accumulated due to a shortage of personnel and a lengthy approval process, which slowed decision-making. Second, excessive enforcement, including broadening the scope of targets of investigation and the overuse of severe punishment, particularly the death penalty. The Gao/Rao Affair provided Deng Xiaoping with the impetus to reform the disciplinary system by introducing a series of institutional changes.

First, election of the supervision committees. Previously, members of a supervision committee were appointed. Under Deng's reforms, they were now to be elected by Party delegates, following the earlier CPSU practices. This change was not merely symbolic but carried important implications. First, it granted the supervision committees a legitimacy rooted in democratic principles, which appointed offices lacked. Second, it allowed the supervision committee to exert authority over and penetrate the autonomy of other Party institutions, a feature that would prove critical in anti-corruption investigation decades later. Third, it enabled the CSC to form, through its membership, a permanent national policy-deliberation platform separate from the Central Committee, a prerogative afforded to no other Party apparatus.

Second, the Party's takeover of state disciplinary functions. Before the CSC's reinstatement, the CCDI's jurisdiction was limited to Party members. Although this restriction was by no means fully followed in practice, a formal division between Party and state disciplinary institutions had nevertheless been upheld in principle. However, after the Anti-Rightist Campaign (1957), which purged nearly all external critics of the Party, the role of state institutions in the overall disciplinary system became significantly weaker.

With the absorption of the MOS in 1959, the Party installed its own supervision outposts in state organs and in lower-level governments in 1962 (Center, 1962). Without any legislative adjustments, the Party effectively crossed its jurisdictional boundary, expanded its reach, and fully absorbed the state disciplinary system (Jiang, 2017). From that point forward, the

CSC and its lower branches became responsible for enforcing all Party-led political campaigns. These campaigns were initiated through resolutions issued by the Party Center, which outlined the required course of actions, without revoking the authority of any state organ.[24]

Third, personnel expansion of the supervision committees. Under Deng's leadership, the number of supervision personnel more than doubled nationwide between 1955 and 1956.[25] Although the CSC experienced staff reduction due to intra-Party purges in the late 1950s, its number was replenished following a new initiative to strengthen the Party's supervisory capacity in 1962 (Wang, 1962). The expansion was remarkable given the country's fiscal difficulties at the time. Alongside increased staffing, the political status of the supervision committees was elevated, with their leaders gaining the second highest position in corresponding Party committees. Unlike earlier CDIs, which were often one-person offices, many supervision committees were now supported by a permanent administrative staff (Dong, 1957; Province A, 1955, 1956). The supervision committees also expanded their reach, establishing a presence in townships and grassroots work units where CDIs had previously been absent. During this period, corruption investigations became a significant part of their workload, though the scale of corruption uncovered at that time was negligible to what it is today.

Four, growing autonomy of supervision committees. Under the previous system, CDIs had little autonomy from the Party committees to which they belonged. Under Deng's reforms, a superior supervision committee was given oversight authority over lower-level supervision committees and was granted the authority to approve or change their decisions (CCP, 1955; Committee, 1957). More importantly, supervision committees were tasked with monitoring disciplinary violations within corresponding Party Committees and reporting such incidents – though not acting on them – to the superior supervision committee (CCP, 1955). This unusual move – allowing a supervision committee to oversee its corresponding Party Committees – raised concerns that it was moving

[24] For instance, during the notorious Anti-Rightist Campaign, the Party issued multiple directives guiding its agents' actions on all aspects of the campaign, including its pace, the scope of investigations, and the criteria for identifying and classifying "rightists," and so on. The state legislature was involved only when a new punitive measure – education through labor – was introduced at Mao's instruction during the Qingdao Conference in 1957 (Centre, 1957; Mao, 1957). Similarly, the Three-Antis Campaign was carried out under Party directives alone before the issuance of the Anti-Embezzlement Directive by a state organ much later.

[25] CSC (1957) and Dong (1957).

toward vertical integration and seeking independence from the Party Committees. These suspicions were not entirely unfounded, as the supervision committee's expanding role indeed posed a challenge to the cardinal principle of the Party's self-rule: the unified (absolute) command of the Party Center, which will be the focus of the next section.

## Unified (Absolute) Command of the Party Center

The principle of unified (absolute) command of the Party Center (UCOPC or *dangzhongyang jizhong lingdao*) was first introduced by the Politburo through the 1942 resolution Unification of the Party's Leadership in Anti-Japanese Revolutionary Bases and the Adjustment of the Organizational Relations (Politburo, 1942). This resolution, passed after Mao gained dominance over the Politburo, established the plenipotentiary authority of the Party Center over all domains and regions, while granting regional and local Party branches a measured degree of autonomy. More specifically, the UCOPC principle positioned the Party Center as the single highest commanding authority, overseeing all affairs in every territorial unit under the Party's control.

It is important to note that the Party Center is an official term deliberately employed with strategic ambiguity (Li, 2020a,b). It is among the least defined but most frequently used terms in Party discourse, appearing in Party leaders' speeches, policy papers, and regulations without ever specifying the referenced entity.[26] For instance, Article 5 of the Central Directive on the Work of the Central Committee (2020) states: "The Central Committee, the Politburo, and its standing committee are the brain and the nerve center of the organizational system of the Party. Only the Party Center can make decisions and interpret its decisions on issues with nationwide and party-wide impacts." The seamless transition between subjects in these two adjacent sentences suggests that the Party Center can refer to any or any combination of the Central Committee, the Politburo, the Politburo Standing Committee, and arguably, the National Party Congress as well.[27]

[26] For instance, in an analysis of over a thousand articles published by the CCDI, Carolin Kautz found that the term "Party Center" appeared 547 times. In 40 percent of these instances, it was unclear which specific institution or decision-making body the term referred to. See Kautz (2022, p. 153).

[27] This is because the Party Charter has consistently declared that the Party's highest decision-making body is the National Party Congress and the Central Committee elected by the former.

The UCOPC principle operates across three key dimensions. First, lateral dimension. It elevates the executive body of a territorial Party Committee above all its components, including subcommittees, departments, functional divisions, and all state organs within the same territorial unit. Second, vertical dimension. It subjects lower-level territorial Party Committees to the command of those at the higher levels, forming a command chain that ultimately leads up to the Party Center. Third, intra-executive dimension. It established power hierarchies within executive bodies, creating an order of power both among different tiers of decision-making bodies and among individual actors of the same body.

The UCOPC principle aims to regulate both institutional and individual behavior to safeguard a unidirectional chain of command that originates from the Party Center, extending laterally to its various components and vertically down to smaller territorial units from regions to prefectures, counties, and townships.

The introduction of the UCOPC in 1942 was largely a reaction to incidents where other Party leaders acted contrary to Mao's instructions. One such case was the Hundred-Regiments Offensive, a major anti-Japanese military campaign led by Peng Dehuai, which Mao had opposed. Another instance involved Zhou Enlai and Wang Ming, who, in the name of the Party Center, issued declarations in support of a unified-front policy toward the KMT – a stance Mao also opposed – while stationed at the Yangzi Bureau at Wuhan (Gao, 2000). By elevating the territorial Party Committee as the highest commanding authority within their respective territorial units and then subordinating them, level by level, to the Party Center, where Mao held dominance, the UCOPC strengthened Mao's personal control over the entire Party (He, 2019).

A key derivative of the UCOPC principle is the autonomy of regional and local territorial Party Committees from other components of the Party-state apparatus. This means that even central Party organs or national state regulatory bodies cannot issue direct orders to a regional territorial Party Committee without the Party Center's approval, despite the fact that the former institutions enjoy a national jurisdiction. Instead, only the Party Center has the authority to command regional territorial Party Committees, which in turn direct lower-level territorial Party committees, and so on, until the order reaches the grassroots level (Center, 1996, 2012).

In contrast, the power structure within state organs diverges from that of the Party in two significant ways. First, flattened authority structure.

Unlike territorial Party Committees, which follow a strict hierarchical chain, state organs operate under a fragmented command system. Taking the State Council as an example, the State Council Party-group led by the Premier cannot command the Party-group embedded in ministries. Instead, ministerial Party-groups report directly to the Party Center.[28] Second, conflicting loyalties in local governance. While territorial Party Committees must unconditionally comply with the Party Center's directives, government agencies do not owe the same allegiance to superior state organs. This means that, for example, if the Beijing mayor (head of the government) received conflicting instructions – one from the State Council and one from the Beijing Party Committee – his primary loyalty lies with the latter.

Hence, if the State Council seeks to introduce a policy with stronger enforcement, it must obtain the Party Center's approval and circulate the policy through the Party's primary chain of command.[29] These arrangements deliberately fragmented the authority of the central government, thus weakening its capacity of policy implementation. However, they align perfectly with the UCOPC principle as they ensure that the State Council – despite controlling massive economic resources and regulatory powers delegated by the Party, cannot outgrow or rival the authority of the Party Center.

## Significance of Deng's Disciplinary Regime

Seen through the lens of the UCOPC principle, Deng's establishment of the CSC was revolutionary. Mandating the supervision committee to monitor and report misconduct of the corresponding territorial Party Committee was to allow the former to encroach upon the autonomy of the latter. This directly challenged the UCOPC principle, which dictates

[28] See Center (2019, chapter 4). As a result of these arrangements, the constitutional authority of the Premier – who, according to the PRC Constitution, is mandated to "direct the work of the State Council" – is undermined. The disparity between the commanding power of a Party chief in a territorial Party Committee and a Party leader in the government of the same territorial unit is well acknowledged in studies of governance and public administration in China. For instance, see Chen (2020), Xiang (2021), Yu (2021a), and Zhou and Huang (2022). For further discussions on the difference of the authority of a territorial Party Committee and of a Party-group, one can refer to an explainer by a professor from the Party-Building Department of the Central Party School (Liu, 2021a). Also see Chu and Yu (2015).

[29] For more on the recent expansion of this co-signing practice, see Feng (2021).

that a territorial Party Committee must submit only to the command of the higher territorial Party Committee, not to the functional apparatus of the latter, such as the supervision committee.

Thus, it is not unsurprising that the operation of the supervision committee raised great concern within the Party when the reform was introduced. Cadres from other central Party apparatuses feared that the supervisory institutions would assume too much power at the expense of undermining the territorial Party Committees.[30] This concern was not unfounded. In the late 1950s, several divisional leaders at the then MOS advocated for complete autonomy, seeking freedom from Party control. Some even proposed granting supervisory bodies the power to suspend funds to state financial institutions and to intervene in policy enactment and implementation before, rather than after, decisions were made.[31] As one could expect, these demands met strong resistance within the Party (Young, 1984).

As a response, Deng Xiaoping repeatedly assured critics that the CSC would not compromise the UCOPC principle or infringe upon the autonomy of the territorial Party Committees.[32] During the Anti-Rightist Campaign in 1958–1959, which Deng himself oversaw, those who had advocated for supervision committee autonomy and vertical integration were condemned as rightists and expelled from the Party.

More critically, Deng's 1955 disciplinary regime first introduced the "dual-leadership" arrangement, which would later catalyze the institutional expansion of the Party's disciplinary system from 1982. The dual-leadership arrangement placed the CSC under the command of the Central Committee and all lower-level supervision committees in the command of their corresponding Party Committees, thus adhering to the UCOPC principle. At the same time, the supervision committees were also empowered (1) to monitor Party leaders appointed by their corresponding Party Committees, (2) to monitor, albeit to a limited degree,

30 Party Committee (1960a,b).

31 Based on disciplinary decisions regarding three cadres of the MOS: Chen Dazhi (Deputy Head of the Research Office), Peng Da (Deputy Head of Division 2), An Rutao (Deputy Head of Division 1). All three were expelled from the Party, removed from their posts, and punished to perform manual labor under supervision. Decisions are on file with the author.

32 Yet, in his later years, Deng became more outspoken in his rebuttal. In a 1980 speech, he blamed the UCOPC principle for causing an excessive concentration of power, which, he argued, led to bureaucratism, autocratic tendencies, and various other governance issues (Deng, 1980).

those appointed by their superior Party Committees and (3) to approve or change the disciplinary decisions of lower-level supervision committees (CCP, 1955).

During this period, the Party supervisory committees grew considerably in strength and capacity. Compared to its predecessor, which had limited presence and influence, the CSC emerged as a critical enforcement agency of the Party Center, playing an indispensable role in the political campaigns launched by the latter. In these campaigns, supervision committees served dual roles: as the Party's "taming instrument," detecting and punishing noncompliance, and as the Party's ombudsman, handling complaints, tempering radical conduct, and correcting mistakes (Center, 1962).

During this era, the Party's disciplinary framework also began to take shape. Several regulations were issued to standardize disciplinary practices. Conferences were held periodically, where supervision cadres across the country gathered to exchange experience and receive policy updates. In 1962, the Party even authorized the CSC to install outposts in State Council ministries (Center, 1962), which would, as will be discussed in Chapter 6, be revitalized five decades later in the critical anti-corruption campaign led by the new Party leader Xi Jinping.

Deng's 1955 disciplinary system was, however, halted by the Cultural Revolution, as power struggles at the top dismantled the institutional cohesion of the Party.[33] The supervision committees were under attack. In 1969, Kang Sheng, head of the Party's intelligence agency, conducted an investigation of the CSC and reported that 80 percent of its members and half of its administrative staff were traitors, spies, and/or counter-revolutionary revisionists (CCDI, 1980).[34] As the disciplinary system was factually paralyzed, the CSC was dissolved in 1969 and most of its staff were sent to labor camps (Zheng, 2015).[35] At the same time, key disciplinary provisions were removed from the Party Charter. Routine disciplinary functions, such as policy enforcement, political education, and handling of grievances, had also ceased. Instead, the Party relied on "Special Case Investigation Teams," which, unlike the supervision committees, lacked any institutional oversight (Schoenhals, 1996). This chaotic period also saw the breakdown of the state legal system, with courts

[33] Fan and Yao (2010, Chapter 8, section 4).

[34] During the investigation, fourteen out of fifteen standing members of the CSC were brutally treated, six of whom died in custody.

[35] CCDI (2014b), Fan (2011), and Peng (2010).

and procuratorates ceasing operations and law enforcement being effectively handed over to the military.

## Revival of Deng's Disciplinary Regime

After Mao's death in 1976, efforts to rebuild the Party-state began. In 1978, the Party resurrected the CCDI as its central disciplinary apparatus. According to Article 44 of the Party Charter (1982), the CCDI and its lower counterparts were authorized to carry out the following activities:

1. To uphold [the authority of] the Party Charter and other important Party regulations;
2. to assist Party Committees in rectifying Party-styles;[36]
3. to inspect the implementation of the Party's line, principles, policies, and decisions;
4. to conduct routine disciplinary education for Party members, rendering decisions to uphold Party discipline;
6. to investigate and handle serious and complicated cases regarding violations of the Party Charter, Party disciplines, state laws and regulations, approving or revoking disciplinary sanctions in these cases;
7. to receive and process allegations and complaints from Party members.

Also in 1978, Chen Yun was elected as the head of the new CCDI. Since he simultaneously held a seat in the Politburo Standing Committee, his appointment elevated the CCDI's political standing above all other central functional departments. Immediately after its establishment, the CCDI was tasked with overseeing the preparation of the two most prominent political trials of the time, one against the so-called Gang of Four and one against Lin Biao and his clique (Li & Chen, 2018). In addition, the CCDI, alongside the Central Organizational Department (COD), took on the responsibility of rehabilitating cadres who had been wronged during previous enforcement excesses. The mandates of these two institutions overlapped considerably, and the COD played a key role in reestablishing the CCDI in 1978 (Jin & Chen, 2015, p. 1524). It was presumably no coincidence that Chen

[36] For a more elaborate account of the meaning of party-style, see Young (1984).

Yun, the newly appointed head of the CCDI, had also led the COD for nearly a decade in the 1930s and 1940s.

The process of fully staffing the CCDI began in 1982. That year, the Party authorized detailed staffing plans to "equip" CCDI departments, outposts, and lower CDIs with politically loyal Party cadres (CCDI, 1983). The number of CCDI members doubled compared to the peak size of the previous CSC (CCDI, 2013a). Two new chapters on Party discipline and disciplinary institutions were introduced to the Party Charter, forming the constitutional foundation of the Party disciplinary system which remains in effect today. The CCDI and the lower CDIs retained their elective status with a notable change: while the 1956 Party Charter had mandated the Central Committee to elect the CSC; the 1982 Party Charter stipulated that the CCDI would be elected by the National Party Congress, the same body responsible for electing the Central Committee, seemingly suggesting that the CCDI and the Central Committee would be equal in power and political status, as both were elected by the Party's most representative body. However, the same Party Charter (1982) also explicitly stipulated that the CCDI should answer to the Central Committee, ensuring that no false impression of equality between the two institutions could arise.

The new disciplinary regime also adopted the dual-leadership model introduced by Deng Xiaoping in 1955. This means that a CDI answers to both its corresponding Party Committee and to the superior CDI. A CDI could report misconduct of members of its corresponding Party Committee to the superior CDI but could not take actions on the information on its own. The superior CDI had the power to oversee the work of lower CDIs in case-handling. Under these arrangements, the CCDI became the only central Party apparatus allowed to form a vertical power substructure, a prerogative that is extended to no other Party apparatus.

As shown in Figure 5.1, the primary and strongest chain of command – illustrated by the enhanced solid arrows – runs from the Party Center to the territorial Party Committees along administrative divisions. The CDIs report to both the higher CDI and their corresponding territorial Party Committees, as indicated by the thin solid arrows in Figure 5.1. A CDI not only shares the power of its corresponding territorial Party Committee in monitoring disciplinary violations of leaders appointed by the latter but also has the independent authority to direct the work of the lower CDIs in the investigation of earmarked cases.

By contrast, as depicted in Figure 5.2, other functional departments of the Party Center do not have commanding authority over their

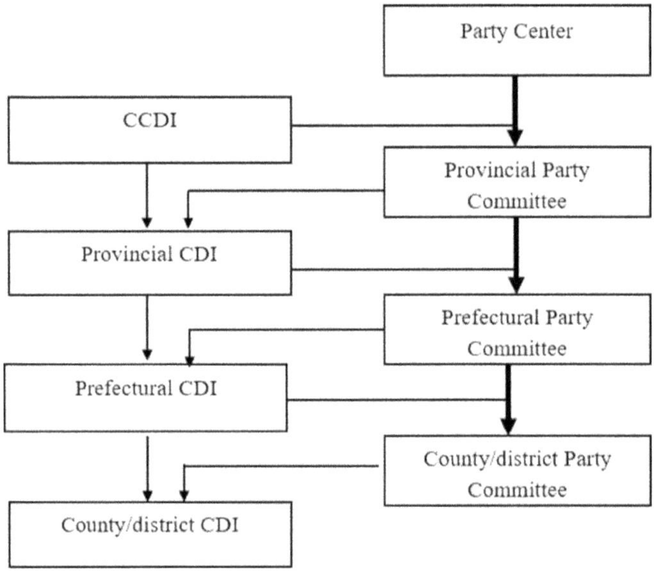


**Figure 5.1** Dual-leadership of the CDIs.

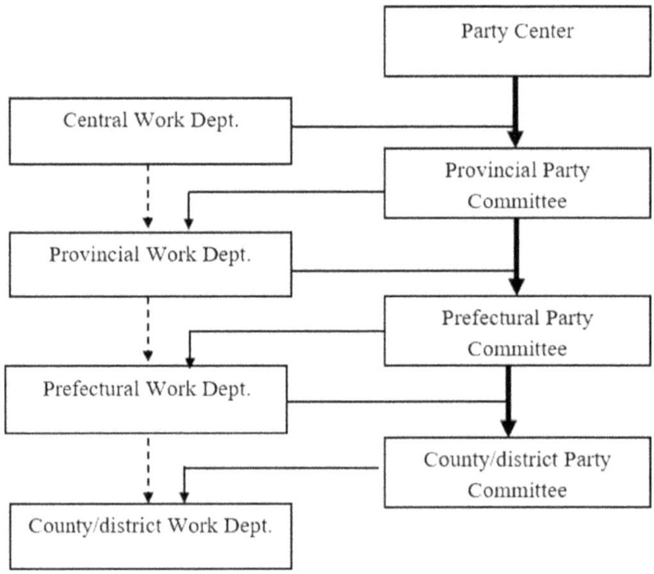


**Figure 5.2** Single leadership of other work departments.

counterparts at the lower administrative levels, as indicated by the broken arrows in the figure. Instead, these lower-level departments primarily answer to their corresponding territorial Party Committees, adhering to the UCOPC principle.

By the mid-1980s, regional and local CDIs had been established at all administrative levels, extending their reach even to grassroots Party organizations. In 1993, the MOS was once again merged into the CCDI while retaining its nominal legal status as an internal disciplinary institution of the administrative branch of the state. After the "annexation," the CCDI expanded to twenty-seven departments and bureaus with more than 1,000 employees (Guo, 2014b). At the same time, the Party introduced an increasing number of disciplinary regulations to standardize disciplinary practices. It was also during this period that corruption began spreading rapidly, as opportunities for corruption exploded during the transition from the planned to the market economy. In response, the Party broadened the scope of disciplinary enforcement to address various forms of corrupt conduct. However, the pace of corruption growth far outstripped the Party's efforts to curb it. By the end of the 1980s, public discontent over corruption and related social problems escalated, culminating in an unprecedented democratic social movement (Manion, 1996; Sun, 1991).

## Disciplinary Decision-Making Structure

Under the "dual-leadership" arrangement, the Party aimed to empower the CCDI while ensuring it remained under its control. To achieve this, it developed a tiered, interlocking decision-making mechanism in which the disciplinary power was distributed among four entities: the CDI, its corresponding territorial Party Committee, the superior CDI, and the superior territorial Party Committee. Specifically, disciplinary matters were first classified based on two criteria: the rank of the Party member under investigation and the severity of the offense. The disciplinary decision-making process was then segmented into multiple stages, creating checkpoints at which different decision-makers could review the case and intervene when necessary.

The initial normative foundation of this disciplinary decision-making structure was laid down in the 1982 Party Charter. It upheld the principle that the higher the rank of the accused and the more severe the sanction, the greater involvement of the higher decision-making bodies.

The Party classified its members into two broad ranking categories: Party Committee members or alternate members and rank-and-file Party members. These categories were further refined in the Rules on the Jurisdictions of Disciplinary Decisions against Party Members introduced by the CCDI in 1983 (hereinafter "Jurisdiction Rules 1983"), detailing which ranking authorities could impose which types of disciplinary sanctions on Party members of which rank-group.

The Jurisdiction Rules (1983) authorized the CCDI to render or approve, depending on the rank of the accused and the sanction proposed, disciplinary decisions against all cadres managed by the Party Center, which included (1) "ministers, vice-ministers, directors, vice-directors, secretaries and vice-secretaries of the Party-group of the Supreme People's Procuratorate, the Supreme People's Court, ministries, ministerial-level committees and offices of the State Council, and secretaries and vice-secretaries of the Party-groups of bureaus and general bureaus directly affiliated with the State Council"; (2) middle-management-level directors and vice-directors of the aforementioned institutions and cadres of enterprises and nonprofit public institutions affiliated with the aforementioned institutions and now managed by the Party Center; and (3) cadres of both provincial and prefectural ranks. As the workload became overwhelming, the Party eventually decentralized the disciplinary power, which went in tandem with the decentralization of the Party's appointment power.[37]

The other factor that determines how the disciplinary power is allocated is the type of sanctions. For example, Article 40 granted the territorial Party Committees the authority to impose sanctions – including removal from office, suspension of Party membership or expulsion from the Party – against their members or alternate members. However, decisions to prosecute these members must be rendered by the executive bodies of the territorial Party Committee – their Standing Committees. The same article further specified: "Disciplinary sanctions against a member or alternate member of the Central Committee who is deemed to have committed a serious crime (and requires prosecution, note by author) must be rendered by the Politburo (not the Central Committee, note by author)." The Party's classification of the disciplinary sanctions closely resembles the system used by the CPSU under Stalin (Cohn,

[37] For more on the distribution of the appointment power, see studies on the nomenklatura system, for instance Burns (1989), Chan (2004), and Heilmann (2000).

2021). Specifically, sanctions were divided into three categories based on severity:

I. Warning and serious warning;
II. Removal from office, suspension of Party membership and expulsion from the Party;
III. Expulsion from the Party with criminal offense verified [which means that the case will be referred to the procuratorate for prosecution].

Based on both the rank and sanction factors, the Party Charter (1982) prescribed four decision-making procedures. The first is what I call "peer decision-making." This procedure, also similar to the CPSU practice (Cohn, 2021), requires disciplinary decisions to be made by the peers of the accused. For example, to expel a member of the Central Committee requires a two-thirds majority vote of the Central Committee.

The second is what I call "executive decision-making," which grants the disciplinary power to the executive body of a territorial Party Committee if the accused is involved in a serious criminal act (Category III sanction). This procedure was then extended in 1983 to allow the "Party Center" to retain the disciplinary power regarding Category II offenses accused of its members when "special circumstances emerged." What constitutes "special circumstances" was never clarified.

The third is the "retroactive-affirmation (*zhuiren*)" procedure, which combines elements of both peer and executive decision-making procedures. In essence, it bypasses peer decision-making and replaces it with executive decision-making, thereby subverting the Leninist model. Before 2002, this practice seemed irregular and informal. However, in 2002, an amendment to the Party Charter formally institutionalized it, granting the Politburo the authority to first make an executive disciplinary decision against a Central Committee member or an alternate member and then submit it for "retroactive-affirmation" by the Central Committee when the latter convenes.

No publicly available information indicates whether any executive decision has ever been overturned by the Central Committee, nor what consequences would arise if such a rejection were to occur. In subsequent years, the retroactive-affirmation procedure was used extensively and almost replaced the ordinary peer decision-making procedure, allowing the Party to reform its approach to power struggles at the Politburo, a topic that will be discussed in greater details in the next two chapters.

The last disciplinary procedure introduced by the Party Charter (1982) was "supervisory approval," which applies primarily to disciplinary decision-making at the subnational and local levels. Under this procedure, no disciplinary decision was made by a single institution; instead, all decisions were subject to oversight by at least one superior decision-making body, unless it was an executive decision made by the Politburo. The intensity of this top-down oversight varied depending on the significance of the case concerned. The general principle, as mentioned already earlier, is that the higher the rank of the accused and the more serious the offense, the more approvals were required.

Closely associated with the supervisory approval procedure was the "filing for the record *bei'an*" procedure. Unlike supervisory approval, which was an *ex ante* requirement and conditional for a decision to take effect, *bei'an* was *ex post* and did not affect the validity of a decision under review. The *bei'an* procedure was used to keep supervisory bodies informed of disciplinary actions of secondary importance that had taken place at the subordinate level. For example, Article 1(c-d) of the Jurisdiction Rules (1983) stipulated:

(c) Decisions to impose a category I sanction on a member or alternate member of the Central Committee must be reported to and approved by the Party Center or the CCDI. If the decision is approved by the CCDI, it must be filed with the Party Center for the record.
(d) Decisions to impose a category I sanction on a member or alternate member of a regional or local party committee must be reported to and approved by the superior CDI. The superior CDI is responsible for filing the decision with the corresponding Party Committee for the record.

In summary, the Party's disciplinary decision-making structure involved three levels of authority, who engage in decision-making at different stages and with different degrees of engagement: a decision-rendering authority (*jǘeding jiguan*), an approval authority (*pizhun jiguan*), and a filing-for-the-record authority (*bei'an jiguan*). In most cases, these roles were filled, respectively, by the local CDI, the corresponding territorial Party Committee, and the superior CDI. In cases involving high-ranking officials and severe punishment, the decision-rendering power would be transferred to the territorial Party Committee, while the approval authority shifted to the superior CDI, and the *bei'an* authority to the superior territorial Party Committee.

This tiered decision-making structure produces two outcomes. First, by placing the CCDI under the authority of the Party Center, the Politburo retains the ultimate disciplinary power over all critical disciplinary matters. Second, by subjecting local CDIs to the oversight and command of the superior CDIs, leading up to the CCDI, the Party transformed the CCDI into a vertical power substructure with a measure of autonomy that is unmatched by any other central Party apparatus. Despite the constraints imposed by their corresponding territorial Party Committees, CDIs retained exclusive investigative authority, allowing them to influence and shape disciplinary outcomes. This very prerogative also renders their power susceptible to abuse, prompting the Party to segment the CDI investigations into multiple stages to allow for interim top-down interventions – a mechanism that will be examined in the next section.

## Disciplinary Decision-Making Stages

With more authority delegated to CDIs and more cases to investigate, the CCDI took steps to standardize the disciplinary procedures. In 1987, it issued the "Rules on Conducting Case-Examination Work" (hereinafter "1987 Case-Examination Rules"), followed by the "Rules on Conducting Case Inspection Work" (hereinafter "1988 Case-Inspection Rules") in 1988. These directives established three stages for disciplinary investigations: case opening, case investigation, and case examination. Each stage erects a checkpoint, allowing a supervisory body or individual to review, approve, or reject disciplinary actions. Many of these procedures described here remain in effect today.

Case-opening. The case-opening stage is more consequential than it may seem. Article 10 of the 1988 Case-Inspection Rules stipulated:

> When a CDI receives a complaint or allegation against a Party member or Party institution, it shall conduct a preliminary investigation to verify the information. If the alleged conduct is verified but does not warrant a disciplinary sanction, the investigative body shall issue a warning; if the alleged conduct is verified and meets the threshold for disciplinary action, then the CDI shall open an investigation. (CCDI, 1988)

Article 12 further stipulated that the decision to open a case would be managed based on ranks "*fenji guanli.*" For example, at the central level:

> The CCDI shall conduct a preliminary verification of allegations regarding Central Committee members. If a violation is confirmed, [the CCDI] shall submit a complaint to the Central Committee in accordance with the Party Charter. Upon approval from the Party Center, the CCDI shall launch a full investigation.

Case-investigation. Once a case is opened, it moves to the case-investigation stage,[38] conducted by the specialized case-investigation department. Article 22 of the 1988 Case-Inspection Rules outlines the permissible investigative measures:

> CDIs are entitled to collect evidence from organizations and individuals with relevant information. All Party organizations and Party members are obligated to provide truthful evidence. . . . CDI investigators may conduct interviews with the accused or witnesses, inspect crime scenes and examine relevant documents.

The 1988 Case-Inspection Rules explicitly prohibited coercion and the use of criminal investigative measures such as "detention, summons, search and seizure, investigation, and movement-tracking," which remain the jurisdiction of state law enforcement agencies.

Upon completing the investigation, Articles 25 and 30 of the 1988 Case-Inspection Rules require a written report summarizing the case. The report should include: the grounds for opening the case, the key facts of the violation, the nature of the offense, the level of accountability of the accused, the remorsefulness of the accused regarding their offense, and recommendations for disciplinary actions. CDI leaders shall review the report and decide whether to close the case or to proceed by referring the case to the case-examination department.

Case-examination. The case-examination department assesses the evidence and applies disciplinary rules. Under the 1987 Case-Examination Rules, each case is assigned an examination team, which presents its findings for collective deliberation at the department. The deliberation evaluates: the clarity of the facts, the sufficiency and certainty of the evidence, the accuracy of the characterization of the case, the appropriateness of the recommended sanctions, and the completeness of the documentation. Examiners may consult the work unit of the accused, their supervisory organs or other regulatory bodies with specialized knowledge of the violation.

To finalize the examination, a written report is required. The report shall assess the evidence, determine whether the offense constitutes a crime, provide a reasoned opinion on the nature of the violation and recommend an appropriate sanction proportionate to the severity of the

[38] Following the supervision reform in 2018, the procedure was renamed from case inspection (*anjian jiancha*) to case investigation (*anjian diaocha*) and the department responsible for this function was also renamed accordingly.

offense. The accused has the right to review the report and offer an explanation or rebuttal. If they dispute the findings, their rebuttal must be reviewed and, if deemed reasonable, included in the case file. While the consent of the accused is not required to finalize the report, examiners must document any objections.

The final report is to be submitted to the CDI standing committee for review and approval. Upon approval, the sanction will be enacted, if the CDI is the designated decision-rendering organ on the case based on the rank-based jurisdiction rules. If further approval is required, the decision does not take effect until the final approval is granted. Upon receiving the disciplinary sanction, the accused may lodge a complaint requesting a review; however, this does not prevent the sanction from taking effect. If the offense is deemed criminal, the case will be transferred to the procuratorate for further investigation and prosecution.

By dividing the disciplinary process into distinct stages, the Party set up multiple checkpoints for interim top-down oversight and intervention. This structure mirrors the segregation of the litigation process in courts, with the shared aim of dispersing power, promoting specialization, and implementing internal checks.

## Rise of the CCDI

After the 1989 democratic movement, the Party took an offensive stance against corruption, declaring it an existential battle. This commitment spurred the rapid rise of the Party's disciplinary institutions, in particular, the CCDI. The most significant factor in the disciplinary expansion was the introduction of the 1994 Case-Inspection Rules, which authorized the CCDI and its lower branches to use coercive measures in anti-corruption investigations.

Before 1994, CDIs were authorized only to conduct interviews with individuals or organizations believed to have relevant information and collect documents from "the scene of the violation" (CCDI, 1988). They were explicitly prohibited from applying coercive investigative measures such as detention, search and seizure – powers reserved for state law enforcement agencies. The 1994 Case-Inspection Rules marked a turning point. Article 28 stipulated that the following investigative measures would be permissible during CDI investigations:

i. To examine and photocopy documents, written materials, accounting books, meeting minutes and work notes related to the case.

ii. To instruct relevant organs to provide documents, written materials and other necessary reports related to the case.
iii. To order relevant personnel to explain matters related to the investigation at a designated time and place.
iv. To make audio, video, and photographic records of relevant individuals or activities when necessary.
v. To request forensic assistance from specialized agencies or personnel to examine special [technical, note by author] issues related to the case.
vi. To temporarily hold and seal documentation, written materials, accounting books, receipts, property and illicit income that serve as evidence of disciplinary violation, with approval from a CDI leader at the county-level or above.
vii. To check and freeze assets of the person under investigation in banks or other financial institutions, with approval from a CDI leader at the county-level or above.
viii. To collect all other evidence that can verify the facts of the case.

Among these measures, the third – ordering individuals to appear for questioning – has drawn the most criticism. Commonly known as "two regulations" or *shuanggui,* this practice closely resembles solitary confinement, a method that the Party had historically used against counterrevolutionaries and defectors, only phasing it out after the Cultural Revolution (Liu, 2014b; Sapio, 2008). Under the 1994 Case-Inspection Rules, *shuanggui* was authorized at both the preliminary investigation stage (before a case was formally opened) and the formal investigation stage (after case opening). It allowed the CDI to detain suspects in isolation for months at undisclosed locations – typically hotel rooms or guest houses – without legal representation or recourse (Liu, 2014b; Sapio, 2008). Unlike the detention measures outlined in the Criminal Procedure Law at the time, *shuanggui* lacked the safeguard, however limited, to which criminal suspects were entitled.

When *shuanggui* was introduced in 1994, it was not a new invention but rather a rebranded version of the "two designations" or *shuangzhi*, a similar measure granted to the state supervision institution, the MOS, through an administrative act by the State Council enacted in 1990. However, the MOS, as a low-ranking institution, lacked the CCDI's authority, limiting the effectiveness of *shuangzhi.* In contrast, the CCDI, as an elected Party institution with a much higher ranking, wielded far greater influence, giving *shuanggui* far more coercive power than *shuangzhi* ever had.

This expansion of power reinforced the CCDI's dominance in anti-corruption investigations, eventually eclipsing the anti-corruption bureaus of the procuratorates (Liu, 2014b), the state agency responsible for anti-corruption investigations at the time. Some procuratorates, in order to extract confessions, even sought to "borrow" the *shuanggui* measure from the CDI, bypassing procedural safeguards and prolonging the detention of suspects in their custody (Liu, 2014b). This practice continued until the PRC Criminal Procedure Law was amended in 2012, granting the procuratorates the authority to impose "residential surveillance at a designated location" (RSDL), a measure functionally equivalent to *shuanggui*, in major corruption cases.[39]

It is important to note that *shuanggui*, as an investigative measure, was resource-intensive. Breaking down the psychological defense of a ranked official accustomed to privilege could take a long time. Throughout this process, the CDI needed to organize three shifts of guards per day, with two personnel per shift, to keep the detainee under twenty-four-hour surveillance (Xiao & Xiao, 2009). Intensive interrogations also required multiple teams of investigators. In addition, since CDIs did not have their own detention facilities, they had to rent space from hotels or other civil or commercial entities. To prevent leaks, CDIs would often rent entire floors or even entire blocks of a building, to ensure controlled access to the detainee. In complex cases, investigations could span several years and involve as many as a thousand agents, guards, handlers, and other support personnel (Xiao & Xiao, 2009).

Due to the immense coercive power of *shuanggui*, the Party's anti-corruption efforts were effective enough to drive corruption underground. Since the 1990s, corruption in China has increasingly relied on *guanxi*-based practices, as discussed in Chapters 2 and 3, involving increasingly complex and networked parochial transactions (Gong 1997, 2008c; Guo, 2008; Wedeman, 2005a).

Parochial corruption is inherently clandestine and notoriously difficult to detect, as it leaves no crime scene, fingerprints, or external witnesses

[39] The RSDL was first introduced into the PRC Criminal Procedure Law in 1996 as a supplementary measure for criminal suspects or defendants who had no fixed residence where residential surveillance or house arrest could be carried out. In 2012, the Criminal Procedure Law was amended to allow state criminal investigation authorities to apply RSDL in major corruption cases, regardless of whether the suspect or defendant had a fixed residence. See Article 73, Criminal Procedure Law (2012).

(Kwok, 2008), making it even more difficult to prove in court. In other jurisdictions, law enforcement agencies rely on covert investigative measures, such as wiretapping, secretive surveillance, informants, and sting operations, to gather evidence and build cases (OECD, 2010). The Party, however, maintains a standing ban on covert methods for intra-Party disciplinary investigations (Liu, 2014b), a stance rooted in deep-seated distrust and fear of abuse of such methods.

Mao Zedong was incensed to learn that his train had been secretly bugged by his assistant – ostensibly to record his formal conversations for documentation – resulting in his private conversations being captured without his knowledge during his travels (Su, 2008). Peng Zhen, head of the Central (Party) Political-Legal Committee (CPLC) in the 1950s and the early 1980s, openly opposed covert surveillance, warning: "Wiretapping will cause endless problems. … The technology now is very advanced. Wiretapping is very easy but we must not use it" (Liu, 2014b, p. 223–4). Peng argued that such measures should be reserved only for struggles against enemies, not for internal disputes. He cautioned that allowing technical investigative measures (wiretapping) within the Party would inevitably lead to paranoia, mutual suspicion, and the erosion of "cordial relations between comrades, intra-Party democracy, solidarity, and an open and lively political atmosphere" (Liu, 2014b, p.223–4).

This aversion to covert surveillance within the Party shaped the operational guidelines of "technical investigations." When the Investigative Technique Bureau (responsible for carrying out wiretapping) was established under the Ministry of Public Security (MPS) in 1955, its activities were governed by two principles. First, the Party maintained absolute control over any aspects of technical investigations, from policymaking to case by case application. Second, technical investigative methods were strictly prohibited in intra-Party disputes and reserved only for struggles against enemies (Procuratorate, 2010; Xie, 2002). In addition, an internal safeguard was later introduced for the use of technical methods in anti-corruption investigations. CDIs were not granted the resources and authority to conduct such measures, including wiretapping, which remained under the jurisdiction of the police.

Covert investigations, of course, have their own ethical concerns, requiring robust regulatory framework for oversight and governance. Nevertheless, they remain essential tools for corruption investigation and deterrence worldwide (Harfield, 2010). Recognizing this, China amended its Criminal Procedural Law in 2012 to authorize the use of "technical measures" in major corruption cases. However, as a district procuratorate president once mentioned these measures were primarily used for tracking suspects' locations to make arrests rather than gathering incriminating evidence (Cheng, 2011). According to another account, investigators could apply for permission to use wiretapping or other surveillance after an investigation is authorized; but the information obtained was mainly used to pressure suspects into confessing their crimes, rather than as admissible evidence in court (Luo, 2012).[40] The use of entrapment or sting operations remains virtually unheard of in China's anti-corruption investigations.

## Problems and Challenges

In 1992, the Party declared the fight against corruption its top priority. From that point on, corruption investigations became the central focus of CDI activities, and corruption – rather than political offenses – became the primary cause for Party disciplinary sanctions. In 2002, anti-corruption was introduced as an official mandate of the CDIs, enshrined in the Party Charter. Parallel to these developments in the Party's disciplinary system, the state also sought to strengthen its own institutions. By the turn of the century, China's state apparatus had expanded significantly compared to two decades earlier. One notable aspect of the state expansion was the rapid growth of the state legal system. With admirable advocacy from the legal professional community, substantial reforms were introduced to improve the quality of the criminal justice system, supported by the swift expansion of legal education and legal services.[41] At the same time, the development of the state legal system had also led to tensions with the Party's disciplinary system.

### *Legal Deficiency of Shuanggui*

One primary issue was the legality of *shuanggui*. As previously discussed, *shuanggui* was authorized by Party rules, not by state law. Legally, PRC laws derive their legitimacy from the sovereignty of the state, as they are

[40] The legal doctrine of "fruits of the poisonous tree," an evidentiary rule in many other legal systems, is widely discussed among legal practitioners and academics in China but is not recognized in current Chinese law or judicial practice.

[41] Already in 2003, the total number of law schools was 6.27 times higher than in 1989 and 48.62 times higher than in 1979. Source of data: Zhu (2007, p. 520).

promulgated by the National People's Congress (NPC) or its Standing Committee, bodies to which the people have conferred the exclusive authority to create laws, particularly those that impose restrictions on personal freedom. In contrast, the Party's normative rules lack such broad legitimacy as they are formulated by Party institutions elected only by Party members not the general public. The Party, therefore, has no constitutional authority to impose and enforce measures that restrict personal freedom through its internal regulations. According to the PRC Constitution, any such restrictive measures must be established through primary legislation passed by the NPC.

A second legal issue was that *shuanggui* disregarded the standard safeguards outlined in the PRC Criminal Procedural Law (2012), which limits the length of detention and grants suspects the right to legal counsel after their first interrogation, which must be carried out within twenty-four hours of detention. This law was violated routinely by the CDIs in their *shuanggui* practices.

The lack of legality for *shuanggui* also created evidentiary challenges in court. When a CDI completed an investigation and determined guilt, it would transfer the case, along with the evidence gathered, to the procuratorate for prosecution. However, under the PRC law, only evidence collected by legally mandated state law enforcement agencies is admissible in court. Since the CDI is not a state organ, evidence it gathered could not be used directly in criminal proceedings. To work around this issue, the procuratorate engaged in a process known as "*evidence conversion*," in which prosecutors would re-conduct interrogations and interviews, documenting the records on their own official stationery, thus converting the inadmissible evidence to the admissible. When this conversion process was not properly carried out, it often became grounds for legal challenges by the defense.

The disparity between the PRC criminal justice system and the use of *shuanggui* became more pronounced as the Party increasingly emphasized its commitment to governing according to the law. This creates a dilemma. On one hand, it became harder for the Party to ignore *shuanggui*'s illegality and its blatant violation of legal principles the Party had pledged to uphold. On the other hand, giving its long-standing resistance to covert investigative measures, the Party had no viable alternatives but to continue to rely on *shuanggui* – especially as corruption had become more hidden and embedded within close-knit personal networks.

### *Jurisdictional Frictions and Procedural Redundancy*

As previously discussed, the Party's normative system and the state legal system derive their legitimacy from different sources and operate within distinct scopes of authority. These differences gave rise to three jurisdictional challenges in anti-corruption investigations.

The first jurisdictional issue concerns officials who are not Party members. The Party's disciplinary system operates on the jurisdictional principle that Party members voluntarily submit themselves to the Party's disciplinary scrutiny upon joining the Party (Zhang, 2024). It follows that the Party has no inherent authority to exercise jurisdiction over public officials working in state organs who are not Party members. This issue was partially addressed in 1992 when the CCDI absorbed the MOS under the conjoined-offices mechanism, allowing the Party to extend its disciplinary reach beyond its members by invoking the MOS's administrative supervisory authority over all public officials in state organs, regardless of their Party membership.[42]

However, two significant problems remained unsolved. First, the administrative act that authorized the MOS to detain suspects under the *shuangzhi* measure clashed with the Legislation Law (2000). This Law, which holds superior legal authority, stipulates that any measure restricting citizens' personal freedom must be enacted in the form of a law (not an administrative act), passed by the National People's Congress, not by an administrative body. Second, the MOS's low administrative rank limited the scope of its enforcement power. In normative terms, this means that the MOS could not enforce its regulation against officials holding ministerial or higher ranks, regardless of their Party membership.[43]

The second jurisdictional problem involves bribers, corruption brokers, and other witnesses of corruption. In the power dynamics between bribe-takers and bribers, the latter group – often private

[42] According to Liu and Xiao, the conjoined-offices practice was introduced after Deng's historic 1992 Southern Tour. Its reintroduction aimed to strengthen disciplinary institutions and align their activities to ensure a smooth transition of the economic reform (Liu & Xiao, 2022, p. 76).

[43] In a separate study, I characterize the administrative ranking system (ARS) as a system that regulates power relations between various institutional and personal actors across key power fields, including courts. I further argue that in China, power – stratified by the ARS – relativizes law in the implementation, application, and enforcement of law. For more details on this "order of power" thesis, see Li (2023).

individuals outside the Party-state structure – lacks the prerogatives, entitlements, networks, and political influence enjoyed by the former group. As a result, they are more vulnerable to intimidation and coercion and more likely to cooperate with investigators. However, since these individuals are often neither Party members nor civil servants, the CDIs hold no mandate or competence to subject them to *shuanggui*. When the CDIs nonetheless detained such individuals, their action could be challenged on legal grounds for exceeding their competence.

The third jurisdictional issue concerns the anti-corruption investigative authority of the procuratorates. Since its reestablishment, procuratorates had been tasked with investigating "duty crimes," – offenses committed by public employees in the course of discharging their official duties, including corruption (Lű, 1992). Following the 1989 democratic movement, the Party strengthened the procuratorates' anti-corruption capacity by authorizing them to establish investigative bureaus specializing in anti-corruption investigations nationwide.[44] These bureaus held a high political and ranking status in the procuratorates and were often staffed with elite agents.[45]

Under the PRC law at the time, procuratorates were mandated to investigate all corruption-related crimes committed by public officials, including those with Party membership, this created a jurisdictional overlap with the CDIs, leading to conflicts. To mitigate these conflicts, procuratorates were required to inform and coordinate with the CDIs when investigating ranked Party officials. However, the extent to which this coordination was actually implemented varied from place to place.

The jurisdictional conflict was further complicated by the fact that, unlike the MOS, the procuratorates were not under CDI control. Instead, they operated within their own hierarchical system, with lower-level procuratorates answering to higher-level procuratorates. This created a parallel chain of command for anti-corruption investigations, separate from the CDI's vertical structure.

Having two institutions with different reporting lines conducting similar work not only led to jurisdictional conflicts but also resulted in procedural redundancy. As discussed earlier, under the PRC Criminal Procedure Law, any case investigated by a CDI and transferred to the procuratorate for prosecution had to be reinvestigated by the procuratorate. The procuratorate's investigation was not so much intended to

[44] Xiao (2009).
[45] Li (2022b).

scrutinize the CDI's work, as procuratorates were never in a position to refuse prosecuting a case transferred by the CDI. Rather, it was more of a legacy design flaw stemming from the fact that when the Criminal Procedure Law was originally drafted, no one had foreseen that the Party would later seek to reclaim coercive investigative power that had been relegated to state organs at the beginning of the reform era.[46]

### *Shortage of Enforcement Resources*

Extensive research on crime control has shown that while law enforcement campaigns can generate strong short-term deterrence (Manion, 2004a; Tanner, 1999, 2007; Trevaskes, 2003; Van Rooij, 2006), their long-term effectiveness diminishes once the mobilized investigative resources are demobilized afterwards. When enforcement resources are demobilized, the chance of detection drops and the targeted offense rebounds.[47]

Corruption investigation is also sensitive to the change of enforcement inputs as it requires substantial enforcement resources, especially manpower. As explained earlier, high-profile investigations could involve hundreds of personnel and span anywhere between six months to several years. Meanwhile, the CCDI alone is responsible for monitoring more than 4,000 senior officials and conducting investigations when offenses are reported.

To address its personnel shortage, the CDIs relied heavily on "loaning" agents from other institutions, particularly the procuratorates (Liu, 2018). While it is common for Party organs or special task forces to temporarily loan staff from other institutions, few had depended on this practice as extensively as the CDIs. In some regions, loaned personnel even outnumbered permanent CDI staff (Lai et al., 2020). This reliance on loaned personnel created several problems (CCDI, 2018; Lai et al., 2020; Qiang & Haotian, 2022; Shu & Liu, 2022).

First, the number of loaned personnel remained insufficient to meet the demands of intensified anti-corruption tasks. Second, since these loaned personnel continued receiving their salaries and routine

[46] When the PRC Criminal Law and Criminal Procedure Law were enacted in 1979, the Party Center issued an instruction prohibiting any institution or individual, other than the police, procuratorates, and courts, from applying lawful coercive measures. For more details, see Center (1979).

[47] Manion (2004b, pp. 155–200) and Wedeman (2005a, pp. 93–116).

political oversight from their home institutions, their loyalty was often divided and their conduct was less strictly regulated. Consequently, loaned personnel were found to be more prone to disciplinary violations, particularly in the leaking of investigative secrets. Third, loaned personnel lacked motivation because their contribution to CDI investigations were not always recognized or credited by their home institutions. Lastly, the CDI missed out on opportunities for on-the-job training and institutional capacity-building when a considerable portion of its investigative workforce remained temporary.

### *Incentive Issues*

Under the "dual-leadership" model explained in an earlier section of this chapter, disciplinary affairs were still largely considered local affairs of territorial Party Committees, unless top-down interventions were warranted in individual cases. A territorial Party Committee was responsible for routinely monitoring conduct of officials it had appointed and for imposing disciplinary sanctions when violations were detected. To assist this function, the Party Center also granted territorial Party Committees the power to appoint the leaders of their corresponding CDIs and oversee their work. These arrangements created a fundamental problem: local territorial Party Committee leaders had little incentive to expose and investigate disciplinary violations committed by the very officials they had appointed.

In addition, local Party leaders often treated corruption as a low priority, preferring to exercise their discretion to shield offenders with lenient punishments rather than handing them over for prosecution (Manion, 2004b, p. 153). At the ground level, CDI agents also displayed reluctance to pursue aggressive investigations, a mindset the Party referred to as "nice-guyism (*haoren zhuyi*)," Many CDI agents hesitated to act against colleagues with whom they worked in the same office building, attended the same conferences, collaborated on various tasks, and shared the same social network. Anti-corruption activities were revitalized only during disruptions to local patronage networks – particularly when power shifted between leaders backed by rival patrons in the Party Center. In such cases, anti-corruption activities at the provincial level could increase by up to 20 percent annually (Zhu & Zhang, 2016).

Equally problematic was the fact that CDI agents themselves were not immune to corruption. Before 2012, occasional accusations of CDI corruption surfaced on social media, often brought forward by individuals who claimed to have been wrongfully accused or unfairly targeted. Few of these accusations were formally investigated, and when they were, the findings were rarely disclosed to the public. It was only during a "house-cleaning" campaign launched by the CCDI in 2016 that the extent of the problem became known. This revelation, however, was unsurprising – CDI agents wielded nearly unchecked power, answerable only to their superiors, making them just as susceptible to corruption as the officials they were tasked with monitoring and investigating.

For example, Shen Jia, a divisional head of the provincial CDI in Inner Mongolia, accepted ninety-seven bribes from forty-five individuals in exchange for favoritism in case investigations. Similarly, CCDI agents, who oversaw more than 4,000 Party elites, had access to even more lucrative corruption opportunities. One case involved Wei Jian, a CCDI divisional head, who was once approached by a businessman seeking governmental approval for a development project in Sichuan. Wei leveraged his position to seek a favor, on behalf of the businessman, from Li Chuncheng, then vice Party-secretary of Sichuan, a province under Wei's watch. Li Chuncheng obliged, and in return, Wei Jian received a 10-million-*yuan* bribe from the businessman.[48]

### *Abuse of Shuanggui*

Although torture was officially banned at any stage of an anti-corruption investigation, reports of abuse during *shuanggui* were not uncommon (Sapio, 2008. p 16–20). In extreme cases, mistreatment even led to wrongful death (Sapio, 2008 p. 20). Even in the absence of physical abuse, the coercive effects of prolonged solitary confinement and psychological pressure were so severe that *shuanggui* became the most "productive" method for extracting confessions and intelligence, whether truthful or not, about corruption (CCDI, 1998; Wei, 2001).

Despite the amendment of the Criminal Procedural Law in 1996, which limited the length of detention during preliminary criminal investigation to twelve hours, effectively rendering *shuanggui* a Party-sponsored illegal practice, the Party continued to permit CDI agents to use it.

[48] These cases were reported in the CCDI-produced anti-corruption docuseries (Zhong, 2017).

At the same time, the Party also sought to tighten internal oversight and implement measures to protect detainees' physical safety. In 2000, the CCDI introduced the Provisional Rules on the Application of *Shuanggui* (*Shuanggui* Rules), which established two conditions for authorizing *shuanggui*. The first was the severity of the offense, meaning that *shuanggui* could only be used in cases warranting disciplinary sanctions. The second was the presence of a risk of obstruction of justice, such as concealing or destroying evidence or suborning witnesses. In 2005, the CCDI banned CDI agents below the county level from using *shuanggui* and introduced additional checks to shorten its duration (2005).

Despite these regulatory measures, reports of abuses continued to surface. While physical torture had significantly declined, it was often replaced with "soft" torture, such as placing suspects under constant twenty-four-hour surveillance in solitary confinement, stripping them of all privacy, subjecting them to sleep deprivation, prolonged stress positions and repetitive interrogations, and denying them any communication with the outside world, let alone access to legal counsel (Sapio, 2008, p. 18–20). Moreover, investigators frequently ignored the duration restrictions set by the revised *Shuanggui* Rules.

The secrecy and arbitrariness surrounding the use of *shuanggui* frustrated even Party officials. For example, during a group discussion session of the annual congregation of the Chinese People's Political Consultative Conference in 2009, Sun Yongfu, former Vice Minister of Railways, openly questioned the disappearance of his fellow vice-minister He Hongda, who had been missing for almost two years. Sun remarked, "One day, He Hongda was summoned by the CCDI, and after that, he simply disappeared. Nobody was informed about what was happening. Then we learned that he was placed under *shuanggui*, nothing more. After a while, we were told that the case had been transferred to the (state) justice system, but only a handful of ministry leaders were aware of this. If a vice-minister appointed by the Party Center has been forced to remain absent from work for more than a year, aren't we entitled to some explanation?" (Huanqiu, 2009).

## Conclusion

The historical development of the Party's disciplinary system has been nonlinear. During the revolutionary era, Party discipline was treated as just another aspect of Party affairs, enforced by the same decision-making bodies that handled all other Party matters. It was only after the Party came to power in 1949 that a specialized central disciplinary institution, the CCDI was created. However, in its incipient years, the CCDI's political standing remained weak, its mandate unclear and its operation obscure until it was replaced by the CSC in 1955. Deng Xiaoping was instrumental in creating the CSC. The institutional framework Deng established in 1955–1956 led to a decade of rapid growth of the Party's disciplinary system, which was ultimately dismantled during the Cultural Revolution.

A full-scale institutional rebuilding of the Party's disciplinary system began in 1982, following the CCDI's resurrection in 1978. This rebuilding process can be divided into two main parts. The first concerned the power structure of the disciplinary institutions. Under the new regime, the system was structured around three key principles. First, the CCDI was designated as an elected body, elevating its political status above all other Party functional apparatus and justifying its prerogatives. Second, the CCDI was placed under the direct command of the Central Committee, upholding the unified (absolute) command of the Party Center. Third, at the subnational levels, CDIs operated under the "dual-leadership" model, and answered to both the corresponding territorial Party Committee and the CDI at the higher level. These arrangements made the disciplinary institutions the most integrated power substructure within the Party and prepared them for their growing role in the Party's intensified anti-corruption efforts in the 1990s.

The second part of the institutional rebuilding process centered on developing a normative system to regulate and standardize disciplinary activities. This system had three main features. First, it delegated considerable disciplinary power from the plenipotentiary territorial Party Committees to the specialized disciplinary institutions while reserving close top-down oversight. The delegation and oversight were balanced through a finely stratified scheme based on two factors: the administrative rank of the official involved and the severity of the offense. Second, the system introduced a three-tier interlocking decision-making structure, through which the authorities to make, approve, and veto disciplinary decisions were shared among three authorities: the investigating CDI, the corresponding territorial Party Committee, and the superior CDI. Third, the normative system segmented the disciplinary investigative process into three stages, with each stage providing opportunities for Party leaders to steer, adjust, or alter the course of an investigation, thereby shaping the final disciplinary outcome.

This normative framework enabled the Party to delegate considerable investigative power to the CDIs, fueling its increasingly intensified anti-corruption efforts, while simultaneously maintaining strict oversight over the disciplinary decision-making process. In doing so, the system ensured that the disciplinary power structure remained fully aligned with the UCOPC principle, strengthening the Party Center's top-down control during the crisis of rampant corruption.

Throughout the 1990s and the 2000s, the CCDI experienced a rapid expansion of power, thanks to the authorization of the *shuanggui* measure. However, this expansion also gave rise to several challenges, including questions about the legality of the Party's disciplinary power, jurisdictional frictions, procedural redundancies, resource shortages, incentive issues among CDI agents, and abuse of *shuanggui*. These developments set the stage for Xi Jinping's unprecedented anti-corruption campaign from 2012 to 2017 and the sweeping disciplinary reforms that followed – both of which took political observers around the world by surprise.

# 6

# Post-2012 Anti-corruption Playbook

The year 2012 was a turning point in Chinese politics, a prelude to an era few could have predicted. In that year, Xi Jinping assumed leadership of the Party at the 18th Party Congress. At the time, many analysts – including some of the best-informed observers – viewed Xi as a political lightweight due to his weak power base and unimpressive performance record. Some predicted that he would be forced into more power sharing and collective decision-making at the top of the Party (Li, 2012a, p. 609; Yaita, 2012; Yuan, 2012) and that his tenure would likely be transient rather than transformational (Callahan, 2012).

The predictions could not have been more wrong. Over the next decade, Xi not only elevated himself from a political underdog to a paramount leader – eclipsing all his immediate predecessors – but also transformed the political landscape in China in ways that few had foreseen. By 2022, he had secured a third term as the leader of the Party with absolute dominance over the Politburo Standing Committee, a feat rarely achieved in PRC history. The question then is: How did he manage to accumulate such immense power so quickly, despite his initially weak political capital, in a highly contested political environment such as the Politburo?

On the surface, the answer seems obvious – his sweeping and fearsome anti-corruption campaign, launched immediately after taking office in 2012. Over the next five years, the campaign brought down 66,000 Party officials at county-rank or above, including 43 members or alternate members of the Central Committee and a former member of the Politburo Standing Committee (XinhuaNet, 2017b). It also led to the expulsion of sixty-three generals, including two vice-chairmen and two regular members of the Central Military Committee. Thereafter, Xi could command the Party with no rivals left capable of challenging him.

Yet, one fundamental question remains unexamined: What made Xi's anti-corruption campaign more forceful than those of his predecessors? Anti-corruption was neither a new political platform nor a magical wand that only Xi had access to or had the acumen to wield. Scholars studying previous anti-corruption campaigns noted that these campaigns typically lacked long-term deterrence and sanction credibility due to structural flaws such as selective enforcement and the lack of independent anti-corruption agencies (Chan, 2008; Gong, 2008a; Gong & Ren, 2012; Ma, 2008; Manion, 2004b). So, what set Xi's campaign apart?

In this chapter, I aim to answer this question by analyzing Xi's key anti-corruption strategies, including his signature anti-corruption campaign in 2012–2017 and the subsequent disciplinary/supervision institutional reforms that followed.

## Command and Control

As with military campaigns, the quality of command and control is vital to the success of an anti-corruption campaign. Given the top-down command structure of the Party-state, the most decisive factor that affects the scale and impact of such a campaign is the rank of its commanding authority. This is because, as already discussed in previous chapters, an enforcement agency within the Party-state can only command compliance from those of lower rank (Li, 2023). In other words, the rank of the campaign's leadership determines how widely it will be enforced – the higher the rank, the broader the scope, and the stronger the impact.

Many mistakenly believe that the Central Committee of Discipline and Inspection (CCDI) is the Party-state's highest anti-corruption agency, with exclusive responsibility for all disciplinary decisions related to corruption. This is a misconception for two key reasons.

First, the CCDI is neither independent nor autonomous, despite its special elective status and the fact that its head holds a seat on the Politburo Standing Committee. Rather, the CCDI is a second-tier body under the Central Committee. It means that it has no authority to impose disciplinary measures on other institutions or their leaders of the same or higher rank. Second, while the CCDI is mandated to police Party discipline, significant disciplinary decision-making power is reserved for the Party Center. These include determining whether to launch an investigation, whether to subject a suspect to *shuanggui*, and whether to conclude an investigation with a light sanction or proceed with criminal prosecution. The higher the rank of the suspect, the more power is retained by the Party Center (see more details in Chapter 5).

As later sections of this chapter will show, several critical components of Xi's anti-corruption campaign – most notably, the austerity drive enforcing the Eight Measures (*ba xiang gui ding*) – were commandeered by the Politburo instead of the Central Committee. Politburo authorization gave the drive more force than any preceding ones, compelling Party organizations at all levels to prioritize the drive. It also strengthened the power of the CCDI and its lower counterparts, allowing them to mobilize resources more effectively and coordinate enforcement efforts more efficiently across relevant agencies.

Effective command and control also depends on a deep level of trust between the commander and the enforcer – trust that enables effective communication, seamless coordination and precise execution. The head of the CCDI, as the central authority in charge of enforcing the campaign, played a pivotal role in this equation. For Xi's campaign to succeed, he needed a CCDI leader who could interpret and execute his intentions with precision, maintain direct and effective communication with him, align enforcement strategies with his broader political vision, command the support of other agencies and authorities, and mobilize CCDI agents while countering any bureaucratic inertia and resistance from within. More critically, the CCDI leader had to enjoy Xi's full trust and sufficient autonomy to make swift decisions that would magnify the impact of the campaign.

At the 18th Party Congress, to the surprise of many, Wang Qishan – a Party leader known for his deep political connections and exceptional administrative skills – was selected as head of the CCDI. Many had expected Wang to become the first vice-premier, a role that seemed better suited to his expertise. However, it was later revealed that Wang and Xi shared a long-standing relationship dating back to the 1960s, when both spent time in Shaanxi as "sent down youth." In hindsight, Wang's appointment in 2012 was both deliberate and fateful. Over the next five years, he would prove to be a masterful political operator with an exceptional ability to execute Xi's will. The synergy between them – built on mutual trust, shared objectives, and Wang's political acumen – was indispensable to the success of the campaign. Yet, at the time, few observers would have foreseen the far-reaching consequences of Wang's appointment or the ramifications of the formidable alliance he and Xi would forge.

## Two Phases

Xi's anti-corruption campaign can be divided into two distinct phases, both conceptually and chronologically. Phase I was what I call a shock-and-awe phase that ran through his first term (2012–2017). It is a textbook example of what criminal policy scholars refer to as "enforcement swamping." According to Mark Kleiman, enforcement swamping improves crime control by strategically deploying limited enforcement resources (Kleiman, 2005): Instead of spreading resources thinly, enforcement agencies should focus their enforcement resources on specific offenses and offenders at targeted times and places. At the same time, they should directly communicate enforcement threats to potential offenders, heightening their perception of chance of crime detection. When implemented effectively, this strategy pushes a high-violation equilibrium into a low one with minimized costs. Once crime rates drop to a low equilibrium, routine enforcement can take over, allowing the redeployment of resources to other priorities (Kleiman, 2005; Kleiman & Kilmer, 2009).

Xi's shock-and-awe phase in 2012–2017 had three components, each targeting different types of misconduct and different groups of Party members concurrently: an austerity drive targeting minor infractions, an anti-corruption crackdown targeting major corruption crimes, and a propaganda drive shaping public perception of these enforcement efforts. Together, these efforts created a shock-and-awe effect, raising the perceived risk and costs of corruption while also allowing Xi to establish dominance over the Politburo by the end of his first term.

By 2017, the campaign had generated palpable deterrence. The fear of corruption investigations became so intense that many officials chose to "lie flat" ("*tangping*"), procrastinating, delaying work, or outright stalling government projects to avoid scrutiny. However, as discussed earlier, deterrence from high-intensity enforcement campaigns is usually short-lived. The moment when mobilized enforcement resources are withdrawn, compliance can quickly erode. Party-led anti-corruption campaigns are particularly problematic in this regard, because the Party's interference in these campaigns disrupts routine law enforcement, weakens the state legal system, and undermines the credibility of the justice system that the Party claims to uphold (Manion, 2004b).

Yet, as even skeptical critics acknowledge, Xi's campaign was different from previous ones and had to be "taken seriously" (Manion, 2016). First, it lasted not for months but for years – so uncharacteristically long that it challenges the very definition of a "campaign" – and operated with an unprecedented level of intensity, ensnaring more officials than the campaigns of the previous two decades combined. Second, and more significantly, the campaigns did not stop after the shock-and-awe. Rather, as

Phase I drew to a close, Xi seized the opportunity created by the political disruption and moved swiftly to Phase II.

Phase II of Xi's anti-corruption campaign focused on consolidating the gains of Phase I through a package of far-reaching structural reforms. These reforms sought to reshape not only the legal framework of anti-corruption enforcement but also the constitutional landscape of the Party-state itself. In addition, during Phase II, the Party also institutionalized aspects of its disciplinary system to reinforce centralized control. Some measures aimed to reduce information asymmetry between the Party Center and its functionaries and units, strengthening the unified (absolute) command of the Party Center (UCOPC). Others were introduced to rein in the CCDI, retracting certain disciplinary power that had been previously delegated to it.

In the rest of the chapter, I will explore in greater detail the key components of both phases of this sweeping anti-corruption campaign.

## Austerity Campaign

The 2012–2017 austerity drive aimed to curb unproductive official activities, control overspending of public funds, and eliminate waste of public resources (Zhu et al., 2017). Specific infractions targeted by the drive included personal expenses charged to public accounts, using government vehicles for private purposes, and overseas vacations disguised as official visits, and so on. The Party had issued numerous bans against these activities before. These efforts were often popular among the public but resented by officials and civil servants, who faced cuts to bonuses and benefits. The resentment grew in proportion to the drive's rigidity once it reached a tipping point, resistance could derail the drive and even stall the career advancement of the campaign's organizer.[1] As a result, past austerity drives were typically short-lived, symbolic, and noncommittal. Their deterrence was often limited and temporary, with targeted behaviors quickly rebounding once enforcement subsided.

[1] For example, the ambitious anti-spiritual-pollution campaign initiated by Deng Liqun in 1983 was so unpopular in the Party that it was aborted after just four weeks due to internal opposition. See Shi and Shi (2017) and Su (2007). If not well handled, austerity drives could halt the political career of its organizer. One such instance occurred in the 1980s when an attempt to revoke the practice of supplying special goods to Party leaders sparked significant backlash against Wang Zhaoguo, who had introduced this initiative. See Lianhe (2016).

Another key feature of previous austerity drives was that they were typically ordered by the General Office of the Party Center, and, as such, did not apply to top-ranking officials such as Politburo members. Xi's austerity drive was, however, different. On December 4, 2012, just two weeks after taking office as the General Party-Secretary, Xi oversaw the issuance of Eight Measures (*baxiang guiding*) by the Politburo.[2] The Eight Measures imposed concrete restrictions on official conduct, such as the duration and venue of governmental conferences, and introduced budgetary constraints on eight categories of public expenses, including business meals, office space and government vehicles, and travel expenses.[3] Unlike previous austerity drives, it required Politburo members to take the lead in observing these austerity measures, setting an example for the rest of the Party. While it is doubtful that these budgetary constraints meaningfully impacted the quality of life of Politburo members, their symbolic value was immense – a clear signal that the Party "means business" in enforcing the austerity drive (CCDI, 2016). Within two months, provincial and regional authorities had rolled out detailed implementation plans, many of which were more stringent than the Politburo's original resolution.[4]

To enforce the campaign, the Committees of Discipline and Inspection at subnational levels (CDIs) deployed patrol teams. Unlike major corruption infractions, such as bribery – which are hidden from the public view and difficult to detect and prove – infractions targeted by the Eight Measures were easily observable and highly visible. Some CDI agents would stake out popular restaurants during lunch and dinner hours,

[2] It was taught in Party training programs that one must distinguish the difference between "Eight Measures" and the "spirit" of Eight Measures". The former was issued by the Politburo and applies only to Politburo members. Ordinary Party members are not eligible to be punished according to the Politburo "Eight Measures". Instead, their ground for sanction is based on the "spirit" of the Eight Measures. See Cheng (2019) and Court (2023). For more on the rank-based order of power and how it relativizes the legal order, see Li (2023).

[3] To be more specific, the Eight Measures address the following: (1) logistic arrangements for field visits of Party leaders, (2) productivity and logistic arrangements of work conferences, (3) efficiency in drafting and issuing official documents, (4) logistic arrangements for overseas diplomatic visits of Party leaders, (5) security protocols for official visits, particularly regarding motorcades and traffic control in response to public disturbances, (6) mandatory media coverage of official activities of Party leaders, (7) regulations on publishing Party leaders' manuscripts, public speeches, and the exhibition of their scripts and autographs, and (8) dispensation of perks, benefits, and privileges drawn from public funds. See Politburo (2012).

[4] See CCTV (2013).

**Figure 6.1** Enforcement of Eight-Measures violations (2012–2017).
Source of data: The original data of all figures presented in this article came from the annual work reports of the CCDI between 2002 and 2017, accessed May 5 2017 www.ccdi.gov.cn/.

watching for officials who arrived in government cars or consumed alcohol at public expense. Others conducted unannounced visits to randomly selected offices, catching public employees playing card games or sleeping during office hours. To expand enforcement efforts, inspection teams opened hotlines, created special webpages, and invited citizens to report violations. Reports were taken seriously. Verified infractions were publicly exposed and denounced in the mass media. In 2013, the first year of the campaign, the CDIs investigated over 30,000 instances of Eight Measures violations nationwide, resulting in sanctions for 7,600 officials. As shown in Figure 6.1, enforcement activities doubled the following year and remained at a high level of intensity throughout the campaign.

The austerity drive had undeniably transformed official conduct. "Hedonistic" and extravagant behaviors among public officials were curbed and driven underground, while civil servants became more accessible and responsive, leading to improved public services. However, the austerity drive was never the ultimate goal but only a "point of entry" and a "mobilizing order" (Xi, 2013a) for the purge of major corruption infractions that will be discussed next.

## Crackdown on Major Corruption Infractions

On December 5, 2012, just one month after Xi assumed leadership of the Party, Li Chuncheng – the Party-Secretary of Chengdu, capital of Sichuan, and an alternate member of the Central Committee – became the first "tiger" (high-ranking Party officials) to fall in the 2012–2017 anti-corruption campaign. By the end of Xi's first term, the number of senior officials disciplined for major corruption infractions would reach 440, including 1 retired member of the Politburo Standing Committee, 3 Politburo members, and 17 full Central Committee members. Almost all of them were ultimately convicted and sentenced to long prison terms.

However, what made this campaign exceptional was not just the sheer number of "tigers" and "flies" targeted but also the unconventional enforcement methods that ensured its success. Normally, a large-scale crackdown would require significant expansions in enforcement resources, such as new investigative powers and/or an increase in manpower. Yet, throughout the campaign, there were no substantial changes to the anti-corruption legal framework or to the allocation of investigative resources until its conclusion. Instead, the campaign's effectiveness stemmed from a series of organizational maneuvers, closely aligning with Kleiman's "enforcement swamp" theory discussed earlier (Kleiman, 2005). Among these maneuvers, four are most notable.

The first is a partial amnesty for past corruption offenses. In 2014, the CCDI announced an ultimatum: the campaign would first target those who refused to exercise restraint and continued engaging in corrupt conduct after Xi's assumption of office at the 18th Party Congress in 2012 (Ye, 2016). The amnesty was partial because it did not absolve earlier corruption but served as a selective criterion for investigations. For example, if an official was caught committing corruption after the 18th Party Congress, there was no promise that their corrupt activities before 2012 would be pardoned or overlooked. This partial amnesty narrowed enforcement targets, prioritized recent violations committed after the ultimatum, and maximized the credibility of the ultimatum, thereby reducing resistance.

The second measure was reducing CDI mandates to focus solely on disciplinary enforcement. Before the campaign, many CDIs were overextended, with some participating in more than 100 regulatory committees and task forces, such as public safety inspection, pollution monitoring and reduction, and so on, few of which were related to their core mission.[5]

[5] See Kong (2015).

In 2013, the CCDI led a "mandate-slimming" reform, withdrawing from 111 out of 125 oversight bodies.[6] Lower-level CDIs followed suit, freeing up resources that were redirected toward two new divisions focused exclusively on disciplinary monitoring and investigations.[7]

The third measure was the energized effort to enforce the internal asset disclosure rules. Asset disclosure is a widely used anti-corruption tool requiring holders of public offices to report their wealth before assuming office. The Party first introduced internal asset disclosure rules in 1995, initially requiring Party leaders with supervisory functions to report their salaries, bonuses, honoraria, and income from direct investments (Center, 1995). Over time (Center, 1995, 2010, 2016), the scope expanded to include bank savings, financial assets, real estate holdings, marital status, and the residences of immediate family members, and so on. By 2012, the rules were applied to all officials of the deputy county/divisional (*fu xian/chu*) rank and above.

Despite these expansions, the effect of the disclosure rules was largely symbolic before 2012 because they were not strictly implemented, and even when implemented, the declared information was rarely scrutinized. That changed in 2014, when the Central Organization Department launched a nationwide campaign to verify the accuracy of asset disclosures (COD, 2014). If false disclosure was discovered, it could be used as grounds for initiating a full anti-corruption investigation. Compared to bribery – a clandestine practice that is difficult to detect and prove – false asset declarations are easier to identify, thanks to advances in digital financial tracking, e-banking, e-commerce and e-governance (Center & Council, 2015; Li & Wang, 2004).

The final and perhaps most significant measure was the invigoration of the Central Inspection Teams (CITs). Unlike routine CDI monitoring, CIT inspections could be launched without a formal report of disciplinary violations. The inspection teams had broad powers to interview personnel, review internal documents and records and assess compliance with prioritized Party policies and discipline. Their main function was to reduce information asymmetry between Party leaders at the top and the vast network of Party units spread across different functionaries and regions (Zhou, 2014).

Like the asset disclosure rules, the CITs were not new. The earliest known practice dates back to the 1920s (Wu, 2013b), but more

[6] See CCDI (2014a).

[7] See CCDI (2014a).

institutionalized inspection practices only began after 1989 (Zhou, 2014). The first permanent Central Inspection Office was established in 2003, and a central directive authorizing regular inspections followed in 2009. However, the impact of earlier CITs was barely noticeable. Their inefficacy stemmed from multiple factors, the most significant being institutional capture.[8] Many local governments sought to distract inspectors with lavish entertainment, extravagant banquets, sightseeing tours, and gifts. Meanwhile, inspectors often complained about their lack of clear directives and an overwhelming workload, as they were expected to scrutinize too many institutions, too many officials, and too many documents within a limited time frame.[9]

The 2012–2017 anti-corruption campaign took several measures to rectify these issues. The first was to reduce capture by ensuring that CIT leaders would be appointed for one tour at a time, preventing long-term collusion between the inspectors and the institutions inspected. In addition, the logistics of the inspection tours were centrally arranged and provided for rather than by the institutions under inspection, eliminating opportunities for undue influence. To improve efficiency, the Party clarified that the inspection would focus on the performance of the leadership within an institution (Center, 2017). Each team was given specific instructions regarding their tasks for each tour.[10]

Lastly, to enhance their authority and compel compliance,[11] a significant proportion of the CIT team leaders were drawn from experienced senior Party officials who had previously held ministerial-rank positions. Operating under direct oversight from the Party Center, CITs became a powerful tool for gathering information on negligence, noncompliance, and disciplinary violations of Party leaders at all levels below the Politburo Standing Committee.[12] By 2014, 121 regional and local inspection offices were established nationwide (Zhou, 2014) and CIT inspections were formally incorporated into the Party Charter.

[8] See CCDI (2015a).
[9] See CCDI (2015a).
[10] See CCDI (2013b, 2015a).
[11] See CCDI (2017a).
[12] For instance, the Party-groups of the National People's Congress, the Chinese People's Political Consultative Conference, and the State Council – headed by members of the Politburo Standing Committees – are not subject to CIT inspections. These Party-groups should not be confused with *jiguan dangzu or dangwei*, which are grassroots Party organizations installed in these organs. The latter have a lower ranking and are subject to CIT inspections.

By the end of Xi's first term, 53 CITs had been assembled and dispatched by the Party Center, conducting 12 tours that inspected 277 Party committees and Party-groups directly monitored by the Party Center. These included all provincial-level territorial Party Committees, centrally supervised state-owned-enterprises (SOEs), central financial institutions, and centrally supervised higher education institutions. More significantly, the CITs were sent to powerful central Party apparatuses that had previously been insulated from such oversight, including the COD, the Central Propaganda Department (CPD), the General Office of the Central Committee, and the Central Committee of the Communist Youth League. State institutions that were previously exempt from inspections due to their autonomous constitutional status, such as the Supreme People's Court (SPC) and the Supreme People's Procuratorate (SPP), were also placed under CIT inspection. By 2017, the Party declared that CIT tours had eliminated any blind spot, achieving full oversight coverage across the Party-state.[13]

Revamped and rejuvenated, the CITs became the spearhead of the 2012–2017 anti-corruption campaign. While they were not authorized to conduct individual investigations, their comprehensive and intrusive inspecting power allowed them to generate valuable leads on disciplinary infractions among regional and ministerial Party leaders. According to the CCDI, the CITs were responsible for 60 percent of the leads that resulted in major infraction investigations by the CCDI.

The shock-and-awe effect of the 2012–2017 anti-corruption campaign was undeniable. The number of high-ranking officials punished for corruption in this campaign exceeded that of all similar campaigns launched by Xi's predecessors in the past two decades combined (Figures 6.2–6.4).

In the meantime, anti-corruption campaigns were also launched at the local level, targeting swarms of "flies," – a metaphorical reference to low-ranking corrupt officials. As Figure 6.4 shows, the total number of officials receiving disciplinary sanctions remained relatively stable before 2012, fluctuating between 0.5 and 0.85 million. However, between 2012 and 2017, these numbers surged, nearly doubling the previous peak recorded in 1997–2002. At the height of the campaign in 2014, Shanxi province alone saw 15,450 officials convicted of corruption, with nearly half of its provincial Party leadership arrested (CCDI, 2014c; XinhuaNet, 2015).

13 See CCDI (2017a).

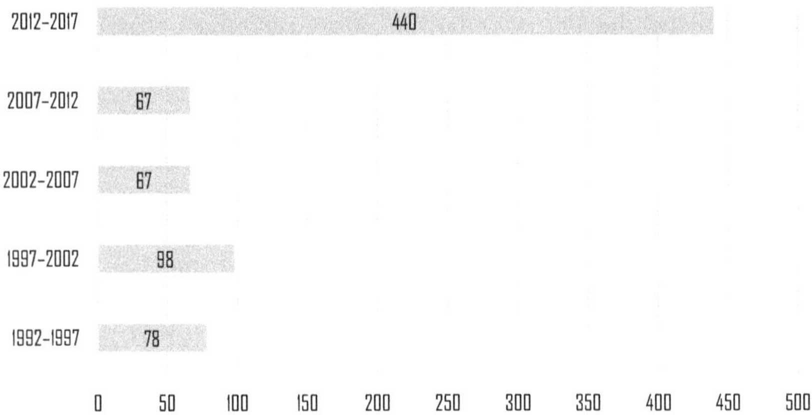


**Figure 6.2** Number of disciplined centrally managed cadres.
*Source*: CCDI Annual Work Reports (1992–2017)

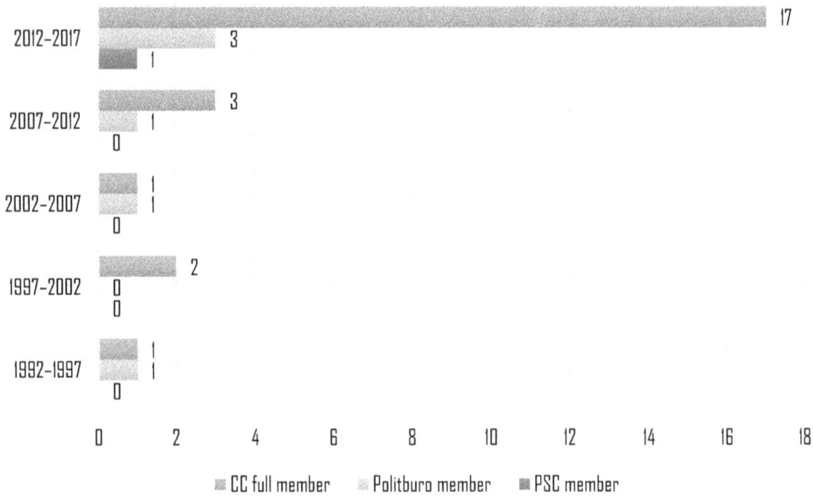


**Figure 6.3** Number of disciplined "giant tigers" (1992–2017).

Another major front of Xi's anti-corruption campaign was the CCDI's house cleaning. Since its reestablishment in 1982, the CCDI had long escaped scrutiny despite complaints of corruption within its own ranks. In 2016, the CCDI launched a campaign to eliminate "blind-spots (*deng xia hei*)" and root out "internal spies (*neigui*)," – agents who leaked

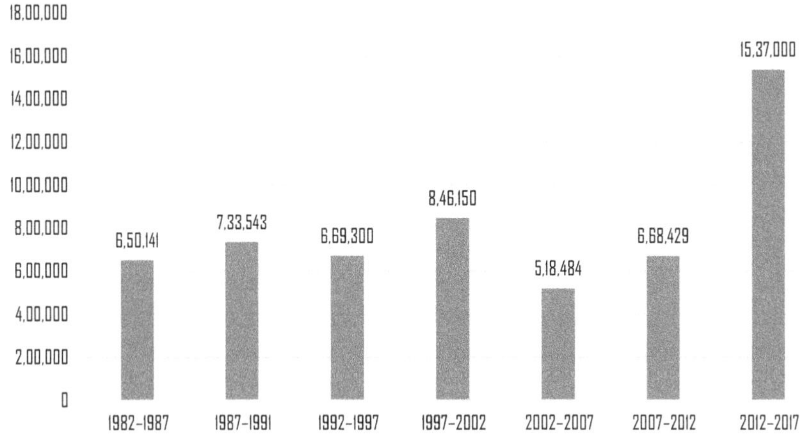


**Figure 6.4** Number of persons who received Party disciplinary sanctions (1982–2017).

investigative information to suspects for bribes or other benefits. As a result, more than 7,200 CDI agents nationwide were punished, including 38 within the CCDI itself. Among them were several divisional leaders of deputy ministerial rank (Wang, 2016).

The shock-and-awe effect of the anti-corruption campaign sent officials into a state of nationwide paranoia. Fearful of attracting attention, many began to forgo privileges they once took for granted (Keliher & Wu, 2016). This cautionary sentiment coincided with a sharp downturn in the global luxury industry (Nitschka, 2018). Over the previous decade, Chinese patrons had fueled rapid growth in the sector, with gifts to Chinese government officials accounting for nearly 50 percent of all luxury sales in China, according to industry experts (Osnos, 2013). However, following the launch of the campaign in 2012, officials would no longer be certain which bribes were safe to accept (Keliher & Wu, 2016), while would-be bribers found themselves uncertain about whom to bribe (Osnos, 2013). The growth rate of China's luxury industry dropped from 11 percent in 2011 to 7 percent in 2012, and further down to 2 percent in 2013 (Ranasinghe, 2014), continuing its decline throughout the campaign (Yoon, 2022).

## Propaganda Drives

Propaganda drives were another key component of the 2012–2017 anti-corruption campaign, designed to control the narrative surrounding corruption and the Party's anti-corruption efforts. These drives operated on two fronts. First, they involve heightened censorship of information originating from unauthorized sources, including accounts from witnesses and victims of corruption. Second, they sought to shape public perception through the strategic dissemination of information curated by anti-corruption authorities. At the onset of the campaign, courts stopped publishing judgments in corruption cases involving mid- and high-ranking officials. None of the rulings against "tigers" were made available to the public. In contrast, state media outlets produced and disseminated a vast amount of sanitized content, ensuring that only officially sanctioned narratives reached the public. By 2012, this tightly controlled, abridged reporting had become virtually the only source of information on high-profile corruption cases in the country.

In early 2013, as the anti-corruption campaign gained momentum, the CCDI was authorized to produce and distribute corruption-related information directly through its own propaganda department, allowing it to bypass the gatekeeping of the Central Propaganda Department, avoiding delays or inaction caused by intricate interdepartmental politics. The newly established CCDI Propaganda Department was headed by Xiao Pei, a former editor-in-chief at major national newspapers, who brought extensive experience in media strategy.

Xiao's first major initiative aimed to "demystify" the CCDI. In September 2013, the CCDI and the Ministry of Supervision (MOS) jointly launched www.ccdi.gov.cn, a website providing official information on anti-corruption policies, disciplinary announcements, procedural guidelines, and educational materials, including a special column featuring confessions from corrupt officials.[14] On January 1, 2015, the CCDI became the first central Party organ to adopt a modern, user-friendly website layout with daily content updates, switching to a sans-serif design for improved readability.[15] A year later, the CCDI/MOS was, once again, the first among central Party organs to launch an official WeChat (China's dominant messaging, social media and payment app) account and a mobile app. With exclusive access to breaking news on anti-corruption investigations, the CCDI website attracted over one million daily visits, marking it China's most-visited government website in 2014.[16] This "demystification initiative" heightened

[14] See Wu (2015b).
[15] See Wang (2014b).
[16] See Wang (2014b).

public awareness of the anti-corruption campaign and reinforced the CCDI's role in corruption discourse.

Beyond raising public awareness of the anti-corruption campaign and the CCDI's presence, the CCDI website also shaped the public narrative on corruption by addressing key questions: why and how did corruption occur? What role did the Party play in combating it? These narratives consistently isolate individual corruption offenders from the Party, thereby insulating the Party itself from the misdeeds of its members. More than admission to institutional flaws, these narratives stress personal moral failings. Officials convicted of corruption were often described as egoistic, power-hungry, dictatorial, or greedy, their misconduct attributed to character flaws, behavioral deviations and mental weakness.[17] These narratives also point at malevolent external influence, mostly from two sources: greedy family members and predatory bribers. Bribers were frequently portrayed as cunning manipulators who deployed "sugar-coated bullets" through *guanxi*-practices to "hunt the officials like prey." In these accounts, corrupt officials were depicted as confused victims, misinterpreting these deceptive inducements or "traps" as gestures of friendship.[18]

Another recurring theme in these narratives was the offender's abandonment of communist ideology. Corrupt officials were said to have strayed from the Party's ethical doctrines, failed to follow Party instructions and adhere to Party discipline, and subsequently, lost their ideological and moral compass (Kautz, 2022). Without spiritual guidance from the Party, these individuals succumbed to temptation and self-indulgence, ultimately falling victim to their own moral weaknesses. This messaging was reinforced through statements of remorse (*chanhuishu*), in which convicted officials typically accepted full responsibility for their crimes and repented for betraying the trust of the Party and the people (Kautz, 2022). In contrast, the Party was consistently portrayed as a trusting and trustworthy authority, occasionally misled by deceitful individuals but ultimately perceptive and able to self-correct.[19] Some of the confessions were then

[17] For example, a report traced the corrupt career of Liu Tie'nan, a senior official at the powerful National Committee of Reform and Development. Under the heading "self-sought shame," Liu's corrupt conduct was framed – through the words of an interviewee – as the inevitable result of his flawed character, described as arrogant and dictatorial. See Yang (2014).

[18] See the interviews of Lű Xiwen and Tan Qiwei at Zhong (2016, Episode 5).

[19] Zhong (2016, Episodes 4 and 8).

selected and compiled into training materials, which would be used in the ideological campaigns – a topic that is discussed in Chapter 7.

## National Supervision Commission (NSC)

During Xi's second term, the anti-corruption campaign continued, albeit with slightly reduced intensity. In 2017–2022, the CCDI placed 261 senior Party leaders under investigation - only 60 percent of the number recorded in 2012–2017, but still three times higher than any term under Hu Jintao or Jiang Zemin. However, what truly defined Phase II of the campaign, and what remains Xi's lasting legacy, was the supervision reform launched as the campaign reached its final crescendo.

The supervision reform was a far-reaching political and legal project aimed at restructuring the Party's disciplinary institutions. This overhaul required major legal revisions, including amendments to the People's Republic of China (PRC) Constitution, the Criminal Procedure Law, the Administrative Supervision Law, the Organic Law of the People's Procuratorates, and the Organic Law of Local People's Congresses and Governments. The reform redistributed power among several anti-corruption agencies in a zero-sum manner, causing a level of disruption that, under normal circumstances, would have made it simply not viable. The sheer scale of institutional upheaval and the associated administrative costs would have typically led to prolonged resistance and bureaucratic inertia, making both consensus building and rapid implementation exceedingly difficult.

It is therefore no coincidence that the reform was introduced at the height of the anti-corruption campaign, when its debilitating effect upon the officialdom was at its strongest. The reform began with a pilot program in late 2016, personally supervised by Wang Qishan, and was carried out in three locations. Unlike conventional trial-and-error local experimentation programs, which serve as a governance approach to foster spontaneous policy diffusion (Heilmann, 2008), the supervision pilot programs were tightly coordinated and deliberately engineered for success. Their purpose was not to test feasibility but to fine-tune implementation before the nationwide rollout. Treated as top-priority political missions, the pilots were swiftly and decisively completed within a year, hailed as a "victory."

In the fall of 2017, as Xi entered his second term, his first executive order was to expand the supervision reform nationwide. Over the next few years, half a dozen fundamental laws, including the PRC Constitution, were either amended or newly promulgated to legalize the changes brought about by the reform. In 2018, the NSC was formally established, replacing the previous MOS. In creating the NSC, the Party achieved three objectives in a single move:

1. Legalizing *shuanggui*.
2. Establishing the Party's exclusive, unified, and encompassing control over public corruption investigations across sectors.
3. Integrating the Party's enforcement apparatus into the state legal system.

Due to its complexity, the substance of this reform will be examined from four key aspects.

The first aspect concerns *shuanggui*, an investigative measure that had long operated in legal limbo. As discussed in Chapter 5, the lack of legal authorization for *shuanggui* was a major issue for the Party's disciplinary operation. This issue was deeply rooted in the Party's earlier abdication of criminal investigative power and its subsequent commitment to a state-based constitutional framework in which such coercive authority could only be granted to a state organ through formal state legislation. However, as the approach of power struggles (a subject explored in Chapter 7) has evolved and anti-corruption has become a central battle ground for such power contestation, the Party's imperative to reclaim this investigative power grew ever stronger.

The supervision reform rectified the issue in three steps. The first step involved a PRC constitutional amendment establishing the NSC as the law enforcement agency for duty crimes, the majority of which involved corruption. The second step was the promulgation of the Supervision Law, which provided the legal framework for the Supervision Commissions (SCs) nationwide. Under this framework, SCs are authorized to use detention (*liuzhi*), replacing *shuanggui*, along with other coercive measures for their investigations. At the same time, the Criminal Procedural Law was also amended to incorporate the SCs into the criminal justice system and formalize their investigative powers. The third step was the merger of the CDIs and the SCs under the conjoined-offices mechanism. Conjoined-offices (*heshu bangong*) is a powerful yet often overlooked administrative instrument that transfers, in one basket, all mandates, powers, and resources granted by the state legal system to the SCs directly to the CDIs, thereby placing them entirely at the Party's disposal.

The second aspect of the reform concerns the jurisdictional boundaries of the Party's criminal investigation power. Before the reform, the Party exercised de facto authority over the investigation of essentially three types of corruption offenses, bribery, embezzlement, and misappropriation of public assets and funds, when committed by a Party member. After the reform, this authority was significantly expanded to cover 101 offenses categorized as duty crimes, as long as the offense was committed by a public official in any public institution, including Party institutions, state organs, State-owned enterprises and other publicly funded entities regardless of whether they are a Party member or not. The new legal framework also authorized the SCs – and by extension the CDIs – to apply coercive measures in investigating crimes committed by non-public officials, such as bribers. Moreover, before the reform, as explained in Chapter 5, the procuratorates were also mandated to investigate corruption-related crimes. The reform revoked that power from the procuratorates, leaving the Party, through the device of conjoined-offices, with *exclusive* control over anti-corruption investigations.

The third aspect of the reform concerns human resources. The reform not only stripped the procuratorates of their anti-corruption investigation power but absorbed their anti-corruption investigation personnel. As a key component of the reform, the SCs took in the entire staff of three anti-corruption units from the procuratorates: the anti-embezzlement and bribery bureau, the bureau of anti-dereliction and rights infringement, and the bureau of duty crime prevention. These units accounted for roughly one-fifth of the procuratorates' total personnel (Li, 2017d). What the procuratorates lost, the CDI/SC gained. By the end of the reform, 61,151 personnel had been transferred from the procuratorates to the SC/CDIs nationwide (Qiu, 2018; Yu & Yang, 2019), increasing the CDIs' manpower by 17 percent.[20] An inter-agency personnel transfer of this scale is unprecedented in recent PRC history.

The fourth aspect of the reform concerns rank. As discussed in greater detail elsewhere (Li, 2023), under the power structure of the Party-state, the commanding authority of a law enforcement agency is constrained by its rank relative to the rank of the individual or entity it seeks to investigate or enforce actions against.[21] Before the supervision reform, the MOS

20 In this calculation, the total number of the CDI personnel nationwide was 360,000, based on Guo (2014c).

21 Discussions on the importance of the ranking status of public institutions in China can also be found in Cartier (2016), Chung and Lam (2004), Jahiel (1998), Lieberthal and Lampton (1992), and Ma and Ortolano (2000).

was merely a ministry, a subordinate entity under the State Council. The NSC, established by the reform, holds a rank equal to the State Council rather than being positioned one level below it. This rank elevation is not a decorative embellishment for the NSC but has important implications. It expands the rank-based personal jurisdiction of the NSC, enabling it to investigate higher-ranking officials who were beyond the reach of the previous MOS. After the reform, the personal jurisdiction of the NSC is fully aligned with that of the CCDI. Furthermore, being "conjoined" to the CCDI, the NSC enjoys a measure of political prerogative in the judicial process, making it even more difficult for the procuratorate or the court to dismiss or question cases sent for prosecution by the CDI/SCs.

The effects of the supervision reform were immediate. According to statistics provided by Beijing CDI/SC, the cases they investigated had increased by 51.8 percent in the first year after the reform and the average time that a suspect spent under detention decreased from 78.7 days to 64.4 days.[22] The rapid growth of the SC/CDI's investigative capacity was achieved at the direct expense of the procuratorates. Anti-corruption investigations had been the most valuable mandate of the procuratorates, granting them substantial political clout. This authority also allowed them to seize and confiscate the illicit gains from the corrupt officials and bribers, at least a portion of which might be used to replenish their "little coffer (*xiao jinku*)."[23] The supervision reform weakened the procuratorates significantly in terms of both power and resources.

Given the extent of disruption to the existing order, it is difficult to imagine that the supervision reform could have been implemented so swiftly and smoothly without the shock-and-awe achieved by Phase I of Xi's anti-corruption campaign. It therefore makes sense that the supervision reform was introduced not at the start of the campaign but rather toward its end. Xi may have been motivated to introduce the reform immediately after taking office in 2012, as creating the shock and awe required a substantial boost of enforcement resources. But such an attempt would almost certainly have failed given the reform's profound impact on the constitutional order, the debilitating loss for the procuratorates, and the significant administrative strain – factors that would

22 See CCDI (2017b).

23 The "Little coffer" is a common practice in many public institutions, despite being banned by the Party and state regulations. Funds from these coffers are often distributed among staff as year-end bonuses or used to cover occasional shortfalls in the institution's operational budget (Li & Yuan, 2015; SPP, 2015; Xiang, 2015).

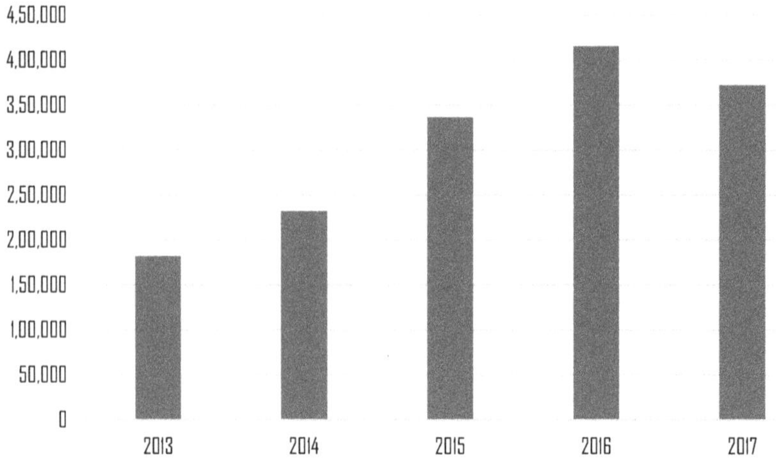


**Figure 6.5** CDI disciplinary investigations nationwide (2013–2017).
Source of data: CCDI Annual Work Report 2014–2018.

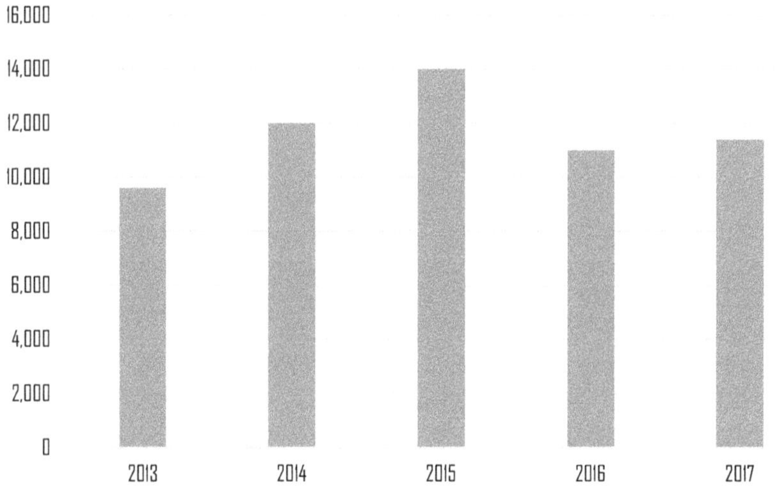


**Figure 6.6** Cases prosecuted nationwide (2013–2017).
Source of data: CCDI Annual Work Report 2014–2018.

have provoked strong resistance from the state legal institutions and a more liberal-minded legal community at the time.

Instead, as we can see from Figures 6.5 to 6.8, the reform was introduced after the anti-corruption campaign had peaked, when the chilling

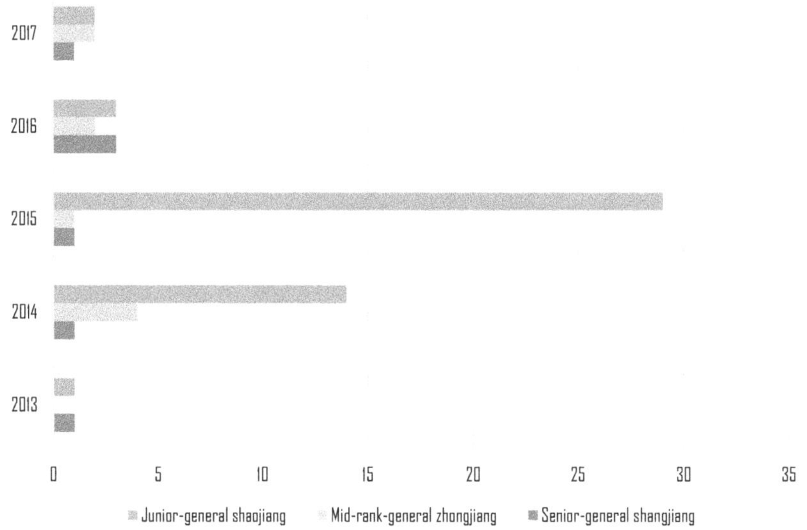


**Figure 6.7** Disciplined top-brass military leaders (2013–2017).
Source of data: This self-compiled dataset is based on the Wikipedia entry Anti-corruption Work of the CCP since the 18th Party Congress as appeared on February 21, 2021 (Wikipedia, 2023). Each case is checked for corroboration with official press release by the author and cases that cannot be corroborated are excluded.

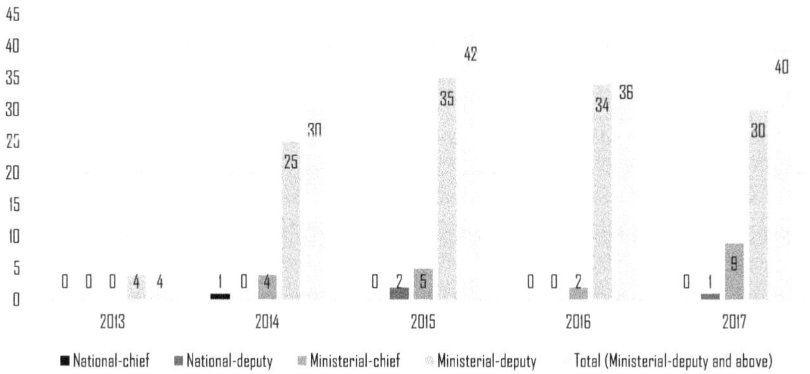


**Figure 6.8** Elite Party leaders placed under investigation (2013–2017).
Source of data: The dataset is also based on the Wikipedia entry "Anti-corruption Work of the CCP since the 18th Party Congress" as it appeared on February 21, 2021 (Wikipedia, 2023). Each case is checked by the author for corroboration with official press releases. Cases that cannot be corroborated are excluded. Note that this dataset only concerns officials who enjoyed full or alternation membership of the Central Committee, which should not be confused with "centrally managed cadres," a category covering a much larger pool of officials - reportedly more than 4,000 persons.

effects were the strongest. Concurrently, a nationwide ideological campaign was carried out to reinforce political compliance. These effects had deterred not only public officials but also compelled critics to hold back their dissent and criticism. Consequently, the supervision reform faced little pushback from the procuratorates when the CDIs absorbed their "crown units." Nor did the legal community mount sustained opposition, despite the reform's challenge to constitutional principles.[24]

## Integration and Outreach of the CCDI

As explained in Chapter 5, under the UCOPC principle, namely, the principle of unified (absolute) command of the Party Center, a territorial Party Committee is responsible for implementing central policies within its territorial boundaries. To achieve this, it exercises discretionary power to adapt central policies to local conditions and is granted the plenipotentiary authority to command all Party functionaries and state organs in its territory to take actions toward the objectives laid down by the Party Center. This authority extends to disciplinary matters, meaning that the CDI functions as a subunit of the corresponding territorial Party Committee and answers to it. This arrangement creates a fundamental flaw in the Party's anti-corruption institutional design, as the most powerful institution in a given administrative unit is tasked with combating corruption, the very offense to which it itself is most susceptible.

To address this issue, some proposed removing the CDIs from local power structures and subjecting them to the exclusive "vertical command" of the CCDI (Gan, 2007; Nie, 2015a). Readers may recall that similar proposals emerged in the late 1950s after the establishment of the first Central Supervision Committee (CSC), as discussed in Chapter 5. Deng Xiaoping, who led the supervision reform at the time, unambiguously rejected the idea. This was because placing the CDIs under "vertical supervision" would have created a new power center under the CCDI,

[24] Scholarly discussions on the constitutionality of the reform only began after the pilot program was already underway, likely because scholars were neither informed of nor consulted on the matter beforehand. While some scholars voiced objections, their critiques were not intended to halt the reform but rather to advise the Party on making necessary legislative adjustments. See these discussions in Han (2017), Jiao and Ye (2017), Li (2018), Qin (2017a, b,c), Ye (2017), and Zhai (2017).

potentially undermining the absolute authority of the Party Center and violating the UCOPC principle.

As a compromise, CDIs were placed under a "dual-leadership" model,[25] requiring them to report both vertically to the higher CDI and laterally to its corresponding territorial Party Committee. The design was intended to allow the CDIs to escalate cases in which the territorial Party Committee had a conflict of interest to the higher CDI. However, in practice, the CDIs rarely reported misconduct of the territorial Party Committee as their leaders were appointed by the same committee they were meant to oversee.

Recognizing this problem, the Party began removing appointment power from territorial Party Committees in the 2000s. During Hu Jintao's last term, half of the provincial CDI leaders were "parachuted" from the CCDI or transferred from other regions by the Party Center.[26] This trend was accelerated under Xi Jinping. In 2014, the CCDI established its own organizational department, gaining greater influence over the vetting and nomination of provincial CDI leaders and CCDI outpost heads.[27] During 2012–2020, no provincial CDI leader was appointed locally (Xiang, 2022). Instead, "parachutes" from the CCDI to provincial CDIs and transfers in the reversed direction had increased drastically (Xiang, 2022).

Beyond strengthening vertical control, the Party Center also introduced incentives to encourage CDI leaders' loyalty and performance. A CCDI editorial revealed that an internal "convention" allowed CDI leaders to extend their retirement age by three years (Capitalnews, 2015; CCDI, 2015b). For example, an ordinary member of a provincial Party Standing Committee must retire at the age of sixty, whereas the provincial CDI head is allowed to retire at sixty-three (Capitalnews, 2015). Furthermore, CDI leaders with strong performance were promised better prospects of promotion. Career mobility – how frequently an official is transferred to different posts of equal rank – is widely acknowledged as a key indicator of potential rank advancement (Xiang, 2022). Frequent transfers provide officials with diverse governance experience, which enhances their competitive edge when vying for high-ranking

[25] This dual-leadership model has been applied not only to the CDIs but also to various state institutions. A typical example is the police, which is subjected to the dual leadership of both the police at the superior level and the territorial Party Committee.

[26] See Dongnan (2013).

[27] See General Office (2015).

positions. According to a study of the biographical data of provincial CDI leaders, the career mobility of provincial CDIs had increased by 30 percent during 2010–2020 compared to 2000–2009 (Xiang, 2022).

Under Xi Jinping, the CCDI also expanded its reach by establishing permanent outposts in central Party-state organs. Different from the CIT, which operates on an *ad hoc* and rotating basis, the CCDI outposts are permanently stationed within the institutions they monitor. The practice of CCDI outposts already began under Jiang Zemin (Guo, 2014c), but early implementations were limited. Only about one-third of state agencies were monitored by CCDI outposts. Additionally, these early outposts had restricted mandates, as they could observe, write reports, and make recommendations but lacked punitive authority (CCDI, 2017c; Guo, 2014c). They were also vulnerable to capture by their host institutions (Li, 2015b). Several changes were introduced between 2012 and 2022.

First, during Xi's first term, the CCDI began dispatching outposts to powerful central Party apparatuses, including the COD, the CPD, the General Office of the Central Committee – institutions that had long been insulated from external monitoring (CCDI, 2015c). By the end of Xi's second term, the CCDI had, for the first time in Party history, achieved "full coverage" of all 139 central-level Party-state organs, 53 centrally managed SOEs, 15 centrally managed financial institutions, and 31 centrally managed higher education institutions (CCDI, 2022). Correspondingly, generous staffing quotas were granted to the CDIs and their outposts. According to an annual budgetary report of a county CDI in northeast Chongqing, in 2022, its headquarters had fifty staff members, while its thirteen outposts collectively employed an additional fifty-four staff (CDI, 2022).

Second, the chain of command between CDI and its outposts was strengthened to reduce institutional capture. In 2022, the Party Center issued the Rules on the Operation of CDI Outposts, stipulating that the CDI outposts report exclusively to their dispatching CDIs and that the outpost leader is entitled to a seat in the Party-group of the host institution.

Third, the CDI outposts were granted direct authority to handle, organize, or oversee anti-corruption investigations involving cadres supervised by the host institutions (CCDI, 2017c). Previously, CCDI outposts rarely exercised punitive power. For example, in 2005, the CCDI outposts launched only seventy-one investigations (Guo, 2014c), whilst in 2016, after the reform, they launched 780 (CCDI, 2017c).

The impact of the CDI outposts reform is best illustrated by the 2020–2022 anti-corruption crackdown in the financial sector. With support from CCDI outposts stationed in all 15 centrally managed financial institutions and their regional branches (Xue, 2021), the campaign led to investigations of 106 senior officials from major banks and various financial regulatory bodies – an unprecedented scale in the Party's anti-corruption history (Daily, 2022; Fu, 2023).

## Decline of the "Anti-corruption Czar"

Despite lacking total autonomy and independence, the CCDI's power continued to grow for three decades. By the end of Phase I of Xi's anti-corruption campaign, the CCDI had undoubtedly become the most powerful institution among all central Party apparatuses. It was also the only Party apparatus permitted, albeit under close supervision by the Party Center, to penetrate the autonomy of territorial Party Committees and form a vertical power substructure within the Party. Given the sensitivity of power balance in high politics, the more power the CCDI amassed, the greater the potential threats it posed to the cardinal UCOPC principle.

Beginning with Xi's second term, efforts were made to rein in the CCDI. The first step was to weaken the power base of the CCDI head, Wang Qishan, who, as noted earlier in this chapter, played an indispensable role in Phase I of Xi's anti-corruption campaign. The campaign between 2012 and 2017 could not have achieved the same scale of impact, *ceteris paribus*, without Wang's administrative acumen, deep political networks, relentless work ethic, and rigorous enforcement of Xi's program. Before their fallout, Wang was widely regarded as Xi's "closest ally" (Mitchell, 2018), "most trusted crisis manager" (Nakazawa, 2018), and "right-hand man" (Tse & Ong, 2018). He was even seen as the second most powerful figure in the Party (Economist, 2015), despite holding only the sixth seat on the Politburo Standing Committee.

The exact cause of the fallout between Xi and Wang remains a mystery. However, a pivotal moment in Wang Qishan's political trajectory was an unorthodox whistleblowing campaign launched against him from a luxury penthouse on Fifth Avenue in New York City. The name of this whistleblower was Guo Wengui, also known as Miles Kuo, a billionaire-in-exile wanted by the Chinese law enforcement on an assortment of criminal charges. Before fleeing to the United States in 2014, Guo controlled a property empire in China with a net worth of US$2.6 billion. Despite his opulent wealth, he had remained largely unknown outside elite circles until 2017. His low profile was, at least in part, due to his other identity – Guo was a contracted fixer for the PRC intelligence service and was handled by Deputy Minister of State Security Ma Jian. His assignments included, for example, establishing connections with "politically sensitive figures" abroad, such as the Dalai Lama and Kim Jong-un (Forsythe & Weiser, 2023). Guo was reportedly an acquaintance of foreign political leaders, such as Tony Blair, who vouched for his character when he purchased a co-op unit in the Sherry-Netherland Hotel in New York (Friedman, 2022).

Guo Wengui's high-level connections also brought him into contact with Wang Qishan. In 2002, Guo's company acquired a plot of land known as Morgan Center, adjacent to what would become the sites of two 2008 Olympics landmarks, the Water Cube and the Bird Nest. However, his development plans faced complications due to rezoning and disputes with constructors. By 2005, when Morgan Center was near completion, the Beijing government decided to reclaim the land. Guo, hoping to retain the property, pleaded with Wang Qishan, who had just assumed office as Beijing's mayor (Guo, 2017). Wang redirected Guo to Vice Mayor Liu Zhihua, who directly oversaw the matter (Gan, 2015). However, Liu refused to reverse the decision, and in 2006, the land was resold to other developers.

To many, what followed was a shocking turn of events. Just two weeks after the land was resold, Liu Zhihua was detained by the CCDI for corruption. The investigation was allegedly triggered by a sex tape secretly recorded by Guo Wengui, who had set up a honey trap for Liu. The tape was delivered through "a special channel" to top Party leaders, who were reportedly outraged and ordered an investigation (Cui, 2015a; Cui et al., 2015; Shenzhen, 2008). Following Liu's arrest, the disputed land was ultimately returned to Guo.

According to Guo, he and his CCDI contacts also secretly gathered evidence implicating Wang Qishan during the corruption probe of Liu Zhihua (Guo, 2017; Guoxing, 2015). Guo claimed that Wang was enraged when learning of these activities. However, no investigation was ever launched against Wang. Instead, in 2012, Wang was promoted to the Politburo Standing Committee and placed in charge of the CCDI. Guo Wengui, once a powerful businessman known as the "war god" (Yin et al., 2015) for his ability to outmaneuver competitors and foes, now faced a drastically different reality in China.

Guo's misfortune began with the detention of his handler Ma Jian, who was placed under CCDI investigation in January 2015. Meng

Huiqing, a CCDI divisional leader who had allegedly led the investigation against Liu Zhihua (Guo, 2017), was also detained by the CCDI in August 2015. Zhang Yue, head of the Party's Political-Legal Committee (PLC) of Hebei province and close associate of Guo, was detained by the CCDI in 2016. All three were later convicted of corruption, accused of having accepted bribes from Guo Wengui (Court, 2018a; Dalian, 2018). In the meantime, Interpol issued a red notice for Guo's arrest, his assets in China were frozen, and his companies were investigated for fraud. His family members, who also held executive roles in his conglomerate, were detained or placed under surveillance. Beginning in March 2015, major business magazines published exposés detailing Guo Wengui's dubious past and fraudulent business practices (Cui, 2015a,b; Wang, 2015; Yin et al., 2015).

It was at this point that Guo Wengui launched what he called the "scoops revolution" (*baoliao geming*) – a whistle-blowing campaign intended to pressure Chinese authorities to release his detained family members and, as he claimed, to influence the outcome of the upcoming Party election taking place thousands of miles away. (Forsythe & Weiser, 2023). Beginning in January 2017, Guo used various online media platforms to level accusations of corruption against Wang Qishan and his family, alleging a vast network of illicit dealings, multiple overseas property holdings, secret stakes in the Chinese conglomerate HNA Group, and lurid stories about Wang's personal life. He provided tantalizing clues and documents, though, like many of his other accusations, they were impossible to verify (Forsythe & Weiser, 2023).

Throughout the campaign, which lasted several months, neither the Party nor Wang Qishan himself publicly repudiated or addressed the accusations. No anti-corruption investigation was openly launched against Wang Qishan. But, during this time, the MPS dispatched several high-ranking officials to the United States in an attempt to persuade Guo to remain silent and voluntarily return to China. MPS officials also sought to engage with the Trump administration to negotiate an extradition agreement. The MPS task force went to great lengths in this pursuit, including attempting to establish contact with the Trump administration through obscure intermediaries such as Malaysian billionaire fugitive Jho Low, rapper-turned-aspirant power broker Pras Michel, and Elliott Broidy, then deputy finance chair of the Republican National Committee (Ames, 2023; Friedman, 2022).

All these attempts failed – Guo was not extradited – but nor was Wang Qishan reelected to the Politburo Standing Committee in 2017. Instead, he retired from all executive bodies of the Party Center and assumed the largely ceremonial role of the PRC vice-Chairman. While many observers saw Wang's vice-chairmanship as evidence of his continued political influence (Mitchell, 2018; Nakazawa, 2018; Zhang, 2018), his political network soon faced grave setbacks. By 2020, several of Wang's longtime associates – including former personal aides and subordinates – were sidelined, removed, or placed under investigation.

Among them was Ren Zhiqiang, a retired SOE leader and childhood friend of Wang Qishan from high school. A few years Wang's junior, Ren considered Wang a "big brother" (Ren, 2013). According to Ren, they remained close and stayed in contact over the years (Ren, 2013). Ren was known for his outspokenness and, throughout the 2010s, frequently criticized the Party's economic policies and ideological campaigns. His remarks were largely tolerated during Xi's first term.[28] In February 2020, amid the Covid lockdown in Wuhan, an essay attributed to Ren began circulating online, criticizing mismanagement of the crisis. By then, Wang Qishan had already left the CCDI for two years. In April 2020, Beijing Xicheng District CDI detained Ren Zhiqiang and launched an anti-corruption investigation. About six months later, a court convicted Ren Zhiqiang for embezzlement, bribery, misappropriation of public funds, and abuse of power, sentencing him to eighteen years in prison.

Ren Zhiqiang's case was only the beginning of a campaign that would debilitate Wang's power base. In October 2020, Dong Hong, Wang Qishan's longtime former aide, was placed under investigation. Dong began working under Wang in 1998 during Wang's tenure as Guangdong's deputy governor (Yu, 2021b). Over the next decade, he followed Wang to various posts in Hainan and Beijing (Ho, 2020). The two were separated in 2006–2012, during which time Wang became a vice-premier of the State Council and Dong was appointed deputy director of the Party-Documents Research Office of the Central Committee. When Wang Qishan was made the CCDI head, Dong rejoined him as a CIT leader until his arrest. The investigation traced Dong's corruption back to 1998, the year when he started to work

[28] When several conservative media outlets accused him of harboring "anti-Party" intentions (Dong, 2016), a CCDI-run newspaper *China Discipline/Inspection and Supervision Daily* published an essay that appeared to defend him (Dong, 2016). Ultimately, the Beijing Xicheng District CDI gave him a mere slap on the wrist, placing his Party membership on a one-year probation with no further action taken – until 2020. See (CDI, 2016).

directly under Wang Qishan. Dong was accused of misusing his power in exchange for 460 million *yuan* in bribes on numerous occasions, including during his time on the liquidation team of Guangdong International Trust and Investment Corp (GITIC), a government project directly overseen by Wang (also see Chapter 2). In 2021, Dong was sentenced to death with a two-year reprieve.

Around the same time in 2022, two other close associates of Wang Qishan also came under investigation. One was Fan Yifei, vice-president of China Central Bank, who had previously worked under Wang at China Construction Bank. Fan was convicted of accepting 386 million *yuan* in bribes between 1993 and 2022 and sentenced to death with a two-year reprieve without parole. The other was Tian Huiyu, president of China Merchant Bank and Wang's former secretary at China Construction Bank (Xinjing, 2013). Tian was convicted for corruption and other financial crimes, receiving a death sentence with a two-year reprieve.

Meanwhile, HNA Group, the conglomerate that Guo Wengui alleged had corrupt dealings with Wang Qishan and his family, also came under criminal investigation. Reports revealed that HNA had an opaque ownership structure, despite being a private enterprise, and enjoyed a exceptional privileges, securing massive loans from state-owned banks totaling hundreds of billions of *yuan* (Xiao & Yu, 2018; Zhao, 2021). Starting from 2017, central authorities cracked down on excessive overseas investment by Chinese conglomerates, including HNA, and warned banks against lending to them (Ning et al., 2021). Without government backing or access to new funds, HNA – once "China's biggest dealmaker" (Stevenson, 2021) – was at the brink of collapse under one of "the world's largest mountains of corporate debt" (Zhao, 2021). Amid the crisis, HNA's co-chairman Wang Jian died from a mysterious fall during a business trip in France in July 2018. HNA's other co-chairman Chen Feng, along with several executives, was arrested in September 2021.

Details about the HNA investigation remain undisclosed. Guo Wengui's claim that Wang Qishan and his family held secret stakes in HNA remains unverified. His other allegation – that HNA chartered Boeing 787 jets to transport high-ranking officials and their families – was refuted by the state news agency Xinhua. HNA responded to Guo's allegations with a defamation lawsuit, seeking US$300 million in damages (Reuters, 2017), though the suit was withdrawn by HNA in 2019 (Podkul, 2019).

More notably, in early 2020, Sun Lijun, the MPS vice-minister who led efforts to extradite Guo Wengui from the United States, was placed under investigation for serious political disciplinary violations and corruption. He was accused of committing some of the most severe political offenses, including political disloyalty, excessive political ambition, spreading fabricated political information, and forming a political clique within the Party. Sun was later convicted of corruption and sentenced to death with a two-year reprieve. Two other senior MPS leaders, Fu Zhenghua and Liu Yanping, both directly involved in the extradition campaign against Guo, were also placed under investigation. Like Sun, both were later convicted for corruption and received a death sentence with reprieve.

Meanwhile, in New York, Guo Wengui's own undoing has driven him to the bitter end of his extraordinary trajectory – from a billionaire Beijing insider to a fugitive critic of the Party and Trump Republican ally, and finally, to an inmate in a US federal prison. His operation of a fraudulent fundraising scheme, along with other illicit activities in the United States, led to eleven criminal charges brought against him (DOJ, 2023). In July 2024, after a seven-week trial in Manhattan, he was found guilty on nine of twelve criminal counts. He now faces the possibility of decades behind bars, and potentially, deportation to China where additional criminal charges await him.

Many would find Guo's behavior appalling, not only because of his guile, vulgarity, and narcissism,[29] but also due to the ease with which he deceived and the ruthlessness with which he eliminated adversaries. His opportunistic alignment with right-wing politics in the U.S. and his audacious fraud schemes have only fueled doubts about his credibility and the truthfulness of the information that he had divulged during his whistleblowing campaign. However, it is also indisputable that he was once deeply embedded in Beijing's political networks – holding a contracted engagement with the Ministry of State Security (MSS) – and enmeshed in shadowy business dealings with senior Party officials. In fact, all information presented in this section regarding Guo's past influence in China stems from or is corroborated by Chinese sources, including legal proceedings in China's courts, press releases from state-run media, and investigative reports from media outlets managed by his adversaries in China.

[29] For instance, Orville Schell described Guo Wengui as "a grifter" and someone who "just understands that whatever system you are in you have to learn how to play it." See Forsythe and Weiser (2023).

## Reining in the CCDI

After Wang Qishan stepped down from the CCDI, he was succeeded first by Zhao Leji and later by Li Xi, both of whom maintained a low profile with minimal and formulaic media coverage.[30] In the meantime, steps were taken to rein in the CCDI, retracting certain disciplinary decision-making power previously delegated to it.

The first sign of the Party Center's move to curb the CCDI's power emerged at the end of Xi's first term. In October 2017, during the 7th Plenum of the Party's Central Committee, the last meeting before the 19th National Party Congress, an unusual item appeared on the agenda: reviewing and approving the CCDI's work report. Previously, the CCDI had independently gathered feedback, revised its report, and submitted it directly to the National Party Congress. However, at the 19th National Party Congress, the procedure changed. For the first time, the CCDI was required to submit its report to the Politburo Standing Committee and then the Politburo for review. Thereafter, the Politburo, not the CCDI, would circulate the report in the Party for comments and, after incorporating the comments, submit the revised work report to the Central Committee for review and approval. Only upon the approval of the Central Committee could the CCDI then submit the report to the National Party Congress (Wan, 2017).

At first glance, this procedural change might seem redundant or pedantic, given that the CCDI work reports, the same as other work reports delivered by other Party or state organs, are largely inconsequential *ex post* self-assessment. However, in a realm where power contestation takes a different form (to be elaborated in Chapter 7), symbolism matters. The procedural change sends a clear message – the CCDI is not autonomous but subjugated to the Party Center. In fact, the insistence on this elaborate procedural change over something so inconsequential only underscores the message.

After Wang Qishan stepped down in 2017, several institutional changes were introduced to the CCDI. The first concerns segregation of

[30] For example, during Wang Qishan's tenure at the CCDI, both his and Xi's activities were reported under the same column "Voices from the Higher Level" on the CCDI website; while activities of other CCDI leaders were reported under the column of "CCDI/MOS leaders." However, after Zhao Leji took office as CCDI chief in 2017, "Voices from the Higher Level" became exclusively dedicated to Xi Jinping, while reports on Zhao were moved to the "CCDI leaders" column. The same practice has continued under Li Xi, who assumed office in 2022.

routine monitoring and case investigation. Routine monitoring, which is preventive in nature, addresses minor infractions through noncoercive measures, such as verifying complaints, making inquiries, maintaining an integrity dossier of monitored officials, and analyzing disciplinary trends. Case investigations, on the other hand, deal with serious infractions that meet the criminal threshold and require coercive investigative measures.

At the beginning of the supervision reform directly overseen by Wang Qishan, CDIs were specifically instructed to integrate the two functions (CDI, 2018; Pei, 2018), although the opposite would have been more logical and practical.[31] CCDI leaders were emphatic at the time that routine monitoring and criminal investigations should be completely fused and all agents should perform both functions.[32] Accordingly, the CCDI set up twelve fused-departments, each responsible for both noncoercive routine monitoring and coercive case investigations within designated geographic areas. Newly transferred agents from the SPP were mixed with CCDI agents, regrouped, and assigned to different fused-departments. Local CDIs followed suit. The fusion made it impossible to distinguish between noncoercive disciplinary activities carried out under the Party rules and coercive criminal investigations authorized by the Supervision Law. It also increased the risk of collusion between the monitors and the monitored, as shown in the case of Wei Jian (see Chapter 5).

Upon Wang's departure, an overhaul reversed the fusion.[33] By mid-2019, segregation of routine monitoring and case investigation became the standard practice and was codified in the revised CDI Operational Rules (2019).[34] Previously fused units were dissected into eleven routine monitoring offices, specializing in inspection, and five case-investigation offices, specializing in coercive anti-corruption investigations (Gao, 2019b; Qu, 2018). To further safeguard the integrity of case investigations, cases

31 It would have been more logical for the CDIs to assign agents newly transferred from the procuratorates – who have stronger legal training in corruption investigations – to the case-investigation division specializing in serious infractions, rather than placing them in routine monitoring roles.

32 See Ga (2019b).

33 Toward the end of Xi's first term, the Operation Rules regarding the Monitoring and Discipline Enforcement (2017) (hereinafter Operational Rules) were introduced. It left an opening for local CDIs to "explore" arrangements that would segregate routine monitoring and case investigations (Article 5). This suggests that decision-makers at the time were likely divided on whether to merge these two functions.

34 See General Office (2019).

will be randomly assigned to *ad hoc* investigation teams to prevent collusion between investigators and suspects or their accomplices (Shi, 2021).

Following the supervision reform, more substantial measures were introduced to rein in the power of the CCDI and its lower counterpart. One such measure concerns redistribution of disciplinary decision-making power between the territorial Party Committees and the CDIs. Previously, CDI leaders had considerable discretion in investigative activities and typically sought to inform or consult the corresponding territorial Party Committee only at the final stage of an investigation (CCDI, 2000; Liang, 2018; Qu, 2018). After the supervision reform, CDIs are now required to obtain authorization from the corresponding territorial Party Committees for all major actions (Shi, 2022, p. 83) and keep the latter informed not only of the outcome of an investigation but also all major steps taken in the investigative process. This marked a shift from an "outcome-oriented" to an "process-oriented" oversight model (Hu, 2017, p. 28). The Operational Rules (2019) further stipulated that the new "process-oriented" oversight also applies to the CCDI.[35] In 2021, the Politburo enacted the Central Directive on the Work of the Party Discipline and Inspection Committees, which specified that the CCDI must report to and seek instructions from the Politburo and the Politburo Standing Committee on all important decisions related to its investigative activities.[36]

The most decisive step in curbing the CCDI's power was taken in 2023, when the Party issued a most elaborate internal regulation – Rules on the Approval Competence of Disciplinary Sanctions – which redistributed the disciplinary decision-making authority among the CCDI, the Politburo and the Politburo Standing Committee and between the CDIs and territorial Party Committees at the lower levels. Compared to the 1983 and 1987 CCDI Jurisdiction Rules, the CCDI's disciplinary authority shrank significantly.

Most notably, the new rules revoked the CCDI's long-standing authority to approve Category I sanctions (warning and serious warning) against senior Party leaders of chief or deputy provincial/ministerial rank.[37] This marked a significant setback for the CCDI, as it could no longer determine, with minimal intervention from the Party Center, whether cases involving provincial/ministerial leaders – the backbone

[35] See General Office (2019, Article 10).
[36] See Center (2021, Article 5).
[37] See Center (2023b, Articles 34 and 35).

of the Party's governing elite – would result in minor reprimands or should escalate into a criminal proceeding. Under the new rules, the CCDI's final disciplinary decision-making power is now limited to its own agents and the lowest-ranking centrally managed cadres.[38]

## Conclusion

This chapter demonstrates that Xi's anti-corruption playbook is both multifaceted and interlinked, unfolding in carefully planned phases over an extended timeline. Phase I launched a shock-and-awe campaign that paralyzed officialdom and suppressed dissent. Phase II seamlessly built upon Phase I, capitalizing on its debilitating effects. This phase began with the pilot program of the supervision reform, which drastically expanded the Party's disciplinary system in reach, resources and investigative capacity. Once the new system was in place, the Party took steps to rein in the CCDI at both the individual and institution levels – weakening the power base of its former leader and introducing new rules and regulations reducing or restricting its disciplinary power.

What is most striking about Xi Jinping's anti-corruption playbook is his distinctive approach to expanding the Party disciplinary system. Instead of dissolving the state supervision organ, as Deng Xiaoping did in the 1950s, Xi elevated its political status, expanded its mandates, armed it with legalized coercive power, and then absorbed it into the Party through the critical – and almost "magical" – conjoined-offices mechanism, which was once merely an administrative tool for government downsizing. This maneuver will continue to challenge Western democratic conception of the relationship between a political party and the state.

From a sociological perspective, Xi's anti-corruption campaign is the outcome of both structural conditions and leadership agency. The campaign would not have generated the same level of shock and awe without Xi Jinping's political resolve, Wang Qishan's executive skills and dedication, and the synergy between them that strengthened the campaign's command and operational effectiveness. At the same time, its impact was also built on a vast array of regulatory instruments, administrative devices and institutional frameworks that the Party had

[38] See Center (2023b, Articles 34 and 35).

developed over decades before Xi came to power. In fact, not a single measure or mechanism in Xi's campaign was created from scratch. His anti-corruption playbook reflects the Party's path dependency as much as it highlights the adaptability of its institutional arrangements – where existing tools, devices, and mechanisms can be revamped, repurposed, and revitalized to different effects by leaders of varying degrees of agency.

# 7

# Power Struggles at the Politburo

Under the Unified (Absolute) Command of the Party Center (UCOPC) principle, power relations in the Party Center and the rest of the Party organizations follow a strict top-down hierarchy. However, within the Party Center itself, the dynamics between its key components – particularly the Central Committee, the Politburo, and the Politburo Standing Committee – become more ambiguous.[1]

According to the Party Charter, the National Party Congress and the Central Committee are the highest decision-making bodies not the Politburo and its Standing Committee. The Politburo and its Standing Committee merely exercise delegated power on behalf of the Central Committee when it is not in session. However, in practice, a hierarchy of personal ranks is applied to members of these bodies that effectively reverses the constitutional order of power – elevating members of the Politburo and its Standing Committee above those of the Central Committee.

As a result, the strictly top-down disciplinary decision-making mechanism – discussed in Chapters 5 and 6 – becomes ineffective when violations occur within the Politburo and its Standing Committee (hereinafter referred to as "the Politburo," as the two had been occasionally conflated in history), since there is no higher authority above them. Thus, initiating disciplinary procedures at the Politburo follows a fundamentally different logic.

In this chapter, I will track and analyze major disciplinary cases initiated at the Party Center from 1940 to the present. The individuals who were primary targets of the selected cases all held Politburo membership or equivalent positions at the Party Center. Specifically, I will

[1] It is also worth noting that for a considerable period in Party history, the Politburo Standing Committee did not exist, making power relations within the Party Center even more fluid.

examine (1) what primary paradigm was used to carry out disciplinary actions against Politburo members and (2) how this paradigm evolved – whether it was maintained, modified, abandoned, or replaced – at different historical junctures and why these changes occurred.

## Yan'an Rectification Campaign (YARC)

In its early years, the Party was small and vulnerable. Rules were few and difficult to enforce as its members constantly faced existential threats. The Party's institutional structure was copied, almost in its entirety, from the Soviet Union, and the operation of the Politburo – particularly the selection of its leadership – was dictated to a large extent by Moscow (Wu, 2015a). By the late 1930s, when the Kuomintang (KMT), the Party's nemesis at the time, was preoccupied with the war against the Japanese invasion, a power struggle[2] emerged at the Politburo in Yan'an, a remote town atop the Loess Plateau in Northern Shaanxi. This was the Party's new headquarters after it had been forced to abandon its Soviet base in Jiangxi and embark on the Long March, an epic military retreat undertaken to escape the KMT's encirclement campaign.

Since joining the communist cause, Mao Zedong had never been a favorite of Soviet leaders. He spoke no foreign language, had never trained in the Soviet Union or elsewhere, and maintained only formal or diplomatic contacts with the Soviet leaders. In the early 1930s, Mao suffered a major setback, losing his military command, and only regained influence during the Long March. After the Party secured control in Yan'an, a group of internationalists, led by Wang Ming, arrived from Moscow in 1937 (Guo, 2014a). Wang had studied at the Sun Yat-sen University in Moscow and had served as a liaison between the Comintern and the Chinese Communist Party (CCP) since the 1920s (Guo, 2014a).

Another key internationalist was Zhang Wentian, who joined the CCP in 1925 after spending a year and a half at UC Berkeley. Shortly after, he was sent to Moscow for five years of study (Cheng, 2006). In 1931, he returned to China and was appointed a Politburo member (Cheng, 2006). Three years later, in 1934, he was promoted to head the Central

[2] In this chapter, power struggles are used as a neutral reference to any internal power contestation at the Politburo that leads to a membership change. Even though power seeking may not be the only driver of these contestations, it remains a definitive aspect of both the goal and the outcome - a change of power structure in the Politburo.

Secretariat, an executive body which at the time functioned as the equivalent of today's Politburo Standing Committee (Cheng, 2006).

By 1938, Mao achieved a critical breakthrough: Moscow recognized him as the "core" of the Party leadership and endorsed his policies at the 6th Plenum of the Central Committee. However, this recognition alone did not translate into full political dominance. Mao's position remained insecure, still facing resistance from key Party leaders on strategic issues such as the Party's military involvement in the war against Japan and its collaboration with the KMT. Internationalists still held top leadership positions, with Zhang Wentian formally serving as head of the Central Secretariat (He, 2019; Liu, 2008).

It was against this backdrop that the Yan'an Rectification Campaign (YARC) was launched. Over time, it evolved to become the paradigm of Politburo power struggle, influencing Party politics for decades, even beyond Mao's death. He Fang, a witness to the campaign and one of the best-informed Party historians on this subject, described its impact as "unparalleled by any other political ideological movement in modern Chinese history" (He, 2019, p. 207). Gao Hua, who wrote the most in-depth historical study on the subject, characterized it as follows:

> The Yan'an Rectification Campaign was the first Party-wide political movement in the history of the CCP. Closely associated with and directly led by Mao Zedong, the campaign involved internal Party purges and reorganizations in various areas, including: Power struggles among the Party leadership and reorganization of the Party's central power apparatus; Ideological remolding throughout the Party; Examination of the personal histories of cadres and "elimination of counterrevolutionaries"; Creation of a new system. Among these, the high-level power struggles and the reorganization of leading organs always occupied a central position. (Gao, 2019a, p. xv)

Most historians mark 1942 as the campaign's starting point, citing a Central Propaganda Department notice issued on April 3, 1942. However, some argue that it began earlier, in 1940–1941, when Mao first openly attacked, at high-level Party meetings, the three "Leftist Lines," policies attributed to two internationalist leaders, Wang Ming and Bo Gu (Deng, 1998; Gao, 2000). It was only after facing no significant pushback that Mao escalated the campaign to a broader audience in 1942 (Gao, 2000).

In February 1942, at the opening ceremony of the Central Party School (the School), Mao called for a campaign to study Marxist classics. At the time, students at the School totaled 300 to 400, drawn from various military units, revolutionary bases, and KMT-controlled areas ("white areas") across the country. These students represented the ideological backbone of the Party. During that period, the School was also hosting a few dozen Party delegates, who came to Yan'an to attend the scheduled 7th Party Congress (Chung, 2018). By April, the School issued a circular requiring all administrative bodies of the Party, local government, schools, and propaganda-related units in Yan'an to organize study sessions.

The campaign's declared objective was to rectify problematic attitudes, in particular, subjectivism (*zhuguan zhuyi*) and sectarianism (*zongpai zhuyi*). A special committee was set up to oversee the campaign. The committee had two chairs – Mao being the first and Kang Sheng the second – and four additional members: Chen Yun, Peng Zhen, Gao Gang, and Li Fuchun.[3] The study sessions involved supervised self- and group study.

At first, participants were required to study a collection of selected reading materials and connect them to their personal experiences. The goal was self-criticism and exposing others' ideological mistakes. To monitor this process, participants were required to record their introspections in notebooks and account for "their personal awakening to the revolution" (Gao, 2019a, p. xii). As the campaign progressed, private self-reflections would be turned into public confessions and accusations, voluntarily at first, but coerced at a later stage if necessary. The materials produced in the process would be filed into personnel dossiers, which may be used as self-implicating materials in future campaigns (Gao, 2019a).

Given that group studies were carried out in Party organizations, the campaign was organically segregated between senior Party leaders and the rank and file (He, 2019). For the former group, the main study material was the "two lines," which historicizes the past and present power strife within the Party. This ideological framework portrayed the policies of targeted leaders as the wrong line, while Mao's own policies were upheld as the correct line. All participants were required to examine and reexamine their personal histories through this lens. In the process, they were compelled first to provide concrete evidence proving the

[3] Historical studies show that, besides Mao, Kang Sheng and Peng Zhen were the most committed to the campaign, and their enabling role was indispensable to its success (Chung, 2018; Gao, 2000; He, 2019).

existence of the divide between the two lines and second to take a side and justify their choice (Gao, 2000; He, 2019).

To achieve the campaign's objectives, participants were required to abdicate their personal sovereignty by actively searching for past mistakes – whether real or imagined – to "authenticate" and substantiate the two-line narrative they were given. Only when such introspection had reached the desired cognitive "depth" would a participant's repentance be accepted and their declared commitment to self-reform be considered genuine. The process would be closely monitored by the campaign organizers, making adjustments whenever it showed signs of deviation or disorientation. By the end of the campaign, all main targets, as well as other top Party leaders, such as Zhou Enlai and Peng Dehuai, had admitted to past mistakes for having followed the wrong-line(s) at one point or another in their careers (Gao, 2000).

The ultimate goal of the campaign, as revealed by Mao himself, was to unify Party cadres' thoughts regarding the correct and the wrong lines and to prepare them for the elections at the 7th Party Congress.[4] Once the participants were believed to have fully understood what the wrong line was and who was responsible for it, then a Party congregation could be convened, where the wrong line would be officially condemned and its leaders held accountable.

For the rank-and-file members, the goal of the rectification campaign was primarily indoctrination. In the words of Liu Shaoqi – Mao's close ally in this campaign – it was to convert participants into "obedient tools of the Party" (He, 2019). The study materials were more diverse in scope and the behaviors under scrutiny were more wide-ranging, including liberalism, demands for equality, or appeal to "extreme democracy" (Gao, 2000; He, 2019). While the campaign proceeded relatively calmly among the senior Party leaders – whose strongest form of resistance was withdrawal – it had encountered some pushback among the rank and file.

The most noteworthy case was about Wang Shiwei, a literary writer working for the *Liberation Daily*. Two months into the campaign, Wang wrote an essay exposing the hypocrisy of the campaign by highlighting the discrepancy between the Party's preached ideal of equality and the

[4] Mao's objective mentioned here was indicated in a telegraph addressed to Rao Shushi and other regional Party leaders, drafted by Mao on behalf of the Central Secretariat. This telegraph, included in the complete collection of Mao's works, is entitled "Studying line issues is the [task] of the more in-depth and advanced phase of the rectification campaign"; see Secretariat (2013).

privileges that Party leaders enjoyed in reality. In response, Wang Shiwei was thrown in prison, and what had begun as an indoctrination campaign escalated into a purge, later known as the "rescue movement (*qiangjiu yundong*)."

During the purge, personal histories were scrutinized for evidence of political disloyalty. Torture was used to extract confessions and to identify spies and enemy informants. However, unlike Stalin's regime, this purge did not culminate in mass executions. Mao issued explicit instructions to prevent another "Futian Incident," referring to the 1930 massacre in the Jiangxi Soviet area during an internal purge.[5] Instead of physical liquidation, the rectification approach was intended to be "therapeutic" – or, in Mao's own words, "to punish the past errors as a measure to prevent future mistakes and to treat the illness in order to save the patient" rather than "to finish someone off with one single strike."[6]

The YARC concluded in victory for Mao, marked by his election as Chairman of the Politburo and the Central Secretariat at an enlarged Politburo meeting in March 1943, granting him the final decision-making power. His dominance at the Politburo was further consolidated two years later at the 7th Party Congress held in 1945, where he was elected, additionally, as Chairman of the Central Committee. The same congress also passed the first resolution on Party history, parsing the correct political line from the wrong lines, solidifying Mao's ideological and political authority. The internationalist Party leaders, who had been the main targets of the campaign, were removed from power – Wang

[5] The Futian Incident is a bloody purge initiated in the Hunan-Jiangxi Soviet Area in the late 1920s. Its goal was to identify and remove spies or other anti-revolutionary members hidden within the Party (Gao, 1999). During 1930–1931, the purge escalated into a liquidation campaign, later known as the Futian Incident. The incident led to the execution of more than 2,000 Red Army officers and men, for which Mao was held responsible (Mertha, 2019). Nearly 100,000 people were killed afterwards when the purge was extended to other areas (Jing, 2005). Despite Mao's instruction not to repeat the Futian Incident in the YARC, Wang Shiwei was nevertheless executed five years later when the Party left Yan'an in 1947. Enduring grievances were harbored by many participants of the 1942 YARC campaign. For instance, at the 7th Party Congress, delegates almost voted Peng Zhen, a key organizer of the campaign, out of the Central Committee, were it not for Mao's intervention (Chung, 2018).

[6] This excerpt is from an address delivered by Mao at the National Conference on Propaganda Work held on March 12, 1957, in preparation for launching the second rectification campaign that year. See Mao (1999, pp. 273–74). Additionally, a guideline disseminated by Liu Shaoqi, director of the campaign to eliminate internal spies, stated that "in principle, no one should be killed [in the campaign]." See Yu (2023, p. 122).

Ming and Bo Gu were both excluded from the Politburo, and Zhang Wentian stepped down as head of the Central Secretariat.

## YARC Model

YARC holds a unique position in Party history as the prototype for the disciplinary paradigm governing power struggles at the top of the Party. It prevailed much of the Party history, and its influence lingers to this day.[7] Before YARC, the removal of a Politburo member was largely dictated by the Comintern, whose superior authority entitled it to exercise top-down supervision over its Chinese branch. While such removals were also frequently framed in ideological terms, their process was much swifter and more straightforward.

Simply put, the YARC functioned as a discrediting campaign designed to facilitate the unseating of internationalist leaders from the Party Center at the 7th Party Congress. The campaign's heavily ideologized rhetoric stemmed, I contend, from the Party's strict ban on personal electoral campaigns.[8] Any personal electoral effort that was not officially sanctioned and organized by the Party's collective decision-making body was labeled a "non-organizational activity (*feizuzhi huodong*)," deemed anti-Party, seditious and illegitimate.[9] However, power contestation is inevitable in any political organization. When such events occur, they must be channeled through *some* kind of regulatory framework. The Party chose an ideological framework, in which competing factions were divided along a binary ideological line, presenting the division as a seemingly incorrigible ideological rift rather than a contest for power.[10]

[7] In earlier Party history, the CPSU exerted considerable influence over the Politburo. The CCP gained its autonomy after the Sino–Soviet split in the late 1950s.

[8] For earlier references on the ban, one can read (Deng, 1955; Zhao & Zhang, 2008). Allegations and condemnations of violation of the ban can also be found in the denouncements of Lin Biao, for instance, see Center (1972).

[9] For example, see the denunciations against Gao Gang, and in more recent cases, against Bo Xilai and Zhou Yongkang.

[10] The use of ideology "to couch a power struggle" was also noted by Andrew Nathan. He argued that ideologization serves three purposes. First, it makes it possible to distinguish one faction from another, "providing a rationale for the continued struggle among such otherwise similar entities;" second, it provides an opportunity to discredit other politicians and to justify oneself on abstract or ideological grounds; and third, the broad programs often include inconspicuous provisions of true strategic political importance. See Nathan (1973, p. 49).

The compulsory study sessions of the YARC were designed to implant an ideologically reconstructed political reality and new power structure into the minds of campaign participants through a unique cognitive process that can be explained as follows.

First, participants were required to study the writings of the campaign's initiator, which were presented as indisputable truth – the correct line. Meanwhile, the words and actions of the campaign's targets – representing the wrong line – were condemned as heresy. It is important that these study sessions were not set up as forums for open discussions and debates; rather, they functioned as exercises in corroborating and buttressing the version of reality outlined in the reading materials with further analytical and empirical support. To this end, participants were expected to actively repress, reject, and denounce alternative viewpoints held by others or themselves. This forced rationalization process compelled campaign participants to internalize the new political order that the campaign organizer sought to introduce and impose.

A crucial mechanism of the YARC was criticism and self-criticism. While similar methods were used in the Soviet Union and Eastern Europe,[11] the Chinese version was distinctive in its broadened application and heightened significance (Dittmer, 1973, p. 710). Under the YARC model, self-criticism went beyond admitting actual mistakes committed – it required individuals to confess to transgressions they had not committed, diminish or deny their self-value, and reinterpret or reconstruct past events they had witnessed or participated in, aligning their accounts with the newly imposed frame of references and political order.

For the campaign's primary targets, such self-criticism was tantamount to an admission of political defeat. Once an individual submitted

[11] Joseph Stalin introduced this concept in his 1924 work *The Foundations of Leninism* and the practice was further expanded under his rule. Viewing self-criticism as indispensable as air or water (Malenkov, 1949), Stalin believed that self-criticism was the only way to purge the ulcers of a body and to eliminate one's shortcomings; and that, without it, the Party could not make any headway (Stalin, 1928). The practice was closely tied to Stalin's demand that all Party members publicly repent for their mistakes, a principle he formally established at a joint plenum of the Central Committee and the Central Control Commission of the CPSU in 1926 (Erik van, 1993). However, despite his belief in the merits of criticism, self-criticism, and repentance, Stalin appeared to have less trust than Mao did in the transformative power of introspection to bring about reform. Unlike the YARC model, which invested significant resources and energy to facilitate ideological transformation, Stalin seemed to regard the use of external control networks, show trials, and physical liquidation as more efficient and effective tools for enforcing discipline.

a self-criticism, the campaign leader could decide whether to circulate it to a wider audience. If the statement was widely distributed, it served as a clear signal to the target's followers, allies, and sympathizers that their leader had capitulated. This often discouraged resistance from the target's faction, pushing them to abandon their stance and align with the dominant political line. Furthermore, once a statement of self-criticism was widely disseminated, the target could not easily recant or modify their position except in the event of a radical political shift.

A YARC-style campaign was typically launched ahead of a critical political event in which major decisions were to be made, such as a national Party congregation. The campaign was launched to ensure that participants were properly conditioned to accept the new political order and reality before being invited to take part in the decision-making at the congregation. This was precisely the case leading up to the 7th Party Congress in 1944–1945 (Gao, 2000; Wu, 2015a, 2018).

In 1945, the Party Charter was amended, to which a new chapter on Party discipline was introduced. Among its provisions was a rule stipulating that a member or alternate member of the Central Committee could be removed from their positions or expelled from the Party for grave violations of Party discipline, provided that the decision was approved by a two-thirds majority of the Central Committee. These rules applied to Politburo members as well since they, per Party rules, retained their Central Committee membership and the Party Charter did not provide separate rules for their removal. This means that two conditions had to be met for a Politburo member's removal: first, the accuser had to prove that the accused committed an offense warranting disciplinary action; and second, consent for the disciplinary sanction must be obtained from a disciplinary panel, which consists of the accused's peers.

Thus, the YARC serves as a preliminary disciplinary platform with two goals: first, to establish the cause for initiating disciplinary proceedings; second, to communicate the new political order to the disciplinary panel and to persuade its members to distance themselves from the accused before the formal disciplinary action begins.

The YARC model's advantage lay in its ability to facilitate power contestation by suppressing rather than fostering policy-based competition within the Party. Unlike conventional power struggles, where a losing faction might consolidate into an opposition, the YARC model ensured that a power struggle did not conclude until 1) the losing faction was ideologically discredited and 2) its key figures capitulated and endorsed the victorious faction's political line (Yan, 1995). Taking these steps helped to close the space for the losing side to reorganize and challenge the new order, thereby ultimately strengthening the Party's cohesion rather than fragmenting and weakening its unity.

In the remainder of this chapter, I will analyze a series of selected historical events to demonstrate how the YARC model was repeatedly deployed to serve the disciplinary process at the Politburo from 1942 until five decades later. Additionally, I will also explore when and why the YARC model was abandoned as well as circumstances under which the Party transitioned to an alternative disciplinary paradigm.

## Showcasing YARC – the Gao/Rao Affair

The Gao/Rao Affair is a pivotal episode in Party history as it marked the first Politburo power struggle since the Party came to power. It also serves as a striking example of how different approaches taken by different actors led to contrasting outcomes. While the Party officially framed the affair as a conspiracy between two Party leaders – Gao Gang and Rao Shushi – my analysis will focus on Gao Gang alone for two reasons: first, for the sake of simplicity, and second, because Rao Shushi's role was largely circumstantial and less significant.

Gao Gang, the "ringleader" of the Affair, was a Party military leader originating from northern Shannxi. He developed a close relationship with Mao in Yan'an, where the Party was headquartered after the Long March. In June 1945, Gao secured a seat on the Politburo, and four months later, he joined Lin Biao and others leading the war against the KMT in the northeastern theater (Zhang, 2011). After the founding of the PRC in 1949, Gao became one of the six vice-chairmen of the PRC Central Government and the chief Party leader of the Northeast Region. In 1952, he was transferred back to Beijing to chair the Central Government Planning Committee, a powerful economic policymaking body also known as the "small" State Council. Despite his dedicated and decorated career within the Party, Gao could never have foreseen the turbulent series of events that would lead to his fatal downfall in 1954–1955.[12]

[12] These events were dramatic and have been the subject of several historical studies. Readers interested in further details of the incident can refer to Chung (1999), Lin (2003, 2017), Teiwes (1990, 2015), Wang (2014a), and Yang (2013).

In early 1953, after moving to Beijing, Gao had several private conversations with Mao, during which he sensed Mao's dissatisfaction with Liu Shaoqi and Zhou Enlai, the second- and third-in-command at the Politburo at the time.[13] Taking Mao's remarks as implicit encouragement, Gao began attacking Liu's policies in Party meetings over the summer. Soon after, he started actively campaigning for Liu and Zhou's replacement, privately lobbying other senior Party leaders. In mid-December, Gao privately approached Xiaoping and Chen Yun separately, seeking their support for his proposal and possibly also hinting at promotions as inducements. However, to Gao's great misfortune, Deng and Chen not only refused to participate but also reported the incident to Mao immediately as a grave disciplinary violation.[14] Upon receiving the report, Mao ordered an investigation into the matter.

At an enlarged Politburo meeting on December 24, 1953, Mao openly criticized Gao Gang with the following allegorical remark: "There are two headquarters in Beijing. One is headed by me, blowing the *yang*-wind and burning the *yang*-fire (positive energy), and the other is headed by Gao Gang, blowing the *yin*-wind and burning the *yin*-fire (negative energy)."

Immediately after the meeting, Mao left for Hangzhou, where he remained for three months. Before departing, Mao instructed Liu Shaoqi and other Party leaders to resolve the Gao/Rao Affair peacefully at the upcoming Central Committee plenary meeting, emphasizing the importance of Party unity. Mao gave Liu specific instructions on how to conduct the plenary meeting as an effort to contain the conflict. As a part of this strategy, Mao advised Liu to make a self-criticism statement at the plenary meeting to balance the tone of the proceedings.[15]

Between February 6 and 10, the Central Committee plenary meeting took place in Beijing in Mao's absence. The meeting lasted five days, during which implicit criticism was directed at Gao Gang and Rao Shushi, though neither was mentioned by name. However, after the

[13] Historical materials do not reveal exactly what Mao said in those conversations. However, given that Mao later launched the Cultural Revolution and ultimately removed Liu from power, it is reasonable to assume that while Mao might have disapproved of Gao's tactics, he was not necessarily opposed to Gao's goal Lin (2003b, 2017); Chung (1999).

[14] In another account, Deng first reported the incident to Zhou Enlai and then Zhou reported it to Mao (Chung, 1999).

[15] Mao's instructions stipulated that there should not be too many speakers, that speakers should only conduct self-criticism not criticism (of others, added by author), and that the meeting should last two days (Lin, 2003 p. 68).

meeting concluded, the Central Secretariat organized two follow-up sessions, during which the discussion took a radical turn.

At one of these sessions, forty-three invited participants delivered speeches, attacking Gao for his alleged "anti-Party" activities (Dai & Zhao, 2011). In contrast, Gao's self-defense appeared weak and ineffective vis-à-vis the organized, vitriolic criticisms directed at him. His self-criticism was deemed shallow, insincere, and inadequate to absolve him of wrongdoing. Feeling betrayed, abandoned, and desolate, Gao attempted suicide on the third day of the meeting, but failed. Following this incident, the Party placed him under house arrest. The meeting continued in Gao's absence and concluded with a formal report outlining his disciplinary violations based on the speeches made by the attendees (Zhao & Zhang, 2008).

Immediately afterwards, a Special Case Investigation Team was assembled, led by Deng Xiaoping, to further investigate Gao's disciplinary violations. Meanwhile, Gao repeatedly requested an audience with Mao, which Mao denied. While the investigation was still pending, Gao made a second suicide attempt, this time killing himself. However, the disciplinary case against Gao did not end with his death. In March 1955, the investigation concluded that Gao had conspired with Rao Shushi to carry out anti-Party activities. An emergent National Party Conference was called upon to deliberate on the case.[16] At the conference, Deng Xiaoping delivered a lengthy report, detailing Gao and Rao's violations, contextualizing their actions, and politicizing their conduct. At the end of the conference, the delegates unanimously agreed to expel Gao (posthumously) and Rao from the Party, officially concluding the disciplinary process (NPDC, 1955).

In retrospect, Gao's half-baked plan to oust Liu Shaoqi and Zhou Enlai from the Politburo was deeply flawed, poorly executed, and ultimately self-destructive. He mistakenly believed he could carry out Mao's bidding (assuming Mao had indeed intended to remove Liu and Zhou) by orchestrating the downfall of two Politburo members of higher standing through his private electoral campaign and lobbying. In doing so, Gao not only underestimated the strength of the political influence of his adversaries (Teiwes, 2015) but also failed to grasp the requirements for

[16] Different from the National Party Congress, the National Party Conference is held *ad hoc* and its members are selected instead of elected. The CCP Charter allows such conferences to be held "under special circumstances."

launching a power struggle at the Politburo and the normative power of the YARC model.

As history would reveal a decade later, removing Liu Shaoqi – the Party's second-in-command and Mao's designated successor – was no easy feat, even when commandeered by Mao himself. It required the launch of a radicalized version of the YARC to initiate a disciplinary process and secure the outcome. The year of 1954 was simply not the right moment for such a move (Teiwes, 2015).

To believe, as Gao did, that such an outcome could be achieved through an unauthorized private electoral campaign was both naive and reckless. Gao's act was such a grave violation of Party discipline that it not only implicated himself but would also have put Mao in a vulnerable position, had Mao's involvement been exposed. Thus, when Deng Xiaoping and Chen Yun reported Gao's lobbying conduct, Mao had no choice but to abandon and condemn him, as Gao's conduct – privately campaigning for electoral offices – was an unambiguous disciplinary violation (Lin, 2003, 2017). Mao's deliberate absence from the plenary meeting is also very telling, reflecting his vulnerable position in the case (Lin, 2003).

In contrast, the counterattack launched by Deng Xiaoping and others was a loyal application of the YARC model – taking steps to expose Gao's misconduct to establish grounds for disciplinary actions, building the case through criticism and self-criticism sessions, and sealing the victory through a formal approval from the disciplinary panel. The key distinction from YARC is that in the Gao/Rao Affair, Deng and his allies did not need to manufacture a cause through a premeditated rectification campaign – Gao Gang's private lobbying provided one for them.

As events unfolded, Deng Xiaoping emerged as the greatest beneficiary of the Gao/Rao Affair, filling much of the power vacuum left by them (Chung, 1999). The affair also provided Deng with the momentum to reform the Party disciplinary system in 1955, the impact of which, as discussed in Chapter 5, far exceeded the Gao/Rao Affair itself.

## Radicalized YARC – Cultural Revolution

The tumultuous Great Proletarian Cultural Revolution (Cultural Revolution) caused the death of countless lives and prolonged anguish and suffering for millions of families. The underlying causes for a political and social upheaval of this scale were undoubtedly complex, multifaceted, and intertwined. Among them, one undisputed driving force was Mao's struggle for absolute dominance in the Politburo (Spence, 2013). Unlike previous power struggles, the targets of the Cultural Revolution were not limited to a single leader or faction but encompassed legions of them. During the Cultural Revolution, 75 percent of high-ranking Party leaders were placed under disciplinary investigations (CCP, 2023). Historians continue to debate whether this scale of persecution was premeditated by Mao or merely the collateral damage of his struggle with the primary target: Liu Shaoqi, the second-in-command in the Party and Mao's chosen successor at the time.

What is of interest to this discussion is not Mao's motivation but the approach of the Cultural Revolution, as a power struggle, through the lens of the YARC model. When examined in this way, one finds that the Cultural Revolution was a radicalized adaptation of the YARC model. On the one hand, the movement followed the main framework outlined by the YARC model, including an ideological campaign to establish grounds for disciplinary actions and consolidation of victory through a collective disciplinary proceeding. On the other hand, the Cultural Revolution also diverged from the YARC in fundamental ways.

As discussed, a key function of the YARC model is to establish a cause for disciplinary action, particularly when the target has not voluntarily committed or exposed an indictable offense. The YARC model prescribes an ideological formula that frames the struggle for power as a struggle between a "wrong line" allegedly held by the accused and a "correct line" proclaimed by the accuser. This framework has little to do with the objective merits of the actual policies advocated by either side of the power struggle. It offers no logically developed criteria by which to objectively assess correctness or incorrectness. Instead, it provides vague guidance to distinguish between the correct and the wrong lines in only the most rudimentary way.[17] The inherent arbitrariness of this process grants the initiator of the power struggle maximum freedom to attack their targets – not on the basis of alleged misconduct but on considerations such as alignment of interests, loyalty, and other tactical calculations, as was starkly evident during the Cultural Revolution.

[17] One tactic for broadening the definition of the wrong line is to use a combined frame of references consisting of two dichotomously opposed types of conduct or policies. For instance, at the YARC, both dogmatism and empiricism were labelled as wrong lines, a combination that could capture virtually any conduct. Similarly, another broad frame of references pairs adventurism with defeatism. For more details, see He (2019).

The Cultural Revolution was not a conventional application of the YARC. It differed in the scope and strength of its targets, leading to a radical adaptation of its strategies. The targets of the 1942 YARC were a handful of internationalists, those leaders who had studied and trained in the Soviet Union. Their leadership positions were largely owed to CPSU backing, and most had limited following and few revolutionary credentials. They were few in numbers and could be easily identified and isolated. By contrast, the targets of the Cultural Revolution had a completely different profile. They were homegrown, decorated and well-connected Party veterans with solid power bases. They held key positions in various Party institutions and were well-versed in the YARC model. In fact, a few of them had played an indispensable role in helping Mao implement the YARC in 1942.[18]

For reasons that remain unclear and continue to be debated by historians, Mao did not launch the Cultural Revolution through the central propaganda apparatus in Beijing. Instead, he turned to an alternative launchpad by enlisting the help of a Shanghai-based group that would later become known as the 'Gang of Four.' Nor did he disclose his true intentions to the Politburo or the Central Secretariat. Rather, he insinuated his belligerent aims by ordering the publication of Yao Wenyuan's polemical essay on the play Hai Rui Dismissed from Office in a Shanghai newspaper. When the central leaders in Beijing ignored the essay,[19] Mao denounced them as a watertight bureaucratic fortress that "no needle can penetrate and no drop of water can sink in" (1966).

Due to the differences in targets, Mao also adapted his strategies of power struggle in the Cultural Revolution. Compared to the orthodox YARC model, the Cultural Revolution introduced two distinctive strategies. First, involvement of the masses. The Cultural Revolution was the first and last instance in which the masses were directly involved in a power struggle at the Politburo level. Previously, such struggles were largely contained within the Party's upper echelons, with senior Party leaders and the rank and file remaining segregated. In the Cultural Revolution, however, Mao sought to "pull the rug under the feet" of his targets by dismantling the Party's primary chain of command, which

[18] For instance, Liu Shaoqi was Mao's key ally in the YARC. Peng Zhen, Zhou Yang, and Lu Dingyi – who were victimized during the Cultural Revolution – were also important facilitators of the YARC in 1941–1942.

[19] Dittmer attributed the initial resistance of the Party establishments, led by Peng Zhen and others, toward Mao's demand to attack the play "Hai Rui Dismissed from Office" also to the increasingly interlocking interest of the Party's cultural establishments and the governing elite. See Dittmer (1973).

linked the Party Center to its various parts and underpinned the power networks of Liu Shaoqi and his associates. To achieve this, he introduced the so-called grand democracy, reversing the existing power structure and authorizing both the rank-and-file Party members and the broader masses to attack Party leaders directly.

Second, to facilitate this power reversal, Mao decentralized the use of violence.[20] In the orthodox YARC model, coercion was centralized and carried out by authorized special investigative units. In contrast, in the Cultural Revolution, the masses were encouraged – or, at the very least, tactically permitted – to use violence to attack their targets and "seize power" from the Party establishments. To that end, the police were relieved from their duty to maintain law and order, the Red Guards were given near-total immunity to publicly humiliate and torture their targets, and the army was deployed to protect and support the radicals in disrupting and reversing the existing power structure.

Alongside the violent seizure of power, a YARC-style ideological campaign was led by a group of radical Party propagandists who produced numerous editorials and other materials attacking Liu Shaoqi and his followers for walking the "capitalist road" – the most egregious offense a Party leader could commit – and for being the most high-ranking anti-revolutionary revisionist in the Party. Liu's self-criticism was circulated to the masses nationwide. Liu and his wife were repeatedly humiliated in public struggle meetings attended by large crowds.

After Liu had completely capitulated and the majority of the Central Committee members had fallen from grace, Mao called for a plenary meeting of the Central Committee, where the formal disciplinary proceeding against Liu Shaoqi took place. Branded the highest-ranking "capitalist roader" as well as a scab, spy, traitor, and running dog of enemy forces, the committee reached a decision to swiftly expel him from the Party, with only one out of 132 members objecting. Liu died the same year of illness in solitary confinement.

## Tactical Abandonment of YARC – Removal of the Gang of Four

The removal of the Gang of Four was a rare event in Party history. It resulted in the ousting of four Politburo members, including two

[20] The scale and intensity of violence during the Cultural Revolution is one of the most well-documented subjects in existing literature. For detailed accounts, see, for example, MacFarquhar (2012), Su (2011), and Wu (2017).

Politburo Standing Committee members, through a single coup, an approach that completely departed from the YARC model.[21]

This coup occurred merely one month after Mao's death, at a time when the Party Center was deeply divided among Mao's designated successor Hua Guofeng, the Cultural Revolution radicals led by the "Gang of Four," the revolutionary elders, and the rest. Although Hua held the highest rank as First Vice-Chairman of the Party, his position was far from secure, let alone dominant in the Politburo. As with any successful intrigue, such an operation could not have been carried out by one person alone. Hua, the mastermind behind the coup, collaborated with General Ye Jianying – also a member of the Politburo Standing Committee – along with other like-minded Party leaders, including Wang Dongxing, the head of the Central Guard Bureau.

The operation, later known as the Huairen Hall Intrigue (*huairentang shibian*) took place at a meeting held at the Huairen Hall in *zhongnanhai* on October 6, 1976. Three members of the Gang of Four were ambushed upon arrival and arrested without an opportunity to resist (Jiang, 2020b). The fourth member, Jiang Qing, Mao's widow, was arrested at her residence. Immediately afterwards, Hua convened an emergency Politburo meeting, at which a proposal was adopted to elect Hua as the Party Chairman. Ten days later, a campaign was launched to denounce the crimes committed by the Gang of Four during the Cultural Revolution and to purge their associates and radical followers. Ten months later, a Central Committee plenary meeting was held, adopting a resolution to permanently expel the Gang of Four from the Party, cementing the victory of the coup. Later, official Party history framed the coup as the rightful retrieval of power from the Gang of Four, omitting the fact that the Gang had been legitimately elected through proper procedures and that their arrests violated the fundamental organizational principles of the Party.

Unlike the YARC model, launching a coup does not require the establishment of a cause for disciplinary action or a formal approval for the use of coercive measures from a formal authority. Once the targets are

[21] It is debated among analysts whether what happened to the Gang of Four at the Huairen Hall Intrigue constitutes a coup. Some argue that it does, since the Gang of Four were physically detained before any disciplinary procedure was launched against them, which contravenes the Party Charter. Others contend that it does not because Hua, as the first-in-command and Mao's heir, had the absolute power to remove any other Party leader. This author took the first view.

physically removed, the victors can employ a range of tools to construct the best-fitting narratives of the coup and legitimize its outcome through formal proceedings that they can now control. However, commensurate with its high rewards, a coup of any form is a highly risky business. Attempting to remove a Politburo member, let alone four at once, through a coup violated any prescribed rules and codes of conduct. It constitutes a high crime, and its illegality is unmistakable. This was well understood among top Party leaders: when Chen Yun, a supporter of the coup, was informed of the operation, he reportedly remarked that "[the coup] should be the first and last exception" (Jiang & Wang, 2014).[22]

Before launching the coup, Hua and his collaborators also considered other options but quickly dismissed the YARC model due to its low viability. Had Hua and his collaborators adhered to the YARC model, their chances of success would have been slim. By the time of the coup, half of the original members of the Politburo Standing Committee had either passed away or remained ousted. The four incumbents were split between the coup plotters – Hua Guofeng and Ye Jianying – and their targets, the Gang of Four, represented by Wang Hongwen and Zhang Chunqiao. Meanwhile, the Central Committee was dominated by members who had been promoted during the Cultural Revolution, making it extremely difficult, if not impossible, to persuade them to switch allegiances, renounce their cause and denounce their leaders while those leaders remained in power. Most critically, the institutions overseeing propaganda and ideology – essential for framing the power struggle and establishing grounds for disciplinary action – were also under the control of the Gang of Four and their associates.

Power struggles at the Politburo level are high-stakes, zero sum games. Hua and his collaborators did not dwell on the legality of their actions for long. Contrary to the common portrayal of Hua as a mild-mannered leader who preferred to avoid confrontations, he seized the first opportunity and executed the coup decisively.

## YARC-Lite in the Deng Era

Politburo power struggles in the 1980s were notably less intense and more contained than those of earlier eras: The punishment was relatively

[22] One researcher questioned the accuracy of attributing the uttering of "the last exception" to Chen Yun, while acknowledging the existence of a discussion about the coup's illegality. (Xu, 2016a).

mild and no wide-scale persecution was launched. When contrasted against the Cultural Revolution, Mao's radicalized YARC model, the struggles in the 1980s marked a clear break from the past: None of them involved the masses or decentralization of violence.[23] However, this contrast is more indicative of the abnormality of Mao's radicalization of YARC in the Cultural Revolution than a fundamental shift from the model thereafter. During the 1942 YARC, for example, none of the primary targets were persecuted either. Wang Ming and Bo Gu were allowed a seat at the Central Committee. Zhang Wentian remained in the Politburo, even being reelected in 1956, albeit as an alternate member. In this sense, Politburo power struggles in the Deng era were more a return to orthodoxy than a new beginning.

Three cases will be analyzed. The first concerns the removal of Hua Guofeng from power. This power struggle was initiated by a group of revolutionary elders led by Deng Xiaoping, Chen Yun, and others who had recently been rehabilitated – ironically, thanks to Hua himself (Ruan, 1992).[24] The power dynamics in this struggle were distinct, making it the most challenging one in the Party history. At the time when the struggle occurred, Hua was officially elected to head all three pillars of the Party-state, the Chairman of the Party, the Commander-in-chief of the military, and the Premier. However, despite this tremendous advantage, he failed to translate these normative authorities into actual power to preempt or counter the power struggle that was plotted against him.

The actions Deng Xiaoping and his allies used to unseat Hua are a textbook example of the YARC model. Dictated by the model, their first goal was to establish a cause for disciplinary action against Hua. This is not as easy as it might seem. At the time, Hua's economic policies were pro-reform but not radical (Ruan, 1992). Politically, he supported the rehabilitation of Party leaders who had been disgraced and victimized during the Cultural Revolution (Teiwes & Sun, 2019). His leadership

[23] After the crackdown of the Gang of Four, the Party launched a campaign to investigate and purge the perpetrators – referred to as the "three types of people" – who attacked the Party establishment during the Cultural Revolution. The investigations were carried out exclusively by Party apparatuses, and the Party issued specific instructions to ban big-character-posters and public debates – hallmarks of the Cultural Revolution – to prevent mass participation. For more details, see Gao (2013).

[24] The term "Deng era" is a simplification commonly used by scholars and analysts to describe the period from Deng Xiaoping's rehabilitation in 1977 until shortly before his death, despite arguments that this era was characterized more by a form of plutocratic rule under multiple Party leaders.

style was congenial and collaborative – so much so that his tenure was regarded by some as "a golden era of collective leadership" in the Party (Torigian, 2022). Under his leadership, political radicalism was halted, the economy was recovering, and China's engagement with the rest of the world had begun. In short, there was no major policy failure significant enough to give cause to justify a disciplinary action.

Was it possible, or even preferable, then, to remove Hua through a coup? There is no historical evidence suggesting that Deng and his allies ever considered this option. However, for the sake of analysis, a coup would have been both risky and difficult. To begin with, a successful coup requires the ability to physically overpower and restrain the target. As Hua later revealed in an interview, Party protocols at the time dictated that, as the Head of the Party, he was the only person permitted to carry a weapon or be accompanied by an armed guard at Politburo meetings. Securing defection and cooperation of Hua's security detail would also have been unlikely, given that the head of the Central Guard Bureau was Wang Dongxing – one of Hua's key allies in the coup against the Gang of Four, whose career was clearly invested in Hua's staying in power rather than in losing it.

In addition, a coup is inherently illegitimate. While the first coup – the removal of the Gang of Four – could be justified on exceptional moral grounds, the same justification could not apply to a coup against Hua, who was lauded for his heroism in that earlier event, from which Deng and his allies had directly benefited. Moreover, a coup would have contradicted the very principle that Deng Xiaoping and his allies had relied on during the 1954 Gao/Rao affair to expel Gao Gang from the Party. A coup would have been a far more flagrant violation of Party discipline than the "non-organizational activities" – private electoral lobbying – that Gao Gang had been accused of. Nothing could have been more "non-organizational" than an orchestrated coup against the Party's paramount leader. If Deng instigated a coup against Hua, it would be a blatant contradiction of the very principles he had preached.

Deng and his allies adopted the YARC model and followed it to the letter. Their first move was to introduce an ideological debate under the banner of "Practice is the sole criterion for testing truth." As dictated by the YARC model, this debate framed past and current Party policies in binary ideological terms, dividing them into "correct" and "wrong" lines. Hua's policies were presented, or, rather, misrepresented (Ruan, 1992; Teiwes & Sun, 2019; Torigian, 2022) as "two whateverism (*liangge fanshi*)," a discourse that held Hua blameworthy for blindly adhering to Maoism without regard for pragmatic governance or truth-seeking.

Also similar to the 1942 YARC, a YARC-style ideological campaign was launched from the Central Party School, now overseen by Hu Yaobang, who would later succeed Hua. Numerous editorials and articles were written and circulated to propagate the ideological attack against the "two-whateverism," Within six months, the new ideological framing had taken hold. In 1978, a national work conference was convened, gathering senior Party officials across the country, where Hua faced direct and intensive criticism. Under pressure, Hua was compelled to admit to his mistakes by the conclusion of the conference. Immediately afterwards, the Central Committee convened, where Deng and his allies court-packed the Politburo with their followers. Weakened and isolated, Hua asked to resign from his posts, which was instantly accepted by the Politburo. The Politburo announced his resignation as one with cause but no disciplinary investigation was launched against him. Hua was allowed to keep his Central Committee membership until 2002.

The second case of power struggle at the Politburo was against Hu Yaobang, who was chosen as the nominal head of the Party after Hua Guofeng's resignation in 1981. During his tenure, Hu faced opposition among conservative Party leaders who objected to Hu's liberal stance on several political issues. In addition, China was at the time undergoing a painful transition, with loosening boundaries between the private and state-owned industries, central and local governments, and state and market forces. This transition led to economic disruptions, inflation, and widespread corruption, fueling popular discontent (Thornton, 2007, p. 212). The 1986 students' protests became the trigger and the disciplinary cause for Hu's removal.

The proceedings reportedly began at a meeting held at Deng's residence, attended by a small group of Party elders. This was followed by a series of Politburo meetings during which Hu faced coordinated criticisms, accusing him of having committed an ideological transgression labelled as "capitalist liberalism." Hu admitted to his mistakes and resigned. The same as Hua's case, Hu's resignation was announced as one with cause but without further disciplinary investigation. Hu was even allowed to keep his Politburo membership.

The third case of power struggle concerned Zhao Ziyang, who had succeeded Hu Yaobang as General Party-Secretary (GPS). His downfall was triggered by his actions in the 1989 democratic movement, not toeing the Party line in support of the students. He was accused of having violated the Party's organizational principles and Party discipline and attempted to divide the Party. Eventually, the Politburo motioned to remove Zhao from all tiers of decision-making bodies of the Party, a move swiftly approved by the Central Committee. Zhao was only allowed to keep his Party membership,[25] but following his removal, a disciplinary investigation was launched into corruption-related accusations against his family. This marked the first time anti-corruption was used as a tool in a Politburo power struggle. The investigation was closed in 1992 with no charge filed.[26]

Following the June 4, 1989 crackdown, the Party launched a sweeping disciplinary campaign targeting active participants and supporters of the democratic movement. Between 1987 and 1992, 13,254 Party members were punished for violations of political discipline, including 1,179 ranked Party leaders of the county-level or above (CCDI, 1992). Although the personal trauma suffered by each victim is immeasurable, the overall purge appears moderate in intensity, especially considering that more than 800,000 Party members and cadres had participated or supported the students' movement (Baum, 2018).

During the same period, the Party's disciplinary institution expanded significantly, as detailed in Chapter 5. In 1989, the Party approved the establishment of the first anti-corruption investigative bureau in the procuratorates. In 1994, the Party granted the CCDI and its local counterparts the authority to use the coercive *shuanggui* measure (a form of internal disciplinary detention) for corruption investigations. By 1997, Jiang Zemin declared that anti-corruption was a matter of life or death for the Party. With all institutional mechanisms in place to empower anti-corruption agencies and substantial enforcement resources dedicated to corruption investigations, anti-corruption was no longer mere political rhetoric but a foundational force that would reshape Politburo power struggles in the following decades.

## Anti-corruption Model – Jiang-Hu Era

Toward the end of Deng's rule, the YARC model was gradually phased out. The model had a significant disadvantage: Before a power struggle

[25] Zhao wrote in his memoir that the Party initially planned to allow him to retain his Central Committee membership. However, unlike Hu Yaobang, who admitted to the mistakes he was accused of, Zhao did not. Instead, he attempted to rebut the accusations, which, according to his own account, led to aggravated punishment (Zhao, 2009).

[26] The decision to close the investigation was mentioned in the Communiqué of the 9th Plenum Meeting of the 13th National Party Congress passed on October 9, 1992.

was resolved, it exposed a split within the Party leadership. Such internal divisions, once revealed, could be exploited by external political forces, as was manifestly the case in the Tiananmen protests.

The removals of Hu Yaobang and Zhao Ziyang marked the last instances of ideologized power struggles at the Politburo. Even in Hu Yaobang's case, the ideological struggle preceding his removal was brief and contained compared to earlier struggles. Zhao Ziyang's removal was even swifter, with the ideological struggle preceding his downfall limited to the Politburo. The 1989 political crisis underscored both the cost and risk of employing the YARC model, leading the Party to favor a model for the handling of power struggles – one that would avoid exposing fractures within the Party Center.

After 1989, two major political developments enabled this paradigm shift. The first was the prioritization of anti-corruption on the Party's agenda. Throughout the 1990s and the 2010s, corruption continued to intensify, becoming deeply entrenched within the Party's power structure at all levels (Guo, 2012; Wedeman, 2005a). In 1997, Jiang Zemin, General Party Secretary in 1989–2002, declared at the National Party Congress that anti-corruption was a matter of life or death for the Party. Around the same time, the Party reframed its anti-corruption discourse, portraying the Party not as a cause of corruption, but as its victim. This discoursal shift enabled the Party to go on the offensive, positioning itself as the guardian of government integrity and the leading force in fighting corruption. It was also during that period that the CCDI was formally designated in the Party Charter as the specialized Party institution for investigating corruption cases against Central Committee members, including Politburo members.

The second but often overlooked political development was the introduction of the age-limit norm. As I discussed elsewhere, this norm functioned as a non-democratic mechanism to facilitate the exits of top powerholders, enabling the redistribution of power *en masse* without resorting to aggressive internal struggles (Li, 2022a). By the early 1990s, the Party urgently needed leadership reinvigoration to push forward the economic reforms, yet the life tenure of Politburo members hindered the process. At the time, Politburo seats were vacated only by illness, death, disciplinary purges following the YARC model or a coup, which were costly and politically disruptive.

Efforts to address this issue began in 1982, when the average age of Politburo Standing Committee members had reached seventy-four-and-a-half years old. The Party experimented with various retirement schemes, including the creation of the Central Advisory Committee (CAC), which removed first-generation Party elders from day-to-day administration while allowing them to influence decision-making from behind the scenes. However, such backseat leadership could be just as disruptive. In 1992, the CAC was abolished, paving the way for the emergence of the age-limit norm.

A full explanation of the age-limit norm is beyond the scope of this discussion, but in essence, it is a set of rules that compels members of different tiers of decision-making bodies of the Party Center to step down upon reaching a designated age at the time of Party elections. Various degrees of exceptions to the rule are granted as prerogatives, depending on the tier of membership.[27] This norm was rather consistently observed at the Central Committee level, as seen in its high turnover rates. While the practices had drifted at the 20th Party Congress in 2022, the violations were deliberate and localized rather than arbitrary and regular (Li, 2022a). The high-performing operational efficiency of the age-limit norm significantly reduced the urgency of power struggles because Politburo seat vacancies were now created with considerable predictability and regularity, eliminating the need for YARC-style "struggles."

The combination of the enhancement of anti-corruption enforcement and the implementation of the age-limit norm led to a paradigm shift in Politburo power struggles. During 1992–2012, three Politburo members were removed, all under strikingly similar circumstances. First, corruption, rather than ideological mistakes, served as the official justification for their removal, marking a clear departure from earlier disciplinary practices. Second, unlike previous power struggles, these cases unfolded without the backdrop of a YARC-style rectification campaign against the targets. Third, the disciplinary process was swiftly followed by a criminal prosecution, culminating in secured convictions and long prison sentences. Lastly, the power struggles were largely contained within the Politburo, avoiding system-wide purges that had characterized earlier Politburo struggles.

The shift marked a decisive break from the YARC model. Rather than exposing internal rifts, the Party leveraged the ubiquity, criminality, and immorality of corruption – repurposing it as a strategic tool for removing political opponents. By using corruption as the new framework for disciplinary action, a YARC-style ideological campaign was no longer

[27] To better understand the effects of the age-limit norm, I developed a stratified framework that reflects the different prerogatives enjoyed by members of different tiers of decision-making bodies at the Party Center. For more details, see Li (2022a).

essential for power struggles. Instead, these campaigns were separated from power struggles and introduced as stand-alone programs for political indoctrination and education. During Jiang Zemin's last term of office, ideological campaigns were rebranded as the Party's Education Programs on Selected Themes (hereinafter Party Education Program or PEP) as a part of the "Party-building" initiative (Gao, 2013). During the PEP, all Party organizations were required to hold regular group meetings where participants studied assigned training materials and conducted self-examination and criticism.[28] However, unlike the YARC-style ideological campaign, these materials were not used to initiate disciplinary actions against the participants.

All these changes led to the complete de-ideologization of Politburo power struggles under Jiang Zemin's leadership. Before 1989, all disciplinary charges against Politburo members involved political offenses, such as counterrevolutionary, capitalist revisionism, dividing the Party, or engaging in anti-Party conspiracies. Under the leadership of Jiang Zemin and Hu Jintao, all investigations were carried out on grounds of corruption (Li, 2016b).

This de-ideologization benefited the Party in two aspects. First, a YARC-style ideological campaign was highly costly, as it disrupted normal functioning of Party-state governance. Such campaigns required the entire workforce of public institutions to suspend their regular duties and participate in lengthy and immersive rectification programs, significantly hindering administrative and economic operations.

Second, it exposed internal fractures in Party leadership. The Party regarded its ability to suppress differences and project unity as crucial to its revolutionary success (Teiwes, 2001, p. 71). This belief was further reinforced after the Party survived its most serious political crisis in 1989, widely attributed – at least in part – to the open split among its leadership (Teiwes, 2001, p. 72). Nothing would have highlighted internal divisions more clearly than a YARC-style ideological campaign deliberately *designed* to create and exploit an internal conflict.

During the Jiang-Hu era, another important shift in Party practice took place: the relegation of the Central Committee from its role as the sole body to authorize disciplinary action against a Central Committee member (including a Politburo member) to a secondary – and *ex post* – rectifying authority with a much reduced role in decision making.

[28] Xi (2013b).

Beginning in 1983, as discussed in Chapter 5, the disciplinary function of the Central Committee was gradually hollowed out by an informal power group led by Deng, as seen in the ousting of Hu Yaobang and Zhao Ziyang. At the same time, the Party Charter was amended to allow the "Party Center," – under special circumstances (a provision removed in 2017) – to make a disciplinary decision first, with retroactive affirmation from the Central Committee later. By 2002, the Party Charter explicitly stated that such a disciplinary decision would be made by the Politburo, with the Central Committee's role limited to affirming it *ex post facto.*

Transferring the disciplinary decision-making power from the Central Committee to the Politburo significantly accelerated the disciplinary process. The Central Committee, whose membership has grown to around 200 and is scattered across the country, meets only once or twice a year. By contrast, the Politburo, typically composed of twenty to twenty-five members, meets monthly, making it easier and faster to build consensus. Since Politburo power struggles are high-stakes and volatile, timing is critical. A swift decision can preempt attempts by the target and their allies to strategize and rally resistance.

As a result of the centralization of disciplinary decision-making, the time required to remove a Politburo member through disciplinary procedures has decreased significantly over the past thirty years. The case against Chen Xitong in 1995 took twenty-eight months, but by 2002, the removal of Chen Liangyu was completed in twelve months. By 2012, the Bo Xilai case took only five and a half months and in 2014 the cases against Xu Caihou and Zhou Yongkang were both resolved in just four months.

## Politicized Anti-corruption Model – Xi Jinping Era

When Xi Jinping assumed power in 2012, he inherited a fully operational disciplinary system that had taken decades to construct and institutionalize, along with a new model of power struggles built around anti-corruption enforcement. This model enabled the precise removal of rivals or nonloyalists with minimal political disruptions, eliminating the need for full-scale YARC-style ideological campaigns.

However, the anti-corruption model has certain weaknesses that mirror the model's advantages. The model has the advantage of being surgical and less disruptive, isolating targets for removal without system-wide upheaval; yet, this strength becomes a liability when faced with entrenched – or worse, organized – threats, as it lacks the transformative impact of YARC-style campaigns. Additionally, by de-ideologizing power struggles, the anti-corruption model has the advantage of concealing major policy disagreements among the top leaders, preventing external forces from exploiting divisions; however, treating power struggles solely as criminal corruption cases – rather than ideological battles – sends mixed signals about the intent behind these measures and weakens the drive for political compliance.

To counter these issues, Xi responded by politicizing the anti-corruption campaign. This occurred around 2015-2016, when the campaign peaked and generated equally strong resentment among officials of all ranks. The resentment was so visceral that some Party officials openly questioned the legitimacy of the campaign. Such open political defiance is contagious and dangerous; once it begins to spread – especially when facilitated through organized networks – it can gain momentum that may weaken the resolve of the campaign enforcement agents and derail the campaign. It was against this backdrop that the anti-corruption model was politicized.

To that end, Xi first revived the Party's political discipline, a discipline that had been largely disregarded for two decades.[29] Under Jiang Zemin and Hu Jintao, all three Politburo members removed from power were disciplined solely on corruption grounds. Under Xi, the practice changed. Bo Xilai's case best illustrates this shift. In his case, the disciplinary process began under Hu Jintao but the judicial process unfolded under Xi Jinping. When the disciplinary investigation was concluded, the Party's resolution made no mention of any political misconduct.[30] Only after Xi Jinping came to power was Bo Xilai's misconduct reinterpreted and politicized, with additional political disciplinary violations added as grounds for disciplinary action.[31]

During Xi's first term alone, three PEPs were launched, double the intensity of Hu Jintao's three PEPs over two terms. Xi's PEPs ran parallel to his anti-corruption campaign and were essential in politicizing anti-corruption from 2014 onwards. At the outset, the indoctrination focused on the populist mass-line policy, which aimed to align Party cadres' activities closely with the demands of the people. However, beginning with the second PEP, two new subject matters were introduced in the study curriculum: political discipline and political protocols.[32]

[29] Li (2016b).
[30] Xinhua (2012a).
[31] Zhong (2015).
[32] Department (2015).

Political discipline as a distinct concept first appeared in the Party Discipline Directive in 2003. Typical political disciplinary offenses include ideological deviations, violations of policies on religion or ethnic minorities, sedition, treason, and espionage. "Political protocol" was a new concept that emerged in Xi Jinping's speeches and Party media editorials in mid-2014. In one speech, Xi defined "political protocol" by stating: "To follow the Party's leadership, one must follow the converged and unified leadership of the Party Center – this is a fundamental principle of Party protocols." As discussed in greater detail in previous chapters, the unified command of the Party Center (UCOPC) principle has been the cardinal tenet of the Party-state architecture; however, this is the first time that it has been operationalized as an enforceable discipline.

Xi's second PEP coincided with a large-scale anti-corruption operation at the Politburo against several "alpha tigers," including a former Politburo Standing Committee member, two military commanders, and dozens of other high-ranking leaders. After their fall from grace, their disciplinary violations and crimes were politically recontextualized, compiled, and circulated to the PEP participants for study. Some traditional political offenses that had vanished from Party disciplinary activities since the 1990s were reactivated – for example, conducting "non-organizational activities," an offense infamously used during the 1953–1954 Gao/Rao Affair. Ling Jihua, former chief-of-staff of Hu Jintao, became the poster boy for this offense after being accused of organizing a club for the political and business elite who shared his ancestral origin. The club, called Xi'shan Society, was portrayed as a factional clique that not only facilitated corruption but also operated as an underground power network conspiring to undermine the UCOPC principle and the authority of the Party Center.[33] Such "group-forming" and "alliance-making" activities were later classified as a distinct enforceable political disciplinary offense.[34]

In 2015, Xi expanded the scope of political offenses in an address to the CCDI. One new offense that garnered significant media attention was "denigrating the Party Center (*wangyi zhongyang*)." The case of Zhou Benshun, former Party Secretary of Hebei Province, was held up as exemplary for this offense after he was caught making disrespectful remarks about the Party's austerity campaign. Zhou allegedly said that

[33] Jun (2016).
[34] Shen (2015).

the anti-corruption campaign was "unnecessarily stringent and rigid" and that "there is nothing wrong with drinking [at banquets] . . . because it helps create a good spirit for bonding."[35] Other new offenses include deceiving the Party Center with obsequiousness regarding major policies,[36] being disloyal and untruthful to the Party, and resisting investigation.[37]

At the beginning of 2016, as enforcement of political discipline gained momentum, a new PEP was launched. During this PEP, the concept of "core (*hexin*)" was introduced to the study curriculum. The "core" is a privileged political status given to Xi Jinping, elevating him above the collective leadership of the Party Center. A doctrine on upholding the "core" status of Xi was formulated and became a mandatory item for study in the PEP. Ten months later, the doctrine was endorsed by the Central Committee and, one year later, written into the Party Charter and other Party regulations. By mid-2017, 15,000 Party members had received disciplinary sanctions for political offenses – exceeding the total punished during the 1989–1992 post-Tiananmen purges.

Besides expanding political discipline, Xi took another critical step to politicize anti-corruption: linking political offenses to corruption offenses for disciplinary investigation. After grave political offenses by several high-ranking Party leaders were discovered, Xi stressed in a 2016 CCDI address that anti-corruption investigations should prioritize cases against those who committed both political and corruption offenses. This linkage is critical for remodeling power struggles. Before this change, the most severe punishment for political offenses was removal from office and expulsion from the Party. Such punishments are insufficient to prevent offenders from exerting influence through informal networks or launching counterattacks. In contrast, corruption is criminalized with death as the maximal penalty. A political offender convicted of corruption will have their political career effectively terminated and lose the ability to organize political mobilization. For the winning side of a power struggle, this is perhaps the best assurance, next only to physical liquidation – of eliminating threats from the losing side. Moreover, politicizing power struggles makes it easier to purge the political influence and uproot the power base of the targets, including their allies, collaborators, supporters,

35 Wang (2017b).
36 Shen (2015).
37 Chen and Chen (2015), Lu and Zhang (2015), and Tianjin (2016).

and sympathizers, who, if left unchecked, may pose an incalculable safety risk to the winning side.

Thus, when corruption is so pervasive that rising to high office almost necessitates engaging in it, linking political offense to corruption renders political misconduct indictable without formally criminalizing it. This politicized anti-corruption paradigm addresses the "signal problem" of the previous de-politicized approach. In the old approach, with political motives concealed, the winning side of the power struggle could not clearly signal its intent to the broader elite, allowing political noncompliance to persist. Although signaling alone cannot eradicate violations, the "enforcement swamp" theory (see Chapter 6) suggests that strong signals reduce violations, enable timely detection and punishment, and enhance sanction credibility – creating a virtuous cycle without significantly increasing enforcement resources.

On the other hand, politicizing the anti-corruption campaign also increases political disruption. To contain this, the policy linking political offenses to corruption investigation is currently applied primarily to high-ranking elites rather than the rank and file. A survey of the anti-corruption campaign in 2012–2017 shows that enforcement of political disciplines was highly uneven: all four Politburo members and thirteen out of the fourteen Central Committee members removed during this period were disciplined for both political and corruption offenses and the one who was disciplined but *not* prosecuted for corruption is the only one *not* accused of political offenses (Li, 2019). In contrast, fewer than 1 percent of the 1.54 million rank-and-file Party members of lower or no rank who had received disciplinary punishments in 2012–2017 were accused of political offenses (Li, 2019).

The politicized anti-corruption model proved highly effective. As detailed in Chapter 6, within just ten years, Xi oversaw the imprisonment of 1 Politburo Standing Committee member, 4 Politburo members, 70 generals, and approximately 700 senior civilian officials at the ministerial or deputy-ministerial rank, all on corruption charges. This scale of power restructuring at the Party Center is unprecedented since Mao's Cultural Revolution, yet it was achieved without mass mobilization or decentralization of violence, both of which had been central to Mao's approach.

## Conclusion

In this chapter, I have shown that power struggles at the Party Center have been an integral part of the Party's disciplinary system from the beginning. Authorizing and instituting a disciplinary mechanism to unseat a Politburo member is a pragmatic choice, given the ban on open competitive political campaigns for electoral offices under Leninist doctrines. Dictated by the disciplinary system, removing an incumbent Politburo member must meet two conditions: establishing a cause for disciplinary action and securing the disciplinary panel's approval for the proposed sanction.

Mao's YARC model was developed when the Party's disciplinary system was still in its embryonic form. This model is distinct for its heavily ideologized format, portraying power struggles as ideological conflicts and framing real or invented policy differences as binary "line-struggles" arising from intractable ideological divisions. Its advantage lies in its ability to provide a channel for power competition by suppressing instead of fostering political opposition within the Party – the defeated side must capitulate and accept the winning side's correct line, thereby reinforcing the Party's collective will. However, at the same time, it also exposes internal splits before the struggle is resolved, rendering the Party vulnerable to external exploitation and threatening regime stability.

Because the YARC model is ideologically driven, initiating and winning a power struggle requires firm control over both the ideological/propaganda apparatuses and the disciplinary system. My analysis in this chapter also shows that when a power struggle became imperative but the offensive side lacked sufficient control over these institutions, modifications were necessary – as seen in the coup against the Gang of Four.

A paradigm shift occurred after the 1989 political crisis due to two factors. First, the emergence of the age-limit norm. This nondemocratic mechanism facilitates the exits of current powerholders, enabling large-scale peaceful redistribution of power in the Party Center, thereby reducing the need and urgency of the YARC-style power struggles. Second, the 1989 Tiananmen political crisis underscored the inherent shortcomings of the YARC model while also reshaping the Party's awareness and perception of corruption, not merely as a pervasive problem but also as a potential tool for political maneuvering.

For the next two decades, Politburo power struggles became de-ideologized and reduced in both intensity and scope. At the same time, the Party's specialized disciplinary institutions, notably the CCDI, rapidly grew in power and capacity, becoming key players in power struggles at the Party Center. When Xi came to power in 2012, he maximized the anti-corruption model's utility, instituting a power restructuring through anti-corruption on an unprecedented scale. This shakeup also triggered widespread political resentment. To quell this resentment and noncompliance, Xi politicized the anti-corruption model, enabling him to remove not only individual political transgressors but also their power bases. By reactivating political offenses and making them indictable, he rectified the signaling problem inherent in the previous depoliticized anti-corruption model. This modified approach has markedly enhanced political conformity, at least on a superficial level.

# PART III

# Conclusion

# 8

# Governance of a Party-State

Comparative political studies have shown that authoritarian rulers face two fundamental challenges to maintaining power (Svolik, 2012). The first concerns the need to share power with other political elites. To address this, many authoritarian rulers introduce formal "democratic-looking" institutions – such as parties, elections, and parliaments – to demonstrate the credibility of their commitment to a power-sharing arrangement (Boix & Svolik, 2013; Gandhi & Przeworski, 2007; Magaloni, 2008; Slater, 2011; Svolik, 2009). The second challenge concerns the repression of the masses. To manage this, authoritarian rulers rely on state institutions to either suppress political demands or co-opt opposition leaders among the masses (Slater, 2011).

In this book, I show that the Party relies on an overlaid, integral, and complex dual governing system to regulate not only the elites, the masses but also the vast meso-level space between them. Within this intermediary zone, the Party first chains the state and then empowers it to serve the Party. Governing this space requires addressing problems such as: how to construct a power system capable of implementing the Party's multifaceted policies nationwide; how to preserve the structural integrity of the Party-state against centrifugal forces arising from both the center and the periphery; and how to institute a disciplinary system that can reduce the principal–agent problems while motivating an army of agents to carry out the Party's will.

These meso-level governance challenges occupy the space *between* the "ruling coalition" at the top and the controlled masses at the bottom. Different from previous studies that focus either on informal politics or on the state's normative system, my analysis centers on the Party's formal-normative system – an institutional framework that links the Party and the state.

This formal-normative system is quite distinct from the People's Republic of China (PRC) law-based state normative system and may appear alien to many readers. Yet, this dissimilarity does not make this system less "institutional" or ineffective when assessed against its intended purposes. Nor should the existence of such a formal-normative system come as a surprise. For an organization with over ninety million members, the Party cannot function by relying merely on informal politics or patronage networks. Informal politics (as important as it is) does not operate in an institutional vacuum. A sole focus on informal politics risks overlooking more durable structural factors embodied in the Party's formal-normative system. A lack of understanding or appreciation of this system can easily result in misinterpretation and distorted analyses.

A recent example is the 2018 amendment to the PRC Constitution abolishing the term limit of the Head of the State, the PRC chairmanship. Analysts widely interpreted this move as a step to enable Xi Jinping to rule for life. As I have argued in greater detail elsewhere (Li, 2021), this interpretation is deeply flawed because it overlooked several key normative rules and practices.

First, the primary seat of power in the Party-state is the position of Head of Party, not that of the State. Second, there has never been a term limit imposed on the Head of the Party, or, for that matter, on any other Politburo members. The Party Charter is silent on this matter. In other words, there is no formal-normative restriction preventing Xi Jinping from serving a third or additional term as the Head of the Party if he continues to win Party elections. Third, historically only one person retired as the Head of the Party after serving two terms – Hu Jintao's reign (2002–2012) – making the two-term practice an exception rather than a rule. Fourth, the term limit for the Head of State – inserted in the PRC Constitution in 1982 – was never intended to constrain the tenure of the Head of the Party. At the time, the posts of PRC Chairman and General Party Secretary (GPS) were held by two different individuals. It was only one decade later that the GPS began concurrently holding the office of the PRC Chairman.

Therefore, I argue that the 2018 constitutional amendment is significant not because it lifted the term limit for the PRC Chairman but because it marked a profound transformation in the Party-state relationship, signaling a shift from the Party's long-standing defensive stance vis-à-vis the state to a strategy that embraces it, capitalizing on reinforced Party-state integration (see section "Evolution of the Party-state"). The implication of this development would be obscured – or missed entirely – if one were to focus narrowly on the term limit issue without understanding the Party's normative system. However, capturing the contours of the

Party-state is not straightforward, given the limits on access to information and the system's inherent opacity and ambiguity. To navigate these challenges, it is useful to place recent political developments within a longer historical perspective. A longitudinal institutional analysis helps avoid the pitfalls of presentism, broadens the analytical horizon, and allows for the identification of intermittent structural shifts and enduring institutional transformations that may otherwise be overlooked or misinterpreted.

## Contour of the Party-State and Its Mode of Governance

The Party-state is a distinct political system. Its distinctive quality cannot be grasped merely by reference to the number of political parties that are allowed to operate within it. Rather, it stems from the nature and scope of the political prerogative that a political party enjoys in its operation within a sovereign state. This political prerogative is used to bind state organs to the Party as an integrated whole.

At an abstract level, the mode of governance of China's Party-state can be represented as shown in Figure 8.1 (also stylized in the book's cover image). The Party occupies the center of the concentric circles of the state and the society. In this nested structure, the state possesses popular sovereignty. It employs a law-based normative system, consisting of laws that purport to protect rights and to uphold the principle of equality before the law. Authorized by this normative legal system, the state provides order and stability within society and holds the formal-legal authority to exercise coercive policing, investigative, and punitive powers to that end.

The Party, anchored at the core of the power structure, exerts monopolistic control over all state organs. It does not regulate society directly through legal enforcement (except for corruption cases), but governs primarily *through* the state.[1] This, however, does not mean that the Party is segregated from society. On the contrary, it is known for its

[1] The fact that the Party regulates the society only through the state organs does not mean that it is absent at the grassroots level. The Party's grassroots presence is achieved by recruiting Party members from the masses and organizing them into Party-cells. However, these Party-cells do not carry regulatory functions like state agencies. In recent years, the Party has consistently sought to strengthen its connection with the masses, most notably, by organizing voluntary service groups to fill gaps in public services. For detailed anecdotes of such voluntary work, see the Party Member Voluntary Service Federation (CVF) website: www.cvf.org.cn/cvf/channels/12152.shtml. Mittelstaedt (2021) has also detailed some ritualized activities aimed at enhancing the Party's grassroots presence.

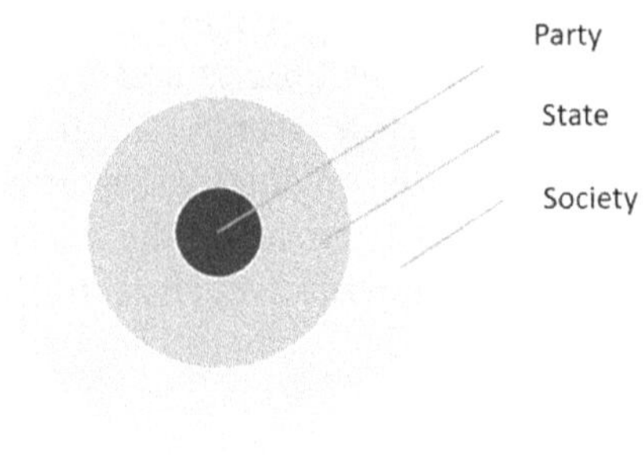


**Figure 8.1** Nested structure of the Party-state-society relations.

capability to penetrate into the grassroots deeper than the state has ever achieved. Yet, such penetration is used more for mass mobilization than for law enforcement. In Imperial China, rulers often maintained distance from the masses, a strategy characterized by some scholars as "top-bottom divided governance."[2] The Party today, while shielded by the state, adopts a similar stance in its structural separation from routine societal administration.

Protected by the state, the Party's operation is self-regulated, self-contained, and subject only to internal scrutiny and selective, voluntary public disclosure. The Party governs itself through an internal formal-normative system that asserts jurisdiction based on Party membership and organizational affiliation. The Party's formal-normative system consists of two main conceptual components: a power system that defines the relations among Party-state organs and offices; and a disciplinary system that polices the conduct of officeholders and enforces the order of power as designated by the Party.

Distinct from the state legal system, the Party's formal-normative system is anchored in the concept of power and serves to protect power-based political prerogatives. Its fundamental goal is to safeguard the unified command – or absolute authority – of the Party Center. This system encompasses both written and unwritten rules. Written rules are the dominant form; they prescribe required conduct and proscribe punishable acts. Unwritten rules – such as the age-limit norm discussed in

[2] The practice can be traced to the legalist philosophy proposed by Han Feizi over two millennia ago: "a wise ruler shall govern the officials not the masses." This philosophy, also referred to as "top-bottom divided governance," had a lasting impact on the mode of governance in imperial China (Cao, 2014, 2011; Zheng, 2020; Zhou, 2016).

Chapter 7 – are equally important, though more difficult to trace or identify. Both types of rules may appear alien to West-trained minds because they address a set of governance problems largely absent in Western democratic systems. Studying them thus requires an endogenous, organic, and ideologically neutral approach – one that assesses the functions of these rules according to their intended purposes, rather than fitting them into normative frameworks developed for entirely different political configurations and problem sets – where conformity is treated as a marker of efficacy and divergence as a sign of deficiency.[3]

## Unified Command of the Party Center

Unified (absolute) command of the Party Center (UCOPC) is the cardinal principle of the Party's formal-normative system. Throughout the Party's centennial history, the UCOPC principle has taken different forms and expressions at different times. Under Mao's rule, it was articulated as "single-unit leadership (*yiyuanhua lingdao*) of the Party." This principle dictated that all decisions concerning military operation, Party affairs, and governmental matters within a given administrative unit under the Party's control were to be made by the Party Committee of that unit (territorial Party Committee).[4] To illustrate this principle, Mao coined the pithy aphorism, "To the east, south, west, north, and the center, the Party must lead in all directions." This phrase has been revived and popularized during Xi Jinping's rule, decades later.

During the reform era, "adherence to the Party's leadership" was enshrined as one of the four cardinal principles of Party-state governance and has remained a consistent political directive. Under Xi's rule, "the Party's leadership" was further elevated in 2018, when it was introduced into the main body of the PRC Constitution and upheld as the "defining feature of the PRC socialist political system." In 2019, the third Resolution on Party History reaffirmed the "concentrated and unified

[3] Similar views advocating a more organic or endogenous approach to studying the Party's normative system can be found in Samuli (2022) and Snape (2019a).

[4] A territorial Party Committee is a Party committee established in an administrative unit. It enjoys the encompassing, plenipotential power over all public affairs within that unit's geographical boundaries. A territorial Party Committee differs from a primary or grass-roots-level Party committee – for example, those set up in universities, state-owned-enterprises, and so on – whose competence is restricted to affairs within its host institution.

leadership of the Party Center" as the primary principle of Party rule (Party, 2019).

Despite changes in terminology, the Party has consistently upheld the UCOPC principle throughout its history. As the cornerstone of the Party-state governance, the Party has institutionalized the UCOPC principle into a two-pronged political prerogative: *exhaustive competence* and *supreme authority*. Exhaustive competence grants the Party Center plenipotentiary power to make decisions across all domains, sectors, and issues of public concern, whether known today or emerging in the future. This notion of plenipotentiary power is fundamentally at odds with Montesquieu's principle of the separation of powers. Rather than a multipolar arrangement, the UCOPC principle concentrates power in a single seat, the Party Center. Supreme authority, in turn, enables the Party Center to demand unconditional compliance from all Party formations, including those embedded within state organs that otherwise enjoy constitutionally conferred autonomy.

The Party Center then delegates its political prerogative to Party organizations at lower levels – a necessity given the scale of the population and territory it governs. This delegation takes place along two dimensions: (1) vertically, through the administrative hierarchy and territorial divides, from the Party Center to subnational territorial Party Committees; and (2) horizontally, across sectoral lines, from territorial Party Committees to specialized Party organs, including those embedded in all state organs and their agencies, of the same administrative units.

The vertical dimension concerns the spatial chain of command along administrative levels and territorial divides, reaching the grassroots. The horizontal dimension is functional, involving a division of labor across sectoral lines, which becomes more refined in the state structure. The Party Center's objective in delegating its political prerogative is twofold. First, it seeks to empower lower-level Party organizations and their agents to implement central initiatives. Where this political prerogative is exercised, it is insulated from third party scrutiny – including from the courts – and is subject only to oversight by the delegating authority, generally the higher Party organization. Second, delegation allows for a degree of implementational flexibility at subnational levels, accommodating diverse local conditions while encouraging regional and local initiatives to foster economic development and improve governance. This arrangement of centrally monitored decentralization – a feature widely recognized by scholars (Chien, 2010; Chung, 2000; Huang, 1996; Lin & Liu, 2000; Liu et al., 2018) and a key distinction between the China model and its Soviet counterparts (Xu, 2024) – enables the Party to govern a country of vast population and immense territorial diversity without committing to a federalist power-sharing constitutional order that requires and guarantees subunit or subsystem autonomy.

In contrast to the Party's concentrated power structure, the power structure in the state system exhibits significant fragmentation. First, in any given administrative unit the state power is divided among several branches – including the legislative, executive, judiciary, procuratorates and (since 2018) supervision – similar to the separation of powers in liberal democracies. Second, power within the executive branch – namely, the State Council, the most powerful and resourceful of all state organs – is further fragmented by the Party-groups embedded in each ministry or ministerial committee. These ministerial Party-groups pledge loyalty to the Party Center rather than to the Premier.

The fragmented power in the state structure becomes united through and only through the territorial Party Committee, which is mandated to coordinate actions of these state organs, adjudicate inter-agency disputes, and resolve policy conflicts. These arrangements chain state institutions horizontally to their territorial Party Committee, and, in turn, link each territorial Party Committee level by level upwards to the Party Center, thus sustaining the unified (absolute) command of the Party Center.

## Problem of Corruption

The Party's formal-normative system is high-performing in terms of safeguarding the absolute power of the Party Center. However, the inherent arbitrariness of absolute power is conducive to corruption. When the Party's political prerogative is delegated to and normalized in all public institutions, it amplifies the principal–agent problem too. System-wide delegation of political prerogative produces a proliferation of corruption opportunities. It means that an otherwise isolatable problem is replicated, multiplied, and spread to all nooks and crannies of the entire structure of the Party-state.

Take courts as an example. As shown in Chapter 2, a court in any given administrative unit is subordinate to its corresponding territorial Party Committee. That Committee is entitled to interfere in judicial decisions within its geographic boundaries to protect the Party's collective interest. Similarly, judges are embedded in an internal power hierarchy within each court, which allows court leaders to impose their will on divisional leaders, who, in turn, impose their will on frontline judges, much like the Party leaders do.

These arrangements transform a court into an official *partial* decision-making body, where law is interpreted on demand by a superior authority to produce a desired outcome. In other words, judges are *obligated* to apply laws partially to satisfy the preferences of their superiors whenever required. As a result, the authority of law is frequently relegated to a secondary role, and impartiality, a hallmark of adjudication, is not just intermittently compromised but systematically eroded. Once this partial decision-making mechanism is institutionalized and normalized, its impacts reverberate far beyond individual cases. The political prerogative delegated to individual leaders, whether inside or outside a court, allows them to camouflage their corrupt intent with thinly veiled political claims and have such intent legitimately translated into partial court decisions through the same mechanism that processes the Party's political demands. Frontline judges, repeatedly exposed to and compelled to engage in these partial practices, may come to see it as acceptable – or even fair – to rule partially in favor of a particular litigant for their own self-enrichment when opportunities arise. Thus, corruption proliferates and festers.

To curb judicial corruption, the Supreme People's Court (SPC) has consistently pushed for reforms. Recently, the SPC garnered support from the Party Center, making its most significant endeavor yet to confront the abuse of political prerogative in the administration of legal affairs. Judicial interference is deemed "improper" and is banned if the interfering leader lacks a mandate to oversee judicial affairs or a legitimate reason to be concerned about a court case. For instance, if a Party leader with a public health portfolio attempts to influence a murder case that has nothing to do with public health, such interference would be considered "improper." When improper interference occurs, the Party relies on the judge affected by the interference to report the incident to his court, which is required to periodically submit these reports to the designated supervisory body.

The reform has not outlawed judicial interference.[5] It cannot because the Party *must* preserve its political prerogative to ensure the desired judicial outcomes in cases of interest through judicial interference. In fact, the reform has not even outlawed improper interference but

[5] Also see Liebman (2007).

merely authorized the affected judge to report it by filling out a form. After receiving the report, the court is under no obligation, nor does it necessarily have the ranking authority, to investigate the incident. Instead, it is up to a higher authority to determine whether an investigation should be launched and a punitive sanction imposed. As with previous reforms surveyed in Chapter 4, the ban on improper interference works at best to redistribute corruption opportunities rather than to eradicate corruption, because it does not tackle the root cause: the universal installation of a judicial decision-making mechanism that honors political prerogative and normalizes judicial partiality.

## Creation of the Party's Disciplinary System

Beyond corruption, the delegation of political prerogative creates another problem: When top-down oversight is frustrated by information asymmetry, overambitious second-tier leaders expand their regions or departments and turn them into "independent kingdoms," threatening both the absolute power of the Party Center and the structural integrity of the Party-state. It was for this reason that the Party began investing in its internal disciplinary system in the wake of the Gao/Rao Affair (1954), the first power struggle at the Politburo since the Party came to power in 1949. In that affair, Gao Gang and Rao Shushi were accused of conspiring to build an "independent kingdom," which provided the impetus for Party leaders, led by Deng Xiaoping, to launch a disciplinary reform in 1955. This reform established the Central Supervisory Committee (CSC), replacing the weak Central [Party] Committee of Discipline and Inspection (CCDI) established in 1949. Over the following decade, the CSC was invigorated and became an indispensable actor of the disciplinary system, which the Party continues to rely upon to this day.

Deng's disciplinary institutional framework consists of the following elements. First, the CSC was to be elected by the National Party Congress, the most representative body of the Party, thus conferring on it a quasi-autonomous constitutional status and allowing it to integrate vertically. Second, despite its electoral status, the CSC was not an equal to, but a functional department of, the Central Committee;[6] its mandate

[6] The Party has used the same approach to manage the tension between the PRC Constitution and the UCOPC principle. In the PRC Constitution, the SPC is granted an autonomous constitutional status but in the administrative ranking system (ARS) it is relegated to a ministerial rank, which is one rank below the State Council. The ranking

was to enforce policies and decisions of the Central Committee. Third, a supervision committee at a subnational level was subject to "dual-leadership" from both its corresponding territorial Party Committee and the higher supervision committee. This "dual-leadership" introduces a measure of heterogeneity to the Party's self-rule and is crucial for the vertical integration of the disciplinary institutions.

As such, the disciplinary system becomes the only vertically integrated power substructure of the Party that is semi-detached from the primary chain of command that runs through the territorial Party Committees. It is no wonder that during the 1955 disciplinary reform some Party leaders questioned whether the new CSC would evolve into an "independent kingdom" itself. To dispel such suspicion, Deng stressed that all supervision committees would operate *under* the leadership of their corresponding territorial Party Committees, not seeking independence from them (Wang, 1962).

During the Cultural Revolution, the CSC was dissolved. The Party operated without specialized disciplinary institutions for over a decade. Eventually, the CCDI was rebuilt, with the same elective status and the "dual-leadership" arrangement – an institutional design drawn by Deng in 1955. In addition, the Party took a further step to grant the head of the CCDI a seat on the Politburo Standing Committee. This practice has been consistently observed to the present, except for a brief interruption during 1992–1997.

In subsequent decades, the CCDI exploited its "license" to its fullest potential, expanding its jurisdiction to oversee the operation of its lower counterparts, including appointments, case work, decision review and approval, and so on. The pace of its "encroachment" became alarmingly noticeable in the late 2000s, giving rise to speculations that the CCDI would seek for full vertical integration by detaching its lower counterparts from the territorial Party Committees. This "rumor" was firmly refuted by the CCDI.[7] Later, following the 2018 supervision reform, the CCDI's capacity had expanded on an unprecedented scale, which had also elicited unofficial discussions for CCDI vertical integration (Nie, 2015b). However, such discussions did not progress far. As I have discussed in Chapter 6, the CCDI was reined in by the Party Center during Xi's second term, a telling testimony to the retractive force of the UCOPC principle.

status of courts is only improved through the "high-equipping" practice, which raises the rank of the court president by one grade.

[7] See Newspaper (2008).

### Regulating Anti-corruption as a Political Prerogative

As I mentioned at the beginning of this chapter, the Party does not directly enforce state-promulgated laws upon the masses but does so through state organs. Anti-corruption laws are an exception. For corruption-related crimes, the Party deploys its own agents to carry out the investigations independently. The Party employs at least 360,000 full-time Committee of Discipline and Inspection at subnational levels (CDI) agents nationwide – about 5 percent of the total number of civil servants – a much higher ratio than, for instance, in Hong Kong and Singapore.[8] Before 2018, public corruption could also be investigated by the anti-corruption bureau of the procuratorate, a state investigative body. After the 2018 supervisory reform, however, investigation of public corruption became an exclusive political prerogative of the Party, making the law on public corruption (or, more broadly, "duty crimes") the only law the Party enforces itself.

Anti-corruption investigations are not only exclusively controlled by the Party but are also managed in a distinctively centralized manner. Under current PRC law and regulations, the power to conduct criminal investigations is largely decentralized on the basis of territoriality. Centralized investigations are required only for two other types of crimes: (1) major crimes that could result in life-imprisonment or the death sentence and (2) crimes involving national security and terrorism. Centralization in the investigation of major crimes is not uncommon elsewhere because such crimes often require more dedicated resources and specialized, sophisticated skills that only a higher-level authority can mobilize and dispense. For crimes related to national security, centralized investigation is warranted also because the primary affected party is the central government, and the investigative authority may require a higher level of clearance. It is therefore not surprising that, in China, investigations of these crimes are centralized at the prefectural level or above and then divided by observing the territoriality principle.

The manner in which investigations of corruption-related crimes are centralized is different: It is not constrained by the territoriality principle.

[8] Just to put it into perspective, the ratio of the anti-corruption agents to civil servants in Hong Kong is 0.72 percent and 0.142 percent in Singapore. Source of the statistical data is from Guo (2014c). However, one must consider that the mandates of China's CDIs are broader than those of the anti-corruption agencies elsewhere, as they involve enforcing the Party's political campaigns or policies not directly related to anti-corruption, such as the campaign to alleviate poverty.

Instead, jurisdiction is determined by the rank of the suspect in the power structure delineated by the administrative ranking system (ARS). (Li, 2023) The rank-based jurisdictional principle dictates that a ranked official can be placed under anti-corruption investigation only by an authority of a higher rank.

The Party enforces anti-corruption laws in a direct, exclusive, and centralized manner because anti-corruption impacts the power field of the Party-state – a domain that only the Party has the prerogative to regulate. Unlike any other crime, every instance of corruption implicates a powerholder in the Party-state structure. If putting a person *in* power is the Party's prerogative, it is only logical that removing a person from power is also the Party's prerogative. In other words, the power to regulate its political prerogative is itself a political prerogative of the Party.

Currently, the administration of appointment power is based on the principle of "one-rank down," which means that a personnel decision-making body of a given rank can only make personnel decisions regarding officials one rank lower. As discussed in Chapter 5, the allocation of disciplinary power is entirely aligned with that of the appointment power. By claiming the exclusive power to conduct anti-corruption investigations and imposing a rank-based jurisdictional rule, the Party preserves the integrity of the top-down power structure and prevents it from being disrupted or challenged by other institutional actors.

## Elite Politics under the Party's Disciplinary System

Rooted in a well-established academic tradition, studies of elite politics in China have long focused on informal practices (Dittmer, 1995; Huang, 2000; Nathan, 1973; Shih, 2022; Tsou, 2002). The "formal rules" are typically referenced only to expose their insignificance (Fewsmith, 2021a; Torigian, 2022). Admittedly, the closer one gets to the apex of power, the fewer rules apply. However, does this necessarily mean elite politics in the Party-state reside in a complete regulatory vacuum? To answer this question, I surveyed major Politburo power struggles since 1940 in Chapter 7. By analyzing and comparing the approaches taken by different actors in power struggles at different historical junctures, I find that the Party's disciplinary system was central in these struggles due to the lack of a regular exit mechanism for Politburo incumbents.

In open political systems, political incumbents can be ejected from offices through regular elections. In a closed Leninist political system, however, a political contestant cannot compel an incumbent to exit via electoral campaigns. Instead, exits had been, before the 1990s – primarily facilitated through the Party's disciplinary system, which resembles an impeachment process. To successfully initiate an impeachment, two conditions must be met: First, a plausible cause must be established – that is, a disciplinary violation; second, the disciplinary panel's consent is required to validate the accusation and impose a sanction.

Chapter 7 shows that the prevailing model for impeaching a Politburo member before 1992 was the one that emerged during the 1941–1942 Yan'an Rectification Campaign (YARC). The YARC model featured a combative ideological campaign, in which power contestation was presented as an ideological clash, whether real or invented. Such a clash, known as "line-struggles (*luxian douzheng*)," is characterized as binary and incorrigible. In Chapter 7, I identified the causal mechanism of the YARC model and used it to explain why the model was observed in some historical cases and modified or disregarded in others. In doing so, I show that actual policy failures or differences were never *intended* as a condition for Politburo power struggles.

From the perspective of the Party's collective interest, the YARC model has the advantage of enhancing rather than weakening the Party's collective will because at the end of a power struggle the losing side must capitulate and submit to the correct line represented by the winning side. However, the YARC model also has a weakness: it accentuates divisions within the Party's top leadership. When exposed, such splits can render the Party vulnerable to challenges – particularly if a rival faction aligns with oppositional mass groups and/or hostile foreign forces.

Following the political crisis in 1989, the approach to Politburo power struggles began to shift from the YARC model to the anti-corruption model. Equally important to this shift was the emergence of the age-limit norm – a mechanism that facilitates the peaceful exits of Politburo incumbents in a regular, predictable, and far less costly manner than would have been possible under the YARC model (Li, 2022a).

Under the anti-corruption model, a Politburo member is removed from power for crimes of corruption, not ideological offenses. In the two decades between 1992 and 2012, power struggles within the Politburo were de-ideologized and reduced in both intensity and scope. When Xi Jinping came to power in 2012, he maximized the utility of the anti-corruption model with an unprecedentedly intensive campaign. Not surprisingly, the resulting shakeup led to equally significant political resentment. Such resentment only subsided, at least on the surface, after Xi politicized the anti-corruption model by reactivating political offenses and indirectly making them indictable.

The Party's disciplinary system holds great normative value as a regulatory platform for power struggles at the top of the Party for two reasons. First, it provides legitimacy to the winner(s) of a power struggle, encouraging political actors to adhere to the disciplinary procedure and prompting the winner(s) to reshape the disciplinary system to secure or enhance their advantages in future struggles. Second, it consists of a loose and fluid regulatory framework, which allows space for manipulation and even transgression by individual political actors with high agency.

## Endured Prevalence of Corruption

By retaining anti-corruption investigative power as a political prerogative, the Party can conduct anti-corruption efforts with enhanced efficacy, leveraging its extraordinary mobilizing capacity. However, even the fiercest anti-corruption campaign sees its shock effect wear off over time. More importantly, with the current "reactive" investigative approach – which relies on reports from witnesses, participants, or victims rather than proactive measures such as entrapment – most offenders of *guanxi*-facilitated corruption remain undetected as long as they avoid predatory behavior and act with sufficient caution. Chapter 4 demonstrates that judicial corruption persisted even at the height of the 2012–2017 anti-corruption campaign and revealed cases show that corruption's long latency period – sometimes spanning more than two decades – has remained remarkably stable and persistent.

In this book, I argue that the root cause for the enduring prevalence of corruption in China stems from the Party's reliance on normalizing its political prerogative as its mode of governance. As discussed earlier, when the Party delegates and normalizes its political prerogative to territorial Party Committees at lower levels and from these Party Committees to other authorities responsible for policy implementation and law enforcement, it establishes a decision-making mechanism susceptible to abuse by all actors in administering public affairs. As long as this mechanism remains in place, it will continue to produce corruption even after occasional purges. Eliminating corruption or reducing its rate to a minimal level would require the Party to relinquish, or at least to de-normalize, its political prerogative – a move that would undermine the foundation of its approach to rule. Viewed from another angle, corruption is not merely an economic and social cost but a trade-off inherent in the political governance of the Party-state.

A second factor contributing to the prevalence of corruption in China is the vitality of the social institution of *guanxi*, which enables corruption to persist despite the Party's robust anti-corruption activities for two main reasons. First, as elaborated in Chapter 3, *guanxi* enhances both external and internal transactional safety of corrupt dealings through a personalized trust-building process. The greater the stakes in a corrupt deal, the more discreet the transactional process becomes. Thanks to this enhanced safety, *guanxi*-driven corruption is notoriously difficult to detect, verify, and prove. This challenge is compounded by the "victimless" nature of corruption, where victims are often unaware of their victimization and/or lack direct evidence of the crime. Consequently, most corruption remains unreported, undetected, uninvestigated, and unpunished despite intensified anti-corruption efforts.[9] When corruption is detected and punished, it is typically the result of accidental exposure – such as an unforeseeable breakdown of trust among participants, chance circumstances (e.g., being in the wrong place at the wrong time or associated with the wrong people), or becoming the target of highly politicized anti-corruption efforts.

Secondly, *guanxi* has improved the transactional efficiency of corruption due to the emergence of professional *guanxi*-brokers. Chapter 3 illustrates how these brokers further reduced the transaction cost of corruption, "democratized" previously exclusive corruption opportunities for a much broader client base, and quasi-marketized parochial corruption.

Thus, on the one hand, the Party's continued reliance on normalizing its political prerogative in governance not only produces but also perpetuates corruption opportunities; on the other hand, the omnipresent social institution of *guanxi* provides an effective mechanism that insulates corruption participants from routine anti-corruption monitoring. This creates an interesting phenomenon: Corruption remains both

[9] CCDI (2023a) data indicate that in 2023, 626,000 disciplinary investigations against Party-state cadres were launched by CDIs nationwide; and 3.9 percent of these investigations led to prosecutions. Assuming that the CDI/SCs monitor a total of 39,180,000 public employees (excluding employees of state-owned enterprises) – a conservative figure deduced from a report by Jia and Li (2009) (a more liberal estimate is 80,000,000) – this means that 15.9 in every 1,000 public employees were investigated for corruption in 2023, among whom 0.59 (out of 1,000) were prosecuted.

hidden and prevalent, producing the perfect environment for selective law enforcement. If any official targeted in a corruption investigation is almost certain to be found guilty, the Party can "hijack" anti-corruption laws to penalize conduct that is otherwise decriminalized – for example, political disloyalty.

As discussed in Chapter 7, adopting anti-corruption as the new model of power struggles offers several advantages over the previous highly ideologized model. First, it confines the details of power struggles to a small circle of insiders. Under the new model, the entire disciplinary process is conducted in a tightly enclosed environment – shielding information not only from the masses but also from the majority of Party members – via a closely monitored procedure not requiring mass mobilization. In fact, since the adoption of the anti-corruption model, even the most informed commentators have been able to offer, at best, only educated guesses about how power struggles at the Party Center began and unfolded. Second, because power struggles under the anti-corruption model no longer require ideological framing, their scale can be more accurately calibrated, thereby reducing enforcement excesses – a hallmark of the previous ideologized model.

These advantages constitute another political trade-off – or "positive" externality – of corruption. This positive externality increases the Party's tolerance for noncompliance with anti-corruption laws and regulations, much as it has tolerated widespread noncompliance with tax laws. China's taxation system, known for its heavy reliance on indirect tax and non-tax revenues (Cui, 2024 (forthcoming); Walder, 2023; Zhang, 2017), has led to under-enforcement of tax laws and ubiquitous tax evasion. However, this "half-taxation regime" (Zhang, 2017) has also worked to the Party's advantage by creating an environment for selective law enforcement, which authorities can exploit to suppress taxpayers' political demands (Zhang, 2017).

In a nutshell, corruption in China is a complex issue – not only in its relationship with economic development (Pozsgai-Alvarez, 2021; Sun, 2004; Wedeman, 2012) but also in its role in the governance of the Party-state. We gain a better understanding of its enduring prevalence by examining not only the economic and social costs it generates but also the positive externality it offers the Party. The positive externality incentivizes even the most principled Party leader to tolerate a high level of corruption in exchange for preserving the Party's mode of political governance, both on the streets and at *zhongnanhai*.

## Evolution of the Party-State

How the Party handled its relationship with the state is a nonlinear historical process. In the early history of the PRC, the Party saw the state as a large, alien life form – intelligent but untrustworthy, slow-moving but in need of high maintenance, bureaucratic but constantly seeking autonomy. Mao, a leader who harbored a deep-rooted general distrust of all institutions, oversaw the drafting process of the PRC Constitution (1954) (Diamant, 2022). His attitude toward state institutions was at best dismissive. Having anchored his power in the Party and the army, Mao believed that laws were a useless instrument of governance; he confessed that he could not remember the contents of the PRC Constitution because there were too many provisions; nor could he see the point of the National People's Congress (NPC) and the State Council since he could more effectively communicate his will to the rest of the Party in face-to-face Party meetings (Mao, 1958).[10]

To dispel any misunderstanding, speculation or false hope regarding the nature of the Party-state, the Party Center circulated a directive in 1958, which stipulated that "the Politburo holds the policy making power; the Central Secretariat is responsible to operationalize the policies; State organs and their Party-groups can provide suggestions in the policymaking process but the decision-making power rests with the Party Center (Chen, 2003)." However, this decree did little to ease Mao's concerns. His distrust of state organs continued to intensify and, during the Cultural Revolution, eventually peaked – culminating in the demolition of most state organs and the imposition of military control over the country.

After Mao's death and the arrests of the Gang of Four, the Party elders, who had been victimized by the Cultural Revolution, were restored to power, and the state organs abolished during that period were reinstated. Soon after, the Party began investing in a law-based state system. To demonstrate its commitment, the Party decriminalized political offenses, relinquished its prerogative to approve criminal penalties, and banned any person or organization other than state law enforcement agencies from exercising coercive investigative and punitive powers (Center,

[10] Mao's view of law was shared by other top Party leaders too. For example, at the meeting where Mao delivered the referenced speech, Liu Shaoqi concurred, adding, "[Do we follow] rule by law or rule by men? I believe we must rely on rule by men. Law can only be a factor for consideration" (Mao, 1958; Network, 2009b).

1979). In 1986, nearly parallel to Gorbachev's *perestroika* and the Party-state separation reform in the Soviet Union (Srivastava, 1999), Deng Xiaoping also authorized a reform that would grant more state autonomy and limit the Party's political prerogatives.

In 1987, the Central Committee even signed off on the General Plan of Political Reform proposed by Zhao Ziyang and his team (Wu, 2013a). The plan was progressive and comprehensive. It presented a roadmap to limit the Party's political prerogatives by downsizing Party organs, restricting the Party's competences to political matters, channeling Party leadership through lawmaking, and, most critical of all, dissolving the Party-groups, the organizational bridge that had bound the state to the Party (Wu, 2014). Between 1987 and 1988, the Party disbanded the Central Party Political-legal Committee (CPLC), abolished the Party-groups in at least half of the ministries and departments under the State Council and reduced its participation in the management of economic and educational organizations (Wu, 2014). However, further implementation was halted due to strong resistance from the Party bureaucracy (Wu, 2023). Then, as the democratic movement erupted and Zhao Ziyang quickly fell from power, the reform was completely abandoned and previously dissolved Party organizations were restored.

In 1992, after witnessing the sudden collapse of the Soviet Union, the Party further tightened its organizational grip on the state. Party-groups were reintroduced into the Party Charter as a mandatory fixture in all state organs, including the people's congress, and were granted the power to make key decisions of those organs. The CPLC was not only restored but had its mandate expanded through the "stability maintenance" operation (Wang & Minzner, 2015). It is also against this backdrop that the practice of conjoining Party-state offices between the Ministry of Supervision (MOS) and the CCDI (see Chapters 5 and 6) was established.

Having tightened its control over state organs, including the NPC, courts, and other legal institutions, the Party increased its investment in the state legal system. Jiang Zemin was the first to introduce a semblance of "rule of law" into the Party's political program. Since 1993, the head of the NPC has been granted a seat at the Politburo Standing Committee and the national legislature has been entrusted with translating the Party's collective will into state laws, which would then be enforced by state agencies. Courts were charged with handling a huge volume of disputes, including administrative litigation against governmental agencies. This trend continued under Xi Jinping's rule. On the one hand,

Party control over state institutions was tightened to the extent that judicial independence was not only discarded as an aspiration but also denounced as a source of Western ideological pollution. On the other hand, the Party authorized unprecedented judicial reforms to expand the "rule of law" project as a form of governance, including a series of Party-state-wide institutional reforms designed to "delocalize" courts through judicial centralization (see Chapter 4).

At this juncture, reflecting on the Party's century-old history, its early approach to governing the Party-state was primitive and highly antagonistic toward the state. Today, having mastered the means to tame the state, the Party views it as both a valuable source of legitimacy and an indispensable instrument of governance. The contrast could not be more striking: During the 1955 disciplinary institution reform, the Party first downgraded the rank of the state supervision institution and then completely absorbed it to exercise total control over disciplinary matters. In the 2016–2018 disciplinary institution reform, the Party upgraded the rank of the state supervision ministry, vested it with immense power, and then appropriated its power and resources *en bloc* through the device of conjoined-offices (see Chapter 6).

It is from this perspective that the constitutional abolition of the term limit of the PRC Chairmanship in 2018 should be examined. As I have discussed at the beginning of this chapter, no term limit has ever been imposed on the Head of the Party, that is, the GPS; nor is the PRC chairmanship a precondition for election as the GPS. Therefore, abolishing the term limit for the PRC Chairman does not "enable" Xi to rule for life; rather, it allows him to retain his hold on the state power system should he continue to rule as the GPS. The office of the PRC Chairman – as the Head of the State and the only national state organ that is represented by a single individual – seems desirable not only for its diplomatic functions (to represent the PRC, conduct state business, and receive foreign convoys (Article 81)) but also for its wide-ranging "ceremonial" powers. Under the current PRC Constitution, the PRC Chairman nominates the premier (Article 62), promulgates laws, appoints top leaders of the State Council, declares a state of emergency and a state of war, and issues mobilization orders, pursuant to decisions of the NPC and its Standing Committee (Article 80).

It has not been tested what happens if the PRC chairman were in disagreement with the NPC on any of these matters. Potentially, the Chairman can hold off on sign-off and effectively veto the passages of critical decisions presented by the legislature if the latter goes "rogue" in times of crises.[11] After having invested so heavily in the state system, it would be imprudent for a paramount Party leader to abdicate that PRC Chairmanship – his only foothold in the state system – before full retirement.

## Modus Operandi of the Chinese Communist Party

In his classic study of Bolshevik strategies and tactics, the late professor Philip Selznick coined the term "organizational weapon" to reveal a key pattern of motivation and action of Bolshevik movements across different countries. As Selznick discovered, this pattern involved Bolshevik leaders using formal organizations as a "weapon" in their pursuit of power (Selznick, 1952). Drawing on Leninist literature and reports on underground activities of communist parties during the first-half of the twentieth century, Selznick argued that the "organizational weapon" initially comprised an elite of reliable agents – skillfully trained, thoroughly indoctrinated, and rigidly disciplined – to carry out any assigned mission. The communist party deployed these agents to infiltrate established state institutions and groups in targeted societies, neutralizing opposition and seizing positions of power, thereby readying itself to displace the constitutional authority of the state when the time came (Blumer, 1952; Selznick, 1952).

Selznick's "organizational weapon" thesis is compelling and its memorable title continues to capture the imagination today. More importantly, its organizational approach provides a sharp analytical tool not only for studying the early operations of the Party when it sought to topple an "enemy state" (as Selznick exemplified) but also for investigating its current operations as the established ruler of a bona fide Party-state – a perspective I adopt in this book.

However, the changing environment in which the Party operates is an important and consequential context to emphasize. When Selznick studied the topic, the Party was struggling to come to power and consolidate its control over vast territories it had just seized. It relied on "conspiratorial" operations to subvert the state and other social organizations that did not necessarily share its political goal or methods. Many of its organizational tactics were deemed "unacceptable to the community as

[11] These crises are not purely hypothetical. For instance, during the Tiananmen crisis in 1989, a number of NPC Standing Committee members motioned to convene an emergent meeting to impeach and remove Li Peng, then Premier, after the latter declared the Martial Order. See Bai (2015) and Yu (2013).

a legitimate mode of action" (Selznick, 1952, p. 2). Today, however, the Party's mission is no longer to seize power but to maintain it. Accordingly, its early modus operandi – institutional infiltration and subversion – though highly effective during its revolutionary phase, must be upgraded. Those former infiltrators, who once operated as covert "foreign" agents within hostile state organs, have since evolved into distinguished and privileged "native residents" within a state structure designed to serve the Party. The once "weaponized" combative organizational devices have to be "naturalized" and converted into peacetime regulatory instruments.

Evidently, while infiltration and subversion were potent tools in the Party's revolutionary past and may still be applicable in new territories – physical or virtual – where the Party has yet to establish control, modernizing a Party-state for sustainable rule requires an updated approach and a more advanced mode of governance to address a myriad of regulatory challenges. As explained at the beginning of this chapter, the Party now relies on an organically developed formal normative system to govern itself and control the state. This system may appear alien to Western audiences because it operates on a logic very different from that of more familiar Western forms: Its language is esoteric and loose, deliberately leaving ample room for varied interpretations; its scope is under-defined; and its contents are often laden with ideological jargon to ensure doctrinal conformity, along with colloquial expressions for the sake of authenticity.

Most importantly, its authority, vis-à-vis state laws, is not clearly delineated, which can lead to profound confusion. A primary example is a statement given by Xu Xianming, a former leader at the CPLC and an esteemed legal jurisprudence professor. In dismissing a discussion that questioned the legitimacy of the Party's supremacy over the law, Xu stated: "the Party is in the law, under the law and above the law at once," a remark that exemplifies the art of dialecticism at its highest form.

In this book, I offer a conceptual interpretative framework to explain the Party's current modus operandi, one that embodies the logic of its formal-normative system. I call this framework the Normalized Political Prerogative (NPP) theory.

## Normalized Political Prerogative Theory

The NPP theory argues that the Party's modus operandi for sustaining its rule is to uphold the UCOPC by normalizing its political prerogative. The causal mechanism underlying this normalization process unfolds in three stages.

First, operationalization. The Party operationalizes the UCOPC principle into a concrete political prerogative comprising two components: plenipotentiary competence and Party supremacy. Plenipotentiary competence grants the Party Center an all-encompassing mandate to make enforceable decisions on every policy field of the Party-state. Party supremacy – or "Party's leadership (*dang de lingdao*)" – ensures the supremacy of the Party Center by constructing a delineated, integrated and regimented power structure for all public institutions, offices and their holders, with the Party Center placed at the top.

Second, normalization. The Party programs its political prerogative into the decision-making mechanism in all Party organizations, including those embedded in the state organs. Thus, the Party normalizes its political prerogative as the primary decision-making principle across all public offices and institutions, enabling it to confidently entrust the state with the resources and authority to regulate society on its behalf.

Third, regulation. Since the Party's political prerogative is susceptible to abuse, it amplifies the principal–agent problem when the Party Center delegates its political prerogative level by level and rank by rank to the rest of the Party-state. As a result, opportunities for abuse extend throughout the entire system. Instead of relinquishing its political prerogative altogether, the Party addresses the problem by creating boundaries for exercising the delegated political prerogative – such as limiting its scope or banning its use for self-enrichment – and punishing those who transgress.

Thus, by operationalizing, normalizing, and regulating its political prerogative, the Party Center builds the formal institutional foundation for the governance of the Party-state.

In Part I of the book, I used the NPP theory to show how the Party normalizes its political prerogative in courts to achieve maximal political control over judicial affairs. Specifically, the Party first organizes courts into a power structure and then institutes a decision-making mechanism that normalizes partial judicial decisions in favor of the litigating party in power on the grounds of political prerogative. Part I has also illustrated how, as a result of this normalization practice, system-wide proliferation of corruption has occurred and festered in these courts.

The prevalence and persistence of judicial corruption in China attests to the robustness of the NPP theory. Conversely, the NPP theory offers a different perspective, viewing corruption as an unintended yet inevitable consequence of preserving its mode of governance. Moreover, the NPP and corruption may mutually reinforce each other. On the one hand, the Party's commitment to the NPP will continue to generate corruption, while its anti-corruption efforts will drive it underground, taking the form of parochial corruption underpinned by the social institution of *guanxi*. On the other hand, prevalent yet hidden corruption yields a "positive externality" for the Party, enabling it to penalize political disloyalty through selective investigations, thereby both justifying and sustaining the NPP.

In Part II of the book, I applied the NPP theory to conduct a power-logic-based normative analysis of the operation of the Party's disciplinary system, including its functions, power structure, decision-making mechanism, and historical evolution. This analysis uncovers several salient features of the NPP.

First, its centrality. The UCOPC principle not only shapes the constitutional makeup of the Party's disciplinary institutions but is also deeply and intrusively embedded in the decision-making process of disciplinary proceedings, thereby upholding the prerogative of the Party Center.

Second, the Party's path-dependence on the NPP. Over time, the Party has launched numerous reforms to address the amplified principal–agent problems – an inevitable side effect of the NPP. Despite shifts in format and terminology, the predominant strategy of these reforms has been the redistribution, rather than the abolition, of the political prerogative. This pattern holds true for disciplinary institutional reforms, just as it does for the judicial reforms discussed in Part I.

Third, the duality of the NPP. While the NPP is rigid in regulating hierarchical relations, it is structurally rather fluid in governing equal relations, especially at the apex of power. This duality provides the NPP with a measure of regulatory plasticity when applied in different power spaces, enabling the Party to maintain a single, cohesive self-regulatory system that both enforces its norms across the ranks and channels power struggles at the top. The system's top-level fluidity also explains how Party leaders, depending on their capabilities and determination, exploited it in diverse ways. Some have fully leveraged this fluidity to establish strongman rule within the Politburo, while others – lacking the will or agency – have failed or opted not to do so, resulting instead in a more power-sharing configuration.

The NPP theory fills a gap in studies of Chinese politics and law, where the Party's formal-normative system – despite its indisputable existence and rapid growth – is often either dismissed outright or analyzed only at a discoursal level. The theory complements existing studies on Chinese informal politics, offering a set of conceptual tools for exploring the interactions between the formal and informal practices. Moreover, given the central role and vitality of the Party in the Party-state-society construct, the NPP theory may serve as a stepping stone for advancing Chinese law and society studies in new directions, enabling a more systematic investigation of the interplay between the Party's normative system and the state's normative (legal) system. Finally, by proposing the NPP theory, I hope to help break down the *sui generis* barrier of the Chinese experience by isolating those features that are unique to China's Party-state and presenting them in an analytical framework that enables clearer and more precise comparison with other systems.

# Appendix I(a)

## List of Names in Pinyin and Chinese Characters

An Rutao 安汝涛
Bo Xilai 薄熙来
Chen Dazhi 陈达之
Chen Jiangang 陈建刚
Chen Liangyu 陈良宇
Chen Xitong 陈希同
Chen Yun 陈云
Cheng Wei 程伟
Cheng Xinwen 程新文
Cui Yongyuan 崔永元
Dai Chunning 戴春宁
Dai Wujian 戴伍建
Deng Xiaoping 邓小平
Dong Biwu 董必武
Dong Hong 董宏
Du Wanhua 杜万华
Fan Yifei 范一飞
Fu Zhenghua 傅政华
Gan Rongkun 甘荣坤
Gao Gang 高岗
Gong Gangmo 龚刚模
Guo Shengui 郭生贵
He Hongda 何洪达
Hu Gang 胡刚
Huang Jianzhong 黄建中
Huang Songyou 黄松有
Kang Sheng 康生
Li Chuncheng 李春城
Li Fuchun 李富春
Li Shangfu 李尚福
Li Xiaohua李晓华
Li Zhuang 李庄

Liu Hanqiang 刘汉强
Liu Shaobin 刘少斌
Liu Yanping 刘彦平
Liu Yuansheng 刘远生
Lou Xiaoping 娄小平
Lü Hongmin 吕洪民
Lü Xiwen 吕锡文
Lü Zonghui 吕宗慧
Ma Yong 马勇
Mai Chongkai 麦崇凯
Meng Laigui 孟来贵
Meng Xiang 孟祥
Mu Suixin 慕绥新
Pan Hannian 潘汉年
Peng Da 彭达
Peng Zegao 彭泽高
Peng Zhen 彭真
Qiao Xiaoxu 乔晓绪
Qin Gang 秦刚
Rao Shushi 饶恕石
Ren Zhiqiang 任志强
Shen Deyong 沈德咏
Su Jiafu 苏家福
Sun Lijun 孙力军
Sun Xiaoguo 孙小果
Sun Yongfu 孙永福
Sun Yongyi 孙永一
Tan Qiwei 谭栖伟
Tan Yongxing 谭永兴
Tian Huiyu 田惠宇
Wang Chen 王晨
Wang Dongxing 汪东兴
Wang Hongguang 王洪光
Wang Jiaxiang 王稼祥
Wang Linqing 王林清
Wang Ming 王明
Wang Qishan 王岐山
Wang Shiwei 王实味
Wei Jian 魏健
Wu Min 邬民
Wu Zhenhan 吴振汉
Xi Jinping 习近平

Xi Xiaoming 奚晓明
Xu Caihou 徐才厚
Xu Xianming 徐显明
Yang Xiancai 杨贤才
Yi Zhenwu 易真武
Yu Junyi 于均义
Zeng Jinchun 曾锦春
Zhai Xuejun 翟雪俊
Zhang Jiahui 张家慧
Zhang Jian 张坚
Zhang Ruping 张汝平
Zhang Xiangying 张祥楹
Zhao Faqi 赵发琦
Zhao Zhengbing 赵征兵
Zhao Zhengyong 赵正永
Zheng Wei 郑维
Zhou Benshun 周本顺
Zhou Bin 周滨
Zhou Daoluan 周道鸾
Zhou Wenxuan 周文轩
Zhou Yongkang 周永康
Zhu De 朱德

# Appendix I(b)

## List of Terms and Expressions in Pinyin and Chinese Characters

*baijiu* 白酒
*banfa* 办法
*baoliao geming* 爆料革命
*baxiang guiding* 八项规定
*beian* 备案
*beian jiguan* 备案机关
*bujianwai* 不见外
*bujin renqing* 不近人情
*chanhuishu* 忏悔书
*dadian guanxi* 打点关系
*dang de lingdao* 党的领导
*dangzhongyang* 党中央
*dangzhongyang jizhong lingdao* 党中央集中领导
*deng xia hei* 灯下黑
*difang* 地方
*dongshi* 懂事
*fayuan* 法院
*feizuzhi huodong* 非组织活动
*fenji guanli* 分级管理
*fujuan* 副卷
*fuza* 复杂
*gao guanxi* 搞关系
*goudui guanxi* 勾兑关系
*gouwuka* 购物卡
*guanli* 管理
*guanxi* 关系
*guanxi yunzuo* 关系运作
*guiding* 规定
*guojia* 国家
*guowen* 过问
*hanggui* 行规
*haochufei* 好处费

*haoren zhuyi* 好人主义
*heshu bangong* 合署办公
*hexin* 核心
*hongbao* 红包
*houdao* 厚道
*huairentang shibian* 怀仁堂事变
*huijin* 贿金
*huikou* 回扣
*huilu* 贿赂
*huiyi jiyao* 会议纪要
*huodong guanxi* 活动关系
*jianchayuan* 检察院
*jieshaofei* 介绍费
*jimi* 机密
*juece* 决策
*jueding* 决定
*jueding jiguan* 决定机关
*la guanxi* 拉关系
*laoren* 捞人
*liangge fanshi* 两个凡是
*lingdao ganbu* 领导干部
*lingdao zhiwu* 领导职务
*liuzhi* 留置
*luxian douzheng* 路线斗争
*mianzi* 面子
*mingan* 敏感
*neigui* 内鬼
*pishi* 批示
*pizhun jiguan* 批准机关
*qianfu houji* 前腐后继
*qiangjiu yundong* 抢救运动
*qingshi baogao* 请示报告
*shouhui* 受贿
*shuanggui* 双规
*shuangzhi* 双指
*silei anjian* 四类案件
*tangping* 躺平
*tiaoli* 条例
*tongzhi* 通知
*tuo guanxi* 托关系
*wangyi zhongyang* 妄议中央
*wo'an* 窝案

*xiaojinku* 小金库
*xiaoyisi* 小意思
*xinghui* 行
*xinkufei* 辛苦费
*xiqi* 习气
*yewupai* 业务牌
*yidian biaoshi* 一点表示
*yinan* 疑难
*yiyuanhua lingdao* 一元化领导
*yuehe zhi* 阅核制
*zhengfa* 政法
*zhengjuan* 正卷
*zhihui* 指挥
*zhongda* 重大
*zhongyang* 中央
*zhuguan zhuyi* 主观主义
*zhuiren* 追认
*zongpai zhuyi* 宗派主义
*zou guanxi* 走关系
*zuzhi* 组织

# Appendix II - Sources of Selected Cases

| No. | Types of documents | Issuing entity of the document | Name of defendant | Profession/position of defendant | Year of issuance |
|---|---|---|---|---|---|
| 1 | Court judgment | Shandong Jinan Intermediate Court | Bo Xilai 薄熙来 | Party leader | 2013 |
| 2 | Court judgment | Jinan Ji Yang District Court | Dai Wujian 戴伍建 | Intermediate court judge | 2020 |
| 3 | Court judgment | Beijing 2nd Intermediate Court | Deng Zhan 邓湛 | Ministry of Commerce | 2009 |
| 4 | Court judgment | Beijing East District Court | Guo Jingyi 郭京毅 | Ministry of Commerce | 2009 |
| 5 | Court judgment | Beijing 2nd Intermediate Court | Guo Jingyi 郭京毅 | Ministry of Commerce | 2010 |
| 6 | Court judgment | Beijing East District Court | Huang Jianzhong 黄建中 | High court judge | 2017 |
| 7 | Court judgment | Hebei High Court | Huang Songyou 黄松有 | SPC leader | 2010 |
| 8 | Court judgment | Beijing 1st Intermediate Court | Li Jizhou 李纪周 | Vice-minister MPS | 2009 |
| 9 | Defense statement | Xing Long Law Firm | Li Xiaohua 李晓华 | High court divisional leader | 2006 |
| 10 | Court judgment | Guiyang Intermediate Court | Liu Guoqing 刘国庆 | Procuratorate anticorruption bureau chief | 2008 |
| 11 | Criminal complaint | Beijing 2nd Procuratorate | Liu Wei 刘伟 | State Administration of Industry and Commerce | 2009 |
| 12 | Criminal complaint | Beijing 2nd Procuratorate | Liu Yang 刘阳 | Ministry of Commerce/ lawyer | 2009 |

| | | | | | |
|---|---|---|---|---|---|
| 13 | Court judgment | Hainan Intermediate Court | Lou Xiaoping 娄小平 | High court leader | 2004 |
| 14 | Court judgment | Nanjing Intermediate Court | Ma Xiangdong 马向东 | Party leader | 2001 |
| 15 | Court judgment | Beijing 1st Intermediate Court | Mai Chongkai 麦崇凯 | High court leader | 2009 |
| 16 | Court judgment | Beijing 1st Intermediate Court | Meng Huiqing 孟会青 | CCDI divisional leader | 2016 |
| 17 | Court judgment | Dalian Intermediate Court | Mu Suixin 慕绥新 | Party leader | 2007 |
| 18 | Court judgment | Jinan Ji Yang District Court | Qiao Xuxiao 乔绪晓 | Intermediate court divisional leader | 2020 |
| 19 | Court judgment | Fuoshan Intermediate Court | Sun XX 孙某甲 | Party leader | 2018 |
| 20 | Court judgment | Jinan Tian Qiao District Court | Sun Yongyi 孙永一 | Intermediate court leader | 2021 |
| 21 | Defense statement | Xing Long Law Firm | Tang Jikai 唐吉凯 | Intermediate court leader | 2005 |
| 22 | Court judgment | Huaihua Intermediate Court | Tang Jikai 唐吉凯 | Intermediate court leader | 2006 |
| 23 | Court judgment | Beijing East District Court | Wang Hongguang 王洪光 | SPC divisional leader | 2017 |
| 24 | Court judgment | Hunan High Court | Wang Kuang 王旷 | High court divisional leader | 2005 |
| 25 | Court judgment | Jinan Intermediate Court | Wang Zhaoyao 王昭耀 | Party leader | 2007 |
| 26 | Court judgment | Beijing 2nd Intermediate Court | Wu Zhenhan 吴振汉 | High court leader | 2006 |
| 27 | Court judgment | Sichuan High Court | Xiong Xiaoping 熊晓平 | Intermediate court leader | 2019 |
| 28 | Criminal complaint | Beijing 2nd Procuratorate | Xu Mangang 许满刚 | State Administration of Foreign Exchange | 2009 |
| 29 | Criminal complaint | Guangxi Fanggang City Procuratorate | Xu Peihua 许佩华 | High court divisional leader | 2018 |

(*cont.*)

| No. | Types of documents | Issuing entity of the document | Name of defendant | Profession/position of defendant | Year of issuance |
|---|---|---|---|---|---|
| 30 | Court judgment | Guangzhou Intermediate Court | Yao Hui 姚辉 | Intermediate court divisional leader | 2023 |
| 31 | Court judgment | Changsha People's Procuratorate | Zeng Jinchun 曾锦春 | Provincial CDI leader | 2008 |
| 32 | Court judgment | Tianyuan District Court of Zhuzhou | Zhan Zhiliang 詹支粮 | Intermediate court divisional leader | 2022 |
| 33 | Court judgment | Zhumadian Xincai County Court | Zhang Guoxi 张国喜 | Basic court divisional leader | 2000 |
| 34 | Court judgment | Hainan 1st Intermediate Court | Zhang Jiahui 张佳慧 | High court leader | 2020 |
| 35 | Court judgment | Beijing 2nd Intermediate Court | Zhang Yudong 张玉栋 | Lawyer | 2010 |
| 36 | Court judgment | Chongqing No.5 Intermediate Court | Zheng Wei 郑维 | Party leader | 2007 |
| 37 | Criminal complaint | Shaanxi Yu Yin City Procuratorate | Zhong Zhongyu 张忠玉 | Intermediate court leader | 2021 |
| 38 | Criminal complaint | Beijing 2nd Procuratorate | Zou Lin 邹林 | State Administration of Foreign Exchange | 2010 |

# Appendix III - Regulations (selected)

(Party), NPC. 1922, 1927, 1945, 1956, 1969, 1973, 1982, 1987, 1992, 1997, 2002, 2007, 2012, 2017, 2022. "Party Charter."

(State), NPC. 1954, 1975, 1978, 1982, 1988, 1993, 1999, 2004, 2018. "PRC Constitution."

1979, 1997, 2015, 2020. "Criminal Law 刑法."

1979, 2012, 2018. "Criminal Procedure Law 刑事诉讼法."

1982, 2024. "Organic Law of the State Council 国务院组织法."

1983, 2006, 2018. "Organic Law of Courts 法院组织法."

1987, 2018. "Organic Law of Procuratorates 检察院组织法."

2018. "Supervision Law 监察法."

CCDI. 1980. "Request to Rehabilitate and Completely Rectify the Wrongful Disciplinary Action against Members of the Central Supervision Commission 中共中央纪律检查委员会关于为中央监察委员会彻底平反恢复名誉的请示报告."

1983. "Provisional Rules on Completing the Party's Disciplinary System and Strengthening the Disciplinary Personnel Construction Work 中共中央纪律检查委员会关于健全党的纪律检查系统加强纪检队伍建设的暂行规定."

1987a. "Directive on Conducting Case-Examination for Party Discipline and Inspection Institutions 党的纪律检查机关案件审理工作条例."

1987b. "Notice on the Amendment of the Notice on the Rules of Jurisdiction to Approve Disciplinary Sanctions against Party-Members 中共中央纪委关于修改《关于处分违犯党纪的党员批准权限的具体规定》的通知" in *No. 5*.

1988. "Rules on Case-Inspection Work for Party Discipline and Inspection Institutions (Provisional) 中国共产党纪律检查机关案件检查工作条例（试行）."

1991. "Measures on the Collection, Appraisal and Use of Evidence in the Investigation of Disciplinary Violations of Party Members 关于查处党员违纪案件中收集、鉴别、使用证据的具体规定."

1994a. "Directive on Case-Inspection Work for Party Discipline and Inspection Institutions (Provisional) 中国共产党纪律检查机关案件检查工作条例."

1994b. "Implementation Protocols regarding the Directive on Conducting Case-Inspection Work for Party Discipline and Inspection Institutions 党的纪律检查机关案件检查工作条例实施细则."

1994c. "Opinions on Strengthening and Improving Case Management Work under New Circumstances 关于加强和改进新形势下案件管理工作的意见."

1999. "Disciplinary Opinions on Issues Concerning the Practice of Falungong by Party Members 关于对共产党员修炼"法轮大法"等问题的若干处理意见."

2000. "Rules on the Application of "*shuanggui*" Measure by Disciplinary and Inspection Institutions (Provisional) [关于纪检机关使用"两规"措施的办法（试行）]."

2001a. "Notice on Correct Application of *shuanggui* and *shuangzhi* Measures 中共中央纪委、监察部关于正确使用"两规""两指"措施的通知" in *zhong ji fa [2001] No. 4.*

2001b. "Notice on Further Standardizing the Use of *shuanggui* 中共中央纪委关于进一步规范使用"两规"措施的通知."

2004. "Rules on the Operation of CCDI Outposts [provisional] 中共中央纪委监察部派驻机构业务工作管理暂行办法."

2005a. "Opinions on Perfecting the Coordination Mechanism in Case Investigation and Handling and Further Improve and Normalize Application of *shuanggui* Measure 中央纪委关于完善查办案件协调机制进一步改进和规范"两规"措施的意见." in *zhong ban fa [2005] No. 28.*

2005b. "Opinions on Strictly Abiding the Discipline and the Law to Conduct Case Investigation 关于纪检监察机关严格依纪依法办案的意见."

2005c. "Regulation on CDI's Assistance in Organizing and Coordinating Anti-corruption Work for Party Committees [provisional] 关于纪委协助党组织协调反腐败工作的规定（试行）."

2008. "Regulation on the Management of Compounded or Confiscated Assets Related to Disciplinary Investigations [provisional] 中国共产党纪律检查机关查办案件涉案款物管理暂行规定."

2009. "Interpretation of the CCDI Opinion on Further Strengthening and Normalizing the Work to Conduct Cases 关于进一步加强和规范办案工作的意见解读."

2017, 2019. "Rules of Operation on the Monitoring and Discipline Enforcement of Party Discipline and Inspection Committees 中国共产党纪律检查机关监督纪工作规则."

2018. "Procedures of the Deliberation and Decision-Making on Disciplinary Sanctions and Related Matters [provisional] 党组讨论和决定党员处分事项工作程序规定（试行）."

2020. "Interpretation of the Provisional Opinions on Improving the Mechanism to Coordinate Supervision Enforcement and Criminal Justice Administration《关于加强和完善监察执法与刑事司法衔接机制的意见（试行）》解读."

CCDI, and COD. 1992. "Notice on the Appointment and Approval Procedure Regarding the Appointment of Leaders of CDIs at the Provincial Level and in CDI Outposts in Central Party or State Departments 关于省、自治区、直辖市纪委和中央、国家机关各部门纪检组（纪委）领导干部任免审批程序的通知 ".

CCDI, COD, Central Bianzhi Office, and Ministry of *Supervision*. 2004. "Implementation Opinions on Unified Administration of CCDI/MOS Dispatched Outposts 关于对中央纪委监察部派驻机构实行统一管理的实施意见."

CCDI, and CPLC. 1983. "Opinions on Severely Punishing Economic Crimes 关于严惩严重经济犯罪的意见."

CCDI, and MOS. 1998a. "Notice on a Few Issues Regarding the Application of *shuanggui* and *shuangzhi* Measures by Disciplinary Institutions in Compliance with the Law 关于纪检监察机关依法采用"两指""两规"措施若干问题的通知."

1998b. "Notice on Measures to Tighten the Handling of Compounded or Confiscated Assets 关于纪检监察机关加强对没收追缴违纪违法款物管理的通知."

CCDI, MOS, and State Baomi Bureau. 1995. "Regulation on the Classification of State Secrets 纪检监察工作中国家秘密及其密级具体范围的规定."

CCP, National Delegates Conference. 1955. "Decision on the Establishment of Central and Local Party Supervision Commissions 中国共产党全国代表会议关于成立党的中央和地方监察委员会的决议."

CDI, Guian. 2020a. "Functions and Mandates of Guian New District CDI Work Committee 贵安新区纪检监察工委职能职责."

2020b. "Operational Procedure of the CDI Work Committee of Guian New District 贵安新区纪检监察工委工作程序."

CDI, Huai An District of Huai An City 中共淮安市淮安区纪律检查委员会. 2015. "Regulation of the Handling of Investigative Leads/Tip-offs [provisonal] 纪律审查案件线索管理办法（试行）."

CDI, Hulunbuir. 2020c. "Regulation on the Operation of CDI Detention Places [provisional] 纪委监委留置场所管理办法(试行)."

CDI, Sichuan. 1953. "Requirements and Opinions on the Discipline and Inspection Work for the Second Half of 1953 关于1953年下半年各级纪律检查委员会几个工作要求与做法的意见."

Center, Party. 1929. "Resolution on the Expulsion of Chen Duxiu and the Approval of Expulsion Decisions of Jiangsu Provincial Party Committee 中共中央关于开除陈独秀党籍并批准江苏省委开除彭述之、汪译楷、马玉夫、蔡振德四人党籍的决议案."

1937. "Resolution on the Organization of Red Army in Party and Political Organs in the New Period 中央关于红军中党及政治机关在新阶段的组织的决定."

1938. "Resolution on the Work Procedures of the Central Committee 关于中央委员会工作规则与纪律的决定."

1949. "Decision on the Establishment of the Central and Local Committees of Discipline and Inspection 中国共产党关于成立中央及各级党的纪律检查委员会的决定."

1952. "Instruction to Combine the Three-anti Campaign with a Party Rectification Campaign 关于"三反"运动和整党运动结合进行的指示."

1953. "Resolution on Strengthening the Practice of *qing shi bao gao* of All Departments of Central Government and on Strengthening the Leadership of the Party Center over Governmental Work 关于加强中央人民政府系统各部门向中央请示报告制度及加强中央对于政府工作领导的决定."

1957. "Notice on the Determined Criteria for the Identification of Rightists 关于划分右派分子的标准的通知."

1962a. "Decision to Strengthen Party Supervision Organs 关于加强党的监察机关的决定."

1962b. "Notice on Expediting the Certification Process of Party-Members and Cadres 中央关于加速进行党员、干部甄别工作的通知."

1962c. "Resolution on Strengthening Party Monitoring and Inspection Institutions] passed by the 10th Plenary Meeting of the 8th Central Party Committee 关于加强党的检查机关的决定".

1979. "Firmly Safegard the Implementation of the Criminal Law and the Criminal Procedure Law [中共中央关于坚决保证刑法、刑事诉讼法切实实施的指示]."

1980. "Principal Guidelines Regarding Intra-Party Political Life 关于党内政治生活的若干准则."

1982. "Resolution on the Retirement of Senior Cadres 关于建立老干部退休制度的决定." edited by 中发[1982]13号文件.

1988. "Notice on the Preservation of Practices of Clean Governance for Party and State Institutions 关于党和国家机关必须保持廉洁的通知 ".

1990, 2012. "Measures on the Making of Intra-Party Regulations 党内法规制定程序条例."

1995. "Income Disclosure Measures for Leading Cadres at and above County/Division (*xian/chu*) Rank 关于党政机关县（处）级以上领导干部收入申报的规定." edited by General Office of the Party Center.

1996, 2012. “Directive on the Flow of the Submission and Circulation of Official Documents of Party and State Administrations 党政机关公文处理工作条例.”

1999. “Circulation of the SPC Report on Solving the Problems that Obstruct Court Enforcement Work 中共中央关于转发《中共最高人民法院党组关于解决人民法院”执行难”问题的报告》的通知.”

2002, 2013, 2014, 2019. “Directive of the Selection and Recruitment of Party and Governmental Executive Cadres 党政领导干部选拔任用工作条例.”

2003, 2016. “Central Directive on Intra-Party Supervision 中国共产党党内监督条例.”

2010, 2016. “Disclosure Measures of Personal Matters for Leading Cadres 关于领导干部报告个人有关事项的规定.” edited by 中共中央办公厅，国务院办公厅.

2015, 2017, 2024. “Central Directive on Roving Inspection Work 巡视工作条例.”

2016, 2019. “Central Directive on Accountabilities 中国共产党问责条例.” edited by 中共中央.

2017a. “CCP Directive of Inspection Work 中国共产党巡视工作条例.”

2017b. “Rules about the Study Sessions of Party Committees and Party-Groups 中国共产党党委（党组）理论学习中心组学习规则.”

2019a. “Central Directive on [the Operation] of Work Departments of the Party [provisional] 中国共产党工作机关条例（试行).”

2019b. “Central Directive on Political-Legal Work 政法工作条例.”

2019c. “Central Directive on Requesting for Instructions and Reports on Important Matters 重大事项请示汇报条例.”

2019d. “Central Party Directive on Party-Group Work 中国共产党党组工作条例.”

2019e. “Regulation on the Responsibility to Implement Party Regulations [provisional]党内法规执行责任制规定（试行).”

2020. “Rules on the Handling of Complaints and Reporting by Disciplinary/Supervision Organs 纪检监察机关处理检举控告工作规则.”

2021a. “Central Directive on the Work of the Party Discipline and Inspection Committees 中国共产党纪律检查委员会工作条例.”

2021b. “Measures of Organizational Sanctions [provisional] 中国共产党组织处理规定（试行).”

2021c. “Opinions on Strengthening Oversight of the First-in-Command and the Executive Team 关于加强对”一把手”和领导班子监督的意见.”

2022. “Rules of Operation of CDI Dispatched Outposts 纪检监察机关派驻机构工作规则.”

2023a. “Code of Discipline 中国共产党纪律处分条例 “.

2023b. "Rules on the Competence to Approve Disciplinary Decisions 中国共产党处分违纪党员批准权限和程序规定."

Center, Party, and State Council. 2015. "Framework of Measures to Strengthen Auditing Practices and Related Policy Documents《关于完善审计制度若干重大问题的框架意见》及相关配套文件."

Central Party, Special-Case Small Group. 1968. "Examination Report on the Crimes of Traitor, Insider Spy and Work Thief Liu Shaoqi 关于叛徒、内奸、工贼刘少奇罪行的审查报告."

COD. 1989. "Opinions on Registration of Party Membership in Selected Units 关于在部分单位进行党员重新登记工作的意见."

2014. "Transcript of the Press Conference of the COD on the Random Inspection of Disclosure Reports 中组部就开展领导干部个人有关事项报告抽查核实工作答问."

Committee, Central Supervision. 1955. "Work Procedures of the Central Supervision Committee 中共中央监察委员会工作细则."

1957. "Rules on the Competence to Approve Disciplinary Decisions against Party-Members 中央监察委员会关于处分党员的批准权限的规定."

Court, Bo Shan District of Zi Bo City 淄博市博山区人民法院. 2015a. "Regulation of the Work of the Adjudicative Committee 审判委员会工作规则."

Court, Gao Ping District of Nan Chong City 南充市高坪区人民法院. 2013a. "Regulation of the Sign-off of Court Documents 法律文书审核签发责任制度."

Court, Guangdong High. 2021. "Guideline to the Implementation of the Three Regulations to Prevent Judicial Interference 严格执行防止干预司法三个规定工作指引."

Court, Guangxi Daxin County. 2008. "Regulation on the Sign-off of Court Documents and on Case Supervision 案件监督、司法文书审核签发暂行规定."

Court, Heilongjiang Province 黑龙江省高级人民法院. 2017a. "Regulation of the Work of the Collegial Panels 合议庭工作规则."

Court, Huai Shang District of Beng Bu City 蚌埠市淮上区人民法院. 2015b. "Regulation of the Sign-off of Court Documents [provisional]裁判文书签发规定（试行）."

Court, Jing County. 2011. "Regulation on the Sign-off of Court Documents [provisional] 静县人民法院诉讼文书签发规定（试行）."

Court, Lucheng District of Wenzhou City 温州市鹿城区人民法院. 2014a. "Rules on the Distribution of Competence to Sign off Court Documents in Civil or Commercial Cases 民商事案件裁判文书签发权限的规定."

Court, Northern District of Xining City 西宁市城北区人民法院. 2012. "Rules on Sign-off of Judicial Documents 法律文书审核签发制度."

Court, Qi Xing Guan District of Bi Jie City 毕节市七星关区人民法院. 2013b. "Regulation of the Sign-off and Issuance of Court Documents [provision] 裁判文书撰稿校核签发及责任追究制度（试行）."

Court, Rang Hu District of Da Qing City 大庆市让湖路区人民法院. 2015c. "Regulation of the Work of the Adjudicative Committee 审判委员会工作规则."

Court, Shenzhen City 深圳市中级人民法院. 2017b. "Regulation of the Work of the Adjudicative Committee 审判委员会工作规则."

Court, Taizhou City Intermediate. 2016. "Notice on the Measure to Record Instances of Judicial Interference 台州市中级人民法院关于实施干预、过问案件记录制度的通知."

Court, Xian An District of Xian Ning City 咸宁市咸安区人民法院. 2013c. "Regulation on the Practice of Document Circulation [for Instructions, Opinions and Approvals] 文件传阅制度."

Court, Yan Shan District of Guilin City 桂林市雁山区人民法院. 2014b. "Regulation of the Sign-off of Court Documents各类文书审核签发规定."

Court, Zhenjiang City Intermediate. 2020. "Regulation on the Work of the Adjudicative Committee 审判委员会工作规则."

CPLC. 1995. "Notice on Enhancing the Work of Party Committee Political-Legal Committee of All Levels 关于加强各级党委政法委员会工作的通知."

2013. "Regulation on Reliably Preventing Wrongful Convictions 关于切实防止冤假错案的规定." in *No. 27*.

2014. "Opinions on Tightening Regulation on Decisions Regarding Sentence Reduction, Parole, Suspension of Sentence to Prevent Judicial Corruption 关于严格规范减刑、假释、暂予监外执行,切实防止司法腐败的意见."

2015. "Regulation on Documenting Instances of Interference from Internal Personnel and Holding Offenders Accountable 司法机关内部人员过问案件的记录和责任追究规定."

General Office, of the Party Center. 1985. "Notification on Enhancing Cadre Equipment in People's Courts and Procuratorates at All Levels 关于加强地方各级法院, 检察院干部配备的通知."

1991. "Notice on the Use of Public Funds, Resources and Refurbishment of Public Housing by Senior Leaders 中共中央办公厅、国务院办公厅关于处理 党和国家机关正、副省(部)级干部用公款、公物超标准装修住房问题的通知 ".

2012. "Bei an Rules on Party Regulations and Other Normative Documents 党内法规和规范性文件备案规定."

2016. "Pilot Program on the National Supervision Institutional Reform at Beijing, Shanxi and Zhejiang [关于在北京市、山西省、浙江省开展国家监察体制改革试点方案]."

2019a. "Regulation on Parallel Administration of (Leading) Cadre Positions and Civil Servants Ranks 公务员职务与职级并行规定 ".

2019b. "Rules of Inspection and Disciplinary Work of CDIs 中国共产党纪律检查机关监督执纪工作规则."

2020a. "Measures on the Assumption of Primary Responsibility by Party Committees (Party-Groups) to Enhance Party Disciplines 党委/党组落实全面从严治党主体责任规定."

2020b. "Regulation on Party Committees and Party Groups Taking the Primary Responsibility on Strictly Governing the Party 党委（党组）落实全面从严治党主体责任规定."

2023. "Opinions on Strengthening Legal Education and Legal Theoretical Research in the New Era 关于加强新时代法学教育和法学理论研究的意见."

NPC, Standing Committee (State). 1995, 2019. "Law of Judges 法官法."

2021. "Law of Supervision Officials 监察官法."

Politiburo. 1942. "On the Unification of the Leadership of the Party and Relational Adjustment of All Organizations in Anti-Japanese Bases 关于统一抗日根据地党的领导及调整各组织间关系的决定."

SPC. 1990. "Notice on How to Refer up in the Handling of Administrative Litigation Cases and Improving Research Work 关于行政案件如何向上请示及加强调研工作的通知."

1993. "Working Procedure of the Adjudicative Committee 审判委员会工作规则."

1996, 2012. "Notice on Rules Governing the Processing of Official Documents in People's Courts 人民法院公文处理办法."

1999. "Notice on Referring-up (qingshi) Issues in Adjudicative Activities 最高人民法院关于审判工作请示问题的通知."

2000a. "Regulation on Issues Concerning Centralization of Certain Enforcement Work by High Courts 关于高级人民法院统一管理执行工作若干问题的规定."

2000b. "Regulation on the Issuance and Publication of Court Judgments 裁判文书公布管理办法."

2000c. "Rules on the Selection of Panel-Leader in People's Courts (provisional) 人民法院审判长选任办法（试行）".

2001. "Regulation on the Sign-off Competence of the Head, Deputy and Chief-Judge of the SPC Adjudicative Supervision Division [provisional]关于审判监督庭庭长、副庭长、审判长签发法律文书权限的暂行规定."

2002a. "Reply on the Professional Eligibility of Newly Promoted Court Presidents and Vice-presidents 关于对新提任的人民法院院长副院长人选应具备的学历条件的答复意见."

2002b. "Working Procedure of the Collegial Panels."

2004. "Regulation on Court-Auction and Court-Sale in the Enforcement Procedure in Civil Litigations 民事执行中拍卖,变卖财产的规定."

2005. "Several Opinions of the Supreme People's Court on Strengthening the Adjudicative Ability and Raising the Standard of Adjudication 关于增强司法能力提高司法水平的若干意见."

2009. "Notification on Further Enhancing the Quality of Court Judgments 关于进一步提高裁判文书质量的通知." *Fa [2009] No.177.*

2010a. "Opinions on Establishing and Completing the Joint Action Mechanism for Court Judgment Enforcement 关于建立和完善执行联动机制若干问题的意见."

2010b. "Opinions on Formalizing the Adjudicative Working Relationship between the Higher and Lower Courts 关于规范上下级人民法院审判业务关系的若干意见."

2013. "Opinions on the Establishment and Completing the Operating Mechanism to Prevent Wrongful Convictions 关于建立健全防范刑事冤假错案工作机制的意见."

2015a. "Regulation of Implementation of Preventing Leader Cadres from Interfering in Judicial Activities 人民法院落实〈领导干部干预司法活动、插手具体案件处理的记录、通报和责任追究规定〉的实施办法."

2015b. "Several Opinions on Perfecting Measures to Improve Judicial Accountability 最高人民法院关于完善人民法院司法责任制的若干意见."

2017. "Provisional Opinions on Implementing the Judicial Accountability Mechanism and Improving the Administration of Adjudicative Supervision 关于落实司法责任制完善审判监督管理机制的意见（试行）."

2019a. "Notice on the Adjustments of the Acceptance Thresholds of First Instance Civil and Commercial Cases by High Courts and Intermediate Courts 关于调整高级人民法院和中级人民法院管辖第一审民事案件标准的通知."

2019b. "Opinions on Improving and Perfecting the Operational Mechanisms of the Adjudicative Committees of People's Courts 关于健全完善人民法院审判委员会工作机制的意见."

2021b. "Guiding Opinions on the Oversight and Management of "Four Types of Cases" 关于进一步完善"四类案件"监督管理工作机制的指导意见."

2021c. "Rules on How to Determine the Correct Governmenal Defendants of the County-rank or above in Administrative Litigation Cases 关于正确确定县级以上地方人民政府行政诉讼被告资格若干问题的规定."

SPC, and State Archival Bureau. 1991. "Rules on Filing and Archiving Judicial Documents 人民法院诉讼文书立卷归档办法."

SPC, and SPP. 2007. "Opinions on the Prosecution and Adjudication on Cases of the Crime of Bribe-Taking 关于办理受贿刑事案件适用法律若干问题的意见."

2016. "Judicial Interpretation on Issues Concerning the Handling of Criminal Cases Involving Embezzlement and Bribery 关于办理贪污贿赂刑事案件适用法律若干问题的解释."

SPP. 1993. "Further Strengthening the Investigation Work on Major Cases and Important Cases 关于进一步加强大案要案查处工作的通知."

1995. "Rules on the Handling of Case Leads and Preliminary Investigation in Cases Involving Ranked Officials 关于要案线索备案、初查的规定."

2012, 2019. "Regulation on Criminal Litigation by Procuratorates 人民检察院刑事诉讼规则."

# REFERENCES


Adams, Jan S. 1978. "Institutional change in the 1970s: The case of the USSR People's Control Committee." *Slavic Review* 37(3):457–72.

Ames, Michael. 2023. "The Feds say Pras is a foreign agent. Now the Fugee tells his side." *Rolling Stone*. www.rollingstone.com/music/music-features/pras-michel-fugees-jho-low-trial-interview-1234694084/. Accessed on November 2, 2023.

Bai, Mo 白墨. 2015. "CCP Founding Elder – Wan Li [中共元老万里]." *BBC Chinese*. www.bbc.com/zhongwen/simp/china/2015/07/150715_wanli_ profile. Accessed on April 22, 2024.

Bai, Zhaodong 白兆东. 2019. "What do we know about Zhao Zhenyong [赵正永往事]." *Caijing* 《财经》. http://m.caijing.com.cn/api/show?contentid=4563159. Accessed on January 11, 2024.

Barbalet, Jack. 2014. "The structure of guanxi: Resolving problems of network assurance." *Theory and Society* 43(1):51–69.

2017. "Guanxi as social exchange: Emotions, power and corruption." *Sociology* 12:1–16.

Barboza, David, Graham Bowley, and Amanda Cox. 2013. "Forging an art market in China." *The New York Times*. www.nytimes.com/projects/2013/china-art-fraud/index.html. Accessed on January 4, 2024.

Barnett, Arthur Doak. 1969. "Introduction." Pp. xi.–xxvi in *Chinese Communist Politics in Action*, edited by Arthur Doak Barnett. Seattle, WA: University of Washington Press.

Baum, Richard. 2018. *Burying Mao: Chinese Politics in the Age of Deng Xiaoping* (Updated Edition). Princeton, NJ: Princeton University Press.

BBC, Chinese. 2019. "Incident of Judge Wang Linqing's lost case dossier and the conclusion of the investigation of the incident [王林清千亿矿权案卷宗丢失事件与调查结果]." www.bbc.com/zhongwen/simp/chinese-news-47342048. Accessed on February 10, 2024.

Beach, Derek. 2016. "It's all about mechanisms: What process-tracing case studies should be tracing." *New Political Economy* 21:472.

Bennett, Andrew, and Jeffrey T. Checkel. 2015. *Process Tracing: From Metaphor to Analytic Tool*. Cambridge: Cambridge University Press.

Blumer, Herbert. 1952. "Book Review: The Organizational Weapon: A Study of Bolshevik Strategy and Tactics." *Americal Sociological Review* 17(5):630–31.

Bogu, Kailai 薄谷开来. 2013. *Criminal interrogation. interviewed* by SPP agents.

Boix, Carles, and Milan W. Svolik. 2013. "The foundations of limited authoritarian government: Institutions, commitment, and power-sharing in dictatorships." *The Journal of Politics* 75:316.

Buckley, Chris. 2020. "'Drive the blade in': Xi shakes up China's law-and-order forces." In *New York Times*.

Burns, J. P. 1989. *The Chinese Communist Party Nomenklatura System: A Documentary Study of Party Control of Leadership Selection*. Armonk, NY: M. E. Sharpe.

Cai, Eryi 蔡迩一. 2018. "Who are the key characters behind the interaction between the SPC and Cui Yongyuan [最高法和崔永元互动的背后涉及哪些关键人物? ]." *China Youth Daily* 《中国青年报》. http://news.china.com.cn/2018-12/31/content_74329054.htm. Accessed on January 11, 2024.

Cai, Wenjuan 蔡文娟 2021. "38 lawyers implicated in Zhang Jiahui case received sanctions [涉张家慧等案件的38名律师被查处]." Yang Guang Network [央广网]. www.cnr.cn/hn/xwsd/20211211/t20211211_525684976.shtml. Accessed on January 8, 2024.

Caixin. 2008. "Vice-president of Shenzhen Intermediate Court Pei Hongquan was sentenced to life [深圳中院原副院长裴洪泉被判无期]." *Caixin*. https://china.caixin.com/2008-01-07/100058543.html. Accessed on January 4, 2024.

2016. "Work Reports of the SPC and the SPP passed with a high margin, Historical low points should not be forgotten [两高报告高票通过 不应忘记过去"低谷"]." *Caixin*. https://topics.caixin.com/2016-03-16/100920637.html. Accessed on March 10, 2024.

Callahan, William A. 2012. "Who is Xi Jinping, and where will he lead China?" *Le Sud En Mouvement*. www.cetri.be/Who-is-Xi-Jinping-and-where-will?lang=fr. Accessed on June 5, 2023.

Cao, Zhenghan 曹正汉. 2014. "Ruling risk and local decentralization: Three theories of governance in China [统治风险与地方分权：关于中国国家治理的三种理论]." *Society* 《社会》(6).

Cao, Zhenhan. 2011. "Top-bottom division of governance in China and its stability mechanism [中国上下分治的治理体制及其稳定机制]." *Sociological Studies* 《社会学研究》(1).

Capitalnews. 2015. "Can CDI secretaries delay retirement for three years [纪委书记都能多干三年吗? ]." *Chang'an Street News* 《长安街知事》.

Capoccia, Giovanni. 2016. "When do institutions "bite"? Historical institutionalism and the politics of institutional change." *Comparative Political Studies* 49(8):1095–1127.

Capoccia, Giovanni, and R. Daniel Kelemen. 2007. "The study of critical junctures: Theory, narrative, and counterfactuals in historical institutionalism." *World Politics* 59(3):341–69.

Carlson, Allen, et al. (Ed.). 2010. *Contemporary Chinese Politics: New Sources, Methods, and Field Strategies*. Cambridge: Cambridge University Press.

Cartier, Carolyn. 2016. "A political economy of rank: The territorial administrative hierarchy and leadership mobility in urban China." *Journal of Contemporary China* 25(100):529–46.

CCDI. 1980. "Request to Rehabilitate and Completely Rectify the Wrongful Disciplinary Action against Members of the Central Supervision Commission [中共中央纪律检查委员会关于为中央监察委员会彻底平反恢复名誉的请示报告]."

1983. "Provisional Rules on Completing the Party's Disciplinary System and Strengthening the Disciplinary Personnel Construction Work [中共中央纪律检查委员会关于健全党的纪律检查系统加强纪检队伍建设的暂行规定]."

1987. "Work Report of CCDI submitted to the 13th National Party Congress [中央纪律检查委员会向党的第十三次全国代表大会的工作报告（一九八七年十月三十日）]." http://cpc.people.com.cn/GB/64162/64168/64566/65447/4441821.html. Accessed on November 18, 2023.

1988. "Rules on Case-Inspection Work for Party Discipline and Inspection Institutions (Provisional) [中国共产党纪律检查机关案件检查工作条例（试行）]."

1992. "Work Report of CCDI submitted to the 14th National Party Congress [中央纪律检查委员会向党的第十四次全国代表大会的工作报告（一九九二年十月九日）]." www.gov.cn/test/2008-07/04/content_1036091.htm Accessed on November 18, 2023.

2000. "Rules on the Application of "shuanggui" Measure by Disciplinary and Inspection Institutions (Provisional) [关于纪检机关使用"两规"措施的办法（试行）]".

2005. "Opinions on Strictly Abiding the Discipline and the Law to Conduct Case Investigation [关于纪检监察机关严格依纪依法办案的意见]."

2013a. "Historical origin and development of the CCDI [中央纪律检查委员会历史沿革]." CCP News Database. http://cpc.people.com.cn/n/2013/0904/c75234-22804679.html. Accessed on August 19, 2018.

2013b. "An Overview of the CIT Work in 2013 [2013年巡视工作综述]." CCDI Website.

2014a. "Annual Work Report delivered by Wang Qishan at the 3rd Plenum of the 18th CCDI 王岐山在十八届中纪委第三次全体会议上的工作报告."

2014b. "Demystifying CCDI [解密中纪委]." *Today's Click*《点击今日》. http://news.sohu.com/s2013/dianji-1069a/. Accessed on January 17, 2024.

2014c. "Taking lessons from the systematic and crumbling corruption in Shanxi [深刻汲取山西系统性、塌方式腐败教训]." *China Daily Online*. www.chinadaily.com.cn/dfpd/sx/2014-12/09/content_19048842.htm. Accessed on October 29, 2023.

2015a. "Interpretation Series on the CCP Directive of Inspection Work [《中国共产党巡视工作条例》系列解读]." *China Jijian Jiancha Daily* 《中国纪检监察报》.

2015b. "One needs to take responsibility when discharging one's duty, including the duty to monitor appointments [干事要担当 管人也要担当]." *CCDI Website*.

2015c. "Zooming in seven new outposts of the CCDI [走近中央纪委新设的7家派驻纪检组]." CCDI Column. www.gov.cn/xinwen/2015-05/28/content_2870199.htm. Accessed on January 14, 2024.

(Writer) 2016. Documentary series: Always on the Road [永远在路上], Episode 2: Top leaders take the lead [第二集 以上率下]. http://v.ccdi.gov.cn/yyzls2016/. Accessed on February 6, 2024.

2017a. "A comprehensive overview of the Party's inspection work since the 18th Party Congress [党的十八大以来中央巡视工作综述]." *Xinhua Agency*. www.xinhuanet.com//politics/2017-09/28/c_1121741459.htm. Accessed on March 10, 2024.

2017b. "An interview of the Beijing CDI secretary Zhang Shuo [北京市委常委、市纪委书记，市监委主任张硕专访]." http://fanfu.people.com.cn/n1/2018/0110/c64371–29756238.html. Accessed on January 5, 2024.

2017c. "Pushing forward the all-coverage CDI outpost reform and cleaning the lens of the monitoring camera [推进全面派驻 擦亮监督"探头"]." *China Jijian Jiancha Daily*. www.xinhuanet.com//politics/2017-09/28/c_1121737162.htm. Accessed on October 31, 2023.

2018. "Interpretation of the CCDI Work Protocols No. 12 ["工作规则"解读之十二]." *Chinese Discipline and Inspection Magazine* 《中国纪检监察杂志》. Accessed on February 8, 2024.

2022. "CCDI Work Report to the 20th National Party Congress [中纪委在党的二十大上的工作报告]."

2023a. "CCDI/NSC Press Release of Disciplinary Investigation Statistics in 2023 [中央纪委国家监委通报2023年全国纪检监察机关监督检查、审查调查情况]." www.news.cn/politics/20240125/9f867189a2b54d59906a3ca7c642b73c/c.html. Accessed on March 24, 2024.

(Writer) (2023b). Ep. 4 Always on the go [永远在路上], *Forever Charged Bugle Call* 《永远吹冲锋号》.

2024. "Former Head of the 1st SPC Civil Division and Member of the SPC Adjudicative Committee Zheng Xuelin is Expelled from the Party for Grave Disciplinary Violations [最高法审委会原委员、 民一庭原庭长郑学林严

重违纪违法被开除党籍].” www.ccdi.gov.cn/toutiaon/202402/t20240226_330303.html. Accessed on February 26, 2024.

CCDI, 中国纪检监察报. 2023c. “Simple and discreet – Investigating unlawful acceptance of shopping cards [办卡简单、送卡隐蔽 . . . 深挖细查违规收受消费卡].” *China Jijian Jiancha Daily*. https://wap.peopleapp.com/article/7246602/7087107. Accessed on February 11, 2024.

CCP, Information Center. 2023. “Rehabilitation Work [平反冤假错案工作].” CCP Information Center – Major Events [重大事件]. http://cpc.people.com.cn/GB/64162/64167/4512071.html. Accessed on November 17, 2023.

CCP, National Delegates Conference. 1955. “Decision on the establishment of Central and Local Party Supervision Commissions [中国共产党全国代表会议关于成立党的中央和地方监察委员会的决议].”

CCTV. 2013. “Operationalizing Measures of the Eight-Measures Issued by Many Central Agencies and Provinces [多地多部门出台落实八项规定措施].” *People's Network*. http://politics.people.com.cn/n/2013/0107/c1001-20121693.html. Accessed on January 14, 2024.

CDI, Beijing Xicheng District. 2016. “Press Statement of Disciplinary Violations of Four Party Cadres from Beijing Xicheng District [北京西城区委通报 4 起党员干部违纪案件处理情况].” Accessed on November 3, 2023.

CDI, Chengdu. 2018. “A diary of the tranfer of a cadet of the new CDI/SC [一名纪检监察新兵的转隶日记].” *Chengdu Business Newspaper*. www.thepaper.cn/newsDetail_forward_1999205. Accessed on November 5, 2023.

CDI, Dianjiang County. 2022. “Explanation of the Final Financial Statements of Dianjiang County CDI of the year of 2022 [中国共产党垫江县纪律检查委员会 2022 年度部门决算情况说明].” https://rb.gy/fr0bi. Accessed on October 31, 2023.

Center, Party. 1949. “Decision on the Establishment of the Central and Local Committees of Discipline and Inspection [中国共产党关于成立中央及各级党的纪律检查委员会的决定].”

1953. “Resolution on Strengthening the Practice of *qing shi bao gao* of All Departments of Central Government and on Strengthening the Leadership of the Party Center over Governmental Work [关于加强中央人民政府系统各部门向中央请示报告制度及加强中央对于政府工作领导的决定].”

1962. “Decision to strengthen Party Supervision Organs [关于加强党的监察机关的决定].”

1972. “Circular of the Summary Outline of the Conference on Criticizing Lin Biao Rectification Campain among Senior Leaders of Guizhou [贵州省地、师级干部批林整风汇报会议总结提纲（修改稿）].”

1979. “Firmly Safegard the Implementation of the Criminal Law and the Criminal Procedure Law [中共中央关于坚决保证刑法、刑事诉讼法切实实施的指示].”

1995. "Income Disclosure Measures for Leading Cadres at and above County/Division (xian/chu) Rank [关于党政机关县（处）级以上领导干部收入申报的规定]." Edited by General Office of the Party Center.

1996 [2012]. "Directive on the Flow of the Submission and Circulation of Official Documents of Party and State Administrations [党政机关公文处理工作条例]."

2010 [2016]. "Disclosure Measures of Personal Matters for Leading Cadres [关于领导干部报告个人有关事项的规定]." Edited by 中共中央办公厅，国务院办公厅.

2017. "CCP Directive of Inspection Work [中国共产党巡视工作条例]."

2019. "Central Party Directive on Party-group Work [中国共产党党组工作条例]."

2021. "Central Directive on the Work of the Party Discipline and Inspection Committees [中国共产党纪律检查委员会工作条例]."

2023a. "Code of Discipline [中国共产党纪律处分条例]."

2023b. "Rules on the Competence to Approve Disciplinary Decisions [中国共产党处分违纪党员批准权限和程序规定]."

Center, Party, and State Council. 2015. "Framework of Measures to Strengthen Auditing Practices and Releated Policy Documents [《关于完善审计制度若干重大问题的框架意见》及相关配套文件]."

1957. "Notice on the Classification Standards Regarding the Rightists [中共中央关于《划分右派分子的标准》的通知]."

Chan, Hon S. 2004. "Cadre personnel management in China: The nomenklatura system, 1990–1998." *The China Quarterly* 179:703–34.

Chan, Hon S., and Jie Gao. 2008. "Old wine in new bottles: A county-level case study of anti-corruption reform in the People's Republic of China." *Crime, Law and Social Change* 49:97–117.

Chang'an, Network. 2009. "Deputy head of the GITIC liquidation team found bribe-taking ["广国投"破产清算组副组长再被查出 60 万受贿款]." 河南长安网–长安视点. https://china.caixin.com/2009-09-02/100061443.html. Accessed on January 4, 2024.

Chen, Hangping 陈杭平. 2012. "Case-remanding practice in civil litigation from the organizational perspective [组织视角下的民事诉讼发回重审制度]." *Chinese Journal of Law*《法学研究》(1):17–30.

Chen, Hongtai 陈红太. 2003. "Periodical features of the political reform in China from the historical perspective of the changes of party-state relations [从党政关系的历史变迁看中国政治体制变革的阶段特征]." *Zhejiang Academic Journal* 《浙江学刊》. www.bjqx.org.cn/portal/sites/site-111/qxweb/zjk/ShowArtcf822b43-31ce-4bcf-a8da-53cc0047fb51.aspx.htm. Accessed on December 23, 2023.

Chen, Lei 陈磊, and Jiayun Chen 陈佳韵. 2015. "Anticorruption shall pay attention to violations of political disciplines [反腐败需重视"违反政治纪律"问题]." *Legal Daily*《法制日报》. http://fanfu.people.com.cn/n1/2015/1225/c64371-27976621.html Accessed on December 25.

Chen, Sicheng 陈思丞. 2020. "Strip-block disparity and vertical policy diffusion of governments [政府条块差异与纵向创新扩散]." *Sociological Studies*《社会学研究 》(2):146–71.

Chen, Weishan 陈惟杉. 2019. "The art of project operation of the female Hong Kong businesswoman behind Zhao Zhengyong [赵正永背后"女港商"刘娟的项目运作术]." *China Economic Weekly*《中国经济周刊》. http://paper.people.com.cn/zgjjzk/html/2019-02/15/content_1910549.htm. Accessed on January 11, 2024.

Cheng, Lei 程雷. 2011. "On the technical investigatory power of procuratorates [论检察机关的技术侦查权]." *Journal of Political Science and Law*《政法论丛》(5):95–100.

Cheng, Xi 程熙. 2019. "Are the Eight-Measures and the spirit of the Eight-Measures the same? [八项规定和中央八项规定精神一回事么？]." *Online Xinhua Newspaper*. www.xhby.net/index/201910/t20191015_6366743.shtml. Accessed on January 4, 2024.

Cheng, Zhongyuan 程中原. 2006. *A Biography of Zhang Wentian*《张闻天传》. Beijing: Contemporary China Press.

Chien, Shiuh-Shen. 2010. "Economic freedom and political control in post-Mao China: A perspective of upward accountability and asymmetric decentralization." *Asian Journal of Political Science* 18:89.

China, Tech & Wealth in. 2005. "Are we auctioning art works or our souls? [拍卖艺术品还是拍卖灵魂]." *Tech & Wealth in China*《中国科技财富》. http://finance.sina.com.cn/money/collection/yspmarket/20050413/11231513614.shtml. Accessed on January 4, 2024.

Chu, Jianguo 储建国, and Lixin Yu 余礼信. 2015. "Repositioning Party-group: How to improve operational efficiency of party-groups [让党组归位：对中共党组制度有效运转的探索]." *Theories and Reforms* 《理论与改革》(5):33–41.

Chung, J. H. 2000. *Central Control and Local Discretion in China, Leadership and Implementation during Post-Mao Decollectivization*. Oxford: Clarendon Press.

Chung, Jae Ho, and Tao-chiu Lam. 2004. "China's "City System" in flux: Explaining post-Mao administrative changes." *The China Quarterly* 180:945–64.

Chung, Yen-Lin 钟延麟. 1999. "The role and activities of Deng Xiaoping in the Gao/Rao Affair [邓小平在"高饶事件"中之角色与作为]." *Journal of Humanities and Social Sciences*《人文及社会科学集刊 》(12):521–62.

2018. "The role and activities of Peng Zhen in the Yan'an Recitification Campaign [彭真在中共延安整风运动中的角色和活动]." *Historical Journal of National Chengchi University* 《国立政治大学历史学报》 49(5):39–92.

Clarke, Donald. 2022. "Order and law in China." *University of Illinois Law Review* 2022:541–95.

COD. 2014. "Transcript of the Press Conference of the COD on the Random Inspection of Disclosure Reports [中组部就开展领导干部个人有关事项报告抽查核实工作答问]."

Cohn, Edward. 2021. *The High Title of a Communist: Postwar Party Discipline and the Values of the Soviet Regime*. Ithaca, NY: Cornell University Press.

Committee, Central. 2018. "Reform Plan of the Party-state Institutional Overhaul [深化党和国家机构改革方案]." Edited by Third Plenum of the 19th Party Congress.

Committee, Central Supervision. 1957. "Rules on the Competence to Approve Disciplinary Decisions against Party-members [中央监察委员会关于处分党员的批准权限的规定]."

County A, Party Supervision Commission of. 1960. "Case Deliberation Records [会议纪要]."

Court, Luanping County Chengde City 承德市滦平县法院. 2023. "Discipline and Law Classroom: Spirit of the Eight-Measures of the Central Party [纪法课堂: 中央八项规定精神]."

Court, Beijing No. 2 Intermediate. 2017. "Court Judgement Beijing No. 2 Procuratorate v. Meng Huiqing." www.yejils.com/show.php?id=3376 Accessed on November 3, 2023.

Court, Luanping County Chengde City 承德市滦平县法院. 2023. "Discipline and Law Classroom: Spirit of the Eight-Measures of the Central Party [纪法课堂：中央八项规定精神]." https://mp.weixin.qq.com/s?__biz=MzIzNzA0OTcxNA==&mid=2651706924&idx=2&sn=8e512569f71e9cd5a5fec89a7f433f8e&chksm=f337f431c4407d2733171fc17c4976f6399686f2c125ac47aa05b566bb43ab49b047fb8302b4&scene=27. Accessed on February 10, 2024.

Court, Lucheng District of Wenzhou City 温州市鹿城区人民法院. 2014. "Rules on the Distribution of competence to Sign off Court Documents in Civil or Commercial Cases [民商事案件裁判文书签发权限的规定]."

Court, Northern District of Xining City 西宁市城北区人民法院. 2012. "Rules on Sign-off of Judicial Documents [法律文书审核签发制度]."

Court, Shouguang People's. 2001. "The operational model and effect of the 'Grand Case-registering' mechanism [山东省寿光市人民法院"大立案"机制的运行模式与成效]." *Judicial Development and Research* 《司法审判动态与研究》 1(1):95–100.

Court, Yuecheng District Shaoxing City 绍兴市越城区人民法院. 2015. "Measures on the Scope of Adjudicative Administrative Competence of Court leaders and Divisional Leaders [绍兴市越城区人民法院关于规范院、庭长审判管理权限的规定]."

CSC, 中央监察委员会. 1957. "Concluding Summary of the 2nd Conference of National Party Supervision Work [draft] [第二次全国党的监察会议工作总结（草稿）]."

Cui, Wei. 2024. "The Chinese tax system: Where it stands and how we should study it." In *Handbook of Public Finance in China*, edited by Linda Li. https://papers.ssrn.com/sol3/papers.cfm?abstract_id=4680217, Last Accessed on March 23, 2025

Cui, Xiankang. 2015a. "Guo Wengui's hunt of high-ranking officials: From an ally to an adverary [郭文贵围猎高官记：从结盟到反目]." *Caixin*. On file with author. Accessed on November 1, 2022.

2015b. "How did Guo Wengui hunt down high-ranking officials [郭文贵围猎高官记]." In *Caixin*.

崔先康. 2022a. "In the wake of the "missing dossier gate" – Wang Linqing received a 14 years prison sentence for bribe-taking and stealing secrets ["丢卷门"事件后续：王林清受贿、窃密一审获刑 14 年]." *Caixin*《财新》. https://china.caixin.com/2022-05-07/101881723.html. Accessed on January 12, 2024.

Cui, Xiankang崔先康, Ning Yu 于宁, and Ran Liu刘冉. 2015. "Power hunter Guo Wengui [权力猎手郭文贵]." *Caixin*. https://weekly.caixin.com/m/2015-03-27/100795235_all.html. Accessed on November 2, 2023.

Cui, Xiaojun et al. 崔小军等. 2022b. "Guangzhou City People's Procuratorate vs. Yao Hui, Decision Rendered by Guangzhou Intermediate Court on May 19th 2022 [广州市人民检察院诉姚辉刑事判决书 (2022) 粤 01 刑初 30 号 判决日期: 2023 年5月 19 日]."

Dai, Maolin 戴茂林, and Xiaoguang Zhao 赵晓光. 2011. *Biography of Gao Gang*《高岗传》. Xi'an: Shaanxi People's Press.

Daily, China. 2010. "Fake meritorous performance has become the life-saving straw [假立功成贪官"救命稻草"]." *Yang Cheng Evening Paper*《羊城晚报》. https://global.chinadaily.com.cn/dfpd/2010-09/20/content_11330018.htm. Accessed on January 4, 2024.

Daily, Legal. 2022. "Financial anticorruption storm gathers strength [金融反腐风暴越刮越猛]." *Legal Daily*. http://epaper.legaldaily.com.cn/fzrb/content/20220928/Articel04002GN.htm. Accessed on October 31, 2023.

Daily, People's. 2018a. "Former Hebei provincial Party-secretary received 15 years prison sentence for bribe-taking of 150 million yuan [河北省委原常委张越一审被判15年 被控受贿超1.5亿元]." *People's Daily*《人民日报》. www.guancha.cn/politics/2018_07_12_463869.shtml. Accessed on January 14, 2024.

2018b. "Frequent ocurrence of prison corruption is correlated to oversight strength [监狱腐败频发与监督力度薄弱不无关系]." *People's Daily*. https://m.thepaper.cn/kuaibao_detail.jsp?contid=3843704&from= kuaibao. Accessed on January 4, 2024.

Daily, Shaanxi. 2007. "Why is shopping card so popular? [购物卡缘何大行其道]." *Shaanxi Daily* 《陕西日报》. www.daynews.com.cn/sxrb/bban/B1/296497.html. On file with the author.

Dalian, Intermediate Court 大连中级人民法院. 2018. "Former State Security Deputy Minister Received a Life Sentence [前国家安全部原副部长马建被判无期]."

Deng, Liqun 邓力群. 1998. *Post Yan'an Rectification Campaign* 《延安整风以后》. Beijing: Contemporary China Publishing House.

Deng, Xiaoping. 1955. "Report on the Anti-Party Alliance of Gao Gang and Rao Shuhi [邓小平关于高岗、饶漱石反党联盟的报告]." https://banned-historical-archives.github.io/articles/d2dcf2d145. Accessed on February 10, 2024.

1980. "Institutional Reform of the Ruling System of the Party and the State (transcript) [党和国家领导制度的改革]." www.reformdata.org/1980/0818/15396.shtml. Accessed on February 11, 2024.

Department, Central Organization. 2015. "Learn from the Lesson of Zhou Yongkang and Bo Xilai, Adhere Firmly to Political Protocols [汲取周永康薄熙来案件教训 坚守政治规矩]." In Sina News.

Deutscher, Isaac. 1967. *Stalin: A Political Biography*. Oxford: Oxford University Press.

Diamant, Neil J. 2022. *Useful Bullshit: Constitutions in Chinese Politics and Society*. Ithaca, NY: Cornell University Press.

Ding, Lianghua 丁亮华. 2023. "Critical reflections on the judicial delocalization reform [司法"去地方化"改革反思]." *Chinese Journal of Law* 《法学研究》 45(5):96–113.

Dittmer, Lowell. 1973. "The structural evolution of 'Criticism and Self-Criticism'." *The China Quarterly* 56:708–29.

1990. "Patterns of elite strife and succession in Chinese politics." *The China Quarterly* 123:405–30.

1995. "Chinese informal politics." *The China Journal* 34:1–34.

Doig, Alan, and Jon Moron. 2000. "Anti-corruption agencies: The importance of independence for the effectiveness of national integrity systems." Pp. 229–51 in *Corruption, Integrity and Law Enforcement*, edited by Cyrille J.C.F. Fijnaut and Leo Huberts. Leiden, The Netherlands: Brill | Nijhoff.

DOJ. 2023. "Ho Wan Kwok, A/K/A "Miles Guo," Arrested For Orchestrating Over $1 Billion Dollar Fraud Conspiracy." *DOJ Press release: US Attorney's Office – Southern District of New York*. www.justice.gov/usao-sdny/pr/ho-wan-kwok-aka-miles-guo-arrested-orchestrating-over-1-billion-dollar-fraud-conspiracy. Accessed on November 4, 2023.

Dong, Biwu 董必武. 1957. "Speech at the Second National Conference of Party Supervisory Work [在第二次全国党的监察工作会议上的讲话]." *On file with the author.*

Dong, Fang. 2016. "CCDI counterattack, a reversal for Ren Zhiqiang's case? [中纪委反击 任志强案逆转？ ]." *Voice of America*. https://rb.gy/xi5snr. Accessed on November 3, 2023.

Dongnan, Zaobao. 2013. "CCDI making plans to implement the Dual-Leadership System [中纪委制定纪检双重领导体制]." *Southeastern Morning News* 《东南早报》. http://news.163.com/13/1115/10/9DNFE50V00014Q4P.html. On file with the author.

Dou, Zhendong 窦振东. 2021. "An investigative report on the asset recovery work of courts in criminal litigation [关于人民法院刑事诉讼涉案财物处置工作的调查报告]." *Criminal Adjudication Reference* 《刑事审判参考》. www.drxsfd.com/xf/anli.asp?bh=2963. Accessed on March 9, 2024.

Economist, The. 2015. "The devil, or Mr Wang – China's second most powerful leader is admired and feared." *The Economist*. www.economist.com/china/2015/03/26/the-devil-or-mr-wang. Accessed on November 3, 2023.

Erik van, Ree. 1993. "Stalin's organic theory of the Party." *The Russian Review* 52(1):43–57.

Eva, Pils. 2021. "China's human rights lawyers: Rifts and schisms in an era of global human rights backlash." *Made in China Journal* 6:113.

Fairbank, John K. 1983. *The Cambridge History of China: Volume 12: Republican China, 1912–949*. Cambridge: Cambridge University Press.

Fairbank, John K., and Albert Feuerwerker. 1986. *The Cambridge History of China: Volume 13: Republican China 1912–949*. Cambridge: Cambridge University Press.

Faison, Seth. 1997. "China after Deng: The overview." *The New York Times*. www.nytimes.com/1997/02/20/world/deng-xiaoping-is-dead-at-92-architect-of-modern-china.html. Accessed on July 5, 2023.

Falleti, Tulia G., and Julia F. Lynch. 2009. "Context and causal mechanisms in political analysis." *Comparative Political Studies*.

Fan, Guangjie 范光杰等. 2011. "Historical development and features of the Party's disciplinary and inspection system over the past nine decades [九十年来党的纪检监察制度的沿革和特点]." *Research on Mao Zedong Thoughts* 《毛泽东思想研究》 (4):42–7.

Fan, Junli 范军利. 2006. "The rise and fall of the godfather of the auction industry in Shenzhen [深圳拍卖业教父盛衰录]." P. A7 in *Shanghai Securities Newspaper*《上海证券报》.

Fan, Lisi范丽思. 2021. "Reconstruction of the protective mechanism of Court funds after the Unified Vertical Administration Reform [省级统管后法院经费保障机制再造]." *People's Adjudication* 《人民司法》 (22):72–8.

Fan, Ping 范平, and Huan Yao姚桓. 2010. *On the Party Charter*《中国共产党党章教程》. Beijing: Fang Zheng Press.

Feng, Jiang. 2019. "Party regulations and state laws in China: A disappearing boundary and growing tensions." *Chinese Law & Government* 51(5–6): 260–76.

Feng, Lixia 封丽霞. 2021. "Institutional logic and standardization issues of the Party-state joint documents [党政联合发文的制度逻辑及其规范化问题]." *Chinese Journal of Law*《法学研究》(1):3–19.

Festinger, Leon. 1957. *A Theory of Cognitive Dissonance*. Stanford, CA: Stanford University Press.

Fewsmith, Joseph. 1996. "Institutions, informal politics, and political transition in China." *Asian Survey* 36(3):230–45.

2021a. "Balances, norms and institutions: Why elite politics in the CCP have not institutionalized." *The China Quarterly*:1–18.

2021b. *Rethinking Chinese Politics*. Cambridge: Cambridge University Press.

Finder, Susan. 2024. "How China's Supreme People's Court supports the development of foreign-related rule of law." *China Law and Society Review* 8(1–2):62–118.

Forsythe, Michael, David Enrich, and Alexandra Stevenson. 2019. "Inside a brazen scheme to woo China: Gifts, golf and a $4,254 wine." *New York Times (Online)*.

Forsythe, Michael, and Benjamin Weiser. 2023. "The undoing of Guo Wengui, billionaire accused of fraud on 2 continents." *New York Times*. www.nytimes.com/2023/03/30/us/guo-wengui-china.html. Accessed on November 2, 2023.

Friedman, Dan. 2022. "A fugitive Chinese tycoon met Steve Bannon. Misinformation mayhem ensued." *Mother Jones*. www.motherjones.com/politics/2022/02/guo-wengui-miles-guo-gettr-steve-bannon/. Accessed on November 3, 2023.

Fu, Claire. 2023. "China is cracking down on bankers. Here are some of the targets." *New York Times (Online)*.

Fu, Yulin, and Randall Peerenboom. 2010. "A new analytic framework for understanding and promoting judicial independence in China." Pp. 95–133 in *Judicial Independence in China: Lessons for Global Rule of Law Promotion*, edited by Randy Peerenboom. New York: Cambridge University Press.

Fushi, 浮石. 2006. *Celadon*《青瓷》. Changsha: Hunan Art and Literature Press.

Gan, Nectar. 2015. "Chinese tycoon denies colluding with disgraced senior spy Ma Jian." in *South China Morning Post*.

Gan, Yisheng 干以胜. 2007. "CCDI Press Conference on central inspection work [中纪委新闻发布会]." http://news.sina.com.cn/c/2007-08-02/112613579734.shtml. Accessed on December 20, 2023.

Gandhi, Jennifer, and Adam Przeworski. 2007. "Authoritarian institutions and the survival of autocrats." *Comparative Political Studies* 40(11): 1279–1301.

Gao, Bin 高斌 2013. "Ten educational programs rejuvenized the Party [10次教育活动让党焕发活力]." *Procuracy Daily*《检察日报》. https://news.12371.cn/2013/11/05/ARTI1383635452341741.shtml. Accessed on July 5, 2023.

Gao, Hua. 2019. *How the Red Sun Rose: The Origin and Development of the Yan'an Rectification Movement, 1930–1945*: The Chinese University of Hong Kong Press: Hong Kong

Gao, Hua 高华. 1999. "A historical investigation of the purge of AB-league ["肃 AB团"事件的历史考察]." *21st Century*《二十一世纪》. www.cuhk.edu.hk/ics/21c/media/articles/c054-199907002.pdf. Accessed on June 26, 2023.

2000. *How the Red Sun Rose: The Ins and Outs of the Yan'an Rectification Campaign* 《红太阳是怎样升起的：延安整风运动的来龙去脉》. Hong Kong: Hong Kong Chinese University Press.

Gao, Min 高昱, and Xiankang Cui崔先康. 2017. "The beginning and end of Guo Wengui's acquisation of Minzu Securities [郭文贵收购民族证券始末]." *Caixin*. https://china.caixin.com/2017-04-20/101080560.html. Accessed on January 4, 2024.

Gao, Yifei 高一飞, and Yicheng Zhao 赵毅城. 2018. "Current reform on the adjudicative supervision of court leaders and divisional leaders [院庭长审判监督管理机制的当前改革]." *Hunan Social Sciences Journal*《湖南社会科学》(6):64–75.

Gao, Yuyang 高语阳. 2019b. "Sixteen new offices of the CCDI/NSC accounced [中央纪委国家监委16个新设室职责公布]." In *China Youth Daily*《中国青年报》.

Ge, Yan 葛燕. 2020. "A Study of the Law Implementation and Supervision of Local Party Political-Legal Committees [地方党委政法委执法监督工作问题研究]." Inner Mongolia University.

General Office, of the Party Center. 1985. "Notification on Enhancing Cadre Equippment in People's Courts and Procuratorates at All Levels [关于加强地方各级法院, 检察院干部配备的通知]."

2015. "Central Office Circulates Three Measures on Nomination of CDI Secretaries [中办印发三个提名考察办法]." in *People's Daily*.

2019. "Rules of Inspection and Disciplinary Work of CDIs [中国共产党纪律检查机关监督执纪工作规则]."

Gill, Graeme. 1988. *The Rules of the Communist Party of the Soviet Union*. London: Macmillan Press.

Gold, Thomas, et al. 2002a. "An introduction to the study of guanxi." Pp. 1–20 in *Social Connections in China: Institutions, Culture, and the Changing Nature of Guanxi*, edited by Thomas Gold, Doug Guthrie, and David Wank. Cambridge: Cambridge University Press.

(Ed.). 2002b. *Social Connections in China: Institutions, Culture, and the Changing Nature of Guanxi*. Cambridge: Cambridge University Press.

Goldstein, Avery. 1991. *From Bandwagon to Balance-of-Power Politics*. Stanford, CA: Stanford University Press.

Gong, Cheng. 2007. "The secret and confession of a boss of an auction house [一个拍卖行老板的秘密与忏悔]." *Southern Weekly*《南方周刊》. www.infzm.com/content/1929. Accessed on January 4, 2024.

Gong, Ting. 1997. "Forms and characteristics of China's corruption in the 1990s: Change with continuity." *Communist and Post-communist Studies* 30(3):277–88.

2002. "Dangerous collusion: Corruption as a collective venture in contemporary China." *Communist and Post-communist Studies* 35:85–103.

2004. "Dependent judiciary and unaccountable judges: Judicial corruption in contemporary China." *China Review* 4(2):33–54.

2008a. "The Party Discipline Inspection in China: Its evolving trajectory and embedded dilemmas." *Crime, Law and Social Change* 49(2):139–52.

2008b. "The Party Discipline Inspection in China: Its evolving trajectory and embedded dilemmas." *Crime, Law and Social Change* 49:139–52.

Gong, Ting, and Jianming Ren. 2012. "Hard rules and soft constraints: Regulating conflict of interest in China." *Journal of Contemporary China* 22(79):1–17.

Gong, Ting, and Stephen Ma. 2008c. "Corruption and anti-corruption reform in and beyond China [Special Issue]." *Crime, Law & Social Change* 49(1–2):1–6

Graeff, Peter. 2005. "Why should one trust in corruption?" In *The New Institutional Economics of Corruption*, edited by J. G. Lambsdorff et al. London and New York: Routledge.

Guangdong, High Court 广东高级人民法院. 2021a. "Guideline to the Implementation of the Three Regulations to Prevent Judicial Interference [严格执行防止干预司法三个规定工作指引]."

2021b. "Implementation Guidelines of Three Regulations to Prevent Judicial Interference [严格执行防止干预司法"三个规定"工作指引]."

Guo, Dehong 郭德宏. 2014a. *Chronicle of Wang Ming*《王明年谱》. Beijing: Social Sciences Literature Press.

Guo, Wengui. 2017. "Streaming broadcast: Meng Huiqing also investigated Wang Qishan in connection with the case on Liu Zhihua (EP–031) [孟会青调查刘志华时也调查了王岐山]." www.youtube.com/watch?v=keSArPRyAGU. Accessed on January 10, 2023.

Guo, Xuezhi. 2001. "Dimensions of guanxi in Chinese elite politics." *The China Journal* 46(Jul.):69–90.

2014b. "Controlling corruption in the Party: China's Central Discipline Inspection Commission." *The China Quarterly* 219:597–624.

Guo, Yong. 2008. "Corruption in transitional China: An empirical analysis." *The China Quarterly* 194(June):349–64.

Guo, Yong 过勇. 2012. "The reformative process of the Chinese Communist Party's Disciplinary Inspection Committee in the new era [新时期中国共产党纪律检查委员会的改革历程]." *Comparative Studies of Economic and Social Systems* 《经济社会体制比较》 (5):130–44.

2014c. "A study of the outpost practice of the discipline/inspection and supervision institutions [中国纪检监察派驻制度研究]." *Journal of National Administrative College* 《国家行政学院学报》 (2):112–16.

Guoxing, Cao. 2015. "Guo Wengui story: A power battle between intelligence agencies [郭文贵故事：情报机构掌握权之争]." https://rb.gy/j5jmda. Accessed on November 2, 2023.

Guyot, Erik, Henny Sender, and Cathy Chan. 1999. "Gitic creditors are shocked to learn extent of their losses." *The Wall Street Journal.* www.wsj.com/articles/SB924743965101288676. Accessed on March 25, 2025.

Hall, Peter A., and Rosemary C. R. Taylor. 1996. "Political science and the three new institutionalisms." *Political Studies* 44(5):936–57.

Hamrin, Carol Lee, and Suisheng Zhao. 1995. *Introduction: Core Issues in Understanding the Decision Process.* Armonk, NY: M. E. Sharpe.

Han, Dayuan 韩大元. 2017. "Several constitutional issues in the national supervision institutional reform [论国家监察体制改革中的若干宪法问题]." 《法学评论》 (3).

Harding, Jacob. 2014. "Corruption or guanxi? Differentiating between the legitimate, unethical, and corrupt activities of Chinese government officials." *UCLA Pacific Basin Law Journal* 31(2):128–45.

Harfield, Clive. 2010. "The governance of covert investigation." *Melbourne University Law Review* 34:773–804.

Harmon-Jones, Eddie, and Judson Mills. 1999. "Chapter 1: An introduction to cognitive dissonance theory and an overview of current perspectives on the theory." In *Cognitive Dissonance: Progress on a Pivotal Theory in Social Psychology*, edited by Eddie Harmon-Jones, and Judson Mills. Washington, D.C.: American Psychological Association.

He, Fang 何方. 2019. *Notes on Party History: From Zunyi Conference to Yan'an Rectification Campaign (enlarged edition)* 《党史笔记：从遵义会议到延安整风 (增订版)》. Hong Kong: City University of Hong Kong Press.

He, Jiahong. 2016. *Back From the Dead: Wrongful Convictions and Criminal Justice in China.* Hawaii, HI: University of Hawai'i Press.

He, Xin. 2008. "Lack of financial funding and judicial corruption in China's courts [中国法院的财政不足与司法腐败]." *21st Century Bimonthly* 《21世纪双月刊》 (2).

2009. "Court finance and court responses to judicial reforms: A tale of two Chinese courts." *Law & Policy* 31(4):463–86.

2011. "Black hole of responsibility: The Adjudication Committee's role in the Chinese court." *Law & Society Review*.

2021. "Pressures on Chinese judges under Xi." *The China Journal* 85:49–74.

He, Xin 贺欣. 2006. "Ill-functioned basic courts? [运作不良的法院]." *Law and Social Science*《法律与社会科学》1:30–66.

Hedström, Peter, and Petri Ylikoski. 2010. "Causal mechanisms in the social sciences." *Annual Review of Sociology* 36:67.

Heilmann, Sebastian. 2008. "Policy experimentation in China's economic rise." *Studies in Comparative International Development* 43:26.

Heilmann, Sebastian, and Sarah Kirchberger. 2000. "The Chinese nomenklatura in transition." *China Analysis* (1):1–13.

Henderson, Keith. 2007. "The rule of law and judicial corruption in China: Half-way over the Great Wall." in *Global Corruption Report 2007: Corruption in Judicial Systems*, edited by Transparency International. Cambridge: Cambridge University Press.

Hillman, Ben. 2014. *Power and Patronage: Local State Networks and Party-State Resilience in China*. Stanford, CA: Stanford University Press.

Ho, Matt. 2020. "China investigates former aide of Vice-President Wang Qishan for alleged corruption." *South China Morning Post*. https://rb.gy/xn4xik. Accessed on November 3, 2023.

Hou, Meng 侯猛. 2013. "An explanation of the relationship between the Party and the courts – From the perspective of the Political-Legal Committee ["党与政法"关系的展开 — 以政法委员会为研究中心]." *The Jurists*《法学家》(2):1–15.

2021. *The Process of Justice, Based on the Survey of the Supreme People's Court*《司法的运作过程：基于对最高人民法院的观察》. Beijing: China Legal Publishing House.

Hu, Ben 胡贲. 2010. "Leaders' instructive remarks: subtle drafting/interpretative craft and circulation logic ["领导批示"：微妙技巧与传阅逻辑]." *Southern Weekend*《南方周末》. www.infzm.com/contents/47027?source=124&source_1=48527. Accessed on April 9, 2024.

Hu, Jing 胡静. 2017. "Straightly enforcing the *qingshi baogao* protocol [把讲政治贯穿监督执纪全过程 – 严格执行请示报告制度]." *China Jijian Jiancha Magazine*《中国纪检监察》12:28–29.

Hu, Xiabing et al. 胡夏冰等. 2002. "Judicial justice and the reform of the judiciary of China [司法公正与我国法官制度改革]." In *Judicial Reform Review*《司法改革论评》, edited by Weiping Zhang张卫平. Beijing: China Legal Publishing House.

Hu, Xiabing 胡夏冰, and Chunmei Chen 陈春梅. 2012. "Critical reflection and reconstruction of the practice of remanding a case [我国民事发回重审制度：反思与重构]." *Application of Law*《法律适用》(8):53–57.

Hu, Xiaobo. 1994. "Political economy of decentralization and resource allocation in contemporary China." Pp. 261. Durham, NC: Duke University.

Huang, Gufeng et al. 黄固锋等. 2006. "A survey report of bribe-giving conducted by Haizhu District Procuratorate [海珠区检察院对行贿人员的问卷调查报告]." *On file with the author.*

Huang, Jian et al. 黄剑 等. 2018. "The dream and fight of Zhao Faqi [赵发琦的梦想与抗争]." *Southern People's Weekly* 《南方人物周刊》. www.nfpeople.com/article/8054. Accessed on January 11, 2024.

Huang, Jianliang, and Qiuhua Chen. 2005. "A criminological analysis of embezzlement and bribery committed by judges [法官贪污贿赂犯罪分析]." *Rule of Law Review Weekly* 《法制评论周刊》.

Huang, Jing. 2000. *Factionalism in Chinese Communist Politics*. Cambridge: Cambridge University Press.

Huang, Mingyao et al. 黄明耀等. 2008. "Improving documents sign-off practice by court leaders and divisional leaders and responsibility of the collegial panel [合议庭职责和院庭长裁判文书签发权限制度的完善]." *Journal of Southwestern University of Political Science and Law* 《西南政法大学学报》 10(3):85–94.

Huang, Wenyi 黄文艺. 2020. "Normative principles of the PRC political-legal system [中国政法体制的规范性原理]." *Chinese Journal of Law* 《法学研究》 42(4):3–22.

Huang, Xiaoguang 黄孝光. 2021. "Judicial corruption scandal at Ji'nan Intermediate Court: Is it bribe-giving when lawyers gave judges money? [济南中院三法官受贿案：律师送钱"不是行贿"]？." *China Newsweek* 《中国新闻周刊杂志》. https://export.shobserver.com/toutiao/html/385900.html. Accessed on December 28, 2023.

Huang, Yasheng. 1996. "Central-Local relations in China during the reform era: The economic and institutional dimensions." *World Development* 24(4):655–72.

Huang, Zhongshun 黄忠顺. 2015. "In-depth analysis of the mandatory judicial auction reform [司法强制拍卖改革的深度透析]." *Modern Legal Science* 《当代法学》 (1):49–58.

Huanqiu, Network 环球网. 2009. "Commissioner raises questions on the disappearance of a vice-minister of railway [委员质疑铁道部副部级官员被双规1年仍无说法]." Huanqiu Network 环球网. http://news.sina.com.cn/c/2009-03-12/011717387766.shtml. Accessed on January 14, 2024.

Ip, E. C. 2011. "The Supreme People's Court and the political economy of judicial empowerment in contemporary China." *Columbia Journal of Asian Law* 24(2):367–435.

2008. "Judicial corruption and its threats to national governance in China." *Journal of Administration and Governance* 3(1). https://shorturl.at/BM7Yl. Accessed on March 26, 2025

Jahiel, Abigail R. 1998. "The organization of environmental protection in China." *The China Quarterly* 156:787.

Ji, Fa 季玹, and Xinglong Pan 潘兴龙. 2020. "An analysis of the case of former vice-president of Jilin High Court Lü Hongmin [吉林高院原副院长吕洪民严重违纪违法案剖析]." *CCDI Newspaper* 《中国纪检监察报》. www.chinanews.com.cn/gn/2020/12-16/9363208.shtml. Accessed on January 4, 2024.

Ji, Lu 吉陆. 2004. "Developers and officials engage in deceptive corruption [开发商与官员变相腐败]." *Southern Metropolitan Paper*《南方都市报》. On file with the author.

Jia, Nan 贾楠, and Fei Li 李菲. 2009. "The number of cadres of ethinic miniorities keeps rising in our country [我国少数民族干部数量不断扩大]." *Daily, China Youth*《中国青年报》. Accessed on March 24, 2024.

Jia, Yucun贾雨村. 2021. "A Liaoning High Court judge remembered it wrong after taking a bribe [辽宁高院法官收钱后"记反了"]." https://mp.weixin.qq.com/s/KYs9O8pM9yEKoNJVOfDnvQ. Accessed on January 8, 2024.

Jiang, Bixin 江必新. 2020a. "Carefulling constructing the mechanism to dispel illegal interference [认真建构和完善排除非法干预的制度和机制]." *People's Courts Daily* 《人民法院报》. http://rmfyb.chinacourt.org/paper/images/2020-04/08/02/2020040802_pdf.pdf. Accessed on January 8, 2024.

Jiang, Chuan 江川. 2006. "The end of career of celebrity judge Tang Jikai [明星法官跑官买官末路]." *Procuracy Affairs*《检察风云》. http://qkzz.net/Announce/announce.asp?BoardID=16200&ID=453104 Accessed on July 2, 2010. On file with the author.

Jiang, Laiying 蒋来用. 2017. "Historical lessons of and solutions regarding national supervision system reform [国家监察体制改革的实践与对策]." *Journal of National Administrative College*《国家行政学院学报》(2):10–16.

Jiang, Shigong 强世功. 2019a. "Chinese path and model of the rule of law [中国法治道路与法治模式 — 全球视野与中国经验]." *Administrative Management Reform*《行政管理改革》(8):21–8.

Jiang, Xi 蒋曦, and Minchao Wang 王民超. 2014. "Chen Yun in historical junctures [历史转折中的陈云]." *The Paper* 《澎湃》. www.thepaper.cn/newsDetail_forward_1265001. Accessed on July 20, 2023.

Jiang, Xiaotian 蒋小天. 2019b. "The "collapse" of the political legal system of Wuhan [武汉市政法系统"塌陷"]." *Sohu News.* www.sohu.com/a/295955567_161795. Accessed on February 17, 2024.

Jiang, Xinqi 蒋新祺. 2020b. "Unknown histories about Hua Guofeng [听华国锋讲不为人知的往事]." *Hundred-Year Tide* 《百年潮》. https://digest.creaders.net/2021/12/26/2434305.html. Accessed on January 14, 2024.

Jiang, Zongfu 姜宗福. 2010. "Former deputy mayor of Lin Xiang city wrote about the hidden rules in the officialdom [湖南临湘原副市长披露亲身经历官场"潜规则"]." in *Chinese News Network* 中国新闻网.

Jiao, Hongchang 焦洪昌, and Yuanto Ye 叶远涛. 2017. "Constitutional safeguards of the National Supervision Commission reform [论国家监察体制改革的修宪保障]." *Journal of Beijing Administrative College* 《北京行政学院学报》 3: 10–16

Jin, Chongji 金冲及, and Qun Chen 陈群. 2015. *Biography of Chen Yun* 《陈云传》. Beijing: Central Party Literature Press.

Jin, Yan 金焰. 2005. "The trial of the vice-president of Guangxi High Court Yang Duoming [广西高级法院副院长杨多铭受贿案审判纪实]." *Democracy and Rule by Law* 《民主与法制》. https://news.sina.com.cn/c/2005-08-16/14337512522.shtml. Accessed on January 4, 2024.

Jing, Jian 荆剑. 2009. "Four sins of the former president of a Beijing court – Guo Shenggui[京城法院院长郭生贵的四宗罪]." *Law and Life* 《法律与生活》. https://news.sina.cn/sa/2009-02-25/detail-ikftpnny4102527.d.html. Accessed on January 8, 2024.

Jing, Yuchuan 景玉川 2005. "The origin and development of the rehabilitation of Futian Incident [富田事变平反的前前后后]." *Hundred Year Tide* 《百年潮》. www.hxzq.net/aspshow/showarticle.asp?id=2353. Accessed on June 26, 2023.

Jiufeng Office, State Council. 2001. "Emergent notification to ban the issuance and use of vouchers [国务院纠正行业不正之风办公室、国家经贸委、中国人民银行关于严禁发放使用各种代币券（卡）的紧急通知]."

Jones, Carol A. G. 1994. "Capitalism, globalisation and rule of law: An alternative trajectory of legal change in China." *Social & Legal Studies* 3(1):195–221.

Jun, Mai. 2016. "What not to learn from Zhou Yongkang and Ling Jihua." *South China Morning Post*.

Kautz, Carolin. 2022. "The ties that bind: Party social identity and the relevance of ideology for the Chinese Communist Party." in *Philosophischen Fakultät*. Göttingen: Georg August-Universität Göttingen.

Keliher, Macabe, and Hsinchao Wu. 2016. "Corruption, anticorruption, and the transformation of political culture in contemporary China." *The Journal of Asian Studies* 75(1):5–18.

Kipnis, Andrew B. 1997. *Producing Guanxi*. Durham, NC: Duke University Press.

Kleiman, M., and B. Kilmer. 2009. "The dynamics of deterrence." *Proceedings of the National Academy of Sciences USA* 106(34):14230–5.

Kleiman, Mark A.R. 2005. "When Brute Force Fails: Strategic Thinking for Crime Control." Report for the US Department of Justice.

Kong, Miao 孔淼. 2015. "Why is it difficult to abdicate from the deliberation and coordination bodies [职责外的议事协调机构为何难退出]." *China Jijian Jiancha Magazine* 《中国纪检监察杂志》 (8):33–5.

Kwok, Man-wai Tony. 2008. "Investigation of corruption cases." Pp. 140–5 in *The 11th International Training Course on the Criminal Justice Response to*

*Corruption – Visiting Experts' Papers.* UN Asia and Far East Institute for the Prevention of Crime and the Treatment of Offenders (UNAFEI).

Lai, Xing 赖星, Dapeng Feng 冯大鹏, and Nan Zhou 周楠. 2020. "Loan but not transfer – Be alert to the normalizing trend of cadre-loaning practice [借调借调，借而不调！基层随意性借调常态化值得警惕]." Xinhua Net 半月谈. www.xinhuanet.com/politics/2020-12/31/c_1126930038.htm. Accessed on January 14, 2024.

Lambsdorff, J. G. 2002. "Making corrupt deals: Contracting in the shadow of the law." *Journal of Economic Behavior & Organization* 48(3):221.

Lambsdorff, Johann Graf et al. 2004a. "Corruption contracting." Pp. 1–15 in *The New Institutional Economics of Corruption: Norms, Trust, and Reciprocity*, edited by Johann Graf Lambsdorff, et al. London: Routledge.

Lambsdorff, Johann Graf, et al (Eds.). 2004b. *The New Institutional Economics of Corruption: Norms, Trust, and Reciprocity.* London: Routledge.

Lewis, Margaret K. 2012. "Presuming innocence, or rorruption, in China." *Columbia Journal of Transnational Law* 50(2): 287–369.

Li, Cheng. 2012a. "The end of the CCP's resilient authoritarianism? A tripartite assessment of shifting power in China." *The China Quarterly* 211:595–623.

Li, De'en 李德恩. 2017b. "Two-dimensional construction of judicial responsibility [主审法官责任制构建之二维展开]." *Journal of Southeast University* 《东南大学学报》 19(6):101–10.

Li, Dongfang 李东方, and Jian Chen 陈坚. 2018. "Early operation of the CCDI after its restoration [不负党中央重托 打开工作新局面 — 中央纪委重建之初各项工作的展开]." in *China Jijian Jiancha Daily* 《中国纪检监察报》.

Li, Dongwen 李东文. 2005. "Shenzhen Da Shijie in both the black and white worlds ["黑白"之间的东门大世界]." in *Southern Metropolis Newspaper* 《南方都市报》.

Li, Ji. 2017c. "The power logic of justice in China." *The American Journal of Comparative Law* 65(1):95–144.

Li, Ling. 2012b. "The 'production' of corruption in China's courts – The politics of judicial decision-making and its consequences in a one-party state." *Law & Social Inquiry* 37(4):848–77.

2023. "Order of power in China's courts." *Asian Journal of Law and Society* 10(3):490–515.

2015a. "'Rule of law' in a Party-state – A conceptual interpretive framework of the constitutional reality of China." *Asian Journal of Law and Society* 2(1):93–113.

2016a. "The Chinese Communist Party and People's Courts – Judicial dependence in China." *The American Journal of Comparative Law* 64(1):37–74.

2016b. "The rise of the Discipline and Inspection Commission, 1927–2012: Anticorruption investigation and decision-making in the Chinese Communist Party." *Modern China* 42(5):447–82.

2019. "Politics of anticorruption in China: Paradigm change of the Party's disciplinary regime 2012–2017." *Journal of Contemporary China* 28(115):47–63.

2020a. "Appeal of Strategic Ambiguity on Party Centre – Reading the Party Directive on the Operation of the Central Committee (Part I)." https://rb.gy/eo2mxu. Accessed on November 18, 2023.

2020b. "Mapping the power of the Party Centre – Reading the Party Directive on the Operation of the Central Committee." https://shorturl.at/gsEKO. Accessed on November 19, 2023.

2021. "The Muddled Case against Xi Jinping's Third Term." *LSE Blogs*.

2022a. "The hidden significance and resilience of the age-limit norm of the Chinese Communist Party." *The Asia-Pacific Journal: Japan Focus* 20(19).

2023. "Order of power in China's courts." *Asian Journal of Law and Society* 10(3):490–515.

Li, Ling, and Carolin Kautz. 2021. "Corruption." *Oxford Bibliographies – Chinese Studies*.

Li, Mingzi 李明子. 2022b. "Historical account of the establishment of the anticorruption bureau [反贪往事]." *China's Newsweek*《中国新闻周刊杂志》1032.

Li, Na 李娜, and Dingbo Yuan 袁定波. 2015. "Standardizing the practices regarding confiscation of illicit assets and preventing judicial corruption ["两办"规范刑事诉讼涉案财物处置八大举措杜绝暗箱操作司法腐败]." *Legal Daily* 《法制日报》. www.spp.gov.cn/llyj/201503/t20150304_92082.shtml. Accessed on January 14, 2024.

Li, Runwen 李润文. 2008a. "Most officials implicated in the collusive corruption taken place in Fuyang Intermediate Court remain unpunished [安徽阜阳中院腐败窝案大多数涉案官员仍居原位]." *China Youth Daily*《中国青年报》. www.chinanews.com.cn/gn/news/2008/03-31/1206911.shtml. Accessed on January 4, 2024.

Li, Shaowen 李少文. 2018. "NSC Reform Project of Constitutional Amendment – A controlled approach of constitutional changes [国家监察体制改革的修宪工程 — 宪制变革的一种控制方式 ]." *Open Times*《开放时代》. https://rb.gy/z81gt3. Accessed on January 14, 2024.

Li, Shuai 李帅. 2017a. "A study of open access to the secretive case dossier fron the perspective of judicial reform [司法改革视角下法院副卷公开研究]." *Yunnan Social Sciences Journal*《云南社会科学》(5):122–29.

Li, Wei 李伟. 2008b. "An investigation of Jiang Renjie's Hundred-million Bribe [姜人杰亿元贿案调查]." *Sanlian Life Weekly*. www.chinanews.com/gn/news/2008/11-21/1458785.shtml. Accessed on December 27, 2023.

Li, Wenying 李闻莺. 2017d. "An interview with Wu Jianxiong by The Paper News [对话吴建雄]." *The Paper*.

Li, Xiang, and Chenbo Wang. 2004. "Auditing Reform [审计变法]." *China Newsweek*《中国新闻周刊》(25):43–45.

Li, Yuwen. 2002. "Court reform in China: Problems, progress and prospects." Pp. 55–84 in *Implementation of Law in the People's Republic of China*, edited by Chen Jianfu, Yuwen Li, and Jan Michiel Otto. The Hague: Kluwer Law International.

Li, Zhiyong 李志勇. 2015b. "History of the Dispatched Offices of CDIs [纪检监察派驻机构历史沿革]," in *China Jijian Jiancha Daily*《中国纪检监察报》.

Liang, Xiaoxu 梁晓旭. 2018. "How to understand the qingshi baogao protocol in case investigation [如何理解调查过程中的重要事项应集体研究并按程序请示报告]." *China Jijian Jiancha Magazine*《中国纪检监察》. www.zzjjjc.gov.cn/sitesources/zzsjwjw/page_pc/zzsjwjww/yys/ywkt/articlec5f5f9f303a04f209e5f8196da2b769c.html. Accessed on January 14, 2024.

Lianhe, Zaobao. 2016. "How did Wang Zhaoguo miss the opportunity to become the core of the 4th generation of leadership? [王兆国因何错失成为第四代领导核心?]" *Lianhe Zaobao Online Chinese version*《联合早报中文网》. www.kzaobao.com/mon/keji/20170622/38505_3.html. Accessed on January 17, 2024.

Lieberthal, Kenneth, and David M. Lampton (Eds.). 1992. *Bureaucracy, Politics and Decision Making in Post-Mao China*. Berkeley, CA: University of California Press.

Lieberthal, Kenneth, and Michel Oksenberg. 1988. *Policy Making in China: Leaders, Structures, and Processes*. Princeton, NJ: Princeton University Press.

Liebman, Benjamin L. 2007. "China's courts: Restricted reform." *The China Quarterly* 191:620–38.

Lin, Justin Yifu, and Zhiqiang Liu. 2000. "Fiscal decentralization and economic growth in China." *Economic Development and Cultural Change* 49: 21.

Lin, Qian. 2009. "Exploring the litigation master's mode of activities and its characteristics through the case of Yeyong's litigation brokerage." *Peking University Law Review* 10(1):6–24.

Lin, Ying 林莹. 2004. "Vice-president of Hainan High Court sentenced to 11 years in prison [受贿40万元 、85.3万元巨额财产来源不明，省高级人民法院原副院长, 娄小平一审被判11年]." *Southern Metropolitan Paper*《南国都市报》. On file with the author.

Lin, Yunhui 林蕴晖. 2003. "Dissent at the top of the Party on the Gao Rao Affair and the issue on the enhancement of the new democratic order [高岗事件与中共高层在巩固新民主主义秩序上的分歧]." *21th Century*《二十一世纪》(78) August:62–8.

2003. "Unpuzzling Mao Zedong's absence at the 4th plenum of the 7th Party Congress [毛泽东缺席中共七届四中全会释疑]." *21st Century*《二十一世纪》. www.yantan.us/blog/?action-viewthread-tid-75097. Accessed on January 14, 2024.

Lin, Yunhui 林蕴辉. 2017. *A Re-examination of the Gao/Rao Anti-Party Incident*《重考高岗，饶恕石"反党"事件》. Hong Kong: Chinese University of Hong Kong Press.

Liu, Bingxiang 刘炳香. 2021a. "A study on Party-groups and its practices of democratic centralism [关于党组及其民主集中制执行力问题研究]." *Journal of Party School of Tianjin Party Committee.* www.xuexi.cn/lgpage/detail/index.html?id=2872439256918763308&item_id=2872439256918763308. Accessed on March 8, 2024.

Liu, Man 刘嫚. 2021b. "Twenty enforcement judges fell for corruption in one year [一年内20余名执行法官接连落马]." *Sohu News.* www.sohu.com/a/484195256_161795. Accessed on January 4, 2024.

Liu, Min 刘敏. 2014a. "Neither online auction nor traditional court auction can prevent corruption [网络司法拍卖和传统的司法拍卖都难以防止腐败]." www.dyzxw.org/html/article/201406/24/175831.shtml. Accessed on January 4, 2024.

Liu, Mingxing, Victor Shih, and Dong Zhang. 2018. "The fall of the Old Guards: Explaining decentralization in China." *Studies in Comparative International Development* 53(4):379–403.

Liu, Renzhou. 2004. "Zooming in the falling trajectory of Mai Chongkai [聚焦麦崇凯沉沦的轨迹]." *Procuratorial Review* 《检察风云》. www.cnki.com.cn/Article/CJFDTotal-SPMF200403000.htm. Accessed on March 25, 2025.

Liu, Ruirong 刘瑞榕, and Fangquan Liu 刘方权. 2002. "The initiation of criminal litigation procedure: A critique of the current case-registration practices in China [刑事诉讼程序启动研究 — 对我国现行立案制度的质疑]." *Chinese Criminal Law Journal* 《中国刑事法杂志》 (1):80–97.

Liu, Shuyin 刘姝殷, and Ruiming Xiao 肖瑞宁. 2022. "The developmental logic and political meaning of the practice of conjoining offices from the perspective of the national deepening reform – with a focus on the CDI institutional reform [全国深化改革视域下合署办公的演进逻辑与政治意蕴 — 以纪检监察机构改革为中心]." *Public Governance Studies* 《公共治理研究》 34(6):73–82.

Liu, Sida, and Terrence Halliday. 2016. *Criminal Defense in China: The Politics of Lawyers at Work.* Cambridge: Cambridge University Press.

Liu, Songfu 刘松福. 2008. "The shift from collective leadership to dictatorship: The changes of decision-making at the top of the Party before and after the Yan'an Rectification Campaign [集体领导如何演变为个人独断—中共延安整风前后党内高层决策体制之变迁]." *Modern China Studies* (2).

Liu, Tao 刘涛. 2012a. "A Study of the Political and Judiciary Commission in Contemporary China: The Polical and Judiciary Commission of X County as Reference [当代中国政法委员会研究 — 以X县政法委员会为参照]." Jilin University Law School.

Liu, Xuanxi刘绚兮. 2022. "Bureaucratic stratification – Binary structure of personal management in China's courts [科层中的分流 — 中国法院人事管理制度的二元结构." *Peking University Law Journal* 《中外法学》 34(4):885–902.

Liu, Zhe 刘喆. 2018. *Diary of a Procurator*《检察官日记》. Beijing: Peking University Press.

Liu, Zhiming 刘志明. 2005. "Corrupt alliance of Chief Justice Wu Zhenhan [大法官吴振汉的腐败同盟]." *Southern People Magazine (Weekly)*《南方人物周刊》. Accessed on March 25, 2025.

Liu, Zhiqiang 刘志强. 2021c. "Second Press Conference of the Political-Legal Rectification Campaign [政法队伍教育整顿第二次新闻发布会]." www.legaldaily.com.cn/direct_seeding/node_106320.html. Accessed on January 5, 2023.

Liu, Zhong 刘忠. 2012b. "The Production of Court Presidents under the Strip-Block Relations [条条与块块关系下的法院院长产生]." *Global Law Review*《环球法律评论》(1).

2012c. "Scale and Internal Governance: Historical Vicissitude of Court Bianzhi System （1978–2008 ） [规模与内部治理：中国法院编制变迁三十年（1978–2008） ]." *Rule by Law and Society*《法制与社会》(5):47–64.

2013. "The Shaping of the Thought of Party Governing Politics and Law in Organization History (1949–1958) ["党管政法"思想的组织史生成(1949–1958).]" *The Jurists*《法学家》(2):16–32.

2014b. "Reading and Interpreting *shuanggui*: Informal anticorruption procedure from the criminal technical investigation perspective [读解双规 —— 侦查技术视域内的反贪非正式程序]." *Peking University Law Journal*《中外法学》(1):209–33.

Lo, Ming-cheng M, Eileen M. Otis. 2003. "Guanxi civility: Processes, potentials, and contingencies." *Politics & Society* 31(1):131–62.

Lű, Jiao 吕浇. 1992. "Historical development of the conduction of criminal investigation by the procuratorates [我国检察机关自侦工作的历史沿革]." *Procuratorial Theory Research*《检察理论研究》(1):83–7.

Lu, Jinzeng 陆金增. 2007. "Shopping-Card Induces Civil Servant Crimes [购物卡易诱发职务犯罪]." Justice Network [正义网]. www.jcrb.com/200707/ca616445.htm. On file with the author.

Lu, Jun. 2018. "Human rights lawyers' role in rights NGOs in China: History and future." *Fordham International Law Journal* 41: 1197–1214

Lu, Yunda 陆云达, and Yan Zhang 张琰. 2015. "We must put adherence to the Party's political disciplines and political code of conduct in the first place [要把严守党的政治纪律和政治规矩排在首位]." CCDI Press Release.

Lui, Francis T. 1986. "A dynamic model of corruption deterrence." *Journal of Public Economics* 31:215–36

Luo, Jieqi 罗洁琪, and Xin He 贺信. 2012. "The other side of the Li Zhuang Case [李庄案另一面]." *Caixin Weekly.* https://magazine.caixin.com/2012-11-30/100467171.html. Accessed on January 4, 2024.

Luo, Meng 罗猛. 2012. "Technical investigative measures need to be regulated [技术侦查措施要规范适用]." *Procuracy Daily*《检察日报》. www.spp.gov.cn/llyj/201211/t20121102_29181.shtml. Accessed on January 23, 2024.

Luo, Shuping 罗书平. 2002. "The practice of adjudication by seeking approval from the adjudicative committee should be abandoned [审判委员会审批案件制度应予取消]." *Judicial Reform Review*《司法改革论评》3:51–74.

Luo, Yadong. 1997. ""Guanxi": Principles, philosophies, and implications." *Human Systems Management* 16:43–51.

Ma, Haibin 马海斌. 2004. "Characteristics, causes, trends and counter-measures regarding white-collar crimes in contemproary China [当前职务犯罪的特点,原因和发展趋势及其方法对策]." Pp. 346–50, in *Investigative Report on Professional Crimes and its Prevention of China*《中国职务犯罪预防调查报告》, edited by Chinese Society of Criminology Beijing: Criminology Research Society of China.

Ma, Stephen K. 2008. "The dual nature of anti-corruption agencies in China." *Crime, Law & Social Change* 49:153–65.

Ma, Xiaoying, and Leonard Ortolano. 2000. *Environmental Regulation in China: Institutions, Enforcement, and Compliance.* Lanham, MD: Rowman & Littlefield.

MacFarquhar, Roderick. 2012. *Mao's Last Revolution.* Cambridge, MA: Belknap Press.

Magaloni, Beatriz. 2008. "Credible power-sharing and the longevity of authoritarian rule." *Comparative Political Studies* 41:741.

Magazine, China Procuracy. 2011. "An analysis of the corruption case of Yang Xiancai, head of enforcement bureau of Guangdong High Court [广东省高级人民法院执行局原局长、高级法官杨贤才案件剖析]."《中国监察》*China Procuracy Magazine.*

Malenkov, G. M. 1949. "On the Occasion of the 70th Birthday of Joseph Vissarionovich Stalin." *Pravda Articles,* made available by Marxists Internet Archive (December 21, 1949).

Manion, Melanie. 2004a. "Anticorruption campaigns as enforcement mechanisms." Pp. 155–99, in *Corruption by Design.* Cambridge, MA: Harvard University Press.

2004b. *Corruption by Design: Building Clean Government in Mainland China and Hong Kong.* Cambridge, MA: Harvard University Press.

2016. "Taking China's anticorruption campaign seriously." *Economic and Political Studies* 4(1):3–18.

1996. "Corruption by design: Bribery in Chinese enterprise licensing." *The Journal of Law, Economics & Organization* 12(1):167–95.

Mao, Zedong. 1957. "Speech at the Qingdao Conference (Transcript) [在青岛会议上的讲话]." P. 456, in *Selected Works of Mao Zedong*《毛泽东文集》. Beijing: Renmin Publishing House.

1958. "Speech at the Enlarged Politburo Meeting at Beidaihe Part IV [在北戴河政治局扩大会议上的讲话（四）]." *Marxist Philosophy Database.* www.marxists.org/chinese/maozedong/1968/4-052.htm. Accessed on December 23, 2023.

1962. “Speech at the Enlarged Central Work Conference on Jan. 30 [在扩大的中央工作会议上的讲话].”

1999. “Speech delivered at the National Party Propaganda Conference [在中国共产党全国宣传工作会议上的讲话].” Pp. 273–74, in *Collected Works of Mao Zedong* 《毛泽东文集》. Beijing: Renmin Publishing House.

Mauss, Marcel. 1967. *The Gift*. New York: Norton.

Meng, Hualiang 孟焕良. 2015. “Court auction returning back to the autonomous model [司法拍卖回归自主模式].” *Legal Daily* 《法制日报》. http://rmfyb.chinacourt.org/paper/html/2015-02/12/content_93925.htm?div=-1. Accessed on July 4, 2023.

Mertha, Andrew. 2019. “Rectification.” Pp. 207–13, in *Afterlives of Chinese Communism: Political Concepts from Mao to Xi*, edited by Christian Sorace, Ivan Franceschini, and Nicholas Loubere. Canberra: The ANU Press.

Milgrom, Paul R., North, Douglass C., Weingast, Barry R. 1990. “The role of institutions in the revival of trade: The law merchant, private judges and the champagne fairs.” *Economics & Politics* 2(1):1–23.

Mitchell, Tom. 2018. “Xi Jinping ally Wang Qishan confirmed as China vice-president.” *Financial Times*. www.ft.com/content/aa260008-28d3-11e8-b27e-cc62a39d57a0. Accessed on November 2, 2023.

Mittelstaedt, Jean Christopher. 2021. “Rebuilding authority: The Party’s relationship with its grassroots organizations.” *The China Quarterly* 248(S1):244–64.

Mo, Yanzhen 莫燕珍, and Rui Li 李锐. 2006. “A survey report of bribe-taking conducted by Haizhu District Procuratorate [海珠区检察院对受贿人员的问卷调查报告].” On file with the author.

Nakazawa, Katsuji. 2018. “Only Wang Qishan knew what Xi Jinping was going to do.” *Nikkei Asia*. https://asia.nikkei.com/Editor-s-Picks/China-up-close/Only-Wang-Qishan-knew-what-Xi-Jinping-was-going-to-do. Accessed on November 2, 2023.

Nathan, Andrew J. 1973. “A factionalism model for CCP politics.” *The China Quarterly* 53:34–66.

Network, People’s. 2009a. “Former Chifeng City mayor Xu Guoyuan: I can’t remember who had given me money but only those who had not [赤峰原市长徐国元:记不住送钱人专记不送者].” *People’s Network* 人民网. https://china.huanqiu.com/article/9CaKrnJmeRc. Accessed on January 8, 2024.

Network, Phoenix. 2009b. “Liu Shaoqi in the eyes of legal practitioners [法律人眼中的刘少奇].” Modern History of China –Phoenix Network. https://news.ifeng.com/history/zhongguojindaishi/200911/1112_7180_1433081_2.shtml. Accessed on December 23, 2023.

News, Sohu. 2018. “Justice Delayed: Top 10 Recent Wrongful Conviction Case [迟到的公正：盘点近年来十大冤假错案].” www.sohu.com/a/232381683_581209. Accessed on January 4, 2024.

Newspaper, Xinjing. 2005. "Insiders reveal the dirty details behind the antique auctions [知情人揭露文物拍卖黑幕]." *Xinjing Newspaper* 《新京报》. www.cnhubei.com/200502/ca691716.htm. Accessed on January 4, 2024.

2008. "CCDI deputy secretary He Yong: The CCDI has no intention to institute vertical administration [中纪委副书记何勇：中纪委无意"垂直管理"]." *Xinjing Newspaper* 《新京报》. www.chinanews.com.cn/gn/news/2008/03-08/1185872.shtml. Accessed on December 17, 2023.

2017. "Qu Long, Guo Wengui's former business partner aquitted after being wronged for 15 years [蒙冤被判15年郭文贵昔日伙伴曲龙再审改判无罪]." Pp. A12–A13 in *Xinjing Newspaper* 《新京报》.

Newsweek, China's. 2014. "A guide to meritorous performance in prison [狱中立功指南]." *China's Newsweek* 《中国新闻周刊杂志》. https://news.sohu.com/20140123/n394044017.shtml. Accessed on January 5, 2024.

Ng, Kwai Hang, and Xin He. 2017. *Embedded Courts: Judicial Decision-making in China*. Cambridge: Cambridge University Press.

Nie, Huihua. 2015a. "CDIs shall exert complete vertical supervision [建议纪委"全面垂直"监督]." *Southern Metropolitan*《南方都市报》. Accessed on November 1, 2023.

Nie, Huihua 聂辉华. 2015b. "CDI shall be subject to full vertical administration [建议纪委"全面垂直"监督]." *Southern Metropolitan Newspaper* 《南方都市报》. http://nads.ruc.edu.cn/xzgd/9d2e3469fd2149d9b9f4d47c258be4a8.htm. Accessed on December 17, 2023.

Ning, Jingbo 宁静波. 2020. "An empirical study on incentive factors and effects for judges from the Basic People's Courts [基层法院法官激励因素与激励效果的实证研究]." *Journal of Shandong University* 《山东大学学报》 (5):53–63.

Ning, Yu, Wang Juanjuan, and Denise Jia. 2021. "Cover story: HNA Group's final crisis." *Caixin Global*. Accessed on November 3, 2023.

Nitschka, Thomas. 2018. "*Did China's anti-corruption campaign affect the risk premium on stocks of global luxury goods firms?*" Swiss National Bank. Online publication. Link: https://shorturl.at/ju5Ng

Niu, Xiaobo 牛晓波. 2005. "Subtle Entanglement between Judges and Lawyers [法官与律师的微妙纠缠]." *21st Century Economic Report 21*《世纪经济报道》. http://blog.sina.com.cn/s/blog_5b7b36210100apa3.html. Accessed on June 27, 2018.

Noonan, John T. 1984. *Bribes: The Intellectual History of a Moral Idea*. Oakland, CA: University of California Press.

North, D. C. 1990. *Institutions, Institutional Change and Economic Performance*. Cambridge: Cambridge University Press.

NPC, National People's Congress. 2005. "Interpretation of the Civil Servant Law Chapter 3 Functions and Ranks [公务员法释义 第三章 职务与级别]."

www.npc.gov.cn/c12434/c1793/c1852/c2189/201905/t20190522_7594.html. Accessed on March 7, 2024.

NPDC, 中国共产党全国代表会议. 1955. "Central Party's Decision on the Anti-Party Alliance of Gao Gang and Rao Shushi [中共中央关于高岗饶漱石反党联盟的决议]."

OECD, Secretariat of the Anti-Corruption Network for Eastern Europe and Central Asia. 2010. "Proceedings of Expert Seminar 'Effective Means of Investigation and Prosecution of Corruption'."

Office, Center Party History 中共党史研究室. 1966. "Mao's Conversations with Kang Sheng and Jiangqing at Shanghai during 28–30 March 1966." *Party Chronicles 1966* 《中国共产党大事记1966年》. http://cpc.people.com.cn/GB/64162/64164/4416081.html. Accessed on January 14, 2023.

Oksenberg, Michel. 1969. *Sources and Methodological Problems in the Study of Contemporary China*. Seattle, WA: University of Washington Press.

1974. "Methods of communication within the Chinese bureaucracy." *The China Quarterly* 57:1–39.

Osnos, Evan. 2013. "China targets corruption, luxury brands mourn." *New Yorker*. www.newyorker.com/news/evan-osnos/china-targets-corruption-luxury-brands-mourn. Accessed on October 29, 2023.

Paper, The. 2020. "Female judge with a family asset worth 20 million sentenced to 18 years in prison [被举报"身家200亿"的女法官获刑18年]." *The Paper*. https://m.thepaper.cn/baijiahao_10271316. Accessed on January 8, 2024.

Paper, The. 2022. "Court decision to be announed on Wednesday on the subcontractor who is charged for blackmailing Zhang Jiahui [包工头"偷拍张家慧打麻将"敲诈案周三一审宣判]." *The Paper*. https://news.cctv.com/2022/12/27/ARTIK38ePDNsidrqdLqivo5H221227.shtml. Accessed on January 6, 2024.

Party, Centre. 2019. "The CCP Center's Resolution on the Major Achievements and Historical Experience of the Party's Century of Struggle [中共中央关于党的百年奋斗重大成就和历史经验的决议]."

Party Committee, Sichuan Province. 1960a. "Opinions regarding the supervisory work of the year of 1960 [四川省监察委员员关于1960年工作的意见]."

1960b. "Report on the spirit of the provincial supervision conference regarding the Central Secretariat's instructions on supervision work [全省监察工作会议关于中央书记处精神汇报]."

Pei, Minxin. 1996. "Microfoundations of state-socialism and patterns of economic transformation." *Communist and Post-communist Studies* 29(2):131–45.

2016. *China's Crony Capitalism: The Dynamics of Regime Decay*. Cambridge, MA: Harvard University Press.

Pei, Xiaofeng 裴晓峰. 2018. "Shangcheng District Supervision Reform [上城区监察体制改革]," in *Shangcheng District Yearbook*.

Peng, Jinxiu 彭劲秀. 2010. "The establishment, disbandment and restoration of the Central Party Monitoring and Inspection Committee [中共中央监察委员会的创设、取消与重建始末]." *Party History Overview* 《党史纵览》 (5):32–5.

Peng, Shuhua 彭树华, and Jing Li 李菁. 2011. "A personal account of the trial of Pan Hannian [潘汉年审判亲历]." *Sanlian Life Weekly* 《三联生活周刊》. http://old.lifeweek.com.cn//2011/0511/32313.shtml. Accessed on January 7, 2023.

PeopleNet. 2011. "The funny act of touching the bottom of a tiger at the 7000 people conference [七千人大会上，毛泽东表演"摸老虎屁股"惹笑全场]." Renmin Network: Culture and History Channel 人民网: 文化和历史频道. http://history.people.com.cn/GB/205396/16324467.html. Accessed on November 21, 2019.

PeopleNet, 人民网. 2015. "Unveiling the first embezzlement case in the PRC [揭秘新中国第一贪污案始末]." *National Humanities and History* 《国家人文历史》. http://news.sohu.com/20141029/n405584137.shtml. Accessed on March 9, 2024.

Pils, Eva. 2015. *China's Human Rights Lawyers and Contemporary Chinese Law: Advocacy and Resistance.* London: Routledge.

Podkul, Cezary. 2019. "HNA plans to drop defamation suit against exiled businessman Guo Wengui." *Wall Street Journal.* https://rb.gy/llqmj4. Accessed on November 4, 2023.

Politburo. 1942. "Resolution regarding the Unification of the Party's Leadership in Anti-Japanese Revolutionary Bases and the Adjustment of the Organizational Relations [关于统一抗日根据地党的领导及调整各组织间关系的决定]."

1950. "Work Rules of the Central Committee of Discipline and Inspection [中央纪律检查委员会工作细则]."

2012. "Decision of Eight Rules regarding Strengthening Relations with the Masses and Improving the Work Styles [关于改进工作作风、密切联系群众的八项规定]."

Potter, P. B. 2000. "Guanxi and the P.R.C. legal system: From contradiction to complementarity." Pp. 179–95 in *Social Connections in China: Institutions, Culture, and the Changing Nature of Guanxi*, edited by Thomas Gold, et al. Cambridge: Cambridge University Press.

Pozsgai-Alvarez, Joseph. 2021. "China's gilded age: The paradox of economic boom and vast corruption, Yuen Yuen Ang. New York, NY: Cambridge University Press. 2020. 266 pp. $39.99 (cloth)." *Governance* 34(1):251–52.

Press, People's Court. 2004. "Cases of Lü Zonghui, Zhao Zhengbing et al. [吕宗慧，赵征兵案]." *Selection of Cases of People's Courts* 《人民法院案例选》. On file with the author.

Procuratorate, Haining People's. 2010. "The Necessity to Equip Procuratorates' with Technical Investigatory Power [检察机关配置技术侦查权的必要性]." Haining People's Procuratorate.

Province A, CDI. 1953. "Speech of Comrade X at the 1st conference of discipline and inspection work of the Party Committee of Province A [某某同志在中共某省委第一次纪律检查工作会议上的发言]."

Province A, Party Supervision Commission of 1955. "Reply to the inquiry regarding the establishment of X prefecture Party supervision commission [中共X地委纪委关于询问成立监委组织机构问题的答复]."

1956. "Brief on the 1st National Conference of Supervision Work of the Party [党的第一次全国监察工作会议的传达报告]."

Pye, Lucian W. 1995. "Factions and the politics of guanxi: Paradoxes in Chinese administrative and political behaviour." *The China Journal* 34:35–53.

Qiang, Zhang 张强, and Xu Haotian 许浩天. 2022. "Cadre loaning: A relational contract interpretive framework [干部借调：一个关系合约的解释性框架]." *China's Administrative Management*《中国行政管理》(8):52–58.

Qianjiang, Evening Paper. 2010. "Huang Songyou is implicated in the auction of the unfinished real estate development project [中国第一烂尾楼拍卖案牵出黄松有贪腐问题]." *Qianjiang Evening Paper*《钱江晚报》. http://news.sina.com.cn/c/2010-01-15/111719475406.shtml. Accessed on January 4, 2024.

Qin, Qianhong 秦前红. 2017a. "Conundrum, reform and the way out: From a tri-horse carriage to national supervision – reflections on the constitutional framework of the National Supervision Legal System [困境、改革与出路：从"三驾马车"到国家监察 – 我国监察体系的宪制思考]." *Chinese Law Review*《中国法律评论》(1):176–82.

2017b. "An investigation of the legal authorization of the pilot program of the National Supervision Commission reform ["重大改革于法有据"· 国家监察委员会授权考]." *China Law Review*《中国法律评论》. https://rb.gy/dvy4mq. Accessed on January 14, 2024.

2017c. "Logic and method of supervision reform [监察体制改革的逻辑与方法]." *Global Law Review*《环球法律评论》(2).

Qiu, Xueqiang 邱学强. 2018. "Historical lessons and inspiration from the internal institutional reform of the procuracy since its restoration [恢复重建以来检察机关内设机构改革的历史经验与启示]." *Procuracy Daily*《检察日报》. www.spp.gov.cn/zdgz/201811/t20181113_398859.shtml. Accessed on February 25, 2024.

Qu, Peng 瞿芃. 2018. "Separating the front and back stages and installing a checking mechanism ["前台后台"分设相互监督制衡 ——纪检监察机关强化自我监督系列报道（五）]." *China Jijian Jiancha Daily*《中国纪检监察报》. www.moj.gov.cn/pub/sfbgw/jgsz/gjjwzsfbjjz/zyzsfbjjzzlk/202102/t20210223_186328.html. Accessed on January 14, 2024.

Quality Watch, China. 2006. "Court released seized assets and kept it secret from the winning litigant: Supervised by Guangxi Political and Legal Committee [法院隐瞒胜诉方解除查封房产续：广西政法委督办]." *China Quality Watch* 《中国质量万里行》. http://news.sina.com.cn/s/l/2006-11-07/120611448807.shtml. Accessed on January 4, 2024.

Quinn, Stephen. 1996. "Gold, silver, and the Glorious Revolution: Arbitrage between Bills of Exchange and bullion." *The Economic History Review* 49(3):473–90.

Ranasinghe, Dhara. 2014. "Tough times for luxury retail in China." *CNBC*. www.cnbc.com/2014/06/19/tough-times-for-luxury-retail-in-china.html. Accessed on October 29, 2023.

Read, F. 1926. "The origin, early history, and later development of Bills of Exchange and certain other negotiable instruments." *Canadian Bar Review* 4:440.

Rees, E. A. 1987. *State Control in Soviet Russia: The Rise and Fall of the Workers' and Peasants' Inspectorate, 1920–1934*. London: Palgrave Macmillan.

Ren, Hengjun 任恒俊. 2003. *Rules in the Officialdom of Late Qing Dynasty*《晚清官场规则研究》. Haikou, Hainan.

Ren, Jianming, and Zhizhou Du. 2008. "Institutionalized corruption: Power overconcentration of the First-in-Command in China." *Crime, Law and Social Change* 49:45–59.

Ren, Zhiqiang. 2013. "Wang Qishan was like our big brother - An exerpt from Ren Zhiqiang's memoir [初中辅导员是王岐山 就像我们大哥哥]." *China Newsweek* 《中国新闻周刊》. https://web.archive.org/web/20160308123103/http://history.sohu.com/20131029/n389134064.shtml. Accessed on November 3, 2023.

Reuters. 2017. "Chinese conglomerate HNA sues exiled tycoon Guo." *Reuters*. www.reuters.com/article/us-china-corruption-tycoon-idUSKBN1970GP. Accessed on November 2, 2023.

Ruan, Ming 阮铭. 1992. *Deng Xiaoping Empire* 《邓小平帝国》. Taiwan: Reading Times Press.

Samuli, Seppanen. 2022. "Turning the party state inside out: CCP intra-party regulations as a theoretical challenge." *Chinese Journal of Comparative Law* 10:139.

Sapio, Flora. 2008. "Shuanggui and extralegal detention in China." *China Information* 22(1):7–37.

Schoenhals, Michael. 1996. "The Central Case Examination Group, 1966-79." *The China Quarterly* 145:87–111.

Schramm, Matthias, and Markus Taube. 2002. "The institutional economics of legal institutions, guanxi, and corruption in the PR China", in *Corruption: Its Realities in Asia*, edited by J. Kidd. Basingstoke: Palgrave.

Scott, James C. 1972. *Comparative Political Corruption*. Englewood, NJ: Prentice-Hall.

Secretariat, Central 中央书记处. 2013. "Studying line issues is the [task] of the more in-depth and advanced phase of the rectification campaign [研究党的路线问题是整风的深人与高级阶段]." Pp. 255–56 in *Full Collection of Mao Zedong's Works*《毛泽东全集》. Beijing: Run Dong Publishing House.

Selznick, Philip. 1952. *The Organizational Weapon: A Study of Bolshevik Strategy and Tactics*. New York: McGraw-Hill Book Company.

Shen, Mengzhe 申孟哲. 2015. "What are political protocols of the Party [中共的政治规矩是什么]." in *People's Daily (Overseas Edition)*.

Shenzhen, Evening Paper. 2008. "Did Beijing vice-mayor fall because of a sex tape? [性爱录像扳倒北京副市长？]" *Shenzhen Evening Paper*《深圳晚报》. https://news.sina.com.cn/c/2008-10-15/145314578677s.shtml. Accessed on November 2, 2023.

Shi, Binhai, and Yijun Shi. 2017. "The drafting process of Decision on Economic System Reform [《关于经济体制改革的决定》起草过程]." *Yan Huang Chun Qiu*《炎黄春秋》(7):8–14.

Shi, Suo 师索. 2022. "Qingshi protocol in anticorruption criminal investigation [腐败犯罪调查中的案件请示制度]." *Science of Law*《法律科学》(3): 71–84.

Shi, Yanhong 石艳红. 2021. "From inspection and examination in one to separation of front and back stages [从监审合一到前后台分设]." *China Jijian Jiancha Magazine*《中国纪检监察》(2):52–55.

Shih, Victor C. 2022. *Coalitions of the Weak*. Cambridge: Cambridge University Press.

Shin, Solee, and Lake Lui. 2022. "Guanxi and moral articulation: Strategies of corruption during China's anti-corruption drive." *The Journal of Development Studies* 58(6):1124–39.

Shu, Wei 舒炜, and Lan Liu 刘兰. 2022. "Conundrums regarding cadre loaning [借调难题]." *Clean Governance Watch*《廉政瞭望》(8):16–17.

Shu, Wei 舒炜, Xiao Liu 刘霄, and Xiaoxi Yao 姚晓熙. 2014. "Unveil the secret game in the game of the Court Enforcement Bureau [揭秘法院执行"局中局"]." *Clean Governance Watch*《廉政瞭望》. https://baijiahao.baidu.com/s?id=1672368442368848033&wfr=spider&for=pc. Accessed on January 8, 2024.

Shum, Desmond. 2021. *Red Roulette: An Insider's Story of Wealth, Power, Corruption, and Vengeance in Today's China*. New York: Scribner.

Shum, Desmond 沈栋. 2023a. "Be seated [请君入座]." Interview by Xiaojun Liao 廖筱君. Taiwan Plus www.youtube.com/watch?v=JWGS6rL0NTk. Accessed on January 10, 2024.

2023b. "How does Chinese elites get rich [中国权贵如何致富]." Interview by Hao Wang 汪浩. CTS Romance of Three Kingdoms 华视三国演义 www.youtube.com/watch?v=N0rdPtslWXc&t=1s. Accessed on January 10, 2024.

2023c. "Premier Wen Jiabao's White Gloves [温家宝的白手套]." Interview by Kylie & Ken. The KK Show www.youtube.com/watch?v=TBzOZAjT3GE. Accessed on January 10, 2024.

2023d. "Special Interview of Desmond Shum [专访《红色赌盘》作者沈栋]." Interview by Zhongren Dai 戴忠仁. RFA Chat Show [亚洲很想聊]. www.youtube.com/watch?v=DuwfGg59BE0&t=1699s. Accessed on January 10, 2024.

Sina, Finance. 2022. "Dong Hong took bribes during his stint at the GITIC liquidation team [中央巡视组原副组长董宏被判死缓与担任广国投破产清算组成员时受贿有关]." Sina Finance Column. https://finance.sina.com.cn/trust/roll/2022-01-29/doc-ikyamrmz8022690.shtml. Accessed on January 4, 2024.

Slater, Dan, Fenner, Sofia. 2011. "State power and staying power: Infrastructural mechanisms and authoritarian durability." *Journal of International Affairs* 65(1):15–29.

Smart, Alan. 1993. "Gift, bribes and guanxi: A reconsideration of Bourdieu's social capital." *Cultural Anthropology* 8(3):388–408.

Snape, Holly. 2019a. "Party leadership and legislating: Party documents through a Party–State relationship lens." *Chinese Law & Government* 51(5–6): 299–314.

2019b. "Party regulations: Changing the rules of the game?" *Chinese Law & Government* 51(5–6):255–59.

Sohu, Finance. 2010. "Former CDB Vice-President Wang Yi faces trial [原国开行副行长王益受贿千万受审]." Special Column of Sohu Finance. http://finance.sina.com.cn/focus/gkh_wangyi/. Accessed on January 3, 2024.

Sohu, News. 2021. "SPC enforcement division head Meng Xiang fell for corruption who had vowed to punish corruption in his division [最高法执行局局长孟祥落马，曾回应执行人员贪污称要刀刃向内]." *Sohu News.* www.sohu.com/a/477896618_161795. Accessed on January 4, 2024.

Song, Shige 宋时歌. 2005. "The lapsing effect of power-transfer: An interpretation of the elite reproduction and recycle in the process of market transition of socialist countries [权力转换的延迟效应： 对社会主义国家向市场转变过程的精英再生与循环的一种解释]." *Sociological Studies* 《社会学研究》 4:45–61.

SPC. 1999. "[人民法院五年改革纲要 1999–2003]."

2000. "Regulation on issues concerning centralization of certain enforcement work by high courts [关于高级人民法院统一管理执行工作若干问题的规定]."

2005. "Several Opinions of The Supreme People's Court on Strengthening the Adjudicative ability and Raising the standard of adjudication [关于增强司法能力提高司法水平的若干意见]."

2010. "Codes of Judicial Ethics."

2011. "Judgment on the appeal of KQL against XMEI [凯奇莱诉西安地矿勘查院合作勘查合同纠纷案]."《民一终字》:81.

2015a. "Opinions on improving judicial accountabilities in people's courts [关于完善人民法院司法责任制的若干意见]."《法发》:13.

2015b. "Several Opinions on Perfecting Measures to Improve Judicial Accountability [最高人民法院关于完善人民法院司法责任制的若干意见]."

2015c. "[领导干部干预司法活动、插手具体案件处理的记录、通报和责任追究规定]."

2017. "Provisional Implementing Measures on Judicial Accountabilities [最高人民法院司法责任制实施意见（试行）]."

2019. "Notice on the adjustments of the acceptance thresholds of first instance civial and commercial cases by high courts and intermediate courts [关于调整高级人民法院和中级人民法院管辖第一审民事案件标准的通知]."

2021a. "Guiding Opinions on Perfecting the Supervisory Mechanism concerning Four Categories of Cases [关于进一步完善"四类案件"监督管理工作机制的指导意见]."

2021b. "Guiding opinions on strengthening adjudicative supervision of four-types of cases [关于进一步完善"四类案件"监督管理工作机制的指导意见]."

2023a. "Different rationale for the case review and case approval procedures ["阅核"与"审批"不同的理据]." SPC Official Wechat Account. https://mp.weixin.qq.com/s/vbBDSC3SETiNBI_55Y4hKQ. Accessed on December 1, 2023.

2023b. "Work Report of the SPC submitted to the National People's Congress [最高人民法院工作报告]."

SPC, and SPP. 2007. "Opinions on the Prosecution and Adjudication on Cases of the Crime of Bribe-taking [关于办理受贿刑事案件适用法律若干问题的意见]."

2016. "Judicial interpretation on issues concerning the handling of criminal cases invovling embezzlement and bribery [关于办理贪污贿赂刑事案件适用法律若干问题的解释]."

Spence, Jonathan D. 2013. *The Search for Modern China*. New York & London: W.W. Norton & Company.

Sperber, Nathan. 2023. "Party and state in China: Beyond the Soviet model." *New Left Review* 142(Jul/Aug):29–53.

SPP. 2015. "[中央司改办就规范刑事诉讼涉案财物处置工作意见答问.]"

Srivastava, Vinayank N. 1999. *The Separation of the Party and the State: Political Leadership in Soviet and Post Soviet Phases*. London & New York: Routledge.

Stalin, Joseph. 1928. "Against vulgarising the slogan of self-criticism." *Pravda* 11 (No. 146- June 26).

Stevenson, Alexandra. 2021. "HNA was once China's biggest dealmaker. Now it faces bankruptcy." *New York Times*. www.nytimes.com/2021/02/06/business/hna-was-once-chinas-biggest-dealmaker-now-it-faces-bankruptcy.html. Accessed on November 3, 2023.

Su, Chenting, and James E. Littlefield. 2001. "Enter7ing guanxi: A business ethical dilemma in mainland China?" *Journal of Business Ethics* 33:199–210.

Su, Shaozhi. 2007. "Over the thought fence of Party Culture [超越党文化的思想樊篱]." *Modern China Studies*《当代中国研究》.

Su, Weimin苏维民. 2008. "Yang Shangkun talks about the so-called "secretive recording" incident [杨尚昆谈所谓"秘密录音"]." *Hundred Year Tide*《百年潮》(4).

Su, Yang. 2011. *Collective Killings in Rural China during the Cultural Revolution*. Cambridge: Cambridge University Press.

Sullivan, Lawrence R. 1984. "The role of the control organs in the Chinese Communist Party, 1977–83." *Far Eastern Survey* 24(6):597–617.

Sun, Yan. 1991. "The Chinese protests of 1989: The issue of corruption." *Asian Survey* 31(8):762–82.

2004. *Corruption and Market in Contemporary China*. Ithaca & London: Cornell University Press.

Sun, Ying, and Hualing Fu. 2022. "Of judge quota and judicial autonomy: An enduring professionalization project in China." *The China Quarterly*:1–22.

Svolik, Milan W. 2009. "Power sharing and leadership dynamics in authoritarian regimes." *American Journal of Political Science* 53:494.

2012. *The Politics of Authoritarian Rule*. New York: Cambridge University Press.

Taishan, Criminal Defense 泰山刑辨. 2023. "The case of Zhao Yongwei in Neijiang City [内江赵永韦案]." https://mp.weixin.qq.com/s/c6zH_oNNi9QKQXJWL-suHw. Accessed on February 18, 2024.

Tan, Shigui 谭世贵. 2000. *A Study on Judicial Reform of China*《中国司法改革研究》. Beijing: Law Press.

Tanner, Harold M. 1999. "Strike Hard! Anti-crime campaigns and Chinese criminal justice, 1979–1985." Pp. X, 253 S. Ithaca, NY: East Asia Program, Cornell University.

Tanner, Murray Scot. 2007. "Campaign-style policing in China and its critics." Pp. 1 online resource (256 p.) in *Crime, Punishment, and Policing in China*, edited by Borge Bakken. Lanham, MD: Rowman & Littlefield Publishers.

Tanzi, Vito. 1998. "Corruption around the world: Causes, consequences, scope, and cures." *IMF Staff Papers* 45(4):559–94.

Team, CPLC-Led Joint Investigative 中央政法委牵头的联合调查组. 2019. "Investigative report of the missing case dossier of KQL case ["凯奇莱案"卷宗丢失等问题调查结果]". www.gov.cn/xinwen/2019-02/22/content_5367791.htm. Accessed on January 11, 2024.

Teiwes, Frederick C. 1990. *Politics at Mao's Court: Gao Gang and Party Factionalism in the Early 1950s*. Armonk, NY: M. E. Sharpe.

2001. "Normal Politics with Chinese Characteristics." *The China Journal*, no. 45, 69–82. https://doi.org/10.2307/3182368

2015. *Politics and Purges in China: Rectification and the Decline of Party Norms, 1950–65*. New York: Routledge.

Teiwes, Frederick C., and Warren Sun. 2019. "Hua Guofeng, Deng Xiaoping, and reversing the verdict on the 1976 "Tiananmen Incident"." *China Review* 19(4):85–124.

Thelen, Kathleen. 1999. "Historical institutionalism in comparative politics." *Annual Review of Political Science* 2:369–404.

Thelen, Kathleen, and Sven Steinmo. 1992. "Historical institutionalism in comparative politics." Pp. 1–32 in *Structuring Politics: Historical Institutionalism in Comparative Analysis*, edited by Frank Longstreth, Kathleen Thelen, and Sven Steinmo. Cambridge: Cambridge University Press.

Thornton, Patricia M. 2007. *Disciplining the State : Virtue, Violence, and State-making in Modern China*. Cambridge, MA: Harvard University Press.

Tian, Fu 田夫. 2016. "A historical review of the independent exercise of judicial power in China [中国独立行使审判权制度的历史考察]." *Global Law Review* 《环球法律评论》(2):36–47.

Tianjin, Daily. 2016. "Seven examples of violation of political discipline and political protocols [违反政治纪律政治规矩的七种主要表现]." in *Tianjin Daily* 《天津日报》.

Tilly, Charles. 2001. "Mechanisms in political process." *Annual Review of Political Science* 4(1):21–41.

Torigian, Joseph. 2022. *Prestige, Manipulation, and Coercion: Elite Power Struggles in the Soviet Union and China after Stalin and Mao*. New Haven, CT: Yale University Press.

Trevaskes, Susan. 2003. "Yanda 2001: Form and strategy in a Chinese anti-crime campaign." *Australian & New Zealand Journal of Criminology* 36:292.

Tse, Don, and Larry Ong. 2018. "Xi Jinping may turn to top ally to handle US pressure." *The Diplomat*. https://thediplomat.com/2018/02/xi-jinping-may-turn-to-top-ally-to-handle-us-pressure/. Accessed on November 2, 2023.

Tsou, Tang. 1995. "Chinese politics at the top: Factionalism or informal politics? Balance-of-power politics or a game to win all?" *The China Journal* 34:95–156.

2002. "Chinese politics at the top: Factionalism or informal politics?" Pp. 59–98 in *The Nature of Chinese Politics: From Mao to Jiang*, edited by Jonathan Unger. Armonk, NY: M. E. Sharpe.

UNDOC. 2012. "Jakarta Statement on Principles for Anti-Corruption Agencies."

2020. "Colombo Commentary on The Jakarta Statement on Principles for Anticorruption Agencies." edited by United Nations Office on Drugs and Crime.

2024. "Measuring corruption." in *UNODC Module Series on Anti-Corruption*: UNODC.

Unger, Jonathan. 2002. *The Nature of Chinese Politics: From Mao to Jiang*. Armonk, NY: M. E. Sharpe.

Van Rooij, Benjamin. 2006. "Implementation of Chinese environmental law: Regular enforcement and political campaigns." *Development and Change* 37(1):57–74.

Walder, Andrew G. 2023. "China's extreme inequality: The structural legacies of state socialism." *The China Journal* 90:1–26.

Wan County, CDI 万县纪律检查委员会. 1951. "Notice to all county CDIs on December 25 [给各县（市）委纪委会的通知]."

Wan, Peng 万鹏. 2017. "New changes seen from the communique of the 7th Plenum of the 18th Party Congress [从十八届七中全会公报中的"12345"看全会新变化]." *CCP News Online*. http://cpc.people.com.cn/19th/n1/2017/1016/c414537-29589897.html. Accessed on November 5, 2023.

Wang, Congwu 王从吾. 1962. "Concluding summary speech delivered by Comrade Wang Cong Wu at the National Supervision Work Conference [王从吾同志在全国党的监察工作会议上的总结纪要]."

Wang, Duan. 2015. "The covered cards of Guo Wengui [郭文贵的底牌]." in *Caixin Weekly*.

Wang, Guoqiang王国强. 2018a. "What is the hundreds-of-billion Shanbei mining rights case that Cui Yongyuan talked about [崔永元说的陕北千亿矿权案到底是什么案子]." *China Youth Daily* Wechat account《中国青年报》微信客户端. https://shareapp.cyol.com/cmsfile/News/201812/30/web169177.html. Accessed on January 11, 2024.

Wang, Haiguang 王海光. 2014a. "Political dispute and power struggle: Reinterpretation of the origin of Gao Rao Affair [政争与权争："高饶事件"起因再解读]." https://zhuanlan.sina.cn/article?ch=history&id=30301&vt=4&page=2. Accessed on February 10, 2024.

Wang, Heyan 王和岩. 2007. "A detailed analysis of the case of former president of Beijing Xicheng Court, Guo Shenggui [细解郭生贵案]." *Caijing*《财经》. https://magazine.caixin.com/2007-09-17/100084891.html. Accessed on September 17, 2007.

Wang, Jinfu 汪金福, and Weiwei Chen 陈维伟. 1998. "Luo Gan demands to rectify conduct of political-legal cadres at a CPLC tele-conference [罗干在中政委电视电话会议上要求，切实抓好政法队伍教育整顿]." in *People's Daily*.

Wang, Juan, and Sida Liu. 2022. "Institutional proximity and judicial corruption: A spatial approach." *Governance* 35(2):633–49.

Wang, Linqing 王林清. 2018b. "Tape recording of conversation between Wang Linqing and Cheng Xinwen (divisional leader) [王林清和陈新文庭长的谈话录音]." https://twitter.com/zhaofaqi. Accessed on December 10, 2023.

2018c. "Tape recording of conversation between Wang Linqing and Han Mei (head of collegial panel) [王林清和韩玫法官的谈话录音]." https://twitter.com/zhaofaqi. Accessed on March 25, 2025.

2018d. "Three records of internal report and approval instructions on the KQL case [关于凯奇莱的案件批示]." Cui Yongyuan Weibo account. On file with the author.

2018e. "Whistle-blowing written statement of Wang Linqing [王林清自述文件]." https://twitter.com/zhaofaqi. Accessed on December 10, 2023.

2019. "Televised confession of Wang Linqing and the findings of the joint investigative team led by the CPLC broadcast by CCTV 13 [王林清电视认罪]." www.youtube.com/watch?v=2g9O2Vlgeh0. Accessed on February 10, 2024.

Wang, Lungang 王伦刚, and Sida Liu 刘思达. 2017. "An empirical study on how the adjudication committee in basic-level courts makes decisions on cases with external pressure [基层法院审判委员会压力案件决策的实证研究]." *Fa Xue Yan Jiu*《法学研究》(1):90–99.

Wang, Mingsheng. 2021a. "An analysis of Mao Zedong's approach to 'Power Decentralization' Reform." Pp. 209–17 in *The History and Logic of Modern Chinese Politics*, edited by Mingsheng Wang. Singapore: Springer.

Wang, Peng. 2017a. "Face, emotional bonding and corruption: How middlemen facilitate corrupt exchanges in China (Unpublished work)." University of Hong Kong Sociology Department.

Wang, Peng, and Jingyi Wang. 2018. "How China promotes its military officers: Interactions between formal and informal institutions." *The China Quarterly* 234:399–419.

Wang, Qishan. 2016. "把监督执纪的权力关进制度笼子."《中国纪检监察》(24):1.

Wang, Shaojun 王少军, and Fuxing Zhang 张福兴. 2011. "An account of how Mao Zedong made the decision to execute Liu Qingshan and Zhang Zishan [毛泽东下决心处决刘青山、张子善经过]." *People's Digest*《人民文摘》. http://paper.people.com.cn/rmwz/html/2011-03/01/content_795618.htm?div=-1. On file with the author.

Wang, Shu 王姝. 2014b. "Charting public opinion on the most discussed topics in 2014 [中纪委官网登"2014网络舆情热点首爆媒体排行榜"]." 新京报网.

2017b. "Central Committee members who had maliciously dissented against Party center [妄议中央的中央委员]." in *Xin Jing Newspaper*《新京报》.

Wang, Xiaolu 王晓璐, and Ling Lu 陆玲. 2015. "How did Zheng Quan wreak havoc on Fang Zheng [方正政泉劫]." *Caijing Magazine*. https://m.caijing.com.cn/api/show?contentid=3796465. Accessed on January 8, 2021.

Wang, Yueduan. 2020. "Overcoming embeddedness: How China's judicial accountability reforms makes its judges more autonomous." *Fordham International Law Journal* 43:737–66.

2021b. "Detaching" courts from local politics? Assessing the judicial centralization reforms in China." *The China Quarterly* 246:545–64.

Wang, Yuewen 王跃文. 1999. *Chinese Painting*《国画》. Beijing: Renmin Wenxue.

Wang, Yuhua. 2013. "Court funding and judicial corruption in China." *The China Journal* 69:43–63.

Wang, Yuhua, and Carl Minzner. 2015. "The rise of the Chinese security state." *The China Quarterly* 222:339–59.

Wedeman, Andrew. 2005a. "Anticorruption campaigns and the intensification of corruption in China." *Journal of Contemporary China* 14(42):93–116.

2005b. "The intensification of corruption in China." *The China Quarterly* 180:895.

2012. *Double Paradox: Rapid Growth and Rising Corruption in China*. Ithaca, NY: Cornell University Press.

Wei, Changdong 魏昌东. 2018. "Supervision Law and the theoretical logic of the revision of corruption control system with Chinese characteristics [《监察法》与中国特色腐败治理体制更新的理论逻辑]." *Jounal of Eastern Chinese University of Political Science and Law*《华东政法大学学报》(3):28–38.

WEI, Jianxing 尉健行. 2001. "论党风廉政建设和反腐败斗争[On Building Clean Party-Style and Anti-Corruption Struggle]." In *查办案件工作的方针政策 [Guding Principles and Policies on the Investigation and Handling of Cases]*, chaban anjian gongzuo de fangzhen zhengce. 方正出版社 [Fangzheng chubanshe]. http://dangshi.people.com.cn/GB/146570/174891/10456272.html.

Wei, Zhezhe 魏哲哲. 2021. "Anticorruption 30-year backtracking review revealed 15,000 problematic cases in sentence reduction, parole and probation [全国倒查30年来"减假暂"案件 1.5万件存在问题]." *People's Daily*. Accessed on January 4, 2024.

Weigelin-Schwiedrzik, Susanne. 1987. "Party historiography in the People's Republic of China." *The Australian Journal of Chinese Affairs* 17:77–94.

Wikipedia. 2023. "List of fallen officials placed under investigation since the 18th Party Congress [中共十八大后落马官员列表]." https://rb.gy/7qu1d. Accessed on October 28, 2023.

Wu, Gaoqing 吴高庆, and Qi Dong 董琪. 2016. "Whoever hears the case should make the decision: Reform of case approval system [谁审谁判：案件审批制度的改革路径]." *Journal of Shandong University of Science and Technology*《山东科技大学学报》18(3):18–27.

Wu, Guo. 2017. "Outsourcing the state power: Extrajudicial incarceration during the Cultural Revolution." *China (National University of Singapore. East Asian Institute)* 15:76.

Wu, Guoguang. 1995. *"Documentary Politics": Hypotheses, Process and Case Studies*. Armonk, NY: M. E. Sharpe.

2015a. *China's Party Congress: Power, Legitimacy, and Institutional Manipulation*. Cambridge: Cambridge University Press.

Wu, Guoguang 吴国光. 2018. *Theatre of Power: The Operation of the Chinese Communist Party's Congress*《权力的剧场 —— 中共党代会的制度运作》. Hong Kong: Chinese University of Hong Kong Press.

2023. "History of the Party reform in the 1980s, Part 1/2 [80年代中共高层改革往事 上]." Interview by Zhi'an Wang 王志安." Wang Ju Pai An 王局拍案.

Wu, Laosi 吴老丝. 2020. "All secrets in criminal trials are hidden in the secretive case dossier [中国刑事审判的秘密，都藏在法院副卷里]." Personal Wechat Account. https://bit.ly/321qh88. Accessed on January 4, 2024.

Wu, Meihua 吴美华. 2009. "History and functional changes of the Party disciplinary inspection institutions [中国共产党纪检机构的历史沿革及其职能演变]." *Journal of the History of the Chinese Communist Party*《中共党史研究》(3):19–25.

Wu, Wei 吴伟. 2013a. *On stage and backstage: China's political reform in the 1980s*《中国80年代政治改革的台前幕后》. Hong Kong: New Century Publishing House.

2014. "Party-state separation reform after the 13th Party Congress [十三大后的党政分开改革]." *New York Times*. https://cn.nytimes.com/china/20140930/cc30wuwei31/. Accessed on December 17, 2023.

Wu, Yuliang 吴玉良. 2015b. "Background, History and Main Functions of the CCDI Organizational Department and Propaganda Department [中央纪委组织部、宣传部的组建背景、历史沿革和主要职能]." *CCDI Press Release*.

Wu, Zhenjun 吴振钧. 2013b. "Reflections on the Development of the Party's Inspection Work [中国共产党巡视工作发展的回顾与思考]." CCDI Website. www.ccdi.gov.cn/lt/llsy/jdzy/201309/t20130927_45672.html. Accessed on March 25, 2025.

Xi, Jinping 习近平. 2013a. "Eight-Measures is the point of entry and the mobilization order to improve our work styles [八项规定是改进作风的切入口和动员令]." *Selected Works of Xi Jinping*. www.12371.cn/2023/04/18/ARTI1681786741018260.shtml. Accessed on March 25, 2025.

2013b. "Speech at the Work Conference on the Mass Line Educational Campaign [在党的群众路线教育实践活动工作会议上的讲话]." *Party Construction Research*《党建研究》(8):4–12.

2019. "The Party's leadership [党的领导]." *People's Daily*《人民日报》. http://ex.chinadaily.com.cn/exchange/partners/82/rss/channel/language/columns/v0m20b/stories/WS5d1aaf52a3103dbf1432b5b4.html. Accessed on December 2, 2023.

Xiang, Yan 向燕. 2015. "Empirical investigation of disposal of property involved in criminal cases [刑事涉案财物处置的实证考察]." *Journal of Jiangsu Administration Institute*《江苏行政学院学报》84(6):127–32.

Xiang, Yang 向杨. 2021. "Features and logic of the institutional arrangements of Party apparatuses – A comparative perspective [党的机构设置特征及其逻辑：一个比较的视角]." *Theories and Reform*《理论与改革》(9):24–36.

2022. "Vicissitudes of the Party's disciplinary system since the founding of the PRC – An examination of the community of provincial CDI secretaries [新中国成立以来中国共产党纪律检查体制的变迁——基于1949–2020年省级纪委书记群体的考察]." *Jiang Han Forum*《江汉论坛》(2):63–72.

Xiao, Di 肖迪. 2006. "Hu Gang: *Celadon* reflects the first half of my life [胡刚：《青瓷》是我前半生的总结]." *An interview of Hu Gang*. On file with the author.

Xiao, Hui 萧辉, and Ning Yu 于宁. 2018. "The mist enveloping the strange accounting practice of HNA [海航蹊跷走账80亿迷雾]." *Caixin Weekly*. https://weekly.caixin.com/2018-09-14/101326338.html. Accessed on November 3, 2023.

Xiao, Ting 肖亭, and Guannan Xiao 肖冠男. 2009. "CCDI led anticorruption in Chinese style – Eight-step procedure [中纪委领衔中国式反贪 办案需要走八道手续]." *Qi Lu Evening Paper*《齐鲁晚报》. www.chinadaily.com.cn/zgzx/2009-08/07/content_8541681_2.htm. Accessed on July 5, 2323.

Xiao, Yang 肖扬. 2009. "The before and after of the birth of the first anticorruption bureau [新中国第一个反贪局诞生的前前后后]." www.criminallaw.com.cn/article/default.asp?id=1529. Accessed on March 25, 2025.

Xie, Fang 解芳. 2002. "Legislative issues on police technical investigation in China [我国公安技侦工作立法问题研究]." *Investigation Forum*《侦查论坛》1:336–45.

Xie, Haitao, et al. 谢海涛等. 2014. "Le Rouge et le Noir of Zhou Yongkang – Part II [周永康的红与黑 (二)]." *Caixin Magzine*. https://chinadigitaltimes.net/chinese/356311.html. Accessed on July 29, 2023.

Xinhua, News Agency. 2012a. "Central Party decides to revoke Bo Xilai's Party membership and expel him from office [中共中央决定给予薄熙来开除党籍、开除公职处分]." *Xinhua News*. http://news.xinhuanet.com/legal/2012-09/28/c_113248574.htm. Accessed on January 26, 2024.

Xinhua, News Agency. 2012b. "Wang Qishan: Rise of a trouble shooter." *China.org.cn*. www.china.org.cn/china/2012-12/26/content_27514232_2.htm. Accessed on January 4, 2024.

2014. "Hebei courts explores online judicial auction to curb enforcement corruption [河北法院探索"网络司法拍卖"遏制"执行腐败"]." Xinhua Agency. www.gov.cn/xinwen/2014-12/14/content_2790731.htm. Accessed on January 8, 2024.

Xinhua, News Agency. 2015. "How are corrupt officials hunted by the business community [贪官缘何频被商人"围猎"]." https://hainanpc.gov.cn/hainanpc/fzsk/202111050015556 4098/index.html. Accessed on January 8, 2024.

XinhuaNet. 2015. "15,450 cadres received disciplinary sanction last year [山西去年处分违纪干部15450人]." Renmin Wang. http://politics.people.com.cn/n/2015/0210/c70731–26542135.html. Accessed on October 29, 2323.

2017a. "Investigation on Guo Wengui's scoop over HNA [郭文贵海航"爆料"真相调查]." Xinhua Agency. http://m.xinhuanet.com/2017-07/10/c_1121290100.htm. Accessed on November 3, 2023.

2017b. "Overview of the anticorruption and clean government work since the 18th Party Congress [党的十八大以来反腐倡廉工作综述]." http://www.xinhuanet.com//politics/2017-10/05/c_1121764418.htm. Accessed on January 20, 2024.

Xinjing, Newspaper. 2013. "Tian Huiyu succeeded Ma Yuhua as the head of Merchant Bank [马蔚华将卸任招行行长 建行北京分行行长田惠宇接任]." *Xin Jing Bao*《新京报》. http://politics.people.com.cn/n/2013/0509/c70731–21422131.html. Accessed on November 3, 2023.

Xiong, Lianghua 熊亮华. 2015. "Chen Yun at the historical juncture of the 3rd Plenum of the 11th Party Congress 陈云在十一届三中全会的历史转折关头." http://dangshi.people.com.cn/n/2015/0303/c85037–26627804.html. Accessed on July 4 2023.

Xu, Chenggang 许成钢. 2024. "Book talk on organizational DNA: PRC system and the origin of totalitarianism." *Potomac Culture Salon*. Accessed on March 22, 2024.

Xu, Hao 徐豪. 2018. "Twelve-year long dispute over mining rights worth hundreds of billion [陕西千亿矿权12年纠纷："黑金"争夺战背后的权力寻租]." *China Economic Weekly*《中国经济周刊》. www.banyuetan.org/chcontent/sz/jjzs/201827/245348.shtml. Accessed on January 11, 2024.

Xu, Ji'ning 徐冀宁. 2016a. "Did Chen Yun say 'one exception only' in the crackdown of the Gang of Four? [陈云在粉碎"四人帮"斗争中讲过"下不为例"吗?]." *Digest of Party History [Theoretical Section]*《党史博采·理论版》(9):31–34.

Xu, Jiaxin 徐家新. 2017. "Transcript of the press conference by Xu Jiaxin on the judicial accountability reform [就司法责任制等综合改革试点工作答问]." www.chinacourt.org/article/detail/2017/07/id/2913022.shtml. Accessed on January 3, 2024.

Xu, Lei 许蕾 2004. "Mobilization mechanism in political campaigns – the case of the three-antis campaign [政治运动的动员机制：以"三反"运动为个案]." *Journal of Central China Normal University: Humanities and Social Sciences*《华中师范大学学报：人文社科版》(4):48–54.

Xu, Mengxia 许梦侠. 1953. "Concluding speech at the 1st Sichuan Provincial CDI work conference [在中共四川省委第一次纪律检查工作会议上的总结发言]."

Xu, Qianfei 许前飞. 2002. "Re-examing the quality (suzhi) of Chinese judges [再论中国法官的素质]." *People's Adjudication*《人民司法》(1).

Xu, Qing 徐清 2016b. "Local CPC Committee of Political and Legal Affairs in Judiciary: An investigation in W city of Y province [基层政法委员会组织结构论 —— 基于Y省W市政法委员会的实证分析]." *Peking University Law Review*《北大法律评论》17(2):211–38.

Xue, Jiancong 薛健聪, and Huajie Jia 贾华杰. 2015. "'Competent' official Qiu He ["能吏"仇和]." *Caixin Weekly.* https://weekly.caixin.com/m/2015-04-03/100797343_all.html. Accessed on January 8, 2024.

Xue, Peng 薛鹏. 2021. "Punishing financial corruption and controlling financial risks [惩治金融腐败 防控金融风险]." *China Jijian Jiancha Daily*《中国纪检监察报》. www.moj.gov.cn/jgsz/gjjwzsfbjjz/zyzsfbjjzyw/202109/t20210913_437557.html. Accessed on October 31, 2023.

Yaita, Akio. 2012. *Xi Jinping: The Weakest Leader in Communist China*《习近平：共产中国最弱势的领袖》. Taipei: Common Wealth Magazine.

Yan, Huai. 1995. "Organizational hierarchy and the cadre management system." in *Decision-Making in Deng's China - Perspectives from Insiders*, edited by Carol Lee Hamrin and Suisheng Zhao. Armonk, NY: M. E. Sharpe.

Yan, Yaobin 晏耀斌. 2018. "Behind the scenes of the hundreds-of-billion mining rights dispute [西勘院千亿矿权案幕后："一女多嫁"对抗会议纪要]." *China Business Operation Newspaper*《中国经营报》. https://finance.sina.cn/2018-01-27/detail-ifyqzcxh0556233.d.html?vt=4. Accessed on January 11, 2024.

Yan, Yunxiang. 1996. "The culture of guanxi in a North China village" *The China Journal* 35(Jan):1–25.

Yanyu, Faming 烟语法明 2023. "Coming of the era of the case review era [裁判文书阅核制时代来了]." www.163.com/dy/article/IG3TIVK10553P TO6 .html. Accessed on December 2, 2023.

Yan Yu, Fa Ming 烟语法明. 2024. "To what extent can the "three regulations" prevent judicial corruption? [干预司法"三个规定"记录制度，究竟能在多大程度上预防腐败？]" https://mp.weixin.qq.com/s/Kg7QRebiDsioqpDJOoPIcw. Accessed on February 25, 2024.

Yang, Jisheng 杨继绳. 2013. "An interview of Gao Gang's secretary on the Gao Gang Incident [高岗秘书谈"高岗事件"]." *Yan Huang Chun Qiu*《炎黄春秋》(6).

Yang, Kuisong 杨奎松. 2006. "Mao Zedong and the three-antis campaign [毛泽东与三反运动]." *Shi Lin*《史林》(4):51–69.

Yang, Mayfair Mei-hui. 1994. *Gifts, Favors, and Banquets: The Art of Social Relationships in China*. Ithaca, NY: Cornell University Press.

2002. "The resilience of guanxi and its new deployments: A critique of some new guanxi scholarship." *The China Quarterly* 170:459.

Yang, Zhenjie, and Linda Chelan Li. 2023. "Court finance and floundering judicial reform in China." *China Information* 37(2):278–98.

Yang, Zhongxu 杨中旭. 2014. "Tyranny of Liu Tie'nan: I snubbed the dinner invitation from the vice-governor [刘铁男的霸道：副省长请我吃饭 我根

本不理他们].” https://business.sohu.com/20130516/n376154067.shtml. Accessed on January 25, 2024.

Ye, Haibo 叶海波. 2017. “Constitutional constraints over the national supervision institutional reform [国家监察体制改革的宪法约束].” *Journal of Wuhan University [Social Sciences Section]*《武汉大学学报（哲学社会科学版）》(3):110–6.

Ye, Quan 叶泉. 2016. “Why do we have to punish strictly those who have not stopped corruption after the 18th Party Congress [为何十八大以后不收手必须严惩].” *Legal Daily*《法制日报》. www.xinhuanet.com/politics/2016-06/22/c_129082090.htm. Accessed on January 14, 2024.

Yin, Dechang 尹德常. 2013. “Reflection and reconstructon of the sign-off power of adjudicative documents [裁判文书签发权配置的反思与重构].” *Shandong Adjudication*《山东审判》(2):83–87.

Yin, Hongwei 尹鸿伟. 2011. “Collapse of the corruption gang in Chongqing High Court [重庆高院腐败小集团瓦解].” *Nan Feng Window*《南风窗》. https://m.fx361.com/news/2009/0827/5597738.html. Accessed on January 8, 2024.

Yin, Yue, Lu Lin, and Yan Li. 2015. “Who is Guo Wengui [起底郭文贵].” in *Caijing Magazine*.

Yoon, June. 2022. “Lex in depth: Why the luxury market needs to hedge against China.” *Financial Times*. www.ft.com/content/314bb4c9-cb47-4678-971a-5ae6fcf00d9b. Accessed on October 29, 2023.

You, Chenjun 尤陈俊. 2015. “A multi-dimension reconstruction of the interest-seeking image of litigation masters in the Qing Dynasty [清代讼师贪利形象的多重建构].” *Legal Studies*《法学研究》5(5):177–93.

You, Chunliang 游春亮. 2006. “A survey report of bribe-giving conducted by Haizhu District Procuratorate 海珠检察院对行贿人员的问卷调查报告.” *Legal Daily* 《法制日报》. https://client.vpn.chu.edu.cn:4443/https/webvpn33ea9ebda45fc5a5e6600ba84e98508a/20060906/n245192255.shtml. Accessed on January 4, 2023.

Young, Graham. 1984. “Control and style: Discipline inspection commissions since the 11th Congress.” *The China Quarterly* 97:24–52.

Yu, Meisun 俞梅荪. 2013. “Anniversary commemoratory essay about Hu Jiwei, a courageous and wise man in times of crisis [全国人大常委会行使委员权力第一人——社会危机时刻的智勇者胡绩伟周年祭].” *Yibao* 《议报》. https://yibaochina.com/?p=235908. Accessed on April 22, 2024.

Yu, Ning, et al. 于宁 等. 2022. “Judicial business of Shen Deyong’s secretaries [沈德咏秘书们的司法生意].” *Caixin Weekly*. https://weekly.caixin.com/2022-04-16/101871164.html. Accessed on January 8, 2024.

Yu, Olivia. 2008. “Corruption in China’s economic reform: A review of recent observations and explanations.” *Crime, Law & Social Change* 50:161–76.

Yu, Ruxin 余汝信. 2023. *Chronicles of Kang Sheng*《康生年谱》. Hong Kong: New Century Press.

Yu, Wenhao 于文豪. 2021a. “Constitutional connotation of dual responsibility of local governments [地方政府双重负责的宪法内涵].” *China Legal Science* 《中国法学》 (3):90–113.

Yu, Xiaohong 于晓虹. 2017. “Gaming and balancing between delocalization and de-bureaucratization: A re-examination of the provincial level unified judicial administration reform [“去地方化”与”去行政化”的博弈与平衡——2014年以来法检人财物省级统管改革再审视].” *China Law Review* 《中国法律评论》 (5):187–98.

2018. “Re-examining the unified vertical judicial administration reform since 2014 [2014年以来法检人财物省级统管改革再审视].” *People's Rule of Law* 《人民法治》 (1):28–35.

Yu, Xiaohong 于晓虹, and Hui Yang 杨惠. 2019. “A revisit to the logic of the political-legal work under the reconstructed Party-state system [党政体制重构视阈下政法工作推进逻辑的再审视].” *Academic Monthly* 《学术月刊》 11(51):105–16.

Yu, Zeyuan. 2021b. “Former butler of Wang Qishan expelled from the Party and sent for prosecution [曾是王岐山”大管家” 董宏违纪受贿遭开除党籍移送法办].” *Lianhe Zaobao* 《联合早报》. www.zaobao.com.sg/news/china/story20210414-1139242. Accessed on November 3, 2023.

Yuan, Fang. 2012. “Xi To Be ‘Weak’ President.” *Radio Free Asia*. www.rfa.org/english/news/china/xi-jinping-11122012110129.html. Accessed on March 25, 2025.

Yue, Sanmeng 岳三猛. 2017. “Bribers of former Yunnan Party-Secretary exposed [给云南省委原书记白恩培送钱的人 终于全曝光了].” *Fa Zhi Evening* 《法制晚报》. https://m.huanqiu.com/article/9CaKrnK0O1c. Accessed on March 25, 2025.

Zhai, Xingli 翟星理, and Yuelin Chen 陈悦琳. 2022. “Social circle of a fallen female judge, whose husband was a divisional leader at the provincial high court [一位落马女法官的朋友圈，丈夫曾任省高院庭长].” *Southern Weekend* 《南方周末》. www.infzm.com/contents/241347?source=101&source_1=241649. Accessed on April 9, 2024.

Zhai, Xuewei 翟学伟. 2004. *Everyday Authority in Chinese Society: A Historical Sociological Study of “Guanxi” and Power* 《中国社会中的日常权威: 关系与权力的历史社会学研究》. Beijing: Social Sciences Literature Press.

Zhai, Zhiyong 翟志勇. 2017. “Supervision Commission and reshaping of the 1982 Constitutional Order [监察委员会与”八二宪法”体制的重塑].” *Global Law Review* 《环球法律评论》 (2): 105–14.

Zhang, Changdong. 2017. “A fiscal sociological theory of authoritarian resilience: Developing theory through China case studies.” *Sociological Theory* 35(1):39–63.

2021. *Governing and Ruling : The Political Logic of Taxation in China*. Ann Arbor, Michigan: University of Michigan Press. https://ubdata.univie.ac.at/AC16483842.

Zhang, Qianfan. 2006. "The People's Court in transition: The prospects for Chinese judicial reform." in *Debating Political Reform in China: Rule of Law vs. Democratization*, edited by Suisheng Zhao. Armonk, NY: East Gate by M. E. Sharpe.

Zhang, Qing 张青. 2019. "Difficult reality and cause of the judicial salary reform at the grassroots level [基层法官薪酬制度改革的现实困境及其因应]." *Sixiang Zhanxian*《思想战线》(5):147–55.

Zhang, Siquan 张思铨. 2011. *Gao Gang*《高岗》. Beijing: China Humanities and History Press 中国文史出版社.

Zhang, Taisu, and Tom Ginsburg. 2019. "China's turn toward law," *Virginia Journal of International Law* 59(2):306–88.

Zhang, Weiping 张卫平. 2000. "Debureaucratizing People's Courts of China – one approach of court reform [我国法院体制的非行政化——一种法院体制改革的基本思路]." *Review of Law and Commerce*《法商研究》77:3–11.

Zhang, Wenzhong. 2018. "Wang Qishan may play a role more than an "external" Politburo Standing Committee member [王岐山的角色或远不止于所谓"第八"常委]." https://rb.gy/q1hv5q. Accessed on November 3, 2023.

Zhang, Xiaoshuai 张小帅. 2024. "Origin of the hard constraint of Party discipline [党的纪律的刚性约束力来源]." *China Academy of Social Sciences Daily* 《中国社会科学报》. www.cssn.cn/skyl/skyl_skyl/202402/t20240222_5734250.shtml. Accessed on February 22, 2024.

Zhao, Faqi 赵发琦. 2016. "Full statement of Zhao Faqi [赵发琦实名举报全文]." https://rb.gy/jm93oo. Accessed on January 11, 2024.

Zhao, Jialiang 赵家梁, and Xiaoji Zhang 张晓霁. 2008. *Past Stories beneath the Half Tombstone*《半截墓碑下的往事》. Hong Kong: Da Feng Press 大风出版社.

Zhao, Shirley. 2021. "End of an era with the arrest of HNA Group chairman." *Bloomberg*. www.aljazeera.com/economy/2021/9/27/end-of-an-era-with-arrest-of-hna-group. Accessed on November 3, 2023.

Zhao, Ziyang, and Bao Pu. 2009.《改革历程》[*Prisoner of the State: The Secret Journal of Premier Zhao Ziyang*]. New York: Simon & Schuster.

Zhen, Guan 贞观. 2019. "Dialogue with Zhao Faqi: Why do I have the courage to report Zhao Zhengyong [对话赵发琦：我为什么有勇气举报赵正永]." https://chinadigitaltimes.net/chinese/604184.html. Accessed on January 11, 2024.

Zheng, Zhidao 政知道. 2015. "Unveiling the appointment process at the early stage of CDI restoration [揭秘中央纪委恢复成立之初如何用人]." *Social media account of Beijing Youth Newspaper*. On file with the author.

Zheng, Zhihang 郑智航. 2020. "A study of the Party-political mechanism that reshapes the judiciary [党政体制塑造司法的机制研究]." *Global Law Review*《环球法律评论》(6):5–23.

Zhong, Jinyan 钟金燕. 2012. "A revisit to the history and vicissitude of the Political-Legal Committee [政法委历史与演变的再思考]." *China through the Ages*《炎黄春秋》(12).

Zhong, Jixuan. 2017. "Forging Iron Requires A Strong Hammer《打铁还需自身硬》" in *CCDI Program*.

Zhong, Jixuan 钟纪宣 (Writer) 2016. Always on the Road《永远在路上》. In CCDI & CCTV (Producer).

Zhong, Zuyi 仲祖一. 2015. "Unwavering commitment to preserve the authority of the Party center [坚决维护党中央权威]." *Qiushi* (18):62–62.

Zhou, Guangyou 周光佑. 2005. "Seeing through the essence of majhong bribes [看清麻将贿赂的实质]." *People's Procuratorate*《人民检察》:54–54.

Zhou, Hao 周浩 (Writer) 2015. *The Chinese Mayor* 大同. BBC4.

Zhou, Luyang. 2019. "Historical origins of the Party-army relations in the Soviet Union and China." *Communist and Post-communist Studies* 52:207.

Zhou, Qiang 周强. 2017a. "SPC President Zhou Qiang stress: Firmly distancing oneself from the wrong thought of separation of powers [最高法院院长周强：坚决与"三权分立"错误思潮划清界线]." http://news.cnr.cn/native/gd/20170112/t20170112_523471725.shtml. Accessed on January 8, 2024.

Zhou, Shuzhen. 2014. "巡视工作的历史沿革、现实成就和制度创新 [History of the CIT Work, Achievements and Innovation]." in 人民网 [*Renmin Network*].

Zhou, Xueguang. 2017b.《中国国家治理的制度逻辑: 一个组织学研究》*The Institutional Logic of Governance in China: An Organizational Approach*. Beijing: San Lian Bookstore.

Zhou, Xueguang 周雪光. 2016. "Between 'officials' and 'local staff': The logic of empire and personnel management in the Chinese bureaucracy [从"官吏分流"到"层级分流": 帝国逻辑下的中国官僚人事制度]." *Society*《社会》(1):1–33.

Zhou, Zhenchao 周振超, and Hongkai Huang 黄洪凯. 2022. "Strip-block relations: from cooperative co governance to collaborative mutal embeddedness [条块关系从合作共治到协作互嵌]." *Public Administration and Policy Review*《公共管理与政策评论》(1):20–33.

Zhou, Zhuo 周卓. 2022. "Why is it so difficult to acquit when there is reasonable doubt? [疑罪为何难以从无]." www.sqxb.com/2022/sqtj_1227/2970.html. Accessed on January 4, 2023.

Zhu, Jiangnan, and Dong Zhang. 2016. "Weapons of the powerful: Authoritarian elite competition and politicized anticorruption in China." *Comparative Political Studies* 50(9):1186–220.

Zhu, Jiangnan, Qi Zhang, and Zhikuo Liu. 2017. "Eating, drinking, and power signaling in institutionalized authoritarianism: China's antiwaste campaign since 2012". *Journal of Contemporary China* 26(105):337–52.

Zhu, Jingwen 朱景文 (Ed.). 2007. *China Legal Development Report (1979–2004)*《中国法律发展报告》. Beijing: Renmin University Press.

Zhu, Suli. 2010. "The Party and the courts." Pp. 52–68 in *Judicial Independence in China: Lessons for Global Rule of Law Promotion*, edited by Randall Peerenboom. New York: Cambridge University Press.

Zhu, Wei 朱薇. 2009. "Chongqing committed to break the hugh profit chain in enforcement corruption [重庆力破司法拍卖暴利链 源头治理"执行腐败"]." *Liaowang Newsweek*《瞭望新闻周刊》.

Zou, Jianzhen 邹坚贞. 2015. "Cover story: The case of Yunnan lawyer Liu Shaobin [云南律师刘少斌案始末]." *China Economic Weekly*《中国经济周刊》. www.ceweekly.cn/2015/0407/107610.shtml. Accessed on January 4, 2024.

Zou, Keyuan. 2000. "Judicial reform versus judicial corruption: recent developments in China." *Criminal Law Forum* 11:321–51.

Zuo, Fengrong 左凤荣. 2010. "How did power transition take place at the top in Soviet? [苏联最高权力是怎样交接的？]" in *What Truly Happened in Soviet Union*《苏联真相》edited by Nanquan Lu and Zongliang Huang. Beijing: Xinhua Publishing House.

Zuo, Weimin 左卫民. 2016a. "Analysis and prognosis: Provincial-level centralized administration of court personnel and finance [省统管法院人财物：剖析与前瞻]." *Law Review*《法学评论》(3):1–7.

2016b. "An empirical study on the operation of the adjudicative committee [审判委员会运行状况的实证研究]." *Law Review*《法学研究》(3):159–73.

# INDEX

For EU product safety concerns, contact us at Calle de José Abascal, 56–1°, 28003 Madrid, Spain or eugpsr@cambridge.org.

www.ingramcontent.com/pod-product-compliance
Ingram Content Group UK Ltd.
Pitfield, Milton Keynes, MK11 3LW, UK
UKHW060658180126
467089UK00008B/92

*9781009275002*